# A Judicial Odyssey:

# Federal Court
# in Santa Clara, San Benito,
# Santa Cruz, and Monterey Counties

# A Judicial Odyssey:

## Federal Court in Santa Clara, San Benito, Santa Cruz, and Monterey Counties

*Edited by*

Christian G. Fritz      Michael Griffith      Janet M. Hunter

*Published by*
Advisory Committee—San Jose Federal Court
San Jose • 1985

**Library of Congress Cataloging in Publication Data**
Main entry under title:

A Judicial odyssey.

Bibliography: p.
Includes index.
1. United States. District Court (California: Northern District) — History. 2. Courts — California — History. 3. Law — California — History and criticism. I. Fritz, Christian G., 1953-    . II. Griffith, Michael, 1948-    . III. Hunter, Janet M., 1951-    . IV. Advisory Committee — San Jose Federal Court.
KF8755.C28J83   1985              347.73'22              85-6161
ISBN 0-9613690-0-0              347.30702
ISBN 0-9613690-1-9 (pbk.)

ISBN: 0-9613690-0-0
ISBN: 0-9613690-1-9 pbk

*Cover photograph by Ira Nowinski*
*Cover map courtesy The Bancroft Library*
*Back cover photograph courtesy Clyde Arbuckle*

# Authors' Acknowledgments

In the order as their contributions appear in A *Judicial Odyssey*, we present acknowledgments from the authors of those who helped them in their efforts.

John M. Findlay — Gunther Barth, Christian G. Fritz, Janet M. Hunter, and Austen D. Warburton have commented helpfully on the essay, and I gratefully acknowledge their assistance.

Christian G. Fritz — Would like to express his deep appreciation to Marlene Keller for her extremely helpful comments and suggestions on the articles he authored.

Caroline L. Hunt — Dean Joel Franklin, Mrs. D. Sallee of Colton Hall Museum, and Mr. C. Fritz assisted greatly in the preparation of the article.

Michael Griffith — Thanks to Lynn Lundstrom and the staff of the library for the United States District Court, Northern District of California.

Mark Thomas, Jr. — Sincere gratitude to Archivist Michael Griffith without whose research and direction this article would not have been possible. Many thanks are also owed to Magistrates Nordin Blacker and Arthur Atteridge and the late Magistrate Richard Goldsmith, as well to Amelie Elkinton and Frederick Phaneuf for their invaluable help and advice.

Warren C. Moore — A good deal of the credit goes to Daniel R. Cowans, the first permanent referee in San Jose, whose memory of historic events is more vivid or colorful than mine.

Patricia V. Trumbull — Thanks to Frank Ubhaus for his help in reconstructing the early days of the Federal Public Defender's office.

Donald B. Ayer — Appreciation to Helen Voss for refreshing my recollection of names, dates, and events.

Rick Carroll — Thanks to William Cooney, Tom Hall, and Joe Frein, who covered the federal courts daily; and Phil Watson and Carolyn Anspacher who taught me how.

# Table of Contents

**Part One: The Early Years**

## Part Three: An End to the Odyssey — A Home in the Central Coast Counties

## Part Four: A Journalist Remembers. *By Rick Carroll*

# Foreword

The United States Courthouse and Federal Building so recently opened in San Jose was long in the planning. The efforts of those who worked for this embodiment of federal justice are chronicled here, in A Judicial Odyssey: Federal Court in Santa Clara, San Benito, Santa Cruz, and Monterey Counties.

The time will come, very soon, when were it not for distant memories or a book such as this, few would realize that for much of its history, the area was without a federal court. Its people had to take their federal cases to San Francisco: the Santa Clara valley was not thought to have enough business to warrant its own court. The story of the struggle to change that is one that bears writing, for those who would tell it, will not.

There would be no court, no courthouse, no story were it not for them. The authors of this volume give a sense of the commitment and labors of the San Jose court proponents and the importance of their achievements. They describe the events of the protracted struggle and the roles of many of those immediately involved.

At the dedication of the United States Courthouse and Federal Building on October 18, 1984, Robert F. Peckham, chief judge of the United States District Court for the Northern District of California, gave thanks to those proponents. Perhaps it is appropriate then, to introduce and acknowledge them in his voice, taken from his remarks on that occasion.

> The return of the federal court to San Jose in 1967 after an absence of 114 years was the culmination of a valiant, determined effort by a few persons playing various roles. It was not work for the short-winded. We pay tribute today to these leaders. Let me call the roll.
>
> - The indefatigable Robert Beresford, who first advanced in 1946 the idea of the return of federal court to San Jose and who was for years the dogged chairman of the Federal Courts Committee of the Santa Clara County bar until he became a judge.
> - The sage Russell Roessler, who succeeded Judge Beresford as chairman of that committee and who has served as chairman of the Advisory Committee — San Jose Federal Court since its inception. His leadership and counsel have been invaluable.

- The lawyer members of the Advisory Committee from the four central coast counties, who have made a superb contribution.
- The able Congressman Don Edwards, who by virtue of his legislative talents and parliamentary expertise guided the legislation providing for federal court sessions at San Jose to enactment. Let us say that without Congressman Edwards, there would not in all probability be a federal court today in San Jose.
- The late Chief Justice Earl Warren and Chief Judge Emeritus Richard Chambers, who as chairs of the United States Judicial Conference and the Ninth Circuit Council respectively brought these judicial governing bodies to support the legislation for a San Jose court despite vigorous opposition from San Francisco's judicial and legal interests.
- Industrious Congressman Norman Mineta who initiated legislative action to authorize this United States Courthouse and Federal Building. We acknowledge his able leadership in Congress and express our gratitude for his achievement in this regard.
- The members of the Board of Supervisors who magnanimously provided a courtroom and related facilities for the use of the United States District Court from 1967 until 1973. We express our gratitude to them for making those quarters available. The board in those days was composed at various times of Sig Sanchez, Sam Della Maggiore, Ralph Mehrkens, Martin Spangler, Charles Quinn, Dominic Cortese, and Victor Calvo.

Let us talk about the nature of the court that is now housed in this building. The federal court that has returned to San Jose differs significantly from the mid-nineteenth century court of Judge Ogden Hoffman, the first United States District Judge for the Northern District of California. Persons come to today's San Jose Federal Court to redress wrongs over which Judge Hoffman's federal court had no jurisdiction. During the more than a century since the first federal court convened here on April 5, 1852, Congress has provided for federal judicial remedies to enforce civil liberties; to eliminate discrimination on account of race, color, religion, sex, age, or handicap; to protect investors from securities fraud; to restrain environmental destruction and pollution; to deter restraint of trade and price fixing under the antitrust laws; and to grant relief to debtors and creditors under the bankruptcy laws.

Today's federal court attacks the problems of litigation delay and cost in ways unknown and unthinkable to Judge Hoffman. Today's federal judge is umpire and case manager. Today's judge assumes responsibility for the management of a case from the time of filing, sets a reasonable time for discovery and a firm trial date, and holds the parties and their lawyers to that schedule. Alternative dispute resolution mechanisms are provided under which early neutral evaluation can lead to settlement before too much time elapses and substantial costs are incurred. In addition, our judges and magistrates are becoming increasingly effective in obtaining just settlements.

The central coast counties are fortunate that the federal judges who will sit here are able jurists who were distinguished lawyers of this area before assuming the bench. May I present the federal judges who will sit in this new courthouse:

Judge Spencer Williams
Judge William A. Ingram
Judge Robert P. Aguilar
Judge Warren C. Moore
Judge Seymour Abrahams
Resident Magistrate Nordin F. Blacker

It is clear to those of us on the Advisory Committee — San Jose Federal Court that without the unflagging attention of Judge Peckham and of those whom he so graciously acknowledged, the court would yet be a dream.

But as the court could not have been created and completed without the efforts of many, so too the book. On behalf of the committee, we would like to thank the authors and editors for all they have done to transform the story into this book. Christian G. Fritz, chairman of the California State Bar Committee on History of the Law in California, worked on the initial plans for A *Judicial Odyssey*: suggesting subjects, locating authors, and offering them assistance as they researched. In addition, he has contributed two chapters on the early history of the area and its judicial presence.

Michael Griffith, archivist for the northern district, served as coordinator of the project. With his access to the court's documents, he has also written one chapter on the building and two on some of the offices to be housed there: the United States Attorney's and Marshal's offices and the United States District Court Clerk's office.

Janet M. Hunter, a freelance editor, came to the Bay Area after the building itself had been started. She has worked with the authors and the other editors to ensure that this record of the proponents' struggle would be completed and used, just as the court and its building.

All three deserve the highest praise: they have taken an idea and transformed it into this book, preserving for us a history of the court and its odyssey.

In addition, others gave generously of their time and experience to improve the book by suggesting further areas to be covered and by reviewing and refining draft versions of the manuscript. We would like to thank all of those whose efforts and endurance have brought this to completion.

Austen D. Warburton
W. Robert Morgan
Lionel M. Allan

# Preface

The story to be unfolded in A *Judicial Odyssey* is a long one, full of false starts, dogged struggle, small gains, and ultimate success. As editors, it is our hope that this book, having suffered through many of the same stages, will also meet with success in its goal of memorializing the story of the court.

The list of those persons who assisted us along the road to completion is a long one. We would especially like to thank six. Rose G. Weick patiently typed draft after draft of the manuscript, and her work materially aided the book. Michael and Jean Sherrell of Sherrell Graphics provided friendly advice and dedicated service, and their efforts greatly eased production. Ron Robin undertook the large task of proofreading the book as it moved through from manuscript to final form and John D. Gordan, III, generously set aside time in his busy schedule to meticulously inspect the final product. The fine index was provided by Elinor Lindheimer.

Many thanks are due to the authors, who contributed their time and resources: obviously without them, this book would not have been written. Less obvious has been the contribution of those who do not figure prominently in the book, but without whom it could not exist: the Advisory Committee — San Jose Federal Court.

Christian G. Fritz
Michael Griffith
Janet M. Hunter

# Chronology

1777 San Jose, first civil settlement in California, founded.

1846 May 12 — United States declares war on Mexico.

1848 January 24 — The gold rush begins after James Marshall finds first specks of gold beside the American River.
March 10 — Treaty of Guadalupe Hidalgo, terminating the Mexican War is signed and ratified.

1850 September 9 — California admitted to the United States as the thirty-first state.
September 28 — The act of 1850 creates California's two federal courts, dividing northern from southern district by the thirty-seventh parallel. The act also requires the northern district to sit in San Francisco, San Jose, Sacramento, and Stockton and the southern district to sit in Los Angeles and Monterey.

1852 April 5 — First session of federal court held in San Jose (in the State House Building).
August 31 — Ogden Hoffman authorized to act as judge in both northern and southern districts of California. Direct appellate review by the Supreme Court extended to all cases from California district courts.

1854 January 18 — Congress abolishes San Jose as a place of holding federal court.
January 23 — Judgeship for southern district reestablished: Isaac Stockton Keith Ogier appointed.

1866 July 27 — Southern District of California abolished.

1886 August 5 — Southern District of California reestablished.

1949 February 14 — H.R. 2701, a bill to establish a term of the Northern District Court of California in San Jose introduced in Congress by Congressman Jack Z. Anderson.

1961 September 5 — H.R. 9051, providing for a new district on the central coast of California introduced by Congressman Charles Gubser.

1964 January 7 — H.R. 9567, providing for new districts, divisions, and judgeships introduced by Congressman Don Edwards.

1965 February 8 — H.R. 4534, providing for new districts and divisions in California introduced by Congressman Don Edwards.
April 1 — S. 1666, the Omnibus Judgeship Bill, introduced by Senator Olin Johnston.
June 16 — H.R. 9168, the House version of S. 1666, introduced by Congressman Emanuel Celler.
June 30 — S. 1666 passed the Senate.

1966 March 18 — S. 1666 signed into law, as Public Law 89-372, by President Lyndon B. Johnson.

1967 January 16 — United States District Court sits in San Jose in courtroom of the Superior Court Building.

1970 July 31 — Venue rule change issued requiring criminal cases to be filed and heard in San Jose.

1973 June 15 — Temporary United States Federal Building and Courthouse dedicated in San Jose.

1982 January — Ground broken for new United States Courthouse and Federal Building in San Jose.

1983 May 1 — Venue rule change allowing civil cases to be filed and heard in San Jose implemented.

1984 October 18 — United States Courthouse and Federal Building dedicated in San Jose.

# Part 1

## The Early Years

The following chapters set forth the early history of the Santa Clara valley, from the time when it was the undeveloped area known as *Llano de los Robles,* or Plain of the Oaks. One can see the American influence through the years, and finally, the influence of technology in transforming the area into Silicon Valley. The authors provide a sense of the area's intriguing history, its people, and the changes and growth it has undergone in each phase of development.

John M. Findlay, author of a number of works on the area, including a book on the social history of gambling in the American West and Las Vegas, presents the early history of the Santa Clara valley. With his master's and doctorate from the University of California, Berkeley, he is now an assistant professor of American history at Pennsylvania State University.

Christian G. Fritz, an editor of this book, a member of the California State bar, and a doctoral candidate in history at the University of California, Berkeley, provides the reader with the early history of the federal court's presence in San Jose. His first chapter in this part gives a taste of the long and circuitous route that has, at last, provided the Santa Clara valley with federal justice in a court at San Jose.

In a related chapter, Caroline L. Hunt, a faculty law clerk and third-year student at Monterey College of Law, presents a brief history of Monterey's federal district court.

With the historical background set and the federal courts in place, we see one facet of the local history in detail: the early land litigation that arose as a result of the Mexican land grants. The discussion is taken from a preliminary version of several chapters of Mr. Fritz's dissertation-in-progress on the history of the northern district during the tenure of its first judge: Ogden Hoffman.

The last chapter in this part explores the continuing connection between the central coast counties and the federal court. One of the area's famous judges, Maurice T. Dool-

1

ing, United States district judge for the Northern District of California from 1913 to 1924, is profiled in two sketches. Judge Dooling's granddaughter, Alma Dooling Dettweiler, provides a brief biography of the man she knew as "Daddy Bob," clearly showing his character and influence on those around him. Joseph Franaszek, a law clerk in the Northern District of California, next highlights Judge Dooling's positive effect on the court and the law. Mr. Franaszek then sketches another attorney and judge well known in the central coast counties: William Francis James.

# 1

## From *Llano de los Robles* to Silicon Valley: Culture and Society in the Santa Clara Valley, 1769-1980

*John M. Findlay*

The Santa Clara valley serves as a representative slice of a state that defies summary analysis. Over the last two centuries it has been the center of a diverse range of social and cultural developments that exemplify many of the distinctive features of California history. As site of the first civilian settlement as well as the most recent coastal boom, the region embodies both the oldest historic legacy and the newest version of the future that the Golden State has to offer to the nation. As a focus for agriculture as well as for city life, it has typified a state that featured extensive urbanization at the same time that it became a leading agrarian producer. As a home for a succession of ethnic groups dating from precontact native Americans to Indo-Chinese immigrants of the 1970s, the area has been a center for ethnic mixture and cultural change. In all of these respects, the region serves better than any other as a microcosm of two centuries of California's past. Despite such an illuminating history, the Santa Clara valley is perhaps the least studied major population center in the state.

The Santa Clara valley has received less attention than the Los Angeles, San Francisco, and San Diego areas, but its development paralleled theirs. San Jose resembled Los Angeles in its origins as a Spanish pueblo and in its geography, which by the mid-twentieth century was shaped more by automobiles and suburban sprawl than by the natural setting. The Santa Clara valley's development has also been influenced by San Francisco ever since pueblos were founded to produce food for presidios during the late eighteenth century. Following the gold rush, San Jose and its environs became tethered to San Francisco first by stage and steamer, next by railway, and finally by highway. Despite its distinct economic orientation and character, the people of the Santa Clara valley identified with—even voted like—San Franciscans. Each tie to San Francisco seemed to limit development of a distinct identity until after World War II, when San Jose and

3

Silicon Valley gained recognition as an international center for the development of postindustrial technology. In emerging from the shadow of its larger neighbor, San Jose followed the example of San Diego, another boomtown on California's coast that blossomed during the twentieth century.

The Santa Clara valley emerged as late as it did because its environment at first seemed better suited to agriculture than to urban life. The valley has long been recognized as one of the most fertile regions on the Pacific Slope. Lacking the tremendous harbors of San Francisco or San Diego, and the fortune and aggressiveness of Los Angeles, people in the Santa Clara valley contentedly turned to cultivation of their lands. Through the late nineteenth and early twentieth centuries, agriculture and canning served as the economic mainstays. As late as 1920, when more than seventy-five percent of the populations of Los Angeles, San Diego, and San Francisco counties was urban, only about fifty-three percent of Santa Clara County was. As orchards and fields were paved over for highways and parking lots after World War II, Californians lamented the passing of some of the state's finest soils, which had produced crops for urban populations throughout the Far West, but local residents anticipated urban growth that would put their valley on a par with the state's leading cities.

Rural traditions played a large role in sustaining a rich ethnic heritage. Ever since the founding of its missions and pueblo, the makeup of the area's population has been complex. After multiracial settlement during the Hispanic period, the region attracted a broad range of immigrants from Asia, Europe, and eastern North America. During the early twentieth century additional Asian and Latin American immigration underscored the region's role as a melting pot. When the area became the center of advances in electronics, still more migrants came from all over the United States and the world. The valley has adhered to American economic and legal culture since the mid-nineteenth century, but its heterogeneous and mobile population has ensured a diversity of lifestyles that reflected the complex population of the entire state.

Ethnic diversity has been the rule in the Santa Clara valley since 1777, the year in which a Spanish mission was founded to convert Indians into Christians and a pueblo was established by thirty-eight Spaniards, eleven native Americans, six mulattoes, three mestizas, nine children of mulatto-mestiza parents, and one "servant vaquero."[1] Motivated by the advances of other European nations in the Pacific, Spain had begun to strengthen its claim to Alta California in 1769 by establishing presidios and missions at selected locations along the California coast. The presidio at Monterey was founded in 1770, and in 1776 a presidio and mission were started at San Francisco. Colonizers came to the Santa Clara valley after a series of exploring expeditions praised the wide, fertile plain as an ideal place for settlement. In 1776 Pedro Font and Juan Bautista de Anza submitted glowing reports on the region.[2] In January of 1777 Mission Santa Clara was founded along the western bank of the Guadalupe River. Ten months later, the pueblo of San Jose was laid out just upstream from the mission, on the eastern bank of the river.

In playing different roles in Spaniards' ambitious colonizing scheme, mission and pueblo each embodied an important part of the highly centralized form of expansion undertaken in Alta California. Unlike the Anglo-American frontier of the gold rush where fortune-seekers seemed to prevail, the Spanish frontier of the eighteenth century revolved around church and military, the two traditional frontier institutions of Europe. From the outset, Spanish authorities suspected that they would not be able to dispatch enough colonists to populate remote outposts on the northwestern frontier. So they established presidios as a token line of defense and transplanted the mission system from

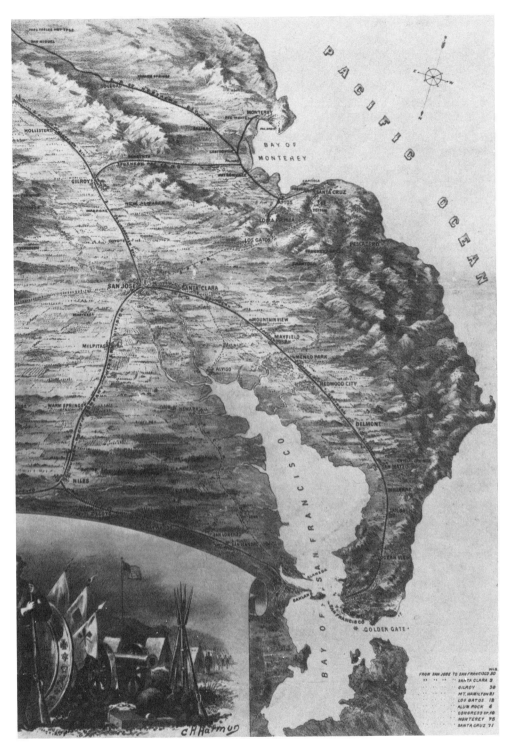

*View of the Santa Clara valley. This picture appeared on the cover of the special Grand Army edition of the* San Jose Mercury *dated June 1880. (Courtesy California State Library.)*

Latin America as a means of converting native Americans into Christian settlers who would validate the king's claims to the territory. Missions not only fulfilled Spaniards' religious obligations in the New World but also functioned as a vital source of colonists. Like the presidios, they were viewed as temporary devices that would dissolve once enough Indians had been converted and prepared to defend the region for Spain. Missions were intended to teach both Christianity and agriculture to the native population. Because colonial authorities expected them to become self-sufficient farms that would also supply presidios, they were generally placed in well-watered, level regions like the *llano de los robles*, or plain of the oaks, as Spaniards termed the Santa Clara valley.

Conceived as temporary institutions, presidios and missions came first, and then died off during the first half of the nineteenth century. Pueblos, on the other hand, developed almost as an afterthought, but have survived in California as the cities of Los Angeles, Santa Cruz, and San Jose. Colonizers established the first town sites once they realized that presidios, which were never intended to be self-sufficient, could not be supplied either by lines of overland and sea transportation from Mexico or by missions such as those at San Francisco and Santa Clara. *Pobladores*, or town settlers, were charged with the responsibility of provisioning soldiers stationed along the coast.

San Jose was the initial pueblo founded in Alta California, with the commission to produce food and other supplies for the presidios at Monterey and San Francisco. Although it has been termed the first purely civilian community in California, its responsibility to the presidios actually made it something of a military town. Many of its leading citizens were presidio soldiers, and economic activities came to be geared strictly to military needs. Pueblos were also viewed by soldiers as pawns in the struggle between church and army for predominance in colonial California.[3] The military and civilian population at San Jose did not often see eye-to-eye with the clerical establishment at Santa Clara.

The Laws of the Indies, the Spanish blueprint for the settlement of the New World, discouraged such close juxtaposition of a mission and pueblo as occurred in the Santa Clara valley. Referring to these regulations, fathers at Mission Santa Clara complained to authorities that men from San Jose abused newly converted, or neophyte, women, exploited Indian laborers, took the mission's cattle, and permitted livestock to trample the padres' fields. Noting that some *pobladores* had been recruited from Mexican jails, the priests also decried immoral behavior at the pueblo, which seemed to be corrupting Indians at the mission. They asked the colonial governors to allocate a wider buffer of lands, but their complaints had little effect.[4] The main boundary between pueblo and mission lands remained the Guadalupe River, and the two frontier outposts managed to coexist. Indeed, mission fathers provided for the spiritual needs of the townspeople until 1803, when a church was erected in San Jose.

The padres' complaints reflected the different attitudes taken by the mission and the pueblo toward native Americans. Prior to the Spaniards' arrival the Santa Clara valley had been occupied by the Tamien tribelet of the Costanoan, or Ohlone, Indians. Deadly epidemics of Old World diseases decimated Indian society, and Europeans helped to undermine native American subsistence patterns and disrupt cultural traditions. Yet it was the mission's responsibility to protect and "denaturalize" the Indian, as Father-President Fermín Francisco de Lasuén said, while *pobladores* viewed the native as a laborer.[5]

Native Americans responded to the various forms of Spanish settlement by seeking to maintain their traditional autonomy and ways of life, and to avoid the dangers inherent

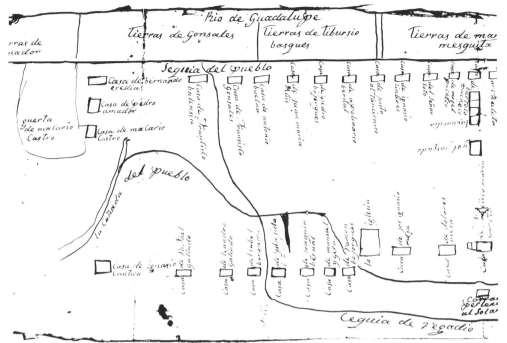

*Map of the pueblo of San Jose in 1802. The clustering of dwellings reflected the pueblo's character as a tightly regulated farming community. (Courtesy Austen D. Warburton.)*

in contact with white peoples. Lasuén lamented the Indians' reluctance to embrace civilization at Mission Santa Clara. Although "these poor creatures" enjoyed so many benefits at the mission, the Father-President wrote, "they see all of this, and yet they yearn for the forest."[6]

The mission has been held partly responsible for devastating the natives' health. Lasuén was present at Santa Clara in 1802 during an epidemic when at least seventy neophytes died. Conditions reached the point where "it was imperative, absolutely imperative to give them permission to scatter through the country...and most of them have been given extreme unction," the Roman Catholic rites given to those who were dying or extremely ill.[7] As local tribes died off, the fathers had to go farther afield to find recruits, and sometimes commissioned soldiers to undertake that task.

Although Indians often resisted the discipline of the mission, relations between *pobladores* and natives were more typically a business arrangement. Indians were in large part responsible for the remarkable productivity of the pueblo, which shipped considerable amounts of goods to the presidios at San Francisco and Monterey. There is some evidence that Indians preferred the pueblo to the mission, perhaps because they were more independent there. One mission father complained that in the towns Indians were "allowed to live with their old freedoms and heathen customs; along with these they have learned other unbecoming vices that they acquaint themselves with in the pueblo, and since they get food for their work they reject submission to the yoke of Evangelicalism."[8]

Relations between *pobladores* and Indians reflected an important dimension of life at San Jose where, as in other parts of northern New Spain and Mexico, settlers came to be viewed as indolent. This ethnocentric and generally mistaken perception resulted from several factors. First, the settlers were remote members of a distant colonial society. Observers who disparaged the Spanish-speaking settlers mostly came from countries where the conversion from preindustrial to industrial attitudes was more advanced than in Spain and Mexico.[9] Colonists in the Santa Clara valley, who followed preindustrial rhythms of work and leisure and often substituted Indian labor for their own, inevitably suffered in foreigners' estimation by comparison to peoples in more industrialized societies.

Critics of Hispanic society in California also overlooked the natural adjustment made by *pobladores* to the lands that they occupied. Much economic activity revolved around livestock, requiring little industrial labor. Colonists often simply permitted their cattle to graze in the wide open valley, where the pasture proved so ideal that herds had to be reduced periodically by slaughter. In addition, the settlers had little institutional incentive to work hard and generally employed Indians to perform much of San Jose's work. Their community had been subsidized from the outset, and to many it offered a better way of life than they had known in Mexico, but there was little room for upward mobility. Surplus crops were sold to the presidio at fixed low prices, discouraging production, and Spanish settlers could not hope to acquire much more land than they had been given at the beginning of the pueblo.[10] There seemed little reason to strive for advance, which may explain why foreign observers viewed the colonists as indolent.

The lack of incentives underscored the Spanish design for colonial villages. Where American frontiersmen tended to disperse themselves, each pursuing fortune in his own way, authorities established San Jose and Mission Santa Clara as the foci for tightly regulated agricultural communities. Pueblo and mission were laid out so that the populations resided close together near the center and worked in fields and pastures around the perimeter. At Santa Clara the mission buildings served as the center of activity, neophyte and gentile Indians lived nearby, and productive fields and pastures surrounded the settlements.[11] Similar patterns prevailed at Mission San Jose to the north (in the present-day town of Fremont) and Mission San Juan Bautista to the south (near Hollister), two nearby links in the chain of missions that were founded in 1797.

In San Jose, settlers' adobes were clustered together in town on *solares*, or building lots, and each head of household was assigned a number of *suertes*, or fields, lying outside the ring of houses. The Spanish king retained ultimate title to these parcels and to all other pueblo lands, so they could not be sold or divided among heirs, but settlers' families were permitted to use the property as their own and were expected to improve it. As agent for the king, the pueblo controlled three other kinds of land: *ejidos*, or vacant lots, which surrounded the town for "ventilation" and limited common usage; *propios*, or lands rented out by the town council as a source of revenue; and *dehasas*, or great common pastures.[12] The early adobes stood close together at the center of settlement; *suertes* lay to the north, west, and south of town; and pasture lay to the east.

Land ownership under the Spanish regime inhibited economic development. This and many other ingredients of society and culture began to change as the Mexicans took over Alta California following a long uprising against colonial control. As Mexico consolidated its new holdings during the 1820s, the restrictive regime imposed by the Spanish was replaced. In fact, the Mexican period between 1821 and 1846 buffered the transition from the highly centralized pattern of Spanish expansion to the individualistic nature of the American frontier.

The transfer to Mexican rule led quickly to at least four major changes in the nature of California society and culture: large parcels of land were transferred to private ownership; trade with foreigners increased; growing numbers of foreigners immigrated to California; and missions were secularized. Each change represented a loosening of political control over the province. The Mexican revolution against Spanish colonialism had in many ways decreased the direct authority of such institutions as the state and the church over the individual, so in part these large-scale changes in Alta California simply reflected the new conditions in Mexico. The decline of central political and cultural direction, however, also reflected Mexicans' inability to govern the province rigorously. Like the Spaniards, they lacked the resources to assert themselves forcefully on the northwestern frontier.[13] Changed patterns of landholding and increased exposure to foreigners worked against a lengthy Mexican reign in California.

Before 1820, only one parcel of land in the Santa Clara valley belonged to a private owner. Over the next twenty-five years, most of the lands in the valley were parceled out in large grants to individual owners. The land distribution undermined strong Mexican control by creating a number of independent landholders who resisted the central authority originating from Mexico City. These land grants, known as ranchos, developed into the basis of power for the ruling elite in California. Power shifted from the missions, presidios, and pueblos to the Spanish and Mexican capital of California at Monterey, where the customs house stood, and to the major landholders who now prevailed in local affairs.

Land grants came from previously unoccupied areas and were also carved out of the holdings of missions and pueblo. Parts of the huge pastures at Santa Clara, San Juan Bautista, and San Jose were turned over to private owners, and most local Indians went to work on ranches and in town. The intention of the redistribution of mission lands was to convert missions into pueblos where Indians could continue to live together and own land, but this system simply proved unworkable during the 1830s and 1840s.[14] The mission and pueblo retained some of their original holdings, but for the most part the valley fell into the hands of private owners.

Individual citizens now not only owned more land but also engaged more freely in trade with foreigners. To be sure, smuggling had been extensive prior to the Mexican takeover of Spanish California.[15] But after 1820 the pace of commerce quickened as English, Russian, and American ships increasingly visited the coasts of California, often in search of sea otter skins. In the vicinity of San Jose, sailors generally came ashore near present-day Alviso at the Embarcadero de Santa Clara. They sold manufactured goods and, with the help of Indian labor, loaded hides and tallow onto their ships. Many Yankees viewed the Mexicans' need for manufactured goods as evidence of another cultural shortcoming, overlooking the economic and political conditions that inhibited economic development in the Mexican-American borderlands, and the real ambitions of Hispanic settlers. In fact, in direct defiance of orders from central authorities, many of the Mexican colonists, or Californios, welcomed *norteamericanos* and the economic vitality that they brought to Mexico's northern frontier.[16]

Increased trade led directly to more interest in California on the part of foreigners. John Gilroy and Robert Livermore were the first Anglo-Americans to pass through San Jose. Beginning about 1830, growing numbers of non-Hispanic whites began to settle in the valley. In 1820, the population of San Jose approached 240; by 1845 it had grown to 900, including about 150 non-Hispanic "interlopers" involved in many forms of economic activity.[17] Many of the calculating newcomers gained substantial landholdings and, often by marrying into Californio society, became accepted into the local power structure. These early arrivals—including Peter Davidson, Pierre Sainsevain, William Fisher, Thomas Campbell, and future alcaldes, or pueblo mayors, James Weeks and John Burton—stood in an ideal position to take advantage of the transfer of territory from Mexican to American hands.

Some newcomers settled in the valley, converted to Catholicism, became Mexican citizens, and reaped financial and political rewards, but most Anglo-Americans who entered the area saw very little to keep them there. Several Yankees who traveled through the valley during the 1840s found the culture interesting but the standard and way of living disappointing. Nicholas Dawson called San Jose a "sleepy village" with "no regular streets" and crude and jumbled housing; Charles Wilkes pointed out the "dilapidated" old mission and the untended gardens; Josiah Belden, who was briefly held prisoner as a suspected foreign agent, commented that the "people lived in a very primitive rude state"; and Edwin Bryant found the rich lands around the mission "entirely neglected" and the San Jose plaza overrun with squirrels.[18]

Such responses reflected a growing sense on the part of Americans that their own culture was best suited to remaking the landscape of the Pacific Coast. Few failed to notice the fertility of the lush valley, and some mentioned that, "if properly cultivated" by "an industrious people," Santa Clara valley could "alone produce breadstuffs enough to supply millions."[19]

The expansionist implications of such remarks were borne out in the Mexican-American War, wherein Alta California and other portions of the Southwest were conquered by the United States. This conflict stemmed clearly from an aggressive outlook on the part of the United States, but in California the American victory was facilitated by the Mexican frontiersman's longstanding dissatisfaction with rule from Mexico City, and by the spirit of independence that had been fostered by social changes following the defeat of Spanish rule. The Treaty of Guadalupe Hidalgo, which terminated the war in 1848, marked a turning point in the development of the Santa Clara valley as Hispanic traditions finally gave way completely to Anglo-American patterns of development.

Americans' attitudes toward the environs of San Jose indicated just how relative the concept of frontier was for different cultures. While Alta California constituted the northern edge of Mexican territory between 1821 and 1846, there was little concentrated effort to reshape the environment. Mexicans were concerned primarily with consolidating their political control of the province, not with taming nature and the Indian. Californios frequently complained about Mexican authority, but seemed relatively satisfied with the cultural landscape. They were more or less satisfied that the frontier had been conquered, and viewed the Mexican province as an ideal place for pursuing autonomy. Their attitude stood in stark contrast to the energetic visions of Americans, who saw the Far West as a rude territory that needed the reforming hand of their culture if its tremendous opportunities for individual and national gain were to be realized. As soon as they began arriving, Yankees earnestly began to remake society in their own familiar image. In this whirlwind of constant change, the Santa Clara valley experienced a second period of frontier development.

Novel designs on the pueblo landscape illustrated the cultural redirection resulting from the American influx. The Spanish founders of San Jose intended ownership and usage of land to be static, and the Mexicans, while distributing more property to private owners, essentially continued to uphold Spanish precepts reserving large tracts for public use and preventing extensive subdivision and speculation. Californios, "who were not assessed for their property and considered it a livelihood, were satisfied with these arrangements. But the Americans, who paid taxes on their real estate and treated it as a commodity, objected to government restrictions on its exploitation."[20] Moreover, as Frederic Hall, the first historian of San Jose and a prominent attorney in local land cases, pointed out, many newcomers understood the Far West as a speculative real estate venture that required clear and predictable definition of property lines.[21] The pueblo of San Jose with its meandering irrigation canals, or *acequias*, plaza, roads, and its large expanses of common pasture, needed to be redrawn in order to support Americans' frontier schemes.

A succession of surveyors imposed a new order on San Jose between 1847 and 1850 by mapping and laying out the town in the standard grid pattern that typified frontier settlements in the United States. Although the perpendicular streets alternated between mud and dust, depending upon the season, and the square reserved as a park was first used as a bull pen, the new shape represented a future of buying and selling town lots. A similar approach was applied to the surrounding pueblo lands. In 1847 James D. Hutton was hired to survey and subdivide the expanse into large tracts, which were subsequently raffled off to willing claimants in order to facilitate development and speculation.[22] A grand project that reflected haste to remake the cultural landscape, this scheme was overturned by American courts.

Notoriously sloppy surveying provided further evidence of the newcomers' carelessness in redefining the land. Chester S. Lyman, Hutton's unhappy successor who continually had to tell property owners that they owned less land than previous surveys had indicated, commented that Hutton had "wretchedly surveyed and as wretchedly mapped" the pueblo lands.[23] Americans' haste to acquire and trade in land ironically delayed title settlements by creating numerous legal disputes. As late as 1870, A.P. Giannini's father, a recently arrived immigrant, advised other newcomers to rent property, rather than buy it, until all titles could be legally confirmed.[24] Litigation seemed as much a part of the American frontier experience in California as land speculation.

Although land titles remained unsettled, the town of San Jose flourished during the early gold rush years. Many residents left for the mines in May and June of 1848, but the wiser ones, like prosperous merchant Josiah Belden, soon returned to reap the more certain profits in commerce and real estate. Trade from travelers on the overland route from San Francisco to both the northern and southern mines in the Sierra buoyed the town's economy. The quicksilver mined at New Almaden provided additional income, and prosperity seemed assured when the state constitutional convention named San Jose the first capital of the newly formed state. The population, which had numbered 900 in 1845 and 850 in 1848, grew to 3,000 by 1850.[25]

Growth did not necessarily mean refinement. San Jose remained a relatively crude town that could not match the sophistication and wealth of San Francisco.[26] The limits of the pueblo were dramatized during the two seasons in which the state legislature convened there. To provide for both legislators and miners wintering in the village, a number of tents and hotels were hastily erected, but housing remained in short supply. When senators and representatives arrived in December 1849, they found that the State House had not yet been completed and that other facilities were meager. Crime increased, idle gold seekers and Californios gambled and danced in the town square, and transience seemed to dominate life in the town. Residents tried to accommodate legislators, but they lacked the resources to retain the capital, and other California communities plotted to secure the state house for themselves. Moreover, San Jose had the misfortune of an especially wet winter during the first legislative session; floods nearly reached the downtown section and rains made most streets nearly impassable. In January 1851, the last legislature to convene in San Jose voted to relocate to Vallejo, and the Santa Clara valley lost the one resource it had to assure steady growth.[27]

The removal of the state capital set the growth of San Jose back for about a decade. Between the early 1850s and the early 1860s, the town's population hovered around 3,000. The population then tripled to 9,118 by 1870, largely as a result of the arrival of the railroad from San Francisco in 1864 and the completion of the transcontinental route in 1869. These lines touched off a spurt of expansion that made San Jose the leading city in the South Bay region, and tied the former pueblo inextricably to the fortunes and influence of San Francisco. But the more fundamental basis for growth, the mainspring behind the town's population increase to 21,500 by 1900, was the development of agriculture in the Santa Clara valley.[28] Whereas gold mining, the state capital, and new rail lines had been short-term sources of growth, farming and ranching became economic staples for the next century.

Observers had recognized the fertility and potential of the soils of the Santa Clara valley since the late eighteenth century expeditions of Pedro Font, Juan Bautista de Anza, and George Vancouver, but to Americans the region remained unproven until it featured flourishing fields laid out in a familiar manner. The valley's reputation for productivity was clearly established by 1861 when William H. Brewer, a professor of agriculture at Yale University, termed the region "the garden of California." Charged with the responsibility of surveying the broad expanses of the state, Brewer wrote that "the Santa Clara valley is the most fertile and lovely of California." The undivided ranchos in the southern end were long used as pasture, thus retaining some of their Hispanic function and flavor. The area around San Jose, on the other hand, had been subdued entirely by the new Yankee culture. "All this is enclosed, in farms, and under cultivation. Farmhouses, orchards, etc., give it an American look."[29]

The reshaping of the landscape of northern Santa Clara valley occurred in the same stages that characterized the development of agriculture in the rest of California, just more quickly. Between 1850 and 1864 stock raising and wheat growing prevailed, over the next decade grains such as wheat and barley became dominant, and then horticulture rose rapidly to prominence. Cattle and sheep were leftover from the Mexican era as products that suited the large landholdings of California and met a strong demand for meat in the mines. Wheat was a particularly apt crop between 1850 and 1875 because it required neither certain land titles, extensive irrigation, nor a sizable labor force, and it suited pioneers' expectations about life and agriculture in California. After 1875, as land ownership became less clouded and the first experiments in other crops proved successful, the more intensive horticulture, with its smaller parcels of land and more profitable products, came to prevail.[30]

Horticulture lent a sense of stability that had not been been apparent during the heyday of livestock and wheat. Spanish settlers at the pueblo and the mission had successfully planted orchards prior to the arrival of Americans, and experimenters like Louis Pellier, who introduced the French prune to California, had demonstrated the feasibility of raising fruits and vegetables in the vicinity, but conditions did not favor extensive development until the last quarter of the nineteenth century when methods of transportation and fruit preservation improved substantially. In 1874 orchards and vineyards covered between two and three percent of the two hundred thousand acres of cultivated land; by 1930 orchards occupied sixty-five percent of the county's cropland, methods of water and soil conservation had become sophisticated, and techniques of

*Packing houses with orchards in the Santa Clara valley during the 1890s. This photograph helps make clear the importance of horticulture in the valley's economy at the turn of the century. (Courtesy The Bancroft Library.)*

drying and canning fruit had improved markedly. Important crops included apples, pears, cherries, peaches, and grapes. The region became an international leader in the production of prunes and apricots. The valley clearly deserved its reputation as "the Garden of the World."[31]

The dramatic rise of horticulture in the Santa Clara valley helped to shape the fusion of urban and rural elements in the population. Concentration on fruit made for a substantial agrarian community, but horticulture required an exceptionally intensive brand of agriculture that accelerated subdivision of farmland into parcels that were relatively small for the state, thus permitting a higher population density. The number of county residents grew from 35,000 in 1880 to 100,000 in 1920.

Almost all crops were grown commercially, which necessitated the development of an adequate market and transportation network, and in many cases the people who worked in horticulture—laborers, managers, and owners—did not live on or near farms, but in cities and towns. During the nineteenth century townships such as Almaden and Alviso had thrived as service centers for outlying farms, but by the early twentieth century they were losing economic strength. Meanwhile, San Jose, with the county seat, a flourishing downtown, a railroad depot, and a crossroads for increasing auto and truck traffic, increased in importance as the predominant city. By 1920 its population approached 40,000.

While San Jose may have seemed an urban anomaly in the rural valley, it actually epitomized the blend of city and country that characterized Santa Clara County. Since the 1850s residents of the town had worked to preserve a rustic setting within city limits. Prominent citizens, including Mayor Thomas Fallon and banker Samuel L. Knox, built homes surrounded by orchards and gardens; sisters from the congregation of Notre Dame de Namur chose to build a college and convent in the town because of the rural setting; and several prominent nurseries were established near the city center.[32] In later years residents divided their time between urban and rural occupations; growers supplemented their income with seasonal work in canneries, and people who worked in town often lived on farms.[33]

These developments were typical. Residential patterns of the wealthy and influential exemplified the urban influence on rural life during the nineteenth century. To be truly successful in business one had to work in a major city. Consequently, Frederic Hall, a respected attorney, moved to San Francisco and later, Los Angeles to pursue his career, and Josiah Belden, a prominent capitalist and early mayor, spent a great deal of time in San Francisco and eventually moved to New York City.[34] Other prominent Californians looked upon the Santa Clara valley as a permanent or temporary place of residence while they made their fortunes in San Francisco. Samuel J. Hensley, president of the California Steam Navigation Company, developed the 25-acre Hensley Gardens near downtown San Jose, and the family of Samuel Osgood Putnam, another partner in Hensley's firm, summered on a farm near Mountain View. Henry M. Naglee, a San Francisco banker, acted as country squire on a 140-acre estate in San Jose, where he grew exotic plants and cultivated grapes for wine and brandy. James Lick, at one time the richest man in San Francisco, built a mansion and mill in present-day Santa Clara, laid out another estate on the road from San Jose to New Almaden, and left much of his fortune for the development of the Mount Hamilton observatory. In the twentieth century, James D. Phelan, banker, mayor of San Francisco, and United States senator, maintained a country estate in Saratoga.[35] By attracting urbanites seeking the benefits of rural life, the Santa Clara valley remained a mixture of city and country through the early twentieth century.

A number of prominent institutions of higher learning added to the cosmopolitan character of the valley during the last half of the nineteenth century. Jesuits founded Santa Clara College in 1851 at the site of the church of the former Mission Santa Clara. The college was chartered by the state in 1855, changed its title to the University of Santa Clara in 1912, and added a law school. The College of the Pacific, the oldest incorporated educational institution in the state, was founded by Methodists in the same year as Santa Clara College. It remained in Santa Clara County until the twentieth century, when it was relocated to Stockton. California State University at San Jose, Californians' first normal school and state college, was started as a private normal school in San Francisco in 1857, made public in 1862, and moved to San Jose in 1870. It was renamed a teachers' college in 1921 and a state college in 1935. Leland Stanford Junior University was founded in 1885 at Palo Alto, and eventually added a law school. Stanford University's nickname, "The Farm," suggested something of the rural milieu in which these centers of higher education were located.

A diverse range of ethnic groups enhanced the cosmopolitan character of society in Santa Clara County. During the American period the populations of native Americans and Californios declined precipitously, while other groups became more prominent.

*Downtown San Jose at the turn of the century. This photograph looks down South Market Street towards the Electric Tower, located at the junction of Market and Santa Clara Avenue. (Photograph by C.C. Pierce, Los Angeles; reproduced courtesy California Historical Society, San Francisco.)*

The initial influx of population came largely from northern Europe and the eastern states so that Irish, French, and Germans figured prominently in the area. After pioneers occupied much of the land, additional newcomers arrived to work as laborers in agriculture. The Chinese became numerous after 1869, toiling in fields and orchards. These immigrants always remained distinctive, and their communities were highly visible. Civic leaders in San Jose opposed a Chinatown near the city center because it conflicted with their ideal of a homogeneous downtown.

Around the turn of the century, the valley's population was swelled by the arrival of Japanese and Italian immigrants. These groups came initially to work as laborers in the fields and canneries, but they eventually succeeded in buying their own land or starting their own businesses.[36] Latin Americans and Asians replaced earlier farm and cannery workers during the twentieth century. Mexicans played a particularly prominent role as laborers in Santa Clara valley agriculture and food processing since the 1920s. Like most immigrants, they came to work in the fields and orchards, but ended up working in canneries. Frequently dwelling in their own communities or in towns, they faced immigrants' traditional problems of poverty, prejudice, and cultural confusion while becoming the largest ethnic group in the area, thus helping to make the area more urban by diversifying the population. Many Mexican-Americans ultimately resided in the barrios of East San Jose, where numerous Californios had lived since the American conquest of the Golden State.[37]

The more agriculture developed in Santa Clara County, the less rural society became. Farming grew steadily more intensive and commercial, permitting greater population density and heightening the importance of such supporting urban services as the canning industry, centralized finance, transport, and commerce, colleges and universities, and government and professional offices. Like industrialists in eastern cities in the United States, growers relied on immigrants for labor and saw their communities become increasingly heterogeneous in makeup. The Santa Clara valley, from 1864 to 1940, exemplified the distinctly modern character of agriculture in California.

The city of San Jose was the focus of urban activity within the valley. As Mexican pueblo, state capital, county seat, and railroad stop, it had advantages that no other community in the South Bay could match. After the arrival of the railroad in 1864 San Jose acquired utility companies, underground sewers, government buildings, streetcar lines, and a downtown core—all the traditional amenities of a respectable American town. Between 1881 and 1915 the city center was marked by the Electric Tower at the junction of Market and Santa Clara streets, a 208-foot high structure that was the largest single source of electric light in the country at the time of its completion. Civic consciousness blossomed during the progressive era when citizens renamed the streets of old downtown vice districts with labels more suited to a thriving urban center, voted for a city-manager form of government that seemed to favor commercial growth, and, after a newspaper headline promised that "Garden City Will Be Made Greater and More Beautiful" following the 1906 earthquake, erected San Jose's first skyscrapers.[38]

The automobile, more than anything else, was responsible for carrying San Jose and environs to the urban forefront of the twentieth century. The Santa Clara valley proved to be an ideal setting for cars and trucks: the population was dispersed on farms and in suburbs, the landscape was mostly rural and flat, the weather was mild, and the people were eager to embrace new means of independent transport. In 1892 one booster boasted, "Probably in no city of its size in the United States are so many private vehicles and horses kept, the well-cared-for, level streets and picturesque country roads offering every inducement for amusement."[39]

Residents of Santa Clara County took to autos avidly. By 1930 one out of every three had a car, and the city of San Jose, which had early undertaken a program to upgrade its streets, "had the greatest week-day auto traffic count in the State, and was the only California city whose week-day traffic count exceeded that of holidays."[40] A host of service and retail businesses appeared in downtown auto rows, major highways to San Francisco and Los Angeles intersected at the city center, San Jose experienced its first traffic congestion, and passenger travel on interurban lines diminished until the last streetcar trip was made in 1938.[41] Automobiles were having their way with the Santa Clara valley.

The initial impact of the auto was to reinforce the existing balance between country and city. Trucks and cars facilitated travel between rural districts and urban centers such as San Jose, San Francisco, and Oakland, tying the two types of settlements more closely together. Once the local population began to grow, however, the automobile and the highway contributed to the process by which city and suburb replaced farmland. Growth did not happen immediately; the area stagnated through the depressed 1930s and the early 1940s. At the end of World War II, city and county leaders worried about

*The automobile reshapes San Jose and the Santa Clara valley. Probably taken between 1910 and 1919, this picture documents the importance of the new means of transportation in the area. It looks northwest along South First Street to the center of the downtown at Santa Clara Avenue. The intersection at the center of the picture is South First and what was then East San Antonio Street. The section to the lower right is now occupied by the new United States Courthouse and Federal Building. (Courtesy California Historical Society, San Francisco.)*

the future. Military demand had increased manufacturing in the valley, but residents feared that the economy still depended too heavily on the seasonal industries of horticulture and canning.[42]

This postwar apprehension about the economy proved unjustified. The Santa Clara valley benefited tremendously from the federal defense spending that had begun during the war. Frederick Terman, a professor of radio engineering at Stanford University, made sure that the region attracted more than its share of government and private investment in advanced research and development. Terman helped to develop Stanford Industrial Park, a meeting ground where academic scientists joined with military planners and major corporations to produce the high technology electronics industry. The industrial park succeeded in attracting Stanford graduates like William Hewlett and David Packard, who built the leading firm of Hewlett-Packard, as well as such promi-

*Silicon Valley in 1981. (Courtesy* San Jose Mercury News.)

nent easterners as William B. Shockley, coinventor of the transistor, who came to Palo Alto in 1955. As new company after new company emerged, and as spending for electronics increased, particularly after the Russians launched Sputnik in 1957, the budding industry spilled beyond the shadow of Stanford to communities like Mountain View, Cupertino, Campbell, Santa Clara, and San Jose. By the 1970s the lowlands of Santa Clara County had been renamed Silicon Valley in honor of the high technology enterprise that seemed to be leading Americans into the postindustrial age.[43]

With economic growth came more people, and with more people came urban expansion that reduced the rural character of the valley. Between 1940 and 1960 San Jose's population grew from 68,500 to 204,000, and the population of the county grew from 175,000 to 642,000. In 1960, all but 40,000 of the people in Santa Clara County lived inside the recently created San Jose Standard Metropolitan Statistical Area. The new census district reflected the burgeoning urban and suburban character of northern Santa Clara valley. Constant city growth ensured that prices, taxes, and use restrictions on cropland increased, pressuring many farmers to sell their holdings. To accommodate the new population, developers built upon and paved over orchards, fields, and pastures. Between 1942 and 1957, 76,000 of the county's 232,000 acres of cultivable soils were converted to nonfarm use, a pattern that continued into the 1960s and 1970s.[44] The northern valley grew steadily more urban and industrial while the agrarian culture that had prevailed for nearly a century declined.

The reshaping of San Jose epitomized urbanization in the Santa Clara valley, and also typified patterns of expansion in midcentury Sunbelt cities in the United States. Between 1945 and 1970 the town's development was directed by a group of business and civic leaders dedicated to aggressive growth. The city manager of the early 1950s, A.P. ("Dutch") Hamann, exemplified the new elite; his critics have often pointed out that Hamann, a former used car salesman, wanted to model San Jose's growth after Los Angeles. Officials administered a very calculating policy of annexation in order to keep the city from being hemmed in on all sides by other growing towns and to ensure that new residential districts as well as outlying shopping centers would be built on city land. Between 1950 and 1970 San Jose grew from 15,000 to 75,000 acres, sprawling over the level terrain that had once been farms, barrios, and small towns, and draining the vitality from the downtown core. By the late 1960s, this single-minded policy of growth had generated an influential group of critics who argued that urban quality-of-life issues should now take precedence over growth in city politics and planning.[45] As residents of the region grew more concerned about protecting and preserving natural and cultural resources, it became clear that the age of unquestioned expansion had drawn to a close.

The new concern for quality of life was one effect of the rapid and extensive social changes that had taken place since World War II. In the space of little more than one generation, the region had been transformed from an agricultural area into a postindustrial, Sunbelt metropolis, with all the problems—air pollution, water shortages, traffic congestion, and ethnic tensions—of a major American city. Huge international corporations now set the pace for an economy once dominated by relatively small farms; a youthful, highly mobile population, mostly made up of recent arrivals from other parts of California and the nation, now thrived in an area once occupied by people with a stronger attachment to the lands of the valley. The cost of living became prohibitively high for minorities and for the lower strata employed in high technology industries, forcing companies to relocate their plants to other regions and other countries, yet Santa Clara County became one of the best-known and wealthiest counties in the nation.[46]

The emergence of Silicon Valley restored San Jose to the prominence it had once possessed as the first pueblo in Alta California and as the first state capital. After the early 1850s, the Santa Clara valley took a backseat to other coastal metropolitan areas, and its importance as a representative example of California culture and society went unrecognized. People occasionally acknowledged the region's ethnic diversity, rural riches, and urban qualities, but greater attention was given to larger cities in the state. Even residents of the Santa Clara valley measured their progress against San Francisco and Los Angeles. With its recent demographic and industrial growth, however, the San Jose area has begun to blossom in its own right by developing distinctive cultural and political styles. The rise of Silicon Valley has ensured that the region receive more attention, particularly from those seeking a glimpse of tomorrow. The Santa Clara valley apparently is as instructive about the future of California as it is about its past.

2

# Federal Court's First Arrival
# in San Jose, April 5, 1852

*Christian G. Fritz*

Holding federal court in San Jose is "a useless and almost ridiculous formality," declared United States District Court Judge Ogden Hoffman, Jr. in 1853. Hoffman, the first judge of the Northern District of California, had been required under the provisions of the act of September 28, 1850 to hold annual terms in four locations: San Francisco, Sacramento, Stockton, and San Jose. Hoffman noted that while San Jose was formerly the state capital it "is now an inconsiderable town" in which sessions lasted less than half an hour. Just enough time, he said, to satisfy the requirements of the statute and return to San Francisco for an extra session to handle the cases crowding his dockets.[1] The gold rush brought many things to California, not the least of which was an enormous amount of business for Judge Hoffman. The young judge — he was only twenty-nine when President Millard Fillmore appointed him in 1851 — complained about holding court in San Jose in a letter to the attorney general of the United States. He urged that legislation be passed giving him discretion to hold court in locations other than San Francisco if and when judicial business warranted.

Despite Judge Hoffman's characterization of San Jose, the South Bay counties, particularly Santa Clara, had early developed a reputation as a more healthful and appealing area than the wind-blown sand dunes of the San Francisco peninsula. San Jose and Monterey had the advantage of being significant towns in Alta California when Yerba Buena, the settlement that eventually grew into the city of San Francisco, was still a hamlet. With the gold rush, San Francisco eclipsed the South Bay towns in economic and later in political importance, but despite the sudden rise of San Francisco, its inhabitants — including lawyers — were not unaffected by the charms of the lower peninsula.

Walter Colton, the first American alcalde at Monterey, lovingly described the town with its "wild waving background of forest-feathered cliffs, the green slopes, and glim-

*United States District Court Judge Ogden Hoffman, Jr. In 1853 Judge Hoffman found holding federal court in San Jose "a useless and almost ridiculous formality." (Photograph by Jose Maria Mora, New York City; reproduced courtesy California Historical Society, San Francisco.)*

*San Jose in the 1850s. During this decade Judge Ogden Hoffman held federal court in the city. (Courtesy The Bancroft Library.)*

mering walls of the white dwellings, and the dash of the billows on the sparkling sands of the bay" which "fix and charm the eye." In 1849, he lamented that

> all eyes are turned to San Francisco, with her mud bottoms, her sand hills, and her chill winds, which cut the stranger like hail driven through the summer solstice. Avarice may erect its shanty there, but contentment, and a love of the wild and beautiful, will construct its tabernacle among the flowers, the waving shades, and fragrant airs of Monterey.[2]

Santa Clara County, too, received its share of praise not only because of its natural beauty and mild weather but because it offered fruits, fresh vegetables, and dairy products. One suffering forty-niner wrote to his wife from San Francisco relating that a doctor had predicted his death if the miner didn't leave the cold city soon. The doctor advised him to go to the Sandwich Islands (Hawaii). Instead, he went to San Jose, where after a month of gorging himself on potatoes, squash, grapes, and fresh dairy products, he returned to San Francisco and astonished his friends with his recovery.[3]

Visitors to the Santa Clara valley, initially drawn to California by the gold rush, often waxed eloquent about the area. One Englishman declared in 1851 that the valley presented "a scene as rich and lovely as ever was portrayed by the delightful pencil of Claude Lorraine." Characterized as a "location for settlement scarcely equaled," Santa Clara valley had both "unapproachable pastoral charms" and a "voluptuous and salubrious climate." While most visitors were struck by the mild climate and natural beauty of the valley, some had reservations about the conditions in early San Jose. One pious immigrant to California, Dr. A.W. Rawson, made a careful study of the Bay Area with an eye to settling down and sending for his family back in Illinois. Although Dr. Rawson found San Jose a place "of many advantages . . . the fact that every hotel in the village had a billiard table or more prevented my making choice of it for a home." The good doctor eventually decided on Santa Cruz, a place with "many advantages over others in respect to morals, social influences, family, and amount of agricultural lands."[4]

In the midst of such perceptions, the federal district court opened its first session in San Jose on April 5, 1852, in the State House Building on the east side of Market Plaza, between San Fernando and San Antonio streets. This two-story structure then housed the county and district courts (predecessor courts to today's superior court) for Santa Clara County. The comity and courtesy shown by the state courts in the mid-nineteenth century towards Judge Hoffman would be repeated in the twentieth century when the federal district court returned to San Jose to a courtroom of the Santa Clara County Superior Court.[5]

Judge Hoffman's characterization of holding court in locations other than San Francisco as "useless" was not strictly correct. At his first San Jose session Hoffman granted motions to transfer three cases then pending in the Third Judicial District Court of California to his court. The third district then included the counties of Santa Clara, Contra Costa, Santa Cruz, and Monterey. The three cases removed reflected characteristics of much of the later legal history of the South Bay counties.[6]

Of special significance is the fact that all three cases concerned disputes over land. The case of *Maria y Bernal de Berryessa v. James A. Forbes et al.* dealt with title to and the profits of the famous New Almaden quicksilver mine. The plaintiffs were represented by two Southerners, Edward W.F. Sloan of South Carolina, and William H. Rhodes of North Carolina. The partnership of Sloan & Rhodes practiced mainly in San Francisco, but the potentially large fees in the adjudication of land claims lured them — as it did

*State House Building, 1849. On April 5, 1852, the building housed the first federal district court session in San Jose. (Courtesy Clyde Arbuckle.)*

many other San Francisco lawyers — to the South Bay. Opposing the plaintiff's motion for an injunction and appointment of a receiver for the profits of the New Almaden mine was Frederick Billings. Billings, a partner in Halleck, Peachy and Billings, one of the most successful and prestigious San Francisco law firms of the day, became general counsel to the British investors that controlled and worked the fabulously rich quicksilver mine. His client, the manager of the mine, was British and Billings sought removal to the federal court on the basis of diversity of citizenship.

Diversity also formed the grounds for removal of the case of *Joseph L. Folsom v. Anna Maria Sparks et al.* Defendants in this action to compel execution on a conveyance were residents of St. Croix, then a part of the Danish West Indies. Billings's firm represented the plaintiffs, opposed by Hall McAllister. Destined to become a preeminent leader of the California bar, McAllister received praise from his peers as a "lawyer's lawyer — being most consulted by other attorneys and by the bench."[7] His father, Matthew Hall McAllister, became a special United States circuit court judge for California in 1855 — the first such position since the ill-fated scheme of the Federalist party to retain control of the judiciary by such judgeships in the wake of President Jefferson's election in 1800.

The last case to be transferred involved an ejectment suit by William Wiggins, John B. Weller, and James M. Jones against John B. Gray and Knowles Taylor. Two of the

*Judge Craven P. Hester of the third district court of California. His refusal to transfer the case of Johnson v. Gordon to federal court was one of the earliest challenges to federal judicial authority in the Far West. (Courtesy California State Library.)*

plaintiffs, Weller and Jones, were lawyers in partnership and handled the suit. Formed in 1849 — the same year they met at California's constitutional convention in Monterey — Weller and Jones provided the earliest if somewhat short-lived example of a law firm headquartered in San Francisco but having a branch office in San Jose. Weller, one of California's first United States senators and later governor of the state, handled the business of the San Francisco office. Jones lived and worked in San Jose. In 1850 Jones received appointment and confirmation as judge of the United States District Court for the Southern District of California; Weller handled the case for the defendants.

The subject matter of the three cases removed to Judge Hoffman's court and the legal talent associated with them forecast the federal court legal history of the four counties. When Congress acted in 1854 (one year after Judge Hoffman's plea for help from the attorney general) and abolished San Jose as a place of holding federal court, more than a century would pass before a federal court would once again hold a session there. Though the institution of the federal court may not have had a situs in Santa Clara County, some of the most important litigation to come before the federal district courts of California in the nineteenth century originated from the area. The Northern District of California, with District Judge Hoffman and Circuit Judge McAllister presiding in San Francisco, heard many of the important land cases that affected the four counties. The New

Almaden mine case alone became one of the most celebrated cases in the northern district's history. Moreover, Santa Clara County set the scene for a fascinating jurisdictional struggle between Judge Hoffman's court and the county's district court.

Just three years after California entered the Union, Santa Clara County provided one of the earliest challenges to federal judicial authority in the Far West. On August 3, 1853, after several days of oral argument, California's Third District Court Judge Craven P. Hester denied a motion to transfer a case from his court to Judge Hoffman in San Francisco. In the first three cases to come before the federal court from Santa Clara County the parties had consented to removal. Now, however, federal jurisdiction itself became an issue when the county resisted the defendant's efforts to remove the case to San Francisco.

Upon its appeal to the California Supreme Court, *Johnson v. Gordon* became the earliest judicial expression by that court of a theory of state sovereignty that southern states later used to justify secession. That the constitutional theories that underlay the South's position during the Civil War should surface in California in the early 1850s was not really surprising. After all, the state's supreme court was for a time dominated by Southerners and many leaders of the prevailing Democratic party in California belonged to the Chivalry, or pro-slavery, wing of that party. Many prominent lawyers in the state, including several from San Jose, were sympathetic to the expansion of slavery. Some of them, when the Civil War came, left California to take up arms for the Southern cause. Others who remained in California refused to take the loyalty oath required by lawyers appearing before the state courts. As a consequence many of these men, including Solomon Heydenfeldt (who as a justice of the California Supreme Court had written the opinion in the *Johnson* case), and prominent lawyers Gregory Yale (who wrote a very influential treatise on mining law) and E.J. Pringle (who became a leading land lawyer), abandoned trial work altogether. Some did quite well as counselors rather than litigators.[8]

Indeed, the attorneys hired by Santa Clara County to resist the transfer to the federal court in San Francisco were prominent South Bay lawyers from states that permitted slavery. William T. Wallace (of Kentucky) and C.T. Rylands (of Missouri) were leaders of the local bar each of whom married daughters of the first American governor of California, Peter H. Burnett, himself a native of Tennessee. The three formed a law partnership that flourished with the talents of Wallace and Rylands and with the political connections established by Burnett.

The case of *Johnson v. Gordon* traces its origins back to a routine debt collection case.[9] On May 17, 1852, James E. Boulden recovered a judgment in the third district court against Henry Clarkson and Jacob D. Hoppe for $12,000 (including $5,000 interest on a loan of $7,000). On February 12, 1853, Joseph W. Johnson, the sheriff of Santa Clara County executed the judgment by selling the interest the debtors had in the Rancho de San Juan Bautista. This rancho consisted of nearly 8,900 acres and included within its bounds the present-day communities of Hillsdale, Robertsville, and Willow Glen as well as much of the Lone Hill vineyard area. The highest bidder, with $5,000, was the flamboyant entrepreneur George Gordon. It was Gordon, more than anyone else, who precipitated the case by subsequently refusing to pay his bid. His motives remain unclear; perhaps the agent bidding on Gordon's behalf overstepped his principal's instructions or simply bought a property Gordon didn't want at that price.[10] In any event, Sheriff Johnson held a second execution sale on March 21; then Lucy Hoppe, the wife of one of the debtors, picked up the property for a mere $151.

Two days later Sheriff Johnson filed an action in the third district court for $5,649 — the difference between the amount recovered in the second sale and the initial bid made by Gordon. Two suits to this effect were filed on behalf of the sheriff, one in March and one in May, and in both instances personal service was made on Gordon. On June 6, 1853, Gordon's attorney William Barber — a United States commissioner (a forerunner of today's federal magistrate) and a good friend of Judge Hoffman — objected to the proceeding on the grounds of the duplication of suits. After Judge Hester overruled his objection, Barber petitioned to transfer the case to Judge Hoffman's court "exercising the powers and jurisdiction of a Circuit Court of the United States." Barber as well as two other witnesses testified that Gordon was English and not a citizen of the United States. Barber cited Gordon's foreign citizenship and noted that the matter in controversy exceeded $500: the threshold amount needed to appear before the circuit court. Judge Hester refused to transfer the case and on August 3, 1853, gave Sheriff Johnson a judgment for $5,649 plus interest at ten percent and court costs. After unsuccessfully renewing his motion to transfer the case to federal court, Gordon appealed to the California Supreme Court on August 30, 1853.

The law firm of Janes, Noyes & Barber handled the appeal for George Gordon, most likely with William Barber making the oral argument. Barber argued that his appearance before Judge Hester on June 6th for Gordon did not constitute an admission of the state court's jurisdiction but was merely to remove the case to the federal court. Given the clear evidence of Gordon's alienage and the appropriate posting of bond, Judge Hester's decree for Sheriff Johnson was "illegal and void." "It was obligatory on the court," said Barber, "and not a matter of discretion, to direct the transfer of this case." Barber took special objection to Judge Hester's decision overruling the motion for a transfer "without in any way indicating the reason of his decision" although all the requirements for transferring a case under the Judiciary Act of 1789 had been met by the defendant.[11]

The argument made by Santa Clara County in support of Judge Hester's decision was a model of pithy alternative pleading, composed of three points scrawled on half a sheet of paper. First, section 12 of the Judiciary Act of 1789 (under which transfers to federal courts were authorized) was unconstitutional. Second, the case did not fall within section 12. Third, even if it did, the "act intends a discretion in the court that authorizes the court to pass both upon the question of alienage and the sufficiency of the bonds. In this case that discretion was properly exercised."[12]

Fourteen months after Gordon appealed, the supreme court rendered its opinion. Justice Heydenfeldt cast the issue before the court as the determination of the relative "power between the federal and state judiciary." After reflecting upon the conflicting political theories, Heydenfeldt declared the arguments of John C. Calhoun more persuasive than those of Alexander Hamilton. He admitted the general acquiescence of the states in federal judicial power but saw "no sufficient reason in this fact for the surrender of a power which belongs to the sovereignty we represent, involving an assumption of power by another jurisdiction in derogation of that sovereignty."[13]

Relying heavily on Calhoun's *Discourse on the Constitution and Government of the United States,* Heydenfeldt denied the United States Supreme Court a role as the final arbiter of the Constitution. Proper construction of the supremacy clause, he argued, did not invest the federal courts with appellate control over the states. Rather, the Constitution mandated a concurrence of judicial power between the federal and state courts. States were only limited if their exercise of jurisdiction "would be absolutely and totally contradictory and repugnant" to that of the federal courts.[14]

*Justice Solomon Heydenfeldt of the California Supreme Court. His opinion upheld Judge Hester's refusal to transfer* Johnson v. Gordon *to federal court by drawing on the doctrines of John C. Calhoun. (Courtesy The Bancroft Library.)*

Only two potential problems might arise from complete concurrent jurisdiction — conflicts over jurisdiction and lack of uniform decisions — but both were "more imaginary than real." No conflicts over jurisdiction need occur, Heydenfeldt argued, if courts followed "the firmly established rule of the common law, that in all cases of concurrent jurisdiction the court which first has possession of the subject must decide it." Heydenfeldt dismissed the lack of uniformity argument by saying that divergent state opinions in matters of federal concern would not be more troublesome than the present "want of uniformity in reference to subjects within the exclusive jurisdiction of the state courts." Besides, "as long as the age of the world continues to be one of great intellectual vigor, uniformity of opinion is and must be unattainable. It is the chimera of an unhealthy brain, because it is incompatible with the known characteristics of the human intellect."[15]

Accordingly, Heydenfeldt held that transfers from a state to a federal court were impermissible and that a writ of error or an appeal from a state court to the United States Supreme Court did not exist. The newspapers referred to *Johnson v. Gordon* as the "nullification decision."[16]

California's high court, wrote the *Stockton Argus*, had embraced "the metaphysical abstractions of John C. Calhoun" by declaring his doctrine "not only the true theory of constitutional law, but . . . *de jure et de facto,* the Constitution *and* laws." "The decision,"declared the *San Francisco Alta California*, "puts the inhabitants of this state without the pale of the Federal Union, so far as the judicial department is concerned, and deprives them of their equal participation in the benefits of the general government instituted by the whole people." Both the *Argus* and *Alta California* correctly represented the decision as a political discussion of the states' rights doctrine.[17]

*Judge Delos Lake of the fourth district court of California. Judge Lake defied the California Supreme Court's ruling in* Johnson v. Gordon. *(Courtesy California State Library.)*

Not all reaction to the decision was unfavorable. The *San Francisco Herald* noted that a San Francisco attorney had recently published a pamphlet entitled "An Inquiry into the Constitutionality of the 12th, 13th and 25th Sections of the Judiciary Act of 1789." The paper observed that the writer "enters into a very able and elaborate examination of the question and contends that all decisions in favor of the constitutionality of the Judiciary Act were Federalist decisions, to which the judges who made them were urged by their political tendencies, and that they should not be held to be binding as established and orthodox precedents."[18]

Legislative response to the decision came immediately. On February 8, 1855, Billington C. Whiting introduced a bill in the state senate entitled an "Act to Provide for Certifying and Removing Certain Cases from the Courts of This State to the United States Circuit Courts, and to Remove by Writ of Error Certain Cases from the Supreme Court of this State to the Supreme Court of the United States." Whiting's bill reenacted the sections of the Judiciary Act of 1789 that authorized transfers and appeals from state to federal courts.[19]

An interesting commentary on the contemporary understanding of the constitutional relationship between state and federal legislatures and judiciaries is reflected in the *San Francisco Herald*'s reaction to the Whiting bill. The paper doubted whether the bill could accomplish its purpose since the state supreme court "made the decision on constitutional grounds, and the direct command implied in the bill . . . to revoke their former decision can be disobeyed by the supreme court on the ground of its unconstitutionality, for if the Constitution of the United States does not authorize the transfer of cases from the state courts to the federal courts, an act passed by the state legislature authorizing that which the constitution does not authorize, can have no binding force."[20]

While Whiting's bill worked itself through the California Senate and the Assembly, two state judges, Delos Lake of the fourth district (which then included San Francisco) and D.O. Shattuck of the Superior Court of San Francisco, defied the ruling in *Johnson v. Gordon*. Both judges granted motions to transfer cases to the federal district court, declaring "that in deciding a constitutional question they felt bound to consider the rulings of the Supreme Court of the United States more binding upon them than those of the state supreme court."[21]

Judge Shattuck's motion arose in a case to recover pay for work in filling in water lots. The defendant, a resident of Virginia, petitioned for a transfer to the northern district court. After Judge Shattuck granted the motion, the plaintiff appealed to the state supreme court, and Shattuck was ordered to show cause why he had ignored *Johnson v. Gordon*. After argument of counsel, the high court issued a writ of mandamus ordering Judge Shattuck to adjudicate the case as if he had not granted the motion to transfer. Judge Shattuck denied a motion *pro forma* that he take the case from the jurisdiction of the federal court, stating he would "take the responsibility of disobeying the mandamus."[22]

The *Alta California* noted "a speck of war here" and constructed a scenario that would test the relative judicial power between the state and federal governments.

> Suppose the venerable Judge Shattuck is imprisoned, and he asks the United States Court for relief, and the United States marshal sets him at liberty, and then the sheriff is ordered to arrest him and lock him up again, and the marshal takes him out again, till finally the two forces of the state and general government are brought into actual conflict, and General Wool, at the head of United States troops and revenue service, and Governor Bigler, commander in chief of the military of California, draw out their forces for battle, to decide which court should be sustained. Why it would be a beautiful commentary on some of the phases of states' rights theories."[23]

Legislative action and not military force broke the deadlock between Judge Shattuck and the California Supreme Court. On April 6, 1855 the *Alta California* reported the passage of the Whiting bill. "It is a rebuke such as, we trust, will not be without its influence, not only on the body it was intended to condemn, but also upon those dissatisfied and unappreciated geniuses who are endeavoring to create dissatisfaction here toward the general government."

The jurisdictional conflict of the *Johnson* case did not result in the military standoff speculated upon by the *Alta California*. Nor was the episode unique. In fact, one year later, the California Supreme Court again denied federal court jurisdiction under the Judiciary Act of 1789.[24] What the *Johnson* case reflected, however, were the sectional tensions and debates over competing theories of constitutionalism that were common to all the states (admittedly with varying degrees of urgency) before 1860. It would take the bloodbath of the Civil War to lay to rest the "constitutional heresy" enunciated in *Johnson v. Gordon*. Only after the war was fought and the North prevailed would federal courts — in Santa Clara or anywhere else in the nation — win the wide and largely unchallenged jurisdiction that they enjoy today.

3

# The History of Monterey's
# Federal District Court, 1851-1866

*Caroline L. Hunt*

Monterey played an important role in California's early history. It was the first capital, the administrative and judicial center of Spanish and then Mexican government of Alta California. Then in 1849 it was the site for the constitutional convention. It was a logical choice as a seat for the United States district court and served as a seat of the southern district from California's statehood in 1850 until 1866 when the southern district was abolished for twenty years.

In the early years of California's statehood, one of the most important social and legal issues was the ownership and control of land. Under the Treaty of Guadalupe Hidalgo of 1848, the United States agreed to fully recognize Mexican land grants, which in many cases were subject to conflicting claims of title. The method of adjudication of property claims in large part determined the economic and social order of the new state; their adjudication was the predominant business of the district court at Monterey. The district court had jurisdiction over appeals from the Board of Land Commissioners, which was established to determine the validity of title to private land claims. Individuals claiming title were required to present documentary evidence and the testimony of witnesses in support of their claims. As is noted by George Cosgrave, a later southern district court judge, claimants were required to deal with an unfamiliar legal system, often in a language foreign to the majority of grant holders: "Fine business for lawyers."[1]

Prior to statehood, California had little need for lawyers. The Mexican government had established a legal system under the regional administration of magistrates or judges, called alcaldes. Walter Colton, the first American alcalde of Monterey writes: "There is not a judge on any bench in England or the United States whose power is so absolute as that of the alcalde of Monterey." Colton writes of the limitations on lawyers under the Mexican legal system:

*Monterey in 1856. This drawing shows the city in one of the years the United States District Court for the Southern District of California sat in it. The drawing is by Henry Miller (fl. 1856-57), known for his views of California towns and missions. (Courtesy The Bancroft Library.)*

We have at this time three young lawyers in Monterey as full of legal acuteness as the lancet cup of a phlebotomist. All want clients, and fees, and the privilege of a practice in this court. Mexican statutes, which prevail here, permit lawyers as counsel, but preclude their pleas. This spoils the whole business, and every effort has been made to have the impediment removed and the floodgate of eloquence lifted. I should be glad to gratify their ambition, but it is impossible. I shall never get through with the business pressing on my hands in every variety of shape which civil and criminal jurisprudence ever assumed. I tell them after the evidence has been submitted, the verdict or decision must follow, and then if any in the courtroom desire to hear the arguments, they can adjourn to another apartment and plead as long as they like. In this way, justice will go ahead, and eloquence too, and the great globe still turn on its axle.[2]

In 1851, Judge James M. Jones was appointed judge of the southern district court and on May 29, 1851, he signed an order adjourning the first session at Monterey until the next year. In a letter concerning the expenses of establishing officers' salaries, rented courtrooms, and furniture for the court, Judge Jones wrote:

The embarrassment arising from the total lack of precedent in the first organization of the courts of California . . . will I trust excuse the particularity of these questions . . . I hope the Department will bear in mind the unusual difficulty, delay and great uncertainty of communication with California, especially the southern part; the extraordinary rate of monthly interest upon money and discount upon drafts on Washington: the total inability to obtain credit without

*United States District Court Judge James M. Jones. The first district court judge for the Southern District of California, Judge Jones died in 1851, less than a year after taking office. This picture was painted in 1845. (Private collection; reprinted from George Cosgrave, "James McHall Jones: The Judge That Never Presided,"* California Historical Society Quarterly 20 *(June 1941): facing page 97.)*

great sacrifice; and the exceeding high prices demanded for rents, labor, furniture, and goods of nearly all descriptions; and so arrange that the salaries of the officers and the expenses of the courts may be transmitted as speedily and certainly as the nature of the case and the rules of the Department will permit.

With great respect I remain, Sir,

Your Obedient Servant

J.M. JONES Judge
Southern District of California[3]

The early problems were resolved, a clerk was appointed at Monterey, and the federal apparatus was reportedly ready to proceed, when Jones died on December 15, 1851, without presiding over a session of the court. The southern district judgeship was left vacant for three years due, at least in part, to political infighting. The General Appropriations Bill of 1852 authorized the judge of the northern district to act as judge for the southern district. Accordingly, Judge Hoffman convened the first session of the Federal District Court of the Southern District, in Monterey on June 5, 1853.

The first case he heard there involved a suit in admiralty against the Steamer *McKim*. William H. Russell appeared for the plaintiff, with Josiah Merritt and Delos R. Ashley intervenors. On Russell's motion, the matter was referred to a master, John A. Monroe, to take testimony and recommend the amount due. The following day, Judge Hoffman approved Monroe's report and ordered the vessel sold. Isaac Stockton Keith Ogier reportedly appeared at this session, having been commissioned as United States district attorney for the southern district on April 6, 1853.

Increasing work generated by appeals from the Board of Land Commissioners put pressure on Judge Hoffman who was attempting to serve both the northern and southern districts. Hoffman complained that the existing law required him to hold sessions in both districts simultaneously, which he submitted was impossible.

Having blocked a previous attempt by President Fillmore to fill the southern district judgeship and in fact having helped abolish the post in 1852, Senator Gwin of California led efforts to re-create and fill the post once Franklin Pierce became president. His act reestablishing the judgeship passed Congress on January 18, 1854. Ogier, after some persuasive lobbying to President Pierce, was appointed southern district judge on January 23, 1854; he resigned as United States district attorney, and the next day took his oath of office as judge. On June 5, 1854, Judge Ogier presided over his first session at Monterey. Since the cases before the court were all land commission appeals, and a new district attorney had not been appointed, Ogier adjourned the court.

The first decision in the land cases was delivered September 24, 1854, in the *Heirs of Felipe Gomez v. United States*. George Cosgrave writes of Ogier:

> It might be well, were anyone in a position to do so, to call the attention of the occupants of the federal bench of a later age to the brevity and clarity that mark the pages of this pioneer character, whose work contributed so materially to the progress of the state. There is no citation of authority. Not a brief was filed. Argument was always oral.[4]

Although Ogier's handling of land cases was swift with a minimum of decision writing, land litigation in California involved a high degree of argument and complexity and was very extensive. In 1846, 10-13 million acres were owned by 800 individuals. While the land distribution had been somewhat changed by 1854, there were still numerous chances for unscrupulous individuals to cash in.

One of the men most successful in acquiring vast tracts in the Monterey area was David Jacks. The city of Monterey had been granted some 30,000 acres of land under Mexican rule in 1830. After statehood in 1850, the city land ended up in the hands of a man who was unable to pay the land taxes. Delos Ashley was retained by Monterey to represent the city before the United States Land Commission in San Francisco for the purpose of regaining title to the public lands, and in 1853 the title reverted to the city of Monterey. Since the city was without funds to pay Ashley's bill for services, the Board of Trustees passed a resolution that the public lands be sold at auction to satisfy the debt to Ashley. On February 9, 1854, Ashley and his partner David Jacks (the only bidders) bought what is now Fort Ord, Del Rey Oakes, Jacks Peak, half of Del Monte Forest, Pacific Grove, most of Monterey, and all of the undeveloped land not in private ownership in and around the Monterey Peninsula for a little over one thousand dollars. Needless to say, Jacks's activities did not endear him to the citizenry of Monterey County. In 1877, the city sued to reclaim its lands, but the California state legislature,

United States District Court Judge
Isaac Stockton Keith Ogier. Judge
James M. Jones's successor, Judge
Ogier presided over federal district
court in Monterey during the 1850s.
(Courtesy California Historical
Society, San Francisco.)

presumably with Jacks's encouragement, had passed a law legitimizing the sale of the Monterey city property, effective one day prior to Jacks's purchase. The case was appealed to the United States Supreme Court, which decided in Jacks's favor. Robert Louis Stevenson wrote of Jacks:

> The land is held, for the most part, in those enormous tracts which are another legacy of Mexican days and form the present chief danger and disgrace of California: and the holders are mostly of American or British birth. We have here in England no idea of the trouble and inconveniences which flow from the existence of these large landholders — land-thieves, land sharks, or land-grabbers, they are more commonly and plainly called. Thus the town-lands of Monterey are in the hands of a single man. How they came there is an obscure, vexatious question, and rightly or wrongly, the man is hated with a great hatred. His life has been repeatedly in danger. Not very long ago, I was told, the stage was stopped and examined three evenings in succession by disguised horsemen thirsting for his blood. A certain house on the Salinas road, they say, he always passes in his buggy at full speed, for the squatter sent him warning long ago.[5]

Another interesting case was adjudicated by Judge Ogier. Vicente Gomez had petitioned for confirmation of the Panoche Grande land claim. The petition was denied by the Board of Land Commissioners and the appeal by Gomez to the district court was heard on June 5, 1857. United States District Attorney Pacificus Ord made no comment when counsel for Gomez stated that the United States did not object to confirmation of the claim. A decree was entered confirming the claim. Ogier later received information that Ord had an interest in the disputed tract, and on his own motion set aside the decree and referred the case to trial. The matter eventually was litigated before the United States Supreme Court. The Court noted that Ord was originally Gomez's attorney, prior to his appointment as United States district attorney on July 1, 1854, and that for nominal consideration of $1.00, Ord had acquired one half of the land subject to the confirmation hearing.[6] The grant was not confirmed and Ord subsequently resigned his position.

By 1861, the year in which Ogier died unexpectedly of apoplexy, the bulk of litigation over land title to private land grants was largely completed, although much litigation would continue over surveys of confirmed grants. Land had always been the chief source of business and with completion of much of the initial litigation the court had little to justify its existence. On August 5, 1861, Fletcher M. Haight was nominated to succeed to the position of district court judge by President Lincoln, after petitions from Monterey citizens. Haight owned a large ranch in Carmel Valley, and was described as "partly" a citizen of Monterey.

Haight presided over the demise of the southern district court. The court minutes reflect a dwindling number of land appeals and numerous adjournments for lack of business. In 1863, Haight ordered that the Los Angeles court records and furniture be removed to Monterey; indeed, "it was humorously said that he moved the court to his ranch."[7] Sessions at Los Angeles were abolished on February 19, 1864. Two years later, the southern district court opened for its last session in Monterey. No judge presided, Haight being near death in San Francisco. "The clerk noted adjourment from day to day, like the failing pulse of the dying, until April 11, when the activities of the court ceased," less than two months after Haight's death.[8]

Bancroft comments that while there was not enough business to occupy the southern district court constantly, there were still many unsettled land titles, sued upon by the United States:

> Many claimants were already ruined by endless law suits; and now the remainder were required to travel with their witnesses several hundred miles to San Francisco, and to incur an expense they were unable to bear. It had been bad enough going to Monterey to attend court, but this was an additional infliction.[9]

# 4

## Litigation over Mexican Land Grants in Santa Clara, San Benito, Santa Cruz, and Monterey Counties

*Christian G. Fritz*

Gold beckoned the world to California in 1848, but relatively few fortunes were made by gold seekers. A historian of the California gold rush has estimated that the average argonaut realized only twenty dollars a day at the end of 1848, which figure quickly declined to an average of three dollars by the mid-1850s.[1] When placed against high inflation, back-breaking labor, and the many hardships the early placer miners faced, their financial rewards were rather meager. The real money to be made in California came from supplying transportation, provision, equipment, and entertainment. Later, of course, the heavily capitalized mining companies exploited the gold-bearing quartz deposits that were beyond the means of the individual miners, sometimes for large profits.

Land was almost as alluring as gold to those seeking quick profits. The tremendous influx of people into California after 1849 quickly increased the demand and hence value of land. Initially, the greatest profits seemed to lie in acquiring some of the recently unoccupied areas in Yerba Buena (later named San Francisco) that were being converted from sand dunes into commercial and residential property. Indeed, many of those already there speculated in "city lots" with good chances of making huge profits. Speculation in water lots, outside lands, and alcalde grants resembled a stock exchange not only in the great number and frequency of transactions but because land values were often tied to the perceived financial health of the city. By 1851 a San Francisco commission to inquire into city property found that some seventy-five percent of all city lots had been sold or granted to individuals between 1846 and 1850. In addition, the state and federal government's disposal of "swamp and overflowed lands," school lands, and various types of land script offered numerous opportunities to acquire wealth, although often at the public's expense.[2]

In the middle of this scramble for land was a special category of property which included some of the most valuable land in California and most of the future urban areas of the state. The Mexican land grants that predated the American conquest in 1846 became the focus of bitter controversy lasting several decades and involving both Californian and federal judges, legislators, and executive officers.[3] The process of quieting title to the lands held under these grants proved tortuous because of the complexity and value of the interests involved. This fact alone insured that the adjudication of titles to and the surveying of confirmed grants would be subjected to crosscurrents of pressure, influence, and manipulation. The counties of Santa Clara, San Benito, Santa Cruz, and Monterey provide a series of cases that illustrate the major themes that characterize the struggle over land in California.

The reason for the bitterness and longevity of that struggle lay less in the procedures Congress established for the settlement of land than in the context of the claims which bred delay, confusion, and ill will. Requiring claimants to seek confirmation before a specially created Board of Land Commissioners and the federal courts was burdensome and expensive, but the actual time involved in the judicial consideration of most claims was relatively short. What caused the most delay between the filing of a claim and its patent, if confirmed, were the lack of initiative on the part of the moving parties, the intervention of third parties, and the extrajudicial maneuverings with departments of the secretary of the interior. The federal trial courts gave wide latitude to the parties in setting the pace of litigation in the mid-nineteenth century. In a day before the concept of court management, the common law judge was largely a passive, if dignified, observer. Claimants and their lawyers had any number of reasons to slow down the process of litigation. Strategy was but one reason. In many cases it behooved a claimant to wait for a more favorable climate of opinion either at the local level (in the United States Attorney's office or the Surveyor General's office) or at the federal level (in the Supreme Court, the Attorney General's office, or in congressional committees).

Some cases, however, were bound to "drag their slow length along" despite the most determined efforts of aggressive lawyers.[4] Some of these claims — including those involving the New Almaden, the New Idria, and the Guadalupe mines — entailed a constellation of interests struggling over millions of dollars of profits from the ore produced by these quicksilver mines. The amounts at stake for the consortiums of investors who held conflicting interests in these mines and the government's interest insured that all branches of both the state and federal government were busied with the fate of the claims for periods of time far disproportionate to their numbers.

Claimants who were unable or unwilling to pay for the costs of litigation accounted for another type of delay. Attorneys whose clients were slow in paying fees or who quibbled over charges had little incentive to vigorously press such claims under their care. Often lawyers took land cases on a contingent or partially contingent basis, frequently advancing legal costs and the investigation of titles themselves.

The heavy costs of litigation, both for confirmation of grants and collateral suits in state courts against settler-squatters, often left the successful claimant with little cash to patent the grant. Initially surveys of confirmed grants were paid for by the government but by the 1860s the financial burden had been shifted to the claimants. To protect the fees of surveyors in California, the commissioner of the General Land Office in the Department of the Interior refused to issue patents until the cost of surveys had been paid. Scores of confirmed grants, some of which had been surveyed, remained unpatented for many years. By the 1870s, the persistence of a large number of land claims yet unpatented induced the land commissioner to seek an appropriation to complete surveys that confirmed grantees had not paid as the only means of getting the cases out of his office.

Lawyers were also a cause of delay in the resolution of these claims. The lure of potentially large fees induced some lawyers to take more claims than they could realistically handle. Sometimes this resulted in shoddy representation or delay, but more often — with claimants who were aware of their interests and who took active roles in preparing the defense of their claims — it resulted in the employment of a different lawyer. The legal histories of many of these claims were complex and each transfer necessarily meant a period of time for the new attorney to familiarize himself with the case. It was not infrequent for over half a dozen different lawyers to be in charge of a claim between its filing before the board and the receipt of a patent from the General Land Office.

Different expectations about land in California provided a context that was bound to delay settlement of titles. The claims of individual grantees to large portions of some of the most desirable land in the state predictably resulted in conflict with the land-hungry settlers and disillusioned miners in California who expected cheap, readily available land. The pattern of freely disposable land to settlers on the western frontier was not repeated in California.

The average size of Mexican ranchos patented under the act of 1851 was roughly 17,600 acres.[5] Many claims were for substantially more, including the fantastic Iturbide claim for over 1.75 million acres in California to be selected by the claimant. The Iturbide claim was rejected, but legitimate concerns arose that huge tracts might receive judicial sanction especially when the Land Board confirmed the notorious Limantour claims in 1856 for half of San Francisco, several islands around the Bay, and part of the Tiburon peninsula. Many settlers accustomed to small holdings with fixed boundaries had difficulty accepting the equity of a single claim for many thousands of acres of unfenced land. The result was prolonged disputes between claimants and settler-squatters over the validity of titles and especially the equitable boundaries of confirmed land grants. Settler-squatters had their champions both in the state legislature and in Congress and the first two decades of California's politics bore the marks of the struggles between land grant claimants and settler-squatters.

Perhaps the greatest source of complication and delay in the settlement of the grants arose from the fact that many other types of landed interests, particularly in urban areas like San Francisco, hinged on these grants. Of vital interest to many landowners, businessmen, and speculators was not only the rejection or confirmation of particular grants, but the extent and boundaries of the land that might be secured under a patent. San Francisco, for example, contained over fifteen claims to private land grants, many overlapping and covering some of the most valuable real estate in California. The fortunes of some of the wealthiest men in the state rested upon their real estate investments and many others had heavy investments that hung on the fate of private land grants. Titles to land granted from the city competed with private land grants, including San Francisco's claim to pueblo lands.

Moreover, there were any number of legal principles and philosophies that could guide the resolution of land titles in California. The contingent nature of titles in San Francisco and the state persisted for decades, buffeted by the alternating and often conflicting decisions of local courts, the California Supreme Court, the federal land board, and the federal courts. Legislative action by the city, state, and Congress introduced new elements and often further delay in the process of settling the conflicts over land. Thus, although the resolution of private land grants forms only part of the story of land in California, it occupied a central role. Its study is in large measure the early history of the state, for no other issue so dominated the attention of California as the efforts to resolve conflicting interests to land during the first three decades of statehood.

Why were the federal courts involved in adjudicating the California land claims? The answer lies in the congressional response to the commitment made in the Treaty of Guadalupe Hidalgo. The treaty provided that Mexican ownership of "property of every kind" within the territory ceded "shall be inviolably respected."[6] It thus committed the United States to recognize the legitimate ownership of substantial tracts of land held by individuals in the new state under Spanish and, for the most part, Mexican grants.

The method Congress adopted to identify legitimate land claims that would be recognized by the United States was the California Land Act of 1851. Most commentators have assumed that the act was responsible for the delays in settling titles in California, needlessly involving the courts and producing litigation that ultimately stripped the Hispanic native Californians (or Californios) of their land. Lamentable delays and unfortunate consequences did result, but the causes of delay were intrinsic in the interests at stake and not primarily produced by the act of 1851.[7]

The act itself had a somewhat checkered background. By the time Congress acted in the matter, the battle lines were fairly well drawn. California settler-squatters and those adverse to the idea of large tracts of land in the hands of individuals had their champion in one of California's United States senators, William M. Gwin. The principal spokesman for the interests of claimants was Senator Thomas Hart Benton of Missouri. The diametric viewpoints of these two politicians were grounded on ideology and self-interest. Gwin's position was in large measure dictated by his effort to consolidate the political support of the settlers in California while Benton could hardly ignore the fact that both his sons-in-law, John C. Fremont and William Carey Jones, owned private land grants in California. In fact, Fremont owned the claim to Las Mariposas, situated in the heart of the gold region and then estimated to be worth ten million dollars.

By the time Congress debated the policy to govern California land grants, two influential — and conflicting — reports had appeared. Together these reports provided most of the information upon which Gwin and Benton drew to make their arguments. One report had been written in 1849 by Captain Henry W. Halleck (later a major general during the Civil War) while he served as a military secretary of state for California. The other had been compiled in 1850 by Benton's son-in-law, William Carey Jones, while he was an agent for the Department of the Interior.

A West Point officer, Halleck experienced a short but very lucrative career before the Civil War as a member of one of the most successful law firms in California. Trained as an engineer rather than a lawyer, Halleck's self-study, particularly of the California land titles, and high reputation in California allowed him to join a major law firm after his resignation from the army in 1854. The firm he became a founder of, Halleck, Peachy and Billings, represented a great number of the claimants who sought confirmation of their Mexican land grants.

Halleck's report concluded that much land in California was held under titles "at least very doubtful, if not entirely fraudulent" that have "been divided up and sold to speculators, who will endeavor to dispose of it to the new settlers at exorbitant profits."[8] Halleck emphasized the inchoate nature of titles and the failure of grants to meet tech-

*William Carey Jones. In his 1850 report, written while a Department of the Interior employee, Jones concluded that Mexican land grants in California were "mostly perfect titles." (Reprinted from* San Francisco News Letter, *22 August 1896, between pages 12 and 13; courtesy California State Library.)*

nical requirements under Mexican law. His report suggested that the Mexican land grants in California should be examined critically, preferably within the context of a trial that would adjudicate titles strictly in accord with the procedures to perfect title under Mexican law.

William Carey Jones, on the other hand, concluded that the grants were "mostly *perfect titles*" and that under Mexican law the holders either had the equivalent of a patent or the equity of a perfected title. Jones conceded the existence of many grants which failed to comply strictly with Mexican procedures for perfecting title to land. But, Jones countered, in the "rude and uncultivated" state of California before the American conquest, "these formalities were to a great extent disregarded" and "the law of custom, with the acquiescence of the highest authorities, overcame, in these respects, the written law." Jones suggested a swift confirmation of titles after their survey, reserving government opposition only to those cases where "there may be reason to suppose a grant invalid."[9]

Whatever the intrinsic merits of Jones's recommendations, his report was hardly that of a disinterested observer. While he was investigating California land titles, Jones bought the twelve league (over fifty-three thousand acres) San Luis Rey and Pala Mission rancho in San Diego. Before he submitted his report, he had acquired interests in at least two additional land grants. Although Jones said he had bought the San Diego rancho after making a "full examination" of its title (it was later rejected by the United States Supreme Court) he had good reasons to favor the swift confirmation of Mexican land grants.[10]

While Halleck apparently did not own any land grants in 1849, his report recommended that the government summarily confirm American alcalde grants in San Francisco: as owner of a dozen very valuable city lots within that description, he had much to gain. Moreover, Halleck's chauvinistic insistence that Mexican law conform to "the spirit of our laws" colored his conclusions.[11] His strict insistence upon written documentation accorded with traditional land settlement practices and common law principles; had all things been equal, it might have been the fairest way of settling the Mexican land grants. Nonetheless, Jones had a telling point: the isolation and ease of obtaining land in California prior to the American conquest had diminished the practical importance of compliance with formalities entailed in granting land. Before the gold rush, land was not a commodity that generated heated disputes. Under those conditions, equity did not demand formal compliance with strict written law as the basis for determining all titles in land. Greater willingness to use oral evidence might have proven useful in establishing the holdings of some of the early grantees. Fraudulent titles would have been a problem whatever approach was adopted, but insistence upon formalities probably stimulated the "manufacturing" of needed, but missing, documents.

Halleck and Jones were in full agreement on one point: the urgency of swiftly moving to settle the private land claims and thus segregating public from private property. Even in 1849 Halleck described land title disputes as "exceedingly numerous" and he stressed the vital importance "to the peace and prosperity of the country that measures be taken without delay for the speedy and final settlement of these titles upon principles of equity and justice."[12] The tardiness of Congress was due in large part to the sectional conflicts that beset the country and were inextricably involved in the issue of whether California should be admitted as a free or slave state. When Congress finally turned its attention to Mexican land grants, the debates drew heavily upon the two land reports: Gwin carried the day, and the bill that ultimately emerged in early 1851 reflected the skepticism of Halleck's report.

The Land Act established a three-man Board of Land Commissioners before whom "each and every person claiming lands in California by virtue of any right or title derived from the Spanish or Mexican government, shall present . . . such documentary evidence and testimony of witnesses as the claimant relies upon in support of such claims."[13] The act thus placed the burden on the grantee to establish title, in the absence of which the land claimed would become public property and open to settlers. The fact that by the time the board began its deliberations many settler-squatters had taken up residence in claimed land, ensured the unpopularity of any decision. Although most of the land claimed under the act of 1851 consisted of Mexican ranchos, many other types of land hinged on the decisions of the board including mission lands, pueblo lands, and smaller tracts.

Both the claimant and the United States could appeal from decisions of the board to the federal district court, and from the latter to the United States Supreme Court. The appeal to the federal district court was essentially a new trial since both sides could introduce new evidence; no new evidence could be introduced at the Supreme Court. Although the board had the final word in only three claims, it was definitely more than a screening committee.[14] In a large number of cases the district court adopted the exact decree of the board, including its description of the grant's boundaries, which had vital bearing on the amount and location of the land eventually patented. Even more significant were the large number of cases, particularly in the southern district, where appeals by the United States were dismissed by the attorney general and the claimant allowed to proceed with the board's decision as a final decree of the district court. Although seemingly a technical point, many vital interests were sometimes at stake depending upon whether or not the decree of the board included a limitation on the amount of land to be surveyed as confirmed land under the boundaries given in the decree. Differences of many thousands of acres were often involved and gave claimants greater control over the more easily manipulated survey process.

The allowance of additional evidence proved to be one of the act's more unfortunate provisions. In some cases, claimants made hasty presentations before the board knowing that they could avail themselves of a full hearing before the district court. Less scrupulous claimants could use the board's adverse opinion citing the deficiencies in a claimant's title as a blueprint to "cure" these infirmities by presenting "new" evidence at the district court. Numerous examples exist of cases in which the district courts, presented with additional testimony, delivered perfunctory confirmations. Certainly some claimants, secure in the bona fides of their titles, saw little wrong with doctoring the record with a little perjury. In the long term, this attitude proved counterproductive: with some evidence of perjury before the courts in land cases, Attorney General Black compiled lists of "professional witnesses" whose appearance in cases raised suspicion about the validity of the grant.[15] In a climate of excessive mistrust, the required technicalities and scrutiny became stricter and it seems reasonable that some valid claims were consequently rejected.

Under the act, the president appointed the members of the board and a law agent to represent the interests of the United States. Both the law agent and a secretary appointed by the board were to be bilingual. Most importantly, the act enumerated, without prioritizing, the sources of law by which both the board and the federal courts were to be governed. It listed the governing sources as "the Treaty of Guadalupe Hidalgo, the law of nations, the laws, usages, and customs of the government from which the claim is derived, the principles of equity, and the decisions of the Supreme Court of the United States, so far as they are applicable."[16] These directives were crucial and the differing weight and interpretation they received at the hands of the board and the federal courts accounts for much of the convoluted legal history of the California land cases.

The land unsuccessfully claimed under the act or not presented to the board within two years automatically became part of the public domain of the United States. Successful grantees, however, were to receive a federal patent after presenting the General Land Office with certification of confirmation and a survey duly approved by the surveyor general of California. The final adjudication of grants under the act of 1851 dealt only with the issue of title between the United States and the claimants. The act specifically reserved the interests and rights of third parties. Inserted by Senator Gwin ostensibly to protect settlers, the reservation resulted mainly in litigation over conflicting surveys usually between claimants although sometimes initiated by settlers. The clause also insured a host of state court actions, often simultaneous with actions before the federal board and courts. The issue of surveys after confirmation of titles promised to be as, if not more, troublesome as determining the validity of the Mexican grants in the first place. At the suggestion of Judge Ogden Hoffman, the first judge of the Northern District of California, Congress passed another act in 1860 (the Hoffman Act) that attempted to deal with the thorny problems involved in surveying confirmed Mexican grants.[17]

The act of 1851 departed from earlier methods Congress had used to resolve land titles held under foreign governments that subsequently became part of the United

States, such as Louisiana and Florida.[18] By vesting final authority in the federal courts rather than in Congress it was hoped that titles might be settled more quickly. Such might have been the case had Congress resisted tampering with the process at the behest of interested parties. Congress extended periods within which claimants could file, mandated the federal courts to hear claims that had not been filed before the board, and conducted innumerable hearings on the validity of grants and the correctness of surveys for a few claims that were kept alive for half a century.

The diversity and sheer number of Mexican land grants in the four counties of Santa Clara, Santa Cruz, San Benito, and Monterey justify generalizaton about the overall experience in California. The northern and southern federal judicial districts were divided by the thirty-seventh degree of north latitude (forming a line slightly north of Santa Cruz at the Pacific through the northern portion of Death Valley National Monument near the Nevada border), so cases from the four counties arose in both judicial districts. All the claims arising out of Monterey and San Benito were in the jurisdiction of the southern district, all the claims from Santa Clara within the northern, and those from Santa Cruz were divided between the two districts. The southern district was abolished after the death of its judge in 1866 and the northern district judge, Ogden Hoffman, assumed jurisdiction over the entire state until 1886 when the southern district was reestablished. Consequently, Judge Hoffman was involved in many of the land cases originally filed in the southern district, especially with respect to new trials mandated by the United States Supreme Court and continuing troubles with surveys.

The four counties accounted for close to twenty-eight percent of the 809 private land claims that were initially filed in California. Some 224 claims were divided among the counties as follows: over eighty claims each from Monterey and Santa Clara and approximately fifty claims split between Santa Cruz and San Benito.

Of even greater importance than the sheer number of claims falling in both judicial districts, however, is the fact that the four counties contain types of land claims that illustrate the different stages and problems encountered in their resolution. To a remarkable degree, a few of the cases from the counties provide the history of the California land claims in microcosm.

The liberal land policy of the Mexican government was embodied in two legislative measures, the Colonization Act of 1824 and the Supplemental Regulations of 1828. The legal foundation of the bulk of the ranchos granted in the period and hence most of the major claims before the board rested on these statutes. While a handful of grants were made under these laws prior to secularization of the missions, beginning in 1833, it was the secularization that stimulated a dramatic increase in the number of ranchos granted. Between 1822 and 1832 less than 5 percent of the total number of ranchos were issued, yet by the end of 1836 the number of ranchos granted totaled 110 or about 25 percent of the total. The last decade of Mexican rule saw an even greater distribution of land: the years 1843 and 1844 alone accounted for 112 rancho grants. By 1846 the total number of ranchos exceeded 470. This trend resulted in the fact that half of the grants for ranchos were less than 6 years old at the time of United States occupancy in 1846.[19]

A simple procedure for granting land emerged under the Colonization Act and its Supplemental Regulations. The first step was for the prospective grantee to submit a petition to the governor, describing the land requested and a statement that it stood vacant. An essential part of the petition was the *diseño*, a rough sketch map that showed the location and proposed boundaries of the grant, often including topographical features, houses, and roads. After receiving the petition the governor normally forwarded the request to a local official, the alcalde, for verification. The alcalde was required to confirm the petitioner's status as a citizen in good standing in the community. If the alcalde's report, known as the *informe*, was favorable, the governor issued a concession, *concedo*, which usually contained special conditions to be fulfilled by the grantee. Virtually all concessions required the grantee to take possession of the land by building a house and occupying it, usually within one year. Another common condition was that if the grantee failed to comply with the conditions, the land could be denounced or claimed by another person and regranted if circumstances warranted. Formalization of the land or title grant was accomplished by placing the grantee in judicial possession of the land, which required a survey witnessed by neighboring rancheros and an act of possession ceremoniously performed by the grantee. After this, the petition, *informe, concedo*, and survey notes were to be submitted to the territorial legislature for its approval.[20]

The earliest land claims to come before the board and the courts thus presented several essential issues, upon which the adjudication of the remaining cases would hinge. A threshold question to be decided was what type of interest (imperfect or perfect title) did a grantee receive with the *concedo* in the absence of approval of the grant by the territorial assembly? Secondly, were the conditions of occupation within one year normally annexed to the *concedo*, conditions precedent or subsequent? The resolution of these interconnected questions would determine the standards by which the validity of grants would be judged.

The first California land grant case to reach the United States Supreme Court involved the San Joaquin or Rosa Morada rancho located in present-day San Benito County. Not one of the original twenty-seven California counties created in 1850, San Benito came into existence as a county in 1874 with land carved from Monterey County. Thus, the claim for San Joaquin filed by Cruz Cervantes on February 20, 1852, with the Land Board was for two leagues (or 8,876 acres) of land in Monterey. On December 18, 1852 the board confirmed Cervantes's claim and ten months later it came before Judge Ogden Hoffman on appeal. Hoffman rejected the claim on October 29, 1853 but the Supreme Court reversed him on May 24, 1854 on the grounds that he had no jurisdiction over the case and remanded it to the southern district. Judge Isaac S.K. Ogier of the southern district confirmed the claim on June 27, 1855 and the Supreme Court affirmed his decision on May 12, 1856.[21]

The case is interesting for what it tells about the state of knowledge in Washington about California affairs. More importantly, it reveals the earliest assumptions and guidelines that largely settled the fate of most of the land claims. Although the merits of the Cervantes claim were only considered by the Supreme Court in 1855 — after the decision in the leading case of the *United States v. Fremont* (1854) — the case involved the earliest arguments for the liberal confirmation of land grants that the Supreme Court would eventually embrace.[22] At the same time, Judge Hoffman's opinion, though rendered moot because of alleged lack of jurisdiction, took a position toward Mexican land grants that was first rejected by the Supreme Court but eventually accepted after five years of experience in dealing with California land claims.

Californians had early developed a grievance against the federal government for the slowness with which the state was admitted to the Union. Sectional conflict did not excuse what seemed to many Californians neglect of their status and interests. Although Congress passed many laws dealing with California after 1850, many of these laws were

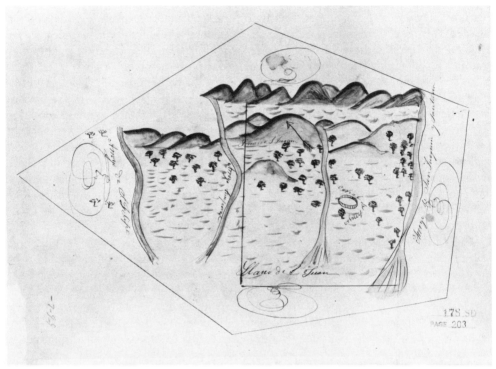

Diseño *of the San Joaquin rancho, located in present-day San Benito County. The rancho figured in the first California land grant case to reach the United States Supreme Court. (Courtesy The Bancroft Library.)*

hastily drawn and were not based on accurate information. Early laws dealing with California's federal courts, in particular, demonstrated considerable ignorance about conditions in California. The original act creating two judicial districts showed a lack of understanding about the judicial business of the state. As divided, the northern district was to have virtually all of the labor, while the southern district bordered on being a sinecure. Moreover, the act required the northern district judge to hold terms in four locations, San Francisco, Sacramento, Stockton, and San Jose. Except for San Francisco, there was little business at the required locations. Nonetheless, Judge Hoffman took the time to travel to the locations outside of San Francisco where he opened and just as quickly closed court for lack of cases. The few cases that were filed outside of San Francisco were summarily transferred to the appropriate dockets in San Francisco. This formality complied with the statute but underscored the types of mistakes that often crept into the laws dealing with California.

In its reversal of Judge Hoffman in the *Cervantes* case, the Supreme Court showed a similar lack of knowledge about statutes that governed California's federal judiciary.[23] Justice John McLean, who delivered the opinion, noted that the San Joaquin grant lay within the boundaries of the southern district and asserted that Judge Hoffman therefore had no jurisdiction over the case. In fact Congress had given Judge Hoffman jurisdiction in both judicial districts. Even Hoffman himself doubted the constitutionality of the act of August 31, 1852 which made him, in effect, judge of the southern district without an appointment by the president. Congress had acted after the death of the first judge appointed to the southern district, James McHall Jones, who died in December of 1851 without conducting any substantive business of the court. As an interim measure Congress imposed upon Hoffman the duties of both courts, and acknowledged the extra work by increasing his annual salary from $3,500 to $5,000.

The growing number of land cases prompted Senator Gwin to introduce a bill (along the lines suggested by Judge Hoffman to the attorney general) that required the appointment of a judge for the southern district. The bill became law in early 1854 and within days of its passage President Pierce nominated Isaac S.K. Ogier for the vacant southern district judgeship. Thus, at the time Judge Hoffman rendered his opinion in *Cervantes* and indeed when Justice McLean reversed and remanded the case to the lower court, Judge Hoffman had jurisdiction over the San Joaquin claim.

More revealing than that error were the assumptions made about Mexican land grants by Judge Ogier in confirming and Judge Hoffman in rejecting the San Joaquin claim. By the time the Supreme Court affirmed Judge Ogier's decision in 1855, the Court had rendered its opinion in the *Fremont* case. William Carey Jones carried the burden of the argument for the claimants in these two cases before the board, the district courts, and the Supreme Court. In accepting Jones's understanding of the nature of Mexican grants and the applicable standards to judge the California claims, the Supreme Court established early precedents that insured easy confirmation of private land grants. As noted, however, there were competing positions on the issue — taken by Judge Hoffman and the representatives of the United States — that only belatedly found favor with the Supreme Court.

After its confirmation by the board, the claim of Cruz Cervantes came on appeal before Judge Hoffman where argument was heard between October 17 and 20, 1853. The board had accepted Jones's assertion that the original grant or concession from the Mexican governors passed a perfect title or estate in fee to the claimant subject only to the condition that the territorial or supreme government might annul the grant. Jones argued that the fifth article of the Supplemental Regulations of 1828 which provided that all grants "shall not be held to be definitely valid without the previous consent of the Territorial Deputation" was in practice ignored by Mexican authorities.[24] He argued that grants issued by governors which did not receive such approval were regarded under the Mexican practice to be good titles and that to regard them as nullities would contravene the Treaty of Guadalupe Hidalgo.

Judge Hoffman, however, read the article as an explicit requirement of positive Mexican law. Without both a concession from the governor and approval by the territorial government, the grantee still had an interest but it was an imperfect or inchoate title to land. In such cases the question, in Hoffman's mind, was whether the United States, succeeding to the rights and duties of the Mexican government, should perfect title to the grant. His conclusion was that in cases where the grantee had performed the conditions, confirmation of the claim should follow. In the San Joaquin claim, Cervantes could only show a concession from the governor. In examining whether Cervantes complied with the conditions of his grant, Hoffman made a second major departure from the ruling of the board.

Whether the United States should perfect title to grantees holding merely a concession was a determination Hoffman felt "must be tested by the principles laid down in similar cases by the Supreme Court."[25] In the *Cervantes* case, Hoffman noted that the evidence showed that there had been a "total neglect" on the claimant's part to comply with any of the conditions (including habitation on the land within one year) for at least five and possibly eight years after the concession in 1836. After reviewing Supreme Court cases dealing with land concessions by the Spanish government in its former dominions in Louisiana and Florida, Judge Hoffman concluded that in the absence of any excuse for the claimant's failure to comply with the conditions of his grant, the title could not be perfected.

Judge Hoffman explicitly rejected the argument advanced by Jones and accepted by the board that the conditions annexed to concessions were conditions subsequent and not precedent. Jones had argued that the only penalty attached to the nonperformance of the conditions was that the land was liable to be denounced by another and, if vacant, regranted by the government. Jones further posited that in such cases where denouncement had not occurred and where the claimant had eventually complied with the conditions, the title ought in equity be confirmed to the claimant. Judge Hoffman was unable to accept Jones's argument in the face of a clear stipulation that if the claimant failed to comply with conditions "he shall lose his right to the land and it shall be denounceable by others." Judge Hoffman indicated that were he "at liberty to follow blindly the dictates" of his own judgment he might have confirmed the San Joaquin claim, but the principles established by the Supreme Court concerning land in Florida and Louisiana dictated the letter and the spirit of applicable rules.[26] He anticipated the Supreme Court might reverse him by modifying or departing from these earlier decisions, but emphasized that such a course was outside of his role as a federal trial judge.

Judge Hoffman was reversed, but only on the grounds of jurisdiction in the *Cervantes* case. His first substantive reversal in a land case occurred with John C. Fremont's claim for Las Mariposas, the first California land case to come before the Supreme Court on its merits. As in the first case to come before the board (the *Cervantes* case), William Carey Jones carried the burden of the claimant's position before the Supreme Court in the *Fremont* case. Jones was fully aware that more than his brother-in-law's mining interests in the gold-bearing claim were at stake. Indeed, Chief Justice Roger B. Taney prefaced his opinion in *Fremont* by noting that "it is understood that many claims to land in California depend upon the same principles, and will, in effect, be decided by the judgment of the Court in this case."[27]

The *Fremont* claim was an anomalous choice for a test case on California land grants for at least two reasons. The claimant, John Charles Fremont, epitomized much more than any other person the struggle that wrested California away from the Californios and Mexico. This impulsive adventurer had achieved national renown for his topographical explorations of the Far West filled with daring and danger and for being the victim, as many thought, of a court martial animated by professional jealousy. Although the Las Mariposas claim had been granted by Governor Micheltorena to Juan B. Alvarado in 1844, Alvarado had sold his interest to Fremont for $3,000 in 1847. Thus the case was not one of protecting the property rights of the conquered Californios under the Treaty of Guadalupe Hidalgo. Rather, at issue was whether Fremont — who had done so much to insure American possession of California — would share in the wealth of the new state and benefit as a purchaser of a Mexican land grant.

Another anomaly was the fact it was a "floating" grant. Unlike most grants which specified an amount of land in terms of given boundaries, the Mariposa grant purported to give the grantee ten square leagues of land (44,380 acres) within an area of one hundred leagues (443,800 acres). Fremont claimed the right to locate his ten-league grant within an area of the Sierra Nevada that contained some of the richest deposits of gold. Indeed, while Fremont's claim was before the board, he obtained a survey of ten leagues of land that included the rich gold mines near Mariposa and Agua Frio and by virtue of a panhandle partition of the survey took in nearly all of the watershed of the Mariposa River. The dispute over the shape of Fremont's grant and his claim to the mineral riches therein proved to be one of the great legal battles waged in the state supreme court and ultimately was laid to rest by that court by the opinion written by Chief Justice Field in *Biddle Boggs v. Merced Mining Co.*[28]

The *National Intelligencer* in Washington, D.C., described the arguments made in the *Fremont* case to be "of unusual public interest."[29] The court's opinion on March 10, 1855, reversed Judge Hoffman and set the context for further adjudication of California land grants. Chief Justice Taney agreed with the board that the land grants made in Louisiana and Florida were fundamentally different from those made in California. While the former grants were conditional upon surveys or other requirements, Taney held that the Mexican governor's *concedo* passed an immediate and present interest in the land. In accepting this understanding with respect to Mexican land grants, Taney in effect denied the applicability of early precedents upon which Judge Hoffman had relied.

Of equal importance was the Supreme Court's acceptance of the board's decision to ignore written law in preference to such departures as were established by custom and usage. The board had been convinced by the testimony of witnesses and arguments advanced by Jones, that many practices contravened the strict letter of the Colonization Act and Supplemental Regulations but had received the sanction of the Mexican authorities. Thus the Supreme Court agreed with Jones that the failure to submit a *diseño*, survey the land, and receive Departmental Assembly approval for the grant were not necessarily fatal to the grant. So too, failure to perform conditions would not prove fatal to a claimant unless the failure to perform conditions was unreasonably delayed or indicated an abandonment of the claim. The existence of hostile Indians on the Mariposa and the general "confusion and disorder of the times" were accepted as legitimate excuses for nonperformance in *Fremont*.[30] As no other person denounced the land in question, Fremont's interest in the grant remained intact and would be upheld.

Both Justice John Catron of Tennessee and Justice John Campbell of Alabama dissented. Both felt that previous decisions of the Supreme Court dealing with Spanish land concessions were applicable and required the rejection of the Mariposa claim. Justice Catron, in particular, felt a long line of the Court's decisions established the necessity of complying with the condition of habitation within one year under Spanish concessions and the invalidity of citing Indian hostility as an excuse for nonperformance in such cases. Justice Catron thus fully endorsed Judge Hoffman's basis for rejecting the claim. Moreover, Catron cited the vague description of Fremont's floating grant as an additional reason for rejecting the claim. Justice Campbell assigned the unspecific description of the grant as the principal reason for rejecting the claim, also citing previous decisions of the Supreme Court. It was Justice Catron, however, who uttered a prophetic statement about the implications of the majority's position in *Fremont*: "If this claim is maintained, all others must likewise be, if the first step of making the concession is proved to have been performed by the acting governor; as no balder case than the one before us can exist in California where the grant is not infected with fraud or forgery."[31]

The strongest rejection of the ruling in the *Fremont* case came from Justice Peter Daniel. Although Justice Daniel did not sit in the *Fremont* case, he took the majority to task in later cases following and even expanding upon the liberal approach taken toward the Mariposa claim. Daniel's most caustic dissent occured in *United States v. Arguello* in which he decried what he saw as the departure from written Mexican law in favor of practices in violation of them, resting upon the testimony of interested persons. Daniel characterized the testimony of Californios as worthless and "marked by the traits which tyranny and degradation, political and moral, naturally and usually engender."[32] Daniel accused his brethren of having been duped into, if not actually abetting, a system of land frauds.

Unlike Justices Catron and Campbell who seemed to rest their dissents principally upon a different interpretation of Mexican law and the applicability of earlier decisions of the Supreme Court, Justice Daniel was violently opposed to the claimants and the existence of large grants of land to individuals. In his eyes, the *Fremont* decision and others following it were "inciting and pampering a corrupt and grasping spirit of speculation and monopoly" in California land that excluded "the honest citizen of small means, by whose presence and industry the improvement and wealth, and social and moral health, and the advancement of the country are always sure to be promoted."[33] In a choice between settlers and large claimants like John C. Fremont, Justice Daniel had little difficulty in concluding that the equities did not favor the grantees.

Given the fact that many members of the Supreme Court, including Chief Justice Taney, shared Justice Daniel's antimonopolistic attitudes and a Jacksonian preference for the small settler against the large grantee, it may well be wondered why the Supreme Court took such a liberal attitude toward the confirmation of Mexican grants. The protection of private property and adherence to the obligations assumed under the Treaty of Guadalupe Hidalgo offer obvious explanations. It would seem, however, that the types of cases first brought before the Court — at the insistence of Jones and other lawyers interested in representing the interest of claimants — may also have influenced the outcome. In each of the first three California land cases to be decided by the Supreme Court the claimants were Americans.[34]

Treaty obligations aside, it may well have been easier to see Americans who favored and fought for American possession of California as beneficiaries under the act of 1851. Despite the fact that title to land rested upon circumstances under which a Mexican governor granted land to the original grantee — usually a Californio — it was impossible for the Court to ignore the fact that the claimants who would benefit were Americans. The Court even validated the claim of an American who became a naturalized Mexican citizen in order to qualify for a land grant in 1844, but who quickly joined the American forces in overthrowing Mexico's hold on California in 1846. As Justice Daniel pointed out in his dissent, the majority had accepted the claimant's "inconsistency of urging a right founded on duties sustained to the Mexican Republic, with the assumption at the same time deduced from the admitted facts of hostility and faithlessness to the government."[35]

Historians who have studied the adjudication of the Mexican land grants in California have noted the importance of the *Fremont* case. If anything, however, they have underestimated its influence and control over the disposition of land claims. The index to Hoffman's *Land Cases*, containing one hundred and twelve opinions written by the northern district judge between 1853-1858, lists some fourteen cases as relying upon the *Fremont* decision. The index lists only cases wherein the *Fremont* case was mentioned by name. A close analysis of the facts and reasoning in Hoffman's opinions, however, reveals that in an overwhelming majority of the cases Hoffman felt compelled to confirm cases because of the Supreme Court's ruling. In case after case, the United States attorney offered no objection or argument against the claims that came automatically on appeal to the district court. Some of this might have been the press of other business or a lack of vigor on his part. But to a large extent, the quiescence of the United States attorney and the many short opinions by Hoffman confirming claims in which he summarized the facts in light of the *Fremont* ruling suggest the great weight given to the *Fremont* case.

Justice Catron was essentially correct in his dissent in *Fremont*: under the broad ruling virtually all claims had to be confirmed unless the government could prove fraud in the *concedo* from the governor to the original grantee. Many of the assumed defects in the process of granting land in California advanced by the government before the board and the Supreme Court in the *Cervantes* and the *Fremont* cases were soon disposed of. Slowly, however, the Supreme Court chipped away at the precedential value of *Fremont*, particularly after Jeremiah S. Black became attorney general in 1857 and sent Edwin M. Stanton (who later became secretary of war under Lincoln) to California as special counsel for the United States. The reason for the shift in attitude by the Supreme Court owed much to the belief of Attorney General Black that many of the land grants were fraudulent and were in danger of being confirmed by the Supreme Court.

A claim involving land in what eventually became San Benito County was illustrative of some of the problems and delays in settling title to land held under Mexican grants. Vicente Gomez's claim was distinctive both for its longevity (filed before the board in 1853, it persisted as a claim until 1900) and for the fact that Bret Harte spun a tale about Panoche Grande.[36]

Quicksilver, or mercury, was of great value in California for its physical properties in amalgamating the gold then being mined. Mercury deposits had already been discovered on the land when Gomez, of Monterey, filed a claim for Panoche Grande before the board. Alleging that he received a grant from Governor Micheltorena in 1844, Gomez had not occupied the land nor could he produce written evidence of a *concedo*. The noncompliance with conditions might have been overcome in the light of the *Fremont* case, but the absence of documentary evidence of the concession and the fact that Gomez produced a *diseño* that bore little resemblance to the claim shed much suspicion on the validity of the grant. On March 6, 1855 the board rejected the claim. After it was erroneously appealed to the northern district, the case was transferred to the southern district.

On June 5, 1857 Judge Ogier confirmed the Panoche Grande claim in a manner that was typical of land cases before his court. When the case came before Ogier, the United States attorney for the southern district, Pacificus Ord, informed the court that he did not oppose confirmation. According to a witness in the courtroom, Judge Ogier "replied that there being no objections this claim would be confirmed as a matter of course." Unlike his northern counterpart, Ogier did not routinely examine the transcript and opinion of the board, but frequently confirmed cases without any opinion beyond his conclusions. Earlier in 1857, Ogier, upon the motion of Ord, vacated the appeal of the United States to the Supreme Court in over fifty land cases he had summarily confirmed. What Judge Ogier did not know — even had he scrutinized the transcript in the Panoche Grande case — was that at the time Ord conceded the validity of the claim, he had become half-owner of it for one dollar.[37]

Ord's malfeasance was eventually uncovered and cited by Special Counsel Stanton in a motion to reopen the case in July 1858. In the meantime, between the time of Ogier's

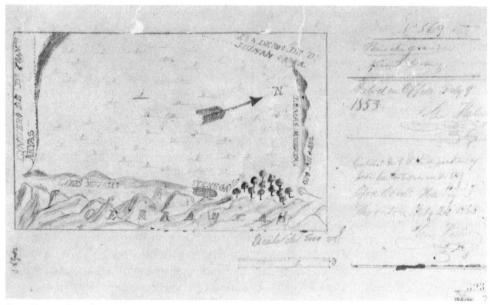

Diseño *produced in support of the Panoche Grande claim in Monterey County. (Courtesy The Bancroft Library.)*

confirmation and before the allegations of fraud, Vicente Gomez sold his claim to William McGarrahan. McGarrahan used all his means to prevent the defeat of the claim even after the Supreme Court mandated its dismissal in 1865. With the value of the mine and the successive companies he arranged to exploit the quicksilver (at one point McGarrahan organized a New York company capitalized at five million dollars), there was plenty of money to fuel a lobbying effort before the Congress, the courts, and the executive departments.

Between Stanton's motion for a hearing in 1858 and the Supreme Court's mandate in 1865, McGarrahan hired top legal talent to vindicate his interests. After the Supreme Court decision, he pursued the matter before Congress for decades and came very close to gaining special legislation that would have assured confirmation. After twenty-one different reports of House or Senate committees, some favorable and some unfavorable, Congress decided to let the issue go before the courts once again. In 1892 both houses approved a measure that so controlled the admissibility of evidence that confirmation was virtually assured. After President Harrison vetoed the measure, sufficient doubts developed among senators that the effort to override Harrison's veto was not carried. Even death could not stop the case, for in 1900, after McGarrahan had died, his heirs and assignees brought it up unsuccessfully for the last time.

The Panoche Grande claim had the dubious distinction of receiving perhaps more congressional attention than any other California land grant. It stands as the most dramatic example of the erosion of Congress' resolve in the act of 1851 to leave the resolution of California land claims to the courts. The combination of congressional investigations and seemingly endless hearings did more than simply delay the final settlement of land titles. The successive hearings and continual introduction of "new evidence" cre-

*United States Circuit Court Judge
Matthew Hall McAllister. Judge
McAllister's participation in the lengthy
New Almaden mine case won him the
title "the venerable Mr. Almaden."
(Courtesy Archives, United States
District Court for the Northern District
of California.)*

ated such a complicated judicial history that proponents of the claim managed to con-vince members of Congress to intervene and rectify an injustice. That the effort almost succeeded was a statement of the morass that typified a number of claims by the 1860s and 1870s. Relatively few cases went through convolutions similar to the Panoche Grande, but those that did left a legacy akin to the interminable chancery suit of *Jarndyce v. Jarndyce* in Charles Dickens's *Bleak House.*

The most famous of California's land grants also involved mining interests: the New Almaden mine in Santa Clara County. Unlike the Panoche Grande claim, however, litigation spanned only some twelve years. Nonetheless, those years were filled with bit-ter wrangling over one of the richest prizes involved in any claim and produced a tran-script running over 3,500 pages. The case consumed so much time that the judges who presided in the district court, Judge Hoffman and Circuit Judge McAllister, were nicknamed "Judge Almaden" and "the venerable Mr. Almaden" respectively. As befits its fame, the New Almaden has its own biographer.[38] Some of the case's history will be presented here to illustrate more general aspects of the adjudication of land titles.

Although the New Almaden case was a *cause célèbre* and in many ways atypical, it had certain features in common with many other land claims. One characteristic of the litigation involving the New Almaden mine, in particular, illustrates the relatively com-mon occurrence that the real parties in interest in much of the litigation before the board and the federal courts were non-Hispanics. From 1852, when the claim to the

New Almaden mine was filed, until 1863, when the United States Supreme Court rejected the claim, the case was pursued under the name of Andres Castillero. Indeed it was Castillero, a Mexican captain of cavalry, who in 1845 claimed the mineral wealth and land around a shallow cave on the eastern side of the foothills of the Coast Range about twelve miles southwest of San Jose. Also in 1845, Castillero formed a partnership of twenty-four shares with four other Hispanics, including General Jose Castro and Padre Real. As early as 1846, however, Alexander Forbes of the British commercial firm of Barron, Forbes and Company based in Tepic, Mexico, began acquiring shares from the five original partners. By 1850, two years before Castillero's claims were filed before the board, the Barron and Forbes group had completely taken over the claim and installed Henry W. Halleck as general manager of the mine at a monthly salary of five hundred dollars.[39]

Validation of Castillero's claim to the mine, however, was only one means of gaining the wealth provided by the fabulous quicksilver deposits. In the event that the claim to the mine itself was rejected, which indeed happened in 1863, the mineral wealth might still be had as part of the land grant upon which the mine was situated. Under Mexican law, minerals were deemed to vest in the government and did not pass to the grantee of land. With the acquisition of California, the United States was assumed to have succeeded to the rights of the Mexican government, but the federal courts ultimately held that a patent to a Mexican land grant vested any minerals in the land in the grantee. This ruling, of course, had profound impact on such grantees as John C. Fremont as well as the claimants to land on which the New Almaden mine was situated.

Two Mexican land grants in Santa Clara potentially covered part or all of the New Almaden mine. The original grantee of one of the ranchos, the San Vicente, was Jose de los Reves Berryessa, a retired San Francisco Presidio sergeant who received his *concedo* from Governor Alvarado in 1842. That same year Alvarado granted Justo Larios the adjacent rancho called Los Capitancillos, an extraordinarily valuable rancho, for within its boundaries was a second mine, the Guadalupe. Thus, if Castillero's claim to the mine and the land surrounding it failed, the claimant who could validate his land grant and insure that its boundaries would embrace the New Almaden would come away with the rich prize. As things turned out, neither Berryessa nor Larios would profit from their valuable grants, even though each was eventually confirmed and patented.[40]

From the moment the state court began functioning in 1850, Berryessa's heirs filed a succession of suits in the third district court of California (which had jurisdiction over Santa Clara County) seeking the profits from the operation of the New Almaden. Indeed, the first case ever transferred from San Jose to the federal court in San Francisco dealt with this very issue. These collateral suits in state court were destined to be inconclusive, not the least because the title to land hinged on decisions of the board and the federal courts. More importantly, the Barron and Forbes interests tried to insure their control over the mine by starting to buy parts of Berryessa's land. Forced to mortgage its lands, the Berryessa family slowly saw its lands slip into the hands of Barron, Forbes and Company at mortgage sales until all of San Vicente was owned by the company in 1861. In this fashion the Barron interests had essentially two chances to win: either on Castillero's claim to the mine itself or Berryessa's valid grant to San Vicente. What the British company did not foresee was the political and financial clout of their American rivals in asserting their claim to New Almaden under Larios's grant to Los Capitancillos.

With an untold promise of wealth in operating a rich quicksilver mine during such a

*Stereo view of the New Almaden mine made during the period 1870 to 1875. This picture of a part of the huge mining works indicates the high stakes involved in the New Almaden mine case. (Courtesy The Bancroft Library.)*

time of high demand for the ore as existed during the gold rush, it was hardly surprising that others began to vie with Barron and Forbes for New Almaden. The earliest competition began in 1848 when a group of distinguished Americans, led by Thomas O. Larkin and Grove C. Cook (who had acquired the Larios claim) asserted that the New Almaden was actually on the Rancho Los Capitancillos. The Larios grant ultimately became known as the Fossat claim, owned by the Quicksilver Mining Company which was composed of investors mainly from New York and Philadelphia. Numerous public officials in Washington, including Secretary of the Treasury Robert J. Walker, had interests in the Fossat claim, a circumstance that goes some way in explaining why the United States persisted in the litigation after the matter became an issue purely between private parties. All the original Hispanic grantees under whom title to the wealth of the New Almaden might vest — Castillero, Berryessa, and Larios — were relatively quickly bought out and precluded from partaking in the spoils of Santa Clara's red cinnabar ore. Thus, a significant aspect of the story of land adjudication in California is how many claims passed out of the hands of Hispanics prior to and during the litigation before the federal courts and how relatively few as a result of the decisions of those courts.[41]

The ultimate result in the struggle over the New Almaden mine also sheds light on the course of the litigation over Mexican land grants after Jeremiah S. Black became attorney general in 1857. Historians of the New Almaden case have often tried to explain why Barron and Forbes lost possession of the mine when the equities seemed clearly in favor of Castillero's claim. Five months after the Supreme Court reversed the district court and rejected the Castillero claim on March 10, 1863, the Quicksilver Mining Company bought out the New Almaden Mining Company for 1.75 million dollars. In 1864 the Supreme Court finally settled the boundaries between the San Vicente and Los Capitancillos ranchos by locating the mine on the Fossat claim and the works and hacienda on the Berryessa property.

Edwin M. Stanton. Sent to California as special counsel to represent the interests of the United States in land cases, Stanton believed every Mexican land claim a fraud. This carte de visite picture after an engraving dates from the late 1860s. (Courtesy The Bancroft Library.)

A number of plausible explanations have been given to account for the outcome, ranging from ignoring the enormous mass of evidence to antipathy toward British claimants during the Civil War to the collusion and corruption of public officials.[42] To some extent all these reasons contributed but the general context of Attorney General Black's administration supplies another reason. Unlike other explanations, which deal with the particular circumstances of the New Almaden, the shift in attitude of the government toward all Mexican grants, accompanied by Black's administration, helps account for a spate of rejections of which Castillero's claim was just one.

Prior to Black's administration neither Californians in general, lawyers, nor government officers involved in the resolution of title to Mexican grants believed that most grants were suspect and that a wholesale system of falsification and perjury existed to perpetrate fraud. American settlers, who objected on principle to large tracts of land claimed under Mexican grants, were the usual source for accusations of fraudulent title. Despite these complaints, the issue of fraud rarely arose in the cases that came before Judge Hoffman prior to 1857. Only a few cases, like the claims of Jose Y. Limantour, evoked immediate and sustained suspicion. Among Limantour's most spectacular claims was his assertion that he held a grant to almost half of San Francisco, several islands in the San Francisco Bay, and much of the Tiburon peninsula. When Limantour filed his claim in 1852, many wealthy and influential San Franciscans found themselves in an awkward position —the irony of which was not lost on the contemporary newspapers. The *San Francisco Alta California* noted that those parties "who have held that the shadow of a Mexican title was sufficient to justify a writ of ejectment" and "who have been most eager to hang the squatters, now, finding they are like to be declared squatters, are for hanging the Mexican grantees."[43]

The Limantour claim was one of the more famous land frauds exposed in the course of adjudication and because of the valuable government property involved, including Fort Point, it received a great deal of attention during Attorney General Black's administration.

The failure to discover a widespread system of fraud in land titles was not a result of incompetence on the part of Black's predecessor. The papers of Caleb Cushing, attorney general between 1853 and 1857, reveal a conscientious official who resisted pressures to acquiesce in the confirmation of claims he or his assistants had not thoroughly examined and yet who appreciated the desirability of settling California's land titles as soon as possible.

What Attorney General Black brought to the adjudication of California land claims was not greater care but an instinctive distrust of Mexican grants and Hispanics who frequently attested to their validity. Black acquired much of his distrust of Mexican grants from the special counsel he employed and sent to California to represent the interests of the United States, Edwin M. Stanton. Stanton believed every Mexican land claim to be fraudulent and himself to be "the chosen instrument to prove this to the world." The exposure of perceived land frauds against the United States in California became for both Black and Stanton "virtually a religious crusade." Indeed, by 1860 Black reported to Congress that twenty-two claims had been rejected on the basis of fraud and noted that some thirty others were pending in the courts on the same grounds, including the Castillero claim to New Almaden.[44]

Black had sent Stanton to California mainly to defend the United States' interest against the Limantour claims that were widely believed to be fraudulent. Soon, however, Stanton gained the impression, which Black came to share, that a great many of the claims besides Limantour's were fabricated. Black instructed Stanton to collect all the Mexican archival records then in California; Stanton had them bound in 400 volumes and sent back to Washington. Even more important was a large volume of photographic copies of official correspondence and seals, with examples of supposedly genuine and fraudulent documents. Although Stanton spent less than three months in California early in 1857 examining grants and collecting the materials, Black believed that the archives collected by Stanton furnished "irresistible proof that there had been an organized system of fabricating land titles carried on for a long time in California by Mexican officials; that forgery and perjury had been reduced to a regular occupation; that the making of false grants, with the subornation of false witnesses to prove them, had become a trade and a business."[45] Thus, Stanton's quickly gathered data provided Black with a potent weapon in his crusade against Mexican grants.

The manner in which Black wielded his weapon almost approached a science. From the records sent by Stanton, Black had lists prepared of "professional witnesses" and others he believed had committed perjury. Moreover, biographies were compiled "of nearly all the men who have been engaged in these schemes of imposture and fraud, from the governors down to the lowest of the suborned witnesses." Finally, Black routinely had photographic copies made (as opposed to handwritten transcripts) of the original papers filed before the Land Board in all cases that came to the Supreme Court on appeal. Comparing the photographs of genuine signatures and seals of the Mexican governors and officials, Black developed an abundant self-confidence in his ability to detect forgeries. With his photographic comparisons, master lists, and biographies, Black declared himself able "to determine, with almost absolute certainty, the truth or the falsehood of any claim."[46]

Black's aggressive scrutiny of Mexican land claims certainly marked a departure from the liberal approach mandated by the *Fremont* case. It seems questionable, however, that Black's influence on the course of land adjudication in California was as beneficial as he believed. While the *Fremont* case created a precedent whose influence tended to overly minimize the formal requirements of Mexican law and precluded scrutiny into doubtful claims, Black's administration erred in the opposite direction. From the legitimate concerns over the Limantour claims, Stanton and Black created an atmosphere in which virtually all grants were suspect and every Californio a perjurer. Some doubt may be entertained about the accuracy of the sources of Black's lists of "professional witnesses" and his photographic volume of genuine and fraudulent documents. His emphasis on documentary evidence from the Mexican archives quite possibly stimulated forged documents by claimants who now saw documentary evidence as a requirement for confirmation. Moreover, in the fascination with the technique of photographic comparison, the substantial equity of some claims may well have been overlooked. Finally, Black's methods often violated the act of 1851 by introducing the photographic comparisons as new evidence before the Supreme Court. Black justified this violation of appellate procedure by asserting that neither the board nor the district courts could have detected the frauds that he had discovered except by use of Stanton's data.[47]

The atmosphere of general distrust of Mexican land grants also affected the resolution of the New Almaden mine case. In 1860, three years before the case reached the Supreme Court, Attorney General Black declared that he had "no doubt at all" that the Castillero claim was "fraudulent and fabricated." Later, in the employ of the Quicksilver Mining Company, Black told the Supreme Court that the government had "always met the claim with uncompromising hostility. From first to last they have shown it nothing but the edge of the naked knife." Coming from the former attorney general, who had done so much to convince the Supreme Court of the ubiquity of fraudulent titles, these were persuasive statements. Whether Black received well over one hundred thousand dollars as his fee in the case, as one source reported, is uncertain. It is certain, though, that the Fossat interests had a great deal of money to dispense to strong advocates of their case.[48]

When both these giant killers of Mexican grants, Black and Stanton, proclaimed the Castillero claim fraudulent, it was not surprising that the Supreme Court concurred. The New Almaden case illustrates the hostile atmosphere in which Mexican land grants were being examined by the Supreme Court after Black became attorney general. After Stephen J. Field's elevation from the California to the United States Supreme Court in 1863, a greater receptivity to such claims could be detected. Thus, the context in which California land claims were adjudicated during Black's administration and before Field's arrival present stark contrasts. Appreciating the hostile judicial environment in which the New Almaden case was decided makes it easier to understand why an apparently valid claim was rejected.

But confirmation of one's land claim presented only half the struggle to a holder of a

Mexican grant. To obtain a patent from the United States — and hence the best security of title — required a survey approved by the federal surveyor general of California and the commissioner of the General Land Office in Washington. After 1860, the claimant or other interested parties could file objections to the survey with the federal district courts, which in turn could either approve them or order another survey. Throughout this period of judicial scrutiny of surveys (from 1860 to 1864) as well as before and after it, parties who objected to the boundaries of a grant could make special appeals to the secretary of the interior and officials of the General Land Office and the Surveyor General's office. Judicial review over surveys diminished the power of interested parties in manipulating the final results, but it often slowed down the process of obtaining a patent. Two principal struggles arose over surveys: those between adjacent grant holders and those between grant holders and settler-squatters. In both cases the disputes over boundaries often saw extensive collateral litigation before the state courts. The experience of the San Andres rancho in Santa Cruz County illustrates the partial range of difficulties that could confront a claimant in terms of settling the boundaries of his grant.

In the case of the Castros, the prominent California family that received the grant to the two-league rancho, San Andres, confirmation of their claim occurred smoothly even though not swiftly. Filed in 1853, the board had no problems with the validity of the grant and confirmed it on February 7, 1854. As the land lay within the southern district, the appeal came before Judge Ogier who summarily confirmed it, albeit three years later. In 1858, when the United States dismissed the appeal to the Supreme Court, the heirs of Joaquin Castro had vindicated their title to the land. Boundary disputes with the owners of the adjacent rancho, Los Corralitos, continued until 1867 and a patent was not issued until 1876.[49]

Actually, the boundary disputes between the two ranchos antedated California's statehood. In 1850 the Castro family filed suit before the Third Judicial District Court in Santa Cruz alleging that Jose de Amesti had succeeded in convincing Walter Colton, the first American alcalde of Monterey, to give de Amesti judicial possession of a large part of San Andres under the mistaken notion that it was part of Los Corralitos rancho. According to the Castros, land which they possessed was awarded to de Amesti in 1847 in an "extraordinary and illegal" jury trial.[50] They claimed that since 1847 they had unlawfully been deprived of almost one half of San Andres. Litigation in the state courts continued for nearly a decade, but the ultimate resolution of the dispute came from the federal courts.

After Ogier approved the survey of San Andres in 1860, the claimants of the grant filed objections early in 1861. The death of Judge Ogier in May of that year postponed matters until his successor, Fletcher M. Haight, was appointed. On June 23, 1862 Judge Haight granted the claimant's objections and ordered a new survey. But in 1865 after numerous procedural maneuverings, the United States surveyor general protested that he could not resurvey San Andres according to the judge's instructions because to do so would appropriate land within Los Corralitos. Although both ranchos had been confirmed, Corralitos had received its patent first. The surveyor general cited an opinion of the attorney general to the General Land Office in which the attorney general advised that after one patent had been issued for land, the Land Office was without authority over such lands "until the former patent is judicially set aside." Judge Haight allowed the claimants to present new documentary evidence relevant to the survey, but before the hearing could be held, Haight died and the southern district went out of existence for

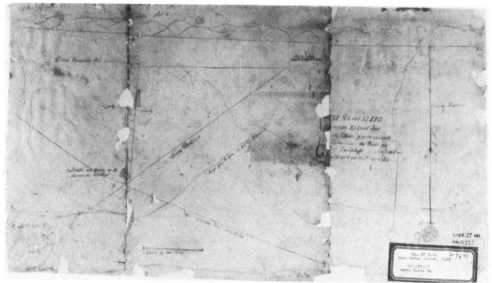

*Diseño of the Rancho Milpitas in Monterey County. Settlement of this claim involved acrimonious boundary disputes between the owners and nearby settlers. (Courtesy The Bancroft Library.)*

twenty years.[51] Judge Hoffman, to whom the matter was referred in 1867, rendered a decision which sustained the General Land Office's surveyor general.

The moral of the San Andres case was that the first claimant to a patent prevailed. The Supreme Court took a firm stand against reexamining title on the basis of fraud after a grant had been patented as a way of avoiding interminable disputes over land. Despite the fact that the state courts, including the third district court and California's supreme court, felt that the equities lay with the Castros, the strategy of expediting the process of patenting rewarded their opponents. Variations of the struggle between the claimants of San Andres and Los Corralitos were repeated all over the state. But controversies over boundaries of grants were not confined to the claimants themselves.

The other main source of disputes over the boundaries of grants in the 1860s and 1870s occurred between grantees whose claims had been confirmed and settler-squatters on or near the grants. The Milpitas grant in Monterey offers a good example of this type of dispute as well as the tendency of grants to expand in size between their filing with the board and patenting by the General Land Office. Milpitas was distinctive: its grantee was an Indian, Ignacio Pastor. Although Santa Clara County contained three ranchos — Los Coches, Posolmi, and Ulistac — granted to ex-mission Indians, the total number of such grants was quite small. The legality of such conveyances under Mexican law was upheld in one of the Supreme Court's earliest opinions on California land grants, *United States v. Ritchie*.[52]

Just as in the *Ritchie* case, the original Indian grantee to Milpitas no longer had possession of the land by the time the grant was confirmed and patented. In Ignacio Pastor's case, his claim for Milpitas found favor before the board who saw the claimant as a member of a "powerless" class deserving "the full measure of protection which the provisions of the treaty and the laws are intended to afford."[53] Shortly after the board's decision, however, Pastor sold his claim to Jose de Jesus Pico and in 1859 the claim was owned by Juan M. Luco.

Unfortunately for Luco, the process of confirming Rancho Milpitas did not go smoothly, though persistence paid off handsomely in the end. In 1856 Judge Ogier rejected the claim summarily, apparently on the grounds that the grant lacked a sufficient description. William Carey Jones, for the claimant, moved to arrest judgment and succeeded in getting Judge Ogier to rehear the case. In 1860, Ogier vacated his earlier decision and confirmed the claim. He admitted that the boundaries of the grant were not as definite "as would be desirable" but declared that it was neither the intent of the act of 1851 nor his intention to apply "the strict legal technical rules of the common [law] to such strong equitable claims as this."[54] The United States dismissed its appeal in 1863 and a patent finally was issued in 1875.

More interesting than Judge Ogier's reversal in favor of the claimant was the manner in which the grant managed to expand in size between 1852, when it was filed, and 1875, when it was patented. When the commissioners confirmed the grant to Pastor in 1853, they spoke of the equities of "these small grants to the Christianized aborigines of the Country." Jones in his petition for Pastor in 1852, however, spoke of the grant containing some three leagues. When the case came to be reheard in 1860, one witness for the claimant estimated that the grant contained between five and six leagues. Even so, Judge Ogier, like the board, continued to describe the grant as a small rancho. After the survey, however, the claimants managed to include some 43,000 acres or nearly ten leagues within their "small grant" which was patented in 1875.[55]

Needless to say, settlers who saw their homes and improvements engrossed by the ever-growing Milpitas rancho bitterly complained. Alleging fraud and illicit manipulation of the survey of the land, settlers in the area formed an association and hired James Stuart as their attorney to resist the patent. As the federal district courts were no longer overseeing the survey process by that time, the settlers sought to offset the influence that the claimant had over the office of the Surveyor General and the commissioner of the General Land Office. The battle raged into the 1870s and 1880s with Stuart vainly petitioning the secretary of the interior, who had authority over both the General Land Office and the surveyor general, and writing an open letter to the president on behalf of the settlers.[56]

Milpitas rancho settlers were not alone in complaining that they had been victimized by settling near grants that expanded to cover their settlements. At least fourteen other grants experienced a dramatic increase in size between what was originally claimed and ultimately patented. The survey process was fraught with disputes, the most bitter of which stemmed from alleged wrongs done to California's settler element.[57] It seems clear that much of the surveying and patenting of Mexican land grants in California remained far too susceptible to the manipulation of interested parties.

The legacy of suspicion of Attorney General Black's administration helped to fan disquiet among the settler-squatter interests. While accommodation and compromise between claimants and settlers occasionally occurred, the history of these clashing interests in California was marked by bitterness and violence. Only with the passage of time would the claims of the settler-squatters be rendered legally moot and their spokesmen relegated to the position of social critics with little political power.

The experience of Santa Clara, San Benito, Santa Cruz, and Monterey counties may not be representative of the adjudication of California's land grants. However, these cases give an indication of the range and complexity of issues and problems that beset the federal courts in attempting to quiet title to these grants.

Further, these cases emphasize the need to study the litigation over land both within a broad context and with close attention to the legal process. The land cases that came before the federal courts in California involved questions having wide impact. They pitted the interests of settler-squatters against large land holders, vast real estate speculation against the public welfare, and the civil law against the common law tradition. The potential economic or political beneficiaries applied much pressure to the judicial process. At the same time the process was constrained by rules of evidence, adherence to precedent, and legislation that significantly shaped the outcome of these disputes. The legal history of land adjudication in the four counties demonstrates the importance of looking carefully into and beyond litigation and judicial decisions.

# 5

## The Continuing Connection: Maurice T. Dooling and William F. James

*Alma Dooling Dettweiler*
*and Joseph Franaszek*

### Maurice T. Dooling
### 1860-1924
*By Alma Dooling Dettweiler*

Maurice Dooling was born in Moore's Flat (a small mining town near Grass Valley in Nevada County, California) on October 12, 1860, the son of Timothy Dooling and Mary Manogue Dooling, both of whom were Irish immigrants. Many of the hard-working miners had not had any formal schooling, and it delighted them when beginning at about five years of age "little Bobby white-head" would read the newspapers to them. Maurice had silver-blond hair as a child, and the nickname "Bob" stayed with him until his death, as did his interest in knowledge and love and concern for people.

Tim Dooling had immigrated to New Canaan, Connecticut from .Tralee, Ireland, in 1847 and worked in the mills there until gold was discovered in California. He worked three years in the gold mines and had quite a savings when he returned to Connecticut to be married to Mary Manogue on April 4, 1853. They did not expect to be living in a gold mining town a few years later, but the bank in which they had their money failed; so they spent about ten years at Moore's Flat working hard to save enough money to invest in a business or farm — Tim said often, "a mining town is no place to raise a family." They moved to San Francisco in 1867 and from there to a small ranch that they purchased near Hollister, California, arriving there on April 1, 1868.

His growing up years were hard but happy. Maurice, or Bob as his family and friends called him, was the middle one of the five Dooling children — Ellen and Catherine

63

*United States District Court Judge Maurice T. Dooling. (Courtesy Archives, United States District Court for the Northern District of California.)*

were older and Patrick and Annie younger. Bob and Pat were just two years apart in age and were the closest of brothers. Each had a keen sense of humor and a good deal of Irish wit. The Tim Dooling ranch was in the Fairview district, just south of and within easy walking distance of Hollister, and some relatives and former friends bought ranches nearby. Most of these farmers raised produce at first and later put in orchards.

But Maurice Dooling's intellectual interests and the broad knowledge he acquired at a youthful age were a source of amazement to his family and friends. Before he completed his public school years in Hollister, he had passed his instructors in his knowledge of Latin and French, and widely read and studied other subjects outside of the required courses. A Protestant minister, his wife, and daughter built and operated Florence College in Hollister for a few years in the 1870s and 1880s. Maurice attended Florence College for a year and then entered Saint Mary's College in San Francisco (before it was moved to Oakland); he graduated in 1880 and got his master's degree in 1881. He had learned some Spanish from friends around Hollister, and asked to room with a Spanish-speaking student at Saint Mary's to perfect his Spanish. Saint Mary's did not have an instructor in Greek when Maurice was a student there, so he and one other student took private lessons in Greek. By the time he completed his studies, he was reasonably proficient in Latin, Greek, French, Spanish, and German. From 1881 to 1883 Maurice Dooling was an instructor at Saint Mary's College in Latin, Greek, Philosophy and possibly one or more modern languages.

The Doolings had little money and it was difficult for them to finance Maurice's college education; so he made an agreement with the college to teach there and also to pay for his brother, Pat, to attend. Maurice hoped that Pat would learn to share his enthusiasm for intellectual pursuits, but Pat hated college and dropped out of Saint Mary's after a year or less.

Apparently no member of Maurice's immediate family had deep intellectual interests; although his oldest sister, Ellen, had some advanced education since she entered the convent and worked for many years at Saint Mary's by the Lake Hospital in Milwaukee, Wisconsin. Maurice's maternal uncle, Patrick Manogue, was a scholar: he worked in the mines to pay for his education to study for the priesthood and selected a difficult theological seminary because he felt it would be more challenging. After he was ordained, Patrick Manogue worked as a priest among the miners, and later became the first bishop of Sacramento. Maurice's mother had learned to read and write as a girl, but his father was illiterate. Tim Dooling was a lovable man with a keen wit. Maurice appreciated his father's mental capacity, and as an example of his father's intelligence said of him, "My father could look out over a field and figure in his head how many acres were planted, what the going price was for each crop, and could make a remarkably accurate estimate of how much money we would get from the crops that year."

But in one area from the time Bob was in his late teens, he was a cause of worry to his family. He would get drunk and Pat would have to bring him home. No one else in his family had this problem; his father and brother seldom took a drink and neither of them ever got drunk. By the time he was at college, Maurice Dooling knew that alcohol affected him differently than it did most of his friends. He would not take a drink for several weeks, but then he'd have a drink with the boys and would keep drinking until he was so drunk they'd have to take him home and put him to bed. Fortunately, he would go for weeks or months without taking a drink so that his occasional drinking did not affect his overall functioning.

In 1883 after teaching for two years, Maurice returned to Hollister to study law in the office of McCroskey and Hudner, and in 1885 was admitted to the bar and began practicing law with J. L. Hudner. In 1884 (while a law student) he was elected as a Democrat to the California Assembly, serving through one regular and one extra session. He was a member of every Democratic State Convention from 1888 to 1912, serving each time on the Platform Committee and was a member of the Democratic State Central Committee for about twenty years.

Maurice T. Dooling and Ida Mae Wagner were married in Hollister in 1887. They had met in grade school after her family moved to Hollister from Illinois. Ida and Maurice had very little money for several years after they were married, and they lived in a three room cabin at the north edge of Hollister until around 1900 when they built a two story home in the same location. Their first child died three weeks after his birth. They had two other children, both boys, Maurice T. Dooling, Jr. born 1889 and Charles W. Dooling born 1891. The early years of their marriage were marred by Bob's periodic drinking bouts. But when their sons were about ages five and three, Bob gave up drinking and never took a drink in the remaining thirty years of his life. In later years he would speak of having been an alcoholic. On one occasion when he heard that a man whom he'd known to be a heavy drinker "never takes a single drink," he said: "That is the only way it can be done."

Meanwhile Maurice Dooling was becoming known as an extremely able lawyer in his area of California. In 1892 he was elected district attorney of San Benito County (Hollister being the county seat) on the Democratic ticket and was reelected on the same ticket in 1894 with Republican endorsement. He was elected judge of the Superior Court, San Benito County on the Democratic ticket in 1896, and was reelected on the same ticket with Republican endorsement in 1902 and 1908. President Woodrow Wilson appointed him to the United States District Court of the Northern District of California in July 1913, and he served as district court judge until his death. Both of his sons were students in Stanford Law School at the time he was appointed to the federal court.

The following excerpts from an article in the July 19, 1913 issue of San Francisco legal paper, *The Recorder* give some sense of Maurice Dooling's reputation.

Judge Dooling is conceded by lawyers generally to be an ideal selection for the district court. He is widely known throughout the state as a judge of unusual character and learning. Early in his first term as San Benito County Judge of the Superior Court, his learning and sound judgment attracted attention beyond his own county, and it was not long before he began to be called into other counties to try difficult cases. When he was first mentioned for the federal bench, he had the record of having held court in twenty-one counties, including San Francisco and Los Angeles.

His best work outside of his own county has probably been done in Los Angeles. Two years ago, when the extra sessions were created, Los Angeles was the first county to establish an extra department. The governor was called upon to designate a judge, and after looking over the state, chose Judge Dooling as the best fitted for the work in hand. On the governor's designation, Judge Dooling held an extra session in Los Angeles for six months steadily. Later in the year, he spent a further three months there, and last year at the request of the local judges, held court for two more terms of three months each. A few months ago, when a bill creating additional judges in Los Angeles was passed, a committee of

Los Angeles lawyers waited on Judge Dooling with the request that he permit the Los Angeles bar to submit his name to the governor for appointment to one of the permanent judgeships.

As showing the extent of his work as a trial judge, his friends point out that in a period of six weeks recently he had four cases before the appellate courts from widely separated parts of the state, and in each case was affirmed. Two of these cases had been tried before by local judges, but had been reversed.

Both on and off the bench, the new federal judge is warmly admired for his kindness and simplicity. He is most approachable in or out of court, but firm and decisive in action. No judge conducts a more dignified and businesslike court, and yet there is no display or affectation about anything he does.

Perhaps nothing better shows his character than the regard in which he is held in San Benito County, as expressed in a recent article in the Hollister *Bee* in which it is said:

"Miss him? Everyone will miss him. There is not a mother or a father in the county who at some time or other has not sought his advice and always acted on it. When in any kind of domestic trouble or public dilemma you asked your neighbor what was best to be done, the answer has always been, 'You'd better ask the judge. He knows best.' And he never refused his opinion, counseling patience in adversity, honesty in action, hope in the future and trust in The Great Judge of all. Yes, we shall all miss him, from the lawyers who have pleaded before him to the humblest citizen in the county unable to speak English."

Bob Dooling loved the people of San Benito County and kept contacts with them. Many a weekend afternoon, he could be found sitting in front of a store on Main Street in Hollister with friends stopping by to say hello or sitting around him for a visit. His friends were many and of a wide range of educational, ethnic and racial backgrounds. He had put his knowledge of languages to practical use in the community and as a lawyer and judge, and probably added the ability to read and speak Portuguese and Italian to the six other languages he spoke in order to be able to talk with a wider range of non-English speaking immigrants in their native tongues. Also, he greatly appreciated the opportunities he had in growing up in the United States in the late 1800s, and actively opposed acts of discrimination or prejudice. In the early 1900s, the first Chinese immigrant child to enroll in the Hollister school was not admitted until Judge Dooling took the boy, Wong U. Fong, with his queue hanging down his back, to the office of the superintendent of schools, and told them they must either admit the child or start a school for him. Fong became a close friend of the Dooling family, graduated from Hollister High School with honors and went on to the University of California where he secured a doctorate in science.

Simple in dress and personal manner, Maurice Dooling always wore a soft-collared, usually colored shirt, a brown or gray suit, and rolled his own cigarettes. This was in a day when business and professional men wore black suits and endured the uncomfortable custom of wearing a stiff collar that was made out of a type of celluloid and attached to the shirt. His old friends were taking bets on whether or not Judge Dooling would dress in the fashion of that day when he was sworn in on the United States District

Court. He arrived in his usual outfit and when he started to enter the courtroom, the bailiff thought he was a lowly citizen and refused to let him enter until someone who knew Judge Dooling told him that this was the new judge. A newspaper article written by Max Stern around 1921 said that Judge Dooling was reported to be the kindest judge in San Francisco, and that he nearly always gave a first offender a second chance. Then Max Stern quoted Judge Dooling as saying, "I try to put myself in the other fellow's place. I've been here eight years. I don't believe I have seen the same fellow up here before me twice. I try to get at the bottom of his crime. There's always a bottom to it." Another article written by Dick Martinsen in the *San Francisco Daily News* on January 17, 1921, referred to Judge Dooling as the "Wonder Man" of the San Francisco district courts in the use of his ability as a linguist in court but, more important, in his manner with defendants. Dick Martinsen wrote:

> But one of the foundations upon which Judge Dooling's prestige rests is his remarkable expertness in criminal psychology, and the peculiar quieting effect he has on defendants who come before him. A United States attorney recently declared that his honor was possessed of a "magic eye." "Two minutes after a defendant is seated near the judge he relaxes, and his whole attitude changes," is the way lawyers who have worked under Dooling put it. "It's really a very simple thing," says the judge, quietly. "I simply try to make them understand that I am quite the opposite of hostile in my attitude towards them."

Judge Dooling's usual manner of speaking was quiet and kindly but he could thrill an audience with his oratory, and he could be stern and even scathing in speaking or writing, particularly if someone tried to use political or personal pull in the courtroom or community.

In November 1909 at a meeting of the San Francisco Bar Association, several members of the California bar gave talks on reform of legal procedure. Excerpts from the speech of Judge Maurice T. Dooling follow.

> For the greatest trouble with the law today, the chief obstacle in the way of its due administration, is the lawyer himself. Yes, and the judges. For the chief thing that tends to bring the legal profession and the law into reproach is the endeavor, so frequently successful, to obtain from the law for some individual or corporation or class that to which he is not entitled. . . . I take for lack of time the simplest and most obvious illustration; the principle is the same and extends through all the complexities of the law, from the poorest fence of the tenderloin in trouble with the police force to the highest merger in New Jersey defending itself before the highest court of the United States. Why, I ask you, should any man who violates the law expect or even hope to escape conviction when brought before a court of justice? For no reason than because the profession itself encourages him in that expectation. Why should any man who is indebted to his neighbor, believe or hope he can escape a judgment against him when brought into court to answer? For no reason than because some member of the bar has encouraged him in that belief. Shall a man go undefended, then? Not at all. Why then, should not an attorney say to his guilty client, "Yes, if you wish I will see that your case is fairly heard. But I don't see how you are going to escape conviction and I don't see why you should"? But you will say,

such a procedure would have a tendency to discourage litigation. That is true. In many instances it would undoubtedly "hurt business." But in every instance I say it would promote justice. And, after all, is not that what your bar association is to be organized for? It would do more. It would elevate the profession and bring it to that high standard where it properly belongs and to that place in the estimation of the people which would make the lawyer what he ought to be: a leader in the cause of right. And ultimately, indeed, while we might have fewer lawyers and lawyers poorer in purse, we would inevitably have better ones. I mean better in the broader sense. For any man who then desired to make vast sums by devious methods would seek some other field, and those who were left would be engaged in the enforcement and not the evasion of the law.

From the time he was a young lawyer, Maurice had been known to always support the cause of justice, even when it brought him no monetary reward. When he had been practicing law for a few years, a potential client made the trip from Watsonville to Hollister because "I heard if you have no money but Dooling feels your case is a worthy one, he'll take your case and will even pay the court costs."

Maurice Dooling had many and varied interests — baseball, a game of cards with friends, the beauty of the country and mountains (it has been said that his life may have been shortened by a car accident when he went with two of his friends on their annual camping trip into the Sierra, probably in 1919), reading, and languages. He enjoyed translating some of the classics into English. He studied Italian after he was forty years old, then translated at least a large part of Dante's "Inferno" into English and then back into his own Italian. During his last illness, he translated "The Gospels" from Greek into English. Latin and Spanish were the two languages he loved best and in which he was most fluent. Slim and of medium height, he was a physically active person until the last few years of his life. But he developed a cough and had periods of difficult breathing; this condition, possibly combined with a weakened heart, caused his death at sixty-four years of age, in 1924. By then both of his sons were practicing law in San Francisco, both had married, and he had three granddaughters and one grandson.

Charles W. Dooling remained a lawyer throughout his life, for most of this time as chief counsel for the Western Pacific Railroad. Maurice T. Dooling, Jr. practiced law for a few years, then in 1928 was appointed judge of the Superior Court in San Benito County where he served for seventeen years, then served as an associate justice on the District Court of Appeal in San Francisco for almost fifteen years, and on the California Supreme Court for two years. He was an amateur poet and wrote three sonnets about his father after his death, and also this poem that takes us back in spirit to when Maurice Dooling was a young man:

> "I see him now as in that long ago
>   He must have been — young, eager, passion swept,
> The tender heart, the spirit all aglow
>   With fires that flamed and leapt.
> I see him now as to her ardent gaze
>   He must have seemed — so fine, so good, so true,
> So noble. It was so in after days
>   I found the man I knew."

Again quoting Maurice T. Dooling, Jr. about his father:

> None, I suppose, can fully appreciate the effect on his own life of the example of his father; but I know, at least, that my father's example furnished me an exacting yardstick of warm-heartedness, judicial and personal rectitude, a passion for justice tempered with human compassion, and a fierce intellectual honesty against which to measure my own conduct. Whatever little I may have contributed to the cause of justice under the law owes some real, if immeasurable part to the memory of his example. I first learned from him that the law is the guardian of those sacred rights of person and property which enoble and enrich the lives of men.

## Judge Dooling's Contribution to the Law in the Northern District of California
### By Joseph Franaszek

At the time Judge Dooling took his seat on the northern district bench, the reputation of that court had fallen a long distance from the high regard it held during the days of its first judge, Ogden Hoffman. More than thirty years after Judge Hoffman's death, the *San Francisco Examiner,* for instance, urged its readers not to be "a blinded people, [who think] sanctity surrounds the lofty bench and [that] ermine [is] the trimming of an untarnished honor. . . . That bunk is over." Now judges were simply "men who . . . seek a place on the bench because they cannot make a living at the bar, and get it through [economic or political] interests." Those interest groups expect to be and are paid back in favorable court decisions.[1]

Judge Dooling's major contribution to the bench was to restore its reputation and to command respect from the public for the office of United States District Court judge. This was not an easy task. As the *Examiner* noted shortly after Dooling assumed the federal bench: "A judge must prove he is honest before anyone will believe it."[2] But during his decade as a federal judge, Dooling did prove the federal bench's integrity. In his court, privilege lost its influence and equal justice demanded by the law was dispensed to everyone: the rich, the poor; the prominent, the insignificant; the robber baron, the beggar.

An examination of Judge Dooling's efforts — on his own initiative — to insure government agents obeyed the Constitution in their attempts to enforce prohibition laws and the Eighteenth Amendment to the United States Constitution in the northern district demonstrates that he took seriously his oath to protect the Constitution.

Attorneys in his court carefully noted Judge Dooling's remarkably short temper with hypocrites — especially those who violated the law while publicly pretending to enforce it. In February 1918, they began to see what the judge would do in cases of official misconduct. The San Francisco papers reported that the judge "scored" federal officers who brought into court a defendant charged with selling liquor to soldiers. Arrested by city police for this federal offense, the defendant was booked in city prison as "en route to the United States marshal's office." But once his cell was locked, the defendant was held incommunicado. The defendant had one thousand dollars he could have put up to meet bail. But no formal charge was lodged against him. It was with considerable difficulty that he succeeded in contacting an attorney.

Judge Maurice T. Dooling of the United States Circuit Court is notable because of his disconcerting methods. For instance, when he started his career by going to the Legislature in 1884 he surprised them and achieved distinction unusual, although not quite unique, by being honest. Later, becoming Superior Judge of San Benito county, he put the jury system, that bulwark of the freeman, out of business by just being fair to all sides. As a result, no civil case was tried before him by jury, litigants preferring trial by the Judge. Becoming Federal Judge in 1913, he enunciated the startling theory that lawyers should see that their clients are tried fairly, but that it is not necessary to resort to trickery and connivance to outwit justice. He looks upon laws as means to work justice, instead of as rules of an intricate and diverting game, and has been known to cut short a windy circumlocution of cross-examination by asking the witness what are the actual facts. We will let him into the notables, but there is no telling what he will do to disconcert us.

*A sketch of Judge Dooling with a brief article. The sketch and article are from the* San Francisco Chronicle, *7 November 1921.*

JUDGE MAURICE T.
DOOLING

71

The attorney took the matter before Judge Dooling's court and Dooling had the defendant produced by prison officials. Hearing the prisoner's uncontested story, the judge exploded: "This sort of thing must stop! Men have been arrested, thrown into jail, forgotten, and left there for months without any charge being placed against them." Jailing suspects by administrative action, as was done here, was unconscionable. "If no charges are filed against the prisoners within twenty-four hours," ordered the judge, "they should be set free." Warning city officials in his most forceful manner, the judge continued, "twenty-four hours is a sufficient length of time in which to place a charge against any prisoner." Then Dooling ordered all prisoners held without an opportunity for bail and without charges being filed to be released immediately.[3]

But if Judge Dooling thought his direct but brief orders on detention of citizens would halt the police practice, he was wrong. He soon discovered it would be a long and difficult struggle. Three months after this first case of a prisoner held incommunicado, another such case came before his court. A twice-decorated war hero faced a charge of selling liquor to sailors. On arrest, he was locked up in city prison, booked as "en route to the [United States] marshal's office." But no charges were brought against him and he was not permitted to contact friends or an attorney. With no immediate prospect of release or of legal process, he was given "one slice of bread for breakfast. . . . For lunch, rice with a little fat mixed in it. . . . Dinner brought forth a slice of bread. This formed the entire day's menu and the trenches [were] heavenly compared with these cells in point of cleanliness," the veteran later told the judge.[4]

In time, this defendant was brought before Judge Dooling. Dooling probed the adequacy of the charge that had eventually been lodged against the veteran. The United States attorney could find no affidavit and had no witness to prove the charge. Accordingly, he withdrew it as meritless. When Judge Dooling heard the prisoner's story, he was outraged. "Who dared disobey my order that no federal prisoner be held for a longer period than twenty-four hours without a warrant?" he asked. "I thought I made it clear to city authorities that no person should be held without first being permitted to communicate with friends and counsel. By whose authority do the city officers hold persons incommunicado. . . . It must be stopped at once! Men do not lose their rights because they are arrested."[5]

The police are not above the law. Police methods must comply with the Constitution. Holding men for a federal crime without warrants for several days, weeks, or months — a common practice of the Police Department, the Department of Justice, and the Army and Navy Intelligence Offices — must end in the Northern District of California. This was the judge's message.

As efforts to control alcohol traffic increased, so too did Judge Dooling's confrontations with police. The Eighteenth Amendment was often enforced by agents who had a special commitment to Prohibition. Their enthusiasm for this law was not shared by many in the "wet" Northern District of California. Accordingly, they felt isolated and frustrated. Some of them had a feeling of self-righteousness and a willingness to do almost anything in order to obtain a conviction.

It was not long before their excesses came to Judge Dooling's attention. For instance, in May 1920, the judge presided in the jury trial of a man charged with violating the prohibition law. An agent was the first government witness to testify concerning a raid on the defendant's California Street hotel. On cross-examination, defense attorney Chauncey Tramulto (later to be a Northern District United States attorney) asked the witness: "Did you have a search warrant" for the raid? As if he had not heard of using warrants before, the reply was "we did not." On hearing this, Judge Dooling stopped the testimony and the introduction of evidence from the raid. To get around this, the United States attorney asked the officer what the liquid seized tasted like. "It tasted like dynamite" was the reply.

Dooling could contain himself no longer. "If we are to enforce the law, we must uphold the law," he declared while expressing amazement that prohibition officers seized property without securing a warrant. As far as the evidence went, he instructed the jury to acquit. The defendants were charged with manufacturing liquor, not dynamite. The government was only able to show that "they manufactured something that tasted like dynamite. It isn't against the prohibition law to manufacture dynamite."[6]

But the judge's activism in protecting defendant's constitutional rights seemed to be constantly tested by prohibition agents. Even in the case of a saloon keeper who unwisely stored — and admitted to storing 30,000 dollars worth of bonded liquors in his Bush Street apartment, the agents could not get around the requirements of the Constitution. In this case, agents did secure a search warrant, but that document's description of the place to be searched and illicit things to be seized was vague and ambiguous.

Dooling rejected the legality of the resulting search. He told the agents that a search warrant could be issued only on probable cause, supported by an affidavit naming or describing with reasonable particularity the property to be searched and the thing to be seized. The affiant must state his belief that "intoxicating liquor is being sold" for there to be probable cause of a Prohibition violation. Mere possession of liquor is insufficient to violate the prohibition laws, the judge ruled. This meant there was no crime in this case (because agents did not state in the affidavit that the defendant was selling liquor) and, in any case, the warrant was impermissibly defective. Prohibition agents cannot expect to convict a man for violating the law when they bring him into court under an illegal process and in doing so have, themselves, violated the law. Nor can they construe mere possession of alcoholic beverages, absent evidence of intent to sell or distribute it, to be a violation of the law. The judge ordered the liquor returned to the defendant's apartment and the defendant released.[7]

These decisions confirmed prohibition agents' belief that they alone understood the nefarious designs of the bootleg trade; it seemed to them that the judge could not understand. Therefore, they channeled their efforts into other projects in which the judge might not be able to help those arrested by the agency. Judge Dooling realized the agents were trying to place themselves above the law and the Constitution and was determined to force a "showdown" on the matter. It came all too quickly.

In 1922 an attorney, representing a Petaluma resident, procured from the northern district court an order directing a prohibition agent to return a truck to his client. The truck had been seized from his client's friend, who had used it to transport four barrels of wine to San Francisco in the truck. The order was presented to the agent, but the agent refused to obey. Judge Dooling's order "makes no difference," declared the agent. "You are not going to get that truck that easy. You . . . ought to be on McNeil Island [prison] for ten years," the agent told the client.[8]

Hearing of this disobedience, "Dooling's wrath then descended" on the agent. At a court hearing, the judge expressed his intent to cite the agent for contempt of court. "I think that at some time we must have a showdown between the prohibition department and the court and see if the orders of the court are going to be obeyed at all, or obeyed at the convenience of the [prohibition] officers." Dooling had the offending agent brought to the court. He allowed the agent to air his views, and then reasoned with him about the necessity of the government's agents, as well as every citizen, to comply with the law. In the end, the judge decided only to reprimand the agent. It would serve as a warning to all other government agents that no one was above the law.[9]

The public, at times, had difficulty understanding the release of persons who clearly violated the law. But they also realized in all this a change from previous years, when the northern district's corporation presidents, political officials, and government operatives could ignore the law's requirements. Under Judge Dooling, everyone — including the government — was subject to the law. This was Judge Dooling's lasting contribution to the administration of justice in the northern district. The idea of equality before the law was an idea apparently so long out of use that its introduction now struck people like a blinding light. They began to tell stories of their Judge Dooling, who "is notable because of his disconcerting methods." As evidence of this, they recalled how, in going to the California legislature in 1884, "he surprised [the political bosses] and achieved distinction unusual . . . by being honest." Others relished the rumor that, while judge of the San Benito Superior Court, "he put the jury system . . . out of business by just being fair to all sides. As a result, no civil case was tried before him by jury, litigants preferring trial by the judge." The Northern District of California had a judge who "looks upon laws as means to work justice, instead of as rules of an intricate and diverting game." All in all, the people of northern California considered Dooling one of their "notables." But many admitted, "there is no telling what he will do to disconcert us."[10]

---

## William Frances James
### 1875-1966
*By Joseph Franaszek*

To all outward appearances, Judge Maurice Dooling's death in 1924 severed the ties of legal community between San Francisco and the central coast counties. Barriers of geography, economy, and custom seemed to render central coast legal practitioners rarities in the federal district court, but the central coast's partnership in the northern district was never completely extinguished. Notable legal figures of the central coast were also notable in the northern district.

An example of this relationship is found in the career of William Francis James. No sooner had Judge Dooling's successor assumed the bench than a new vacancy on that court was created with the demise of Dooling's colleague, Judge John Slater Partridge. In behind-the-scenes jockeying to fill the vacant judgeship in 1927, James, an attorney long attached to the Santa Clara valley and an active and dedicated Republican party member, was a possible nominee for the northern district court bench. President Calvin Coolidge was having difficulties finding a nominee to take the place of deceased United States District Judge John Slater Partridge in San Francisco.

Since Partridge's death, the battle for his court seat had been waged between various San Francisco judges, primary among them, Presiding Superior Judge Harold Louderback — a rather distant, sometimes unapproachable man. Louderback was a prominent supporter of California Supreme Court Chief Justice Waste's campaign for a professional state bench. He was also the choice of the man who had President Coolidge's ear on California federal patronage: California's United States Senator Samuel Shortridge. But in the battle for the district court judgeship, Louderback's appointment hit a roadblock.

*William Francis James. This photograph is dated 1932, a few years after James's candidacy for a federal judgeship on the northern district court. (Courtesy Judge Mark Thomas, Jr.)*

Various San Francisco attorneys charged him with unethical dealings in several cases before his court. Faced with this accusation, the administration delayed announcing Louderback's nomination — at least until the dust cleared — which turned out to be a matter of some two years.

During the tempest over Louderback's possible nomination, the major San Francisco candidates for the northern district bench seemed deadlocked. The president began to look outside San Francisco for a nominee who might arouse less controversy. It was not long before letters made their way to the White House from regions of the northern district where Republican politics were independent of the San Francisco party bosses. For example, citizens of Santa Cruz County urged the president to appoint Hubert C. Wykoff of Watsonville to the federal bench. Others, at Berkeley, actively pressed the administration to nominate their neighbor, Frank D. Stringham. And in summer and fall of 1927, the president received letters from California's central coast region urging the appointment of attorney William F. James of San Jose.

The district attorney for Santa Clara County, a noted Republican, wrote the president that "conditions which have developed" in the struggle over the appointment made Louderback a political liability to the party. The "partisanship displayed by sponsors for the various candidates" made it necessary that the president look outside San Francisco for a nominee. This was especially so because one San Francisco candidate for the district judgeship could not be appointed "without creating some dissatisfaction" in the losing factions. Accordingly, "the best solution . . . can be found in the appointment of someone outside of San Francisco and within the northern district" — namely, William F. James. Mr. James, he reminded the president, "has not [been] through this unhappy partisan strife [which would] render his appointment in any way objectionable."[11]

The need for a federal judge with little connection to San Francisco politics was a recurring theme in letters to the president from the central coast counties. These writers felt that the two judges currently on the northern district bench from the "large cities" — San Francisco and Oakland — were enough. "It seems to me that the country districts should have consideration and that the present vacancy should be filled by one man who is experienced in the problems and litigation of the great farming and fruit growing sections of northern California," declared one farmer.[12]

Not every cow county should have a federal judge. But the central coast region contained few cow counties. The Santa Clara valley was "one of the greatest and richest fruit growing districts in the world." It had "many prosperous towns" such as San Jose with a population of 60,000 persons and was a "community of some importance." Not only was it Secretary of Commerce Herbert Hoover's home, but it was "a Republican community with a patriotic, conservative population — although it occasionally gets sore and votes Democratic" admitted one writer to the Republican president.

If William F. James were appointed, the central coast counties would have little reason to "get sore" and vote Democratic. The lack of consensus among city politicians concerning who should be the district court nominee, the need for a rural-based judge to occupy a seat on the bench where Judge Maurice T. Dooling of San Benito had once sat, and the "absolutely square man" that Mr. James was, made him the logical nominee. The confidence the fruit growers and farmers of rural northern California had in James made it likely that his appointment would bring "general satisfaction throughout the district including the cities." And there was an added advantage to appointing someone from outside the large cities. Namely, with the appointment of James, Coolidge could "please a lot of plain people" and show that he was "really one of us."[13]

The basic argument of the letters to the president on behalf of James bear a remarkable similarity to an argument advanced nearly thirty-five years later in the struggle to get the district court to sit in San Jose. It was the belief that the San Jose area was entitled to "at least one judge . . . who knows our conditions and can understand our viewpoint." In 1927, these writers felt vitally affected by the court in San Francisco, if for no other reason than "a great many of the lawsuits in which the farmers and fruit growers are vitally interested" were heard in the federal court there. One correspondent wrote that James deserved the appointment because "he is not a politician but still is familiar with conditions here" in the Santa Clara valley.[14]

What characteristics were these writers looking for in a United States District Court judge? W. S. Clayton, president of the First National Bank of San Jose, noted that James — fifty-two-years old in 1927 — had worked himself up in the world, being "compelled to support himself at age fifteen." James had the "energy and persistence" of a scholar, demonstrated by "his studies in law, languages, literature, and history." He was well traveled and educated and attended law lectures at Stanford and the University of Denver. He "has been consistently a Republican, as were his father and grandfather before him." Clayton wrote that while James "was reared a Protestant . . . his broad views have won him the friendship of many sincere Catholics." Indeed, the archbishop of San Francisco recently wrote United States Senator Shortridge suggesting that James be appointed to the district court. Just as important as his experience and success in the law was his "very pleasing personality and . . . strong sense of loyalty." As another correspondent wrote the president, "If you appoint Mr. James to the federal court, we will have an honest judge who is a scholar, a thinker, and a gentleman, and who is one of the ablest lawyers on the Pacific Coast."[15] This seemed to sum up all that was required to sit on the federal bench.

But William Francis James did not receive the appointment to the United States District Court for the Northern District of California. San Francisco's Presiding Superior Judge Harold Louderback did.

Although James's supporters had emphasized his facility with law, none cited his experience with the federal court. Unlike most attorneys in the central coast counties, James did appear in the United States District Court in San Francisco.

William F. James was admitted to the California State bar in 1896. In starting solo practice, he attempted to secure any position of prominence in the San Jose legal community. He needed something to set him apart from all other local practitioners. Appearing before the federal court offered one such opportunity for distinction. It was unusual in the normal law practice of the town to handle federal matters — these were usually left to the experts in San Franciso. However, a year after passing the bar, James represented a San Jose resident in the United States District Court for the Northern District of California. His client had been arrested in San Jose and taken to San Francisco, charged with "passing counterfeit coin." James represented the defendant in a preliminary hearing before United States Commissioner Heacock in San Francisco, but was unsuccessful in preventing the commissioner from binding the San Jose defendant over to answer before the federal grand jury of the city. The grand jury subsequently indicted James's client. Apparently, James found a procedural defect in these indictment proceedings. He went before United States District Judge John J. DeHaven in San Francisco with a "motion to squash" [sic] the grand jury indictment. DeHaven granted this motion and the government released James's client from custody; no attempt was made to reindict the San Josean.[16]

A year after this success, James received appointment as a United States commissioner in San Jose. For the recent admittee to the bar, this was a desirable position. It might give James a step above his competitors. It would make him appear more established than he actually was, two years after his admission to the bar. It also could supply a supplementary source of income.

James entered his duties as United States commissioner on March 18, 1898. It was a part-time position; the government paid him, according to a compensation schedule, for each piece of work he did. The duties of this office in San Jose were light, issuing "complaints, warrants, subpoenas, orders, judgments, et cetera."[17] The job did not occupy all of his time, so he also pursued litigation in the local courts.

It is clear that the volume of business this post brought to his practice varied. It certainly was not lucrative. For instance, he was paid a total of $48.89 for his work in this position during the months of April, May, and June 1900. And that was $31.69 more than he received for work in October, November and December that year.[18]

After several years as United States commissioner in San Jose, James seemed to grow disenchanted not only with the position, but also with all the paperwork it required. Therefore he resigned the post before 1906. But this did not free him of the insistent demands of the clerk for the United States District Court for the Northern District of California. Indeed, the demands increased. The clerk charged that James failed to comply with Section 21 of an 1896 act of Congress pertaining to duties of United States commissioners. This act required James give reports on his performance of his duties. The clerk claimed James failed in this vital responsibility.[19]

James seemed bemused at these requests to file his record of proceedings as United States commissioner. James explained that it was unavailable. Apparently, in moving from his old offices in the Porter Building to new offices in the Auzerais Building in San Jose, the record was lost. "I have made a very careful search for this record, not once, but several times," James insisted. "It has apparently been mislaid, or accidentally lost or destroyed."[20]

The clerk's office would not accept this answer and involved the United States attorney for the northern district in an investigation of James's failure to file the report. Assistant United States Attorney A. P. Black was assigned to the case. He met with James in early January 1906. They went down to the clerk's office where James offered the deputy clerk "a bunch of papers wrapped in manila paper, which the deputy clerk understood to be papers in regard to deportation cases." Commissioners need not file these papers and so they were refused.[21]

It seems James satisfied Assistant United States Attorney Black regarding his failure to file this report. But the clerk's office was not so easily mollified and tried, unsuccessfully, to contact him in San Jose. Apparently they kept trying to reach him at his old address, forgetting that James had told them he moved to the Auzerais Building (and that in this move his report was lost). In desperation, the clerk wrote to the postmaster at San Jose asking if James had left San Jose, and if he had, to "furnish me with his present address . . . for government reasons, I am very anxious to locate him."[22]

On hearing of this from the postmaster, James wrote the clerk explaining once again that he had changed his address in San Jose. Indeed, it was in changing his address that this whole problem of the missing report arose. He described once again why he could not file the necessary report. "Very probably the record you desire was mislaid and lost" when James moved his office. But James made an offer of settlement to the persistent clerk: "I have here a number of documents filed with me as . . . commissioner . . . which I offered to file in your office on the visit" of January 1906 with Assistant United States Attorney Black. The clerk's office declined these papers then. Perhaps they might accept these now in lieu of the report? Clearly James was annoyed. What more did these bureaucrats want? "I do not see that I can offer anything" more but those papers refused by the clerk's office, he wrote.[23]

The clerk, not conceding a thing, wrote James that he should send the documents to San Francisco "for inspection so that I may determine whether or not they may be properly received" as the report of the commissioner.[24] Nothing more is known of the resolution of this dispute. Available evidence indicates this marked the end of James's prolonged contact with the United States District Court in San Francisco. It also preceded the beginning of his rise in professional stature. Curiously, it was the 1906 earthquake which was the catalyst for this.

The 1906 earthquake destroyed much of downtown San Jose, as well as James's office in the Auzerais Building. James recalled coming to where his office had been located and finding a pile of rubble. Standing nearby was another attorney who worked in a separate law office that was also in that rubble. "Tell you what," suggested this attorney, Louis Oneal. "You and I would make a good combination. You're a damned good lawyer; I'm not. I'm good at getting business; you're not." So they established this division of duties and started their partnership. Their office did quite well as San Jose began to rebuild. In time, it represented the more substantial business concerns of the region.

Oneal, known as "Mr. Republican" of the Santa Clara valley, was finally able to get James a judgeship — in 1933 as an appointee by Governor Rolph to the Santa Clara County Superior Court. "I got interested in the job of being a judge, and away we went," James once reminisced.[25] And he went far: handling the court's criminal calendar for two decades, deciding important civil matters, and applying his pre-New Deal Republican philosophy to the interpretation of the law. He would remain on the Santa Clara County Superior Court bench nearly thirty years to become the state's oldest practicing judge when he stepped down in 1963. He was then eighty-eight years old, but he could not stop his work with the law and rejoined his old firm, which now included several new partners. Among them was William A. Ingram, who in twelve years would become a United States District Court judge.

When S. 1666 passed Congress in 1966, establishing the San Jose Federal Court, William Francis James was ninety-one years old. That San Jose candidate for the northern district bench in 1927 was still practicing law, although at a slower pace. He had lived to see the legislation to establish a federal court in San Jose, but he would not survive to see its first judge appointed, nor its first trial on the central coast. Still, he did see the reestablishment of those old ties of legal community that bound the central coast counties and San Francisco together as equal partners in the Northern District of California.

# Part 2

## Politics, Persistence, and Principles in the Struggle for a Federal Court on the Central Coast

As we have seen, the residents of San Jose and the central coast counties had federal courts during California's early development. In later days, however, the area lost its federal courts; instead, those with federal issues had to travel the long road to San Francisco. To regain a federal court presence, residents undertook a protracted and difficult campaign, one of seemingly interminable skirmishes and setbacks before the eventual triumph.

In this part, Joseph Franaszek, a member of the California State bar, describes that process. His experience in Washington, D.C. as a fellow with the House Committee on the Judiciary, Subcommittee on Monopolies and Commercial Law, gives him a special knowledge from which to tell the story of the maneuverings on Capitol Hill that ultimately brought the federal court back to San Jose after its long absence.

# 6

## A Cornerstone for the Northern District Court

*Joseph Franaszek*

Spring was rather cool and damp for the Santa Clara valley in 1973, but as mid-June neared, a pleasant, moderate warmth arrived in the air. This brought considerable satisfaction to a small group of local attorneys. To consider them among the region's ranks of sun worshippers would have been a mistake: they had set the fifteenth day of that month, with the approval of the United States District Court for the Northern District of California, for the dedication of the first federal courthouse in San Jose. They realized the rather cramped quarters available in the new court facility would not hold the numbers expected at the dedication, so they had planned an outdoor celebration to mark this significant event in the development and growth of the community. No doubt the prospect of the ceremony in the warm, bright valley sun would remind many that only two decades ago the area was typified by its acres of scented, verdant orchards and cattle grazing on rolling grassy hills. Others would recall that in those days one traveled sixty miles or more to attend the United States District Court for the Northern District of California.

Those planning the dedication wanted it to be a day of celebration for the northern district court, however, many of the court's judges dissented from this view. Only one of the northern district judges who had opposed the federal court's presence in San Jose had cleared his calendar. Although the rest of the judges would not or could not attend the ceremony, more than 150 governmental, judicial, and legal leaders of the valley were present. Consequently, the ceremony marked a reaffirmation of the region's concern for a permanent federal court presence in the area.

The result of a long administrative and political battle for a federal court in San Jose was now marked by two simple buildings. Persons attending the ceremony took great satisfaction in these structures despite their rather makeshift character. The *San Jose*

*Mercury* spoke for many when it called the temporary court complex to be dedicated at the Santa Clara County Civic Center a "much needed home for the federal judges when they preside in San Jose." At the same time, the *Mercury* reflected the general hope that the buildings would not have to serve the northern district court more than a few years. The newspaper quoted the sentiment calling for a more "permanent federal building in San Jose that will house all United States agencies now scattered over the Santa Clara valley."[1]

The dedication ceremony was held in front of the main entrance to the courthouse. The larger main court building housed a clerk's office, chambers, and two courtrooms, so that two federal judges could hold court at the same time. A smaller structure on the right contained a United States Probation office. The spectators sat in long rows of plain metal folding chairs on the level ground beneath a spreading walnut tree. They faced a dais with a waist-high stand and microphone. Behind this podium ranged a single row of eleven folding chairs.

To the right of this platform was a section claimed by the press. There, reporters stood ready as news technicians adjusted their equipment, intently focusing and refocusing on the podium and then on the audience. Spectators sorted themselves out, finding good seats while greeting one another with neighborly gestures and friendly words.

The last members of the Advisory Committee for the San Jose Federal Court arrived. That committee had gathered at 11:30 that morning for a genial meeting and lunch at a nearby restaurant. Not content with the courthouse that would open that day, the committee had already turned its attention to a new problem. Dominating the meeting was the prospect of getting the planning, site acquisition, and construction of a hoped-for 34 million dollar United States Courthouse and Federal Office Building in San Jose off of dead center.[2]

Two-thirty neared and various notables took their places in the chairs on the dais. The temperature, now in the low 70s, lent a vigorous, fresh feeling to the afternoon. Committee Chairman Russell Roessler stepped forward and welcomed the guests to the ceremony. A northwestern breeze joined his welcome, whipping the courthouse flag against its flagpole with playful, metallic clangs.

After this brief opening to the ceremony came a series of speeches. Each speech, although on a different subject, developed a common theme: the history of the region's lawyers and political leaders' struggle to compel the northern district court to sit in San Jose. This history described the discouraging prospects for success that Bob Beresford and later Russ Roessler had faced when they coordinated the movement for a San Jose federal court. Even by the time Congressman Don Edwards joined in this struggle, the chances of success did not appear good. But with persistence and growing expertise in local, state bar association, judicial, and congressional politics, the proponents obtained congressional authorization to have the federal court sit in San Jose.

When this battle had been won, however, a guerilla war persisted led by doubters of the San Jose court. Congress had allowed the northern district court to sit in San Jose, but *compelling* the court to sit there permanently involved much more than legislation. It required that central coast attorneys demonstrate that Judge Chambers's and Judge Peckham's arguments concerning the region's need for a federal court were in fact well founded.

But recounting the northern district court's history in the four central coast counties was merely a means for building consensus about the court's future there. References to the past were designed to indicate just how practical this future might be. There was no assurance that the court would continue to meet in San Jose. The ground for the building dedicated that June 15, 1973, was leased from the City of San Jose and was only a temporary home. Accordingly, many valley attorneys sought an enduring symbol of the court in San Jose — a permanent federal courthouse. Congressman Edwards announced to his listeners that after checking with the General Services Administration in Washington, he was "assured that we have a high priority" for the construction of a permanent federal courthouse. Indeed, the government would build a federal building to house all federal agencies in the area, including the court. The years of argument involved in gaining the simple structures dedicated that spring afternoon made this expectation seem rather ambitious. But, Edwards declared to his listeners, "We intend to have that building and not a decade from now."[3]

This future San Jose federal court building — this symbol of the federal court in the central coast counties — would be founded upon more than the General Service Administration's concrete and steel. Its real foundation would rest upon the vigorous labors of a few whose foresight, imagination, and determination would make federal justice more accessible to the people of the region. This would form the cornerstone for the northern district court in San Jose.

7

# A Long Road and a Vision

*Joseph Franaszek*

This struggle for a federal court presence in the central coast counties, referred to so frequently during the June 15, 1973 dedication ceremony, was being preserved even before the opening of that shed-like United States Courthouse in San Jose. During a late and darkening February afternoon in 1967, Judge Robert Beresford sat with Carl Baar, helping to preserve this legacy. Baar, a twenty-seven- year-old political science graduate student, interviewed him about the politics of establishing a United States District Court in San Jose. Baar had been a congressional fellow with Congressman Don Edwards, a friend of Beresford. In Edwards's office, Baar had frequently heard of Judge Beresford's efforts to procure an accessible federal forum for the area and he decided to write his doctoral dissertation on the politics of the federal courts in California. During his discussion with the friendly and helpful Judge Beresford, Baar inquired as to how the judge had become involved in the problem of the federal courts in the first place. It would be a long story, he was warned. Baar persisted, probing whether attorneys of the central coast used the United States District Court in San Francisco. He learned and reported in his dissertation that it was the "personal inconvenience and consumption of time" traveling the long highway to San Francisco that caused generations of attorneys to avoid any involvement with the United States District Court for the Northern District of California. Baar concluded that the road symbolized how troubling it was to use the federal court in San Francisco.[1] It was an important factor in the tendency of valley attorneys to avoid the federal courts, but the highway alone was an insufficient explanation.

Beresford could recall his experiences on the highways in the late 1940s representing a local business in the United States District Court. Then, as now, on foggy mornings the road seemed to pass through a desolate, bleak, and comfortless wasteland on the flat shoreline between San Jose and San Francisco. Through much of this road, there was lit-

Judge Robert Beresford about 1980. His efforts in the late 1940s initiated the long struggle for a federal court in San Jose. (Courtesy Judge Robert Beresford.)

tle to arrest a traveler's interest. It was a curious road; one traveler of postwar California claimed: "Its scenery is almost non-existent, many times consisting of bleak views of the bay, uninspiring rows of roofs of the subdivisions . . . and a multitude of traffic signs."[2] Over vast stretches of the roadway even these items of slight interest were rare. Populated by occasional gas stations, this narrow strip of land running south from San Francisco retained a rural aspect in some areas, but in other areas, one of hesistant industrial development.

Before World War II, many Peninsula towns were merely the suburbs of San Francisco, providing a restful and nearby escape from the pressures of the city. But an ideal climate, pleasant living conditions, and the promise of growing industrial and business opportunities following the war attracted an ever-increasing residential population which worked where it lived — on the Peninsula. Judge Beresford was among that population: his law practice and his home were located in San Jose.

In 1949, Beresford's difficulties with the highway related to more than the time or strain it took to go from the spacious orchards of the Santa Clara valley to the urban clutter of San Francisco's Mission Street where the federal courthouse stood. As attorney in the Western Well Drilling Company's suit against the United States, Beresford was then making his first appearance as counsel in the United States District Court for the Northern District of California.

Arrival at the federal courthouse on Mission Street brought to Beresford's mind other thoughts than those of the vicissitudes of a long trip. Appearance in court was not an effortless experience for him, and going before a federal court brought additional risks of the unexpected. He always felt ill at ease in court. This was not due to any weakness of his case or arguments. Rather, he simply "didn't go into court enough to be casual about it" and so he tended to be "tense and not at all comfortable" during trial.[3]

He realized, as he surveyed the solemn and impressive classical facade of the court building in which he would argue *Western Well Drilling Co. v. United States,* that this would not be like going before any other court. Only after the trial had started did he realize how much he had over prepared for it. He also realized that there was no impenetrable barrier for a general practitioner to gain expertise in such a court.

At the time of that trial, Beresford had practiced law in California more than three years. Like his colleagues in the Santa Clara valley, he practiced in the local courts rather than in the more distant federal forum. But because Western Well Drilling Company had sued the federal government, the case could be heard only in a federal court. Beresford then had little direct or prolonged experience in the federal courts. He had advised clients about the requirements of federal law, but going to federal court was new.

Federal court practitioners who may have been in court while Beresford presented his case might have found him a quiet and mild-mannered lawyer. This would be quite unlike the picture San Francisco attorneys would later draw of him as irrepressible. He could be as blandly smooth as the best of the city's attorneys when necessary, but he still radiated a general air of commitment and sincerity. No one, seeing Beresford in a room full of lawyers, would imagine that he would play a crucial role in battling judges and the big-city bar associations to correct the concentration of federal justice in the cities of San Francisco and Los Angeles.

Beresford was a compact individual who seemed to shrink on formal occasions. Yet this did not diminish the impact of his performance. While pursuing a just cause, his eyes burned with zeal and impatience. They could be active and quick to sparkle, especially as he varied his arguments with bits of self-deprecating humor. But they would grow dark and stern when he emphasized what he considered critical principles. His manner was gentle and deferential. By nature he was modest — perhaps almost shy — yet he was a man of tremendous activity.

Some would come to consider him a fanatic: "A man that does what he thinks th' Lord wud do if He knew th' facts iv th' case."[4] But this was not true. Beresford was never confident he had all the facts of the case, nor had he the blind pride to think that he knew what the Lord might do. But there were those who felt there was a certain force in Beresford: the force of a crusader. Beresford seemed an individual who perceived a right and against insurmountable odds used his abilities, skills, and powers of endurance and conciliation to achieve that right. Others believed it was not so much the force of a crusader that sparked Beresford, but rather that of a modern-day Don Quixote.

But whether one saw crusader or Don Quixote, there was in Beresford the commitment to righting injustices. That one of the injustices he would fight would be the effective denial of federal justice to citizens of the central coast counties seemed accidental. His early life offered little indication of the role he would play in the development of the central coast area. It seemed unusual that he would end up practicing law in San Jose in the first place. All indications of his early career were that seeking to establish a federal court there would be the least of his concerns.

A graduate of Yale Law School during the Great Depression, he associated with the

Wall Street law firm of Donovan, Leisure, Newton & Lumbard. He had been with the firm for several years when the attack on Pearl Harbor caused him to enlist in the navy. For much of the war, he applied his legal expertise in the Bureau of Ships, arranging the contracts for manufacture of vessel components. This activity, as well as his experience on a navy contract management and negotiating team, altered his perception of the type of law practice he desired.

When he worked for Donovan, Leisure, he had gained considerable experience in business and antitrust law. Some of his activities for the firm required that he travel about the country to study the possible effect federal commercial law might have on clients' activities. This work was basically consultative and he rarely had court appearances, much less any in federal court. He was, however, particularly active in Federal Trade Commission administrative hearings.

This travel and work in a specialized and growing area of law made him realize that in many small communities of the nation, the local bar was "not well equipped with the somewhat sophisticated counsel" offered by the larger firms of New York. In retrospect, this view might have been attributable to a certain clannishness that attorneys in the legal centers of the nation have regarding those practicing out in the country. As Beresford later admitted, in heavily populated trade centers like New York, the bar tends to have "its own set of values," making them feel "superior to attorneys in less populous areas . . . [It was a] . . . kind of snobbishness . . . the lawyers of Wall Street don't think much of the lawyers of Chicago or California or anywhere else."[5]

But Beresford only gained this perspective years after the war. He found that many smaller legal communities appeared to be behind the times. This was especially true with regard to some of the newer developments in the growing body of federal law. Although his work up to 1946 gave him no direct experience in federal court, it left him with a personal interest in the federal courts. He thought that after the war he could offer to the businesses in smaller legal communities the type of advice that, so far, had been available only to firms in the big cities.

Moreover, while big city practice had its enjoyable moments, it was not the type of practice he desired. Besides, his specialized legal knowledge and navy legal experience gave him expertise in techniques of legal negotiation, not confrontation. A final inducement to seek a practice in a small community was that such a practice would be less impersonal than a metropolitan practice could be. In the smaller communities, one's clients were also one's neighbors and friends; this appealed to Beresford.

Having decided to search for a different professional future in the law, Beresford and his wife established criteria for deciding where this future law practice might be. One criterion was that the practice be in a much smaller community than New York, with a population of between 50,000 and 500,000. Another criterion was that the area have a diversified economy. A final criterion was the presence of educational institutions of good standing in the area.

After the war, Beresford and his wife used his navy leave to drive about the country to visit the communities that matched their threefold criteria. It took some time before they pulled into San Jose. As Beresford recalled their arrival, he and his wife "had a good meal — right opposite the Saint Claire Hotel at a moderate price and found a good motel — out on First Street."[6] The town met all the criteria: it had 75,000 people; a diverse economy of agriculture and small, but growing industry; and several nearby universities or colleges of excellent repute. The town offered a restful, serene atmosphere. In the popular notion of the American Main Street of the era, it boasted a mixture of

*Downtown San Jose in 1946. This photograph, which looks northwest along South Second Street, shows San Jose as it was when Judge Robert Beresford moved to the city. The left side of the street, in the foreground, is the site of the new United States Courthouse and Federal Building. (Courtesy San Jose Mercury News.)*

the new and old. It was a seasonal town, liveliest during the harvest and canning season when workers flocked to the area's orchards, fields, and packing plants.

It seemed that no buildings exceeded twelve stories in height; most were lower than five stories. Some of the taller structures indicated their vintage with period decorations — ornate awnings, sculptured decorations in Roman or Greek style. This grandiose architecture of the turn of the century was marred by the fire escapes crawling down the front or sides of buildings. There were few neon signs in the town but transparent plastic signs were popular. Cars parked on both sides of the major streets, which already had parking meters. The streets could be rather wide, having two lanes running one way and two in the other direction, excluding space for parking. Rather old street lamps, Victorian in design, marked off the length of the street.[7]

It was an unpretentious town; it was a friendly community. Reacting to all this, Beresford's intuition brought him to suggest to his wife as they settled down to their first dinner in San Jose that, "This is it!"[8]

He spent his first two weeks going from one business or legal concern to another, checking for job opportunities and assessing whether the town was consistent with the promotions of the chamber of commerce. He found everyone optimistic about the future, everyone except the lawyers. Most of the lawyers suggested that he'd "do better in Sunnyvale." But essentially Beresford's discussions confirmed his belief in the community.

But those outside the Santa Clara valley had a completely different conception of the promise of the region. He found the San Francisco attorneys had a uniformly "sneering attitude about San Jose." This reaction was reflected by many of his friends back East. Even his mother, a well-traveled individual, "somewhat sophisticated in some ways," felt he should settle in "some real place" rather than in San Jose.

His experiences in the navy and with Donovan, Leisure, gave him definite ideas about his desired practice in San Jose. He wanted to serve as counsel to small businesses in the area. He believed there was very little emphasis on preventative law for these companies. Businesses were not getting adequate advisory service which anticipated legal problems and resolved them before litigation occurred. Beresford thought he might offer this type of advisory service, as a "sort of house counsel on a part-time basis," to the moderate-sized firms in the area which usually tried to find an attorney only when dragged into court.

While acting on intuition, Beresford also checked the facts. Would he have the opportunity to practice the type of law he desired in San Jose? He was giving up his position with Donovan, Leisure yet none of the many attorneys and businesses he contacted had offered him a position. He would have to go into solo practice.

Beresford closed out his affairs on the East Coast and found a home in San Jose. He was frustrated for a considerable time by the simple problem of finding available office space in the town and when he was finally able to open his office, he discovered that he was the only attorney in the area practicing an anticipatory approach to the law. The custom of the community was such that clients "did not see the value of paying me fees for keeping them out of trouble."

Businesses shared this general view. Attorneys' fees were to be paid only to get out of trouble. One of Beresford's clients had been represented for years by an attorney considered "one of the best known in town." This practitioner had "never sent them a bill . . . because there was no litigation." There was no charge for advice and the client was expected to reciprocate for the free advice by giving "a present to his lawyer at

Christmas time and the lawyer would be pleased: he expected to outlive his client and he hoped to be rewarded."

Beresford would have to adjust to this custom. But he remained committed to offering some form of anticipatory legal counsel: the type of counsel available to businesses in the large cities. Despite all the setbacks and the accommodations, he was "sold on the community" and would allow himself no second thoughts.

In his early San Jose practice, his concept of legal consulting for local business brought fewer clients than necessary for a thriving concern, so his practice diversified into a range of civil, personal, and family matters: a general legal practice. Eventually his office was well supplied with litigation although Beresford tried to use his skills in settling cases and keeping them out of court. In time he won converts to his form of anticipatory legal counsel, especially since "none of [his] clients got into trouble."

Yet Beresford's practice on this assortment of legal matters brought a disturbing fact to his attention. The nearest federal court was more than sixty miles away over long and often crowded roads. Clients with federal rights to assert could not easily avail themselves of this federal forum. Hiring a San Jose attorney to pursue a matter in the United States District Court in San Francisco could be unduly expensive, perhaps more than the remedy available to the client justified. Because it was uneconomical for the less wealthy and smaller businesses to use the federal court, local attorneys were not well versed in federal practice. This lack of familiarity with federal practice rendered most about as willing to prosecute a case in the federal district court as they would be to prosecute one overseas. Among his new colleagues in the San Jose area, Beresford could not recall any San Jose attorney going to San Francisco to pursue federal cases; he doubted any were going on a regular basis. Some did, but it was rare.[9]

It was as attorney for Western Well Drilling Company that Beresford's interest in the federal courts crystalized. After Beresford opened his San Jose law office in August 1946, he handled several minor matters for N.T. Bradford's local companies. Bradford was one of the people Beresford had called upon in making his decision to settle in San Jose. Their genial relations continued. One day in 1947, Bradford asked Beresford to "handle a dog of a case . . . that he had for one of his companies, the Western Well Drilling Company." Apparently the regular San Jose counsel for Bradford's companies had been confronted with Bradford's contract case involving the federal government. Not very familiar with federal courts or their procedure, he referred the case to an attorney in San Francisco "supposed to be an expert" in such matters. After studying the case, this learned counsel "threw in the sponge" suggesting to Bradford that Western Well Drilling had no cause of action against the government. In any event, the expert argued, the heavy costs of litigation made it ill advised for a small business concern to take on the government.

Probably realizing the slender financial position of Beresford at this stage in his practice, Bradford suggested that he take the case. "I'll give you half of anything you get," he declared, ignoring Beresford's protests that this considerably exceeded the customary contingency fee. With words of prophesy, Bradford dismissed the protests. "Considering what I've gone through with these other lawyers, you take half. You're just starting out: you'll earn it."

Earn it he did. Beresford filed the case in March 1947. It went to trial in 1949. It was decided in April 1951, more than four years after it was filed. "It was a fight every step of the way," recalled Beresford. Not only did he have to learn federal procedure to present the case, but having never filed a complaint before in a federal court, he discovered he had only one week to learn how to do so before the applicable statute of limitations expired.

It was not simply learning federal procedure that compelled the uninitiated to stay away from the federal courts. It was also the distinctly different atmosphere of the federal district court. State superior courts and municipal courts were tied to the community and responsive, to a certain extent, to local custom. San Jose attorneys were familiar with the tempers and thought processes of their local judges. The attorneys knew how best to argue before them and how much leeway the judges would allow. The attorneys did not know any of this for the federal district court judges in San Francisco.

Federal judges and their courts differed. The formal building, its ornate structure incongruous with its deteriorating surroundings on Mission Street, had courtrooms that lent a rather pretentious atmosphere because of their considerable age and august design.

The judge presiding in the Western Well Drilling trial equaled the grandeur of the surroundings. Indeed, he was so impressive that thirty-five years after the trial, Beresford would declare with considerable amusement and with the nostalgia of a rugged survivor, "Oh! I'll never forget him! It was George B. Harris." Beresford found Judge Harris "quite formal" in demeanor and a stickler for proper procedure.

But the judge was receptive to Beresford's arguments, at least initially. "In the first few hours it appeared" to Beresford that Judge Harris "had heard all he wanted to hear" about Beresford's client drilling for water in Utah. Beresford would not voluntarily cut short his presentation. Judge Harris might feel he had heard all the evidence necessary for a decision, but if the case went on appeal, Beresford felt his position "wouldn't stand up factually" unless he incorporated in the record a depressingly protracted set of technical facts.

Beresford considered his position to be critical. His rather "accommodating" judge was "very tired of having all these papers" thrust upon him as evidence. Beresford felt that Harris had ruled against him in "one decision after another." The cold feeling an attorney dreads came upon him: "The judge was against me." He would have to present his case with an eye towards the appellate record. This caused a marked persistence in his arguments, beyond the point of irritating Judge Harris. By trial's end, Beresford felt he "got in everything I had wanted to get in — but not the judge's friendship."[10]

But it was his unfamiliarity with the overloaded federal courts which had made Beresford feel his cause was lost. Judge Harris, in a brief opinion, found for the Western Well Drilling Company. On the evidence parties presented, the court found the drilling company entitled to the full amount prayed for: $9,995.00.[11]

Bradford was pleased with the victory and accordingly insisted on his initial agreement. The company would take half the recovery and Beresford the other half. Even so, the four years of effort held no monetary gain for Beresford. "After the case was over and we got the money, I figured out I got about $2.00 an hour for the work in the case." The drive to San Francisco was a considerable inconvenience, consumed volumes of time, and accounted for much of this slender return. If the opportunities lost to Beresford while he pursued the work for Western Well Drilling were counted, he lost money. Beresford now understood the quizzical looks given him by valley attorneys who learned he was handling a federal case in San Francisco. It was plainly uneconomical. It followed that valley litigants incurred the considerable inconvenience of finding a San Francisco firm to represent them and at a substantial cost and at a great distance.

Beresford thought this unacceptable. In his travels and in his work, he had passed through numerous communities with federal district courts and populations only a fraction of San Jose's. He could not help wondering about the San Jose attorneys' attitudes towards all this. Why weren't they sensitive to the business they lost to the San Francisco law firms because of the absence of a federal court in the central coast area of California?

The reason turned on their general lack of experience with the federal courts. This lack formed a barrier to their learning to use the northern district court. Beresford understood that many attorneys of the region would not enter a federal court, even if it moved to downtown San Jose. "They were afraid to go before a federal court — a real fear — as if [they were required to present a case in] a foreign land. They would have to learn the federal rules — and so they just didn't want to get involved" in worrying about all this.[12]

In trying to gain access to federal court for those in the San Jose area, Beresford would be challenging the powerful inertia of that court's history. The location of the United States District Court was a result of a political decision. Changing that location would involve politics. This was confirmed when Beresford wrote to a friend who drafted Senate legislation as a member of the United States Senate Office of Legislative Counsel. Beresford inquired about having Congress take the necessary steps to authorize the northern district court to hold hearings in San Jose. His friend wrote back that the whole issue was a political matter and briefly mapped out some of the considerations Beresford should keep in mind.[13]

This confirmation of the role of politics in this question of judicial organization might have deterred an inexperienced attorney. Beresford, however, was no political novice. His time with Donovan, Leisure was filled with preparations for hearings before the Federal Trade Commission in Washington, D.C. When this did not occupy his time, he found himself constantly in contact with politics. He lived near Rock Creek Park at the Shoreham Hotel, which was a "pretty lively place in those days." Actors in the political process in Washington — congressmen, executive branch officials, and lobbyists congregated there when not in the halls of power. This exposure made Beresford feel "really comfortable in dealing . . . with people involved in the federal [political] picture."[14] He began to acquire a strong sense of how to get things done politically.

This helped him develop a tentative strategy for getting the United States District Court to San Jose. First, he defined reasonable goals. All he desired was for the court to hold several short sessions in the town; there was not enough federal business in San Jose to keep the court busy full time. Hardly anyone in San Jose at that time realized a local federal court was missing; he must convince people that they needed one. The call for a local federal court must come from all segments of San Jose society: attorneys and fruit pickers; Republicans and Democrats; businessmen and union members.

The remaining question involved creating an interest in an institution with which few local people had any experience. Beresford decided that the best way to do this was to tie a federal court presence with the efforts to transform San Jose into an industrial city.

Although San Jose did not benefit from much war-time industrial growth, by the late 1940s, growth had become a major topic of concern. An estimated half of the work force in the area was then employed in canneries. But in 1944, Progressives were elected to city offices as voters endorsed their plan "to build something they all wanted, a new metropolis, in the place of sleepy San Jose."[15]

With the years, this slow pursuit of development grew. By the early 1950s, the implicit strategy for attracting new industry became more explicit. The town's new civic

*Congressman Jack Z. Anderson. In 1949 Congressman Anderson introduced the first modern bill authorizing a term of the northern district court in San Jose. (Reprinted from* California Blue Book 1950, *(Sacramento, 1950), 40; courtesy California State Library.)*

improvements brought about a commitment to building "a city organization that provided the right atmosphere for the developer and subdivider." One participant recalled that at that time the people emphasized "togetherness . . . We seemed, in those days, to be united in a big ongoing effort and each new step was hailed with enthusiasm."

Between 1950 and 1965 the chamber of commerce would spend nearly a million dollars advertising the virtues of San Jose in Eastern newspapers. Elaborate growth formulas were established. It was estimated the advertising brought at least 50,000 a year to the San Jose area. Recalled one official, "We all learned the formula that if you created a new job through a new plant, you supplied two and a half additional jobs in service and other fields: doctors, bus drivers, barbers, clerks, not to speak of policemen and probation officers."[16] Presumably this also included a need for more lawyers.

Beresford hoped to work his federal court idea into the growing efforts to develop the town. Until the local bar got used to using the federal court, it would serve a booster role. It would be a symbol of equality with San Francisco; that San Jose could match San Francisco in industry and in the law.

Beresford searched for a mechanism to bring and keep the issue before the public. This involved interesting those directly concerned with the courts in the desirability of his project. On November 29, 1948, Beresford introduced a resolution at a Santa Clara County Bar Association meeting. The resolution called for the establishment of a federal court committee to "make an investigation of the feasibility of having the United States District Court sit in San Jose." If the committee found it feasible, it was to take appropriate measures to accomplish that end.[17]

It cannot be said that the resolution sparked much interest or excitement. Beresford recalled that, "No one at the outset said: 'Oh! That's a great idea!'" Some members were amused. Others, while encouraging any pet project of a colleague, were skeptical about the whole project's practicality. But the resolution was carried without dispute.[18]

Beresford convinced the president of the Santa Clara County bar to appoint men to the committee who "had some standing in the profession and were somewhat well known in the community." But membership on the committee did not indicate the nature of one's involvement or commitment to the project. For most of the committee's first participants, this idea of a local federal court was a "great idea" but altogether too visionary to warrant much time, work, or bother. Like most of the local bar, they saw it as having little chance of success. One was not expected to be active on such a committee: one was lending one's name, professional reputation, and a minimum of time to a colleague's pet project. Beresford did "all the struggling" for the committee; the others lent some credibility to his enterprise.[19] In its first year, the committee tended to be a rubber stamp for Beresford's activities. Then it was rare for the committee to have even a quorum.

The first step was to lay the foundation for the court to come to San Jose: Congress must authorize the northern district court to hear cases in that city. The committee contacted Congressman Jack Z. Anderson, whose district included Santa Clara County. Anderson was not an attorney, but he recognized an influential group of constituents and responded to their desires. On February 14, 1949, he introduced H.R. 2701. The bill sought to establish a term of the northern district court in San Jose.

Notwithstanding its eventual lack of success, H.R. 2701 gave several benefits to San Jose court proponents. It provided a vehicle to focus and organize support for a local federal court. Beresford, on behalf of the Federal Court Committee, solicited support for the bill from community organizations. The local chamber of commerce, labor groups, and local government bodies endorsed the bill. But many of these endorsements were given without much conviction or understanding of the issues involved. Often Beresford found himself drafting the resolutions and statements for these endorsers to issue. This was the nature of the political game, however, and he realized that it was difficult for people to get too excited about the whole issue of a federal court.

Congressman Anderson's attitude reflected this lack of local enthusiasm. Beresford realized that H.R. 2701 was a courtesy bill, introduced at the behest of constituents — Beresford's Federal Court Committee. Anderson did not expect it to go anywhere. Yet, it wàs "all very impressive to see that there [was] a bill . . . it looked like we were making progress."[20]

A subcommittee of the House Committee on the Judiciary included the bill in hearings chaired by Congressman Emanuel Celler of New York on August 15, 1949. In support of H.R. 2701, the San Jose Federal Court Committee submitted Beresford's two typewritten pages arguing for a session of the northern district court in San Jose. In this submission, Beresford identified the nation's federal court districts with smaller populations than San Jose. The half million people of the central coast counties should have the same opportunity to bring their claims to federal court.

The prospect of success on the bill seemed so remote that neither Beresford nor anyone from San Jose traveled to Washington to testify personally. However, Congressman Anderson spoke to the committee, using a speech written for him by Beresford.

Arguments in opposition to H.R. 2701 also reached the House Committee on the Judiciary. These arguments contested Beresford's assumption that "people use courts the way they use hospitals. If there's no medical care available they can still live but they don't get any special care." The opposition focused not on those excluded from court; in fact, the opposition completely ignored Beresford's assertions about the denial of federal court justice to a half-million people. Rather, the opponents focused on "efficiency": the ability to provide justice to those already in court. Division of the northern district would not help people already inclined to use the court.

The court's calendar system allowed judges to specialize in certain types of tasks. It was feared that if the judges now in San Francisco were spread about the northern district, this same number of judges would hear fewer cases. Pending litigation in San Francisco would be delayed unless more judges were appointed to the court.[21]

Opponents of H.R. 2701 considered Beresford's arguments about the population of the San Jose area irrelevant. The population of the central coast area could not adequately indicate the volume of federal litigation that would arise in the region, they argued. In addition, the prevailing theory of judicial administration disfavored more than one place for holding court in a district. While there were many places in the nation with a federal court but with considerably lower population than San Jose, judicial administration theorists argued that this arrangement was obviously inefficient. Congress should consolidate the districts, not subdivide them.

These considerations in opposition to H.R. 2701 were expressed by the United States Department of Justice and the Administrative Office of the United States Courts. The judges of the northern district did not make their views known to the House Committee on the Judiciary, but their opposition was well known and killed whatever slim chances the bill had of passing.

During the debate on the bill, Beresford had traveled to San Francisco, calling upon northern district Chief Judge Michael Roche. Chief Judge Roche complained to Beresford that the northern district judge sitting in Sacramento, as required by congressional legislation similar to H.R. 2701, "doesn't have enough to do." Keeping that judge in Sacramento was inefficient and unfair to litigants on the crowded dockets in San Francisco.[22] Roche's geniality did not mask his view that having the court sit in San Jose would result in another Sacramento situation.

The chief judge of the Ninth Circuit, William Denman, was no more amenable to Beresford's idea of a San Jose court. He was a hard-driving, no-nonsense judge, who would not even extend to the Santa Clara County Bar Association the courtesy of inquiring about their goals in H.R. 2701. A native San Franciscan of patrician demeanor, Denman found very little in the measure to commend. He refused to recognize that the Santa Clara County bar might have some reason for dissatisfaction with the federal district court. Since few attorneys from the central coast region ever appeared before the northern district court, why should he now pay much attention to their complaints about the federal court?

In 1949, Beresford faced the unified opposition of the United States judicial-administrative establishment. Not only did the local federal judges oppose the San Jose court, but so did the Department of Justice, the Administrative Office of the Courts, and probably the chairman of the House Committee on the Judiciary. Moreover, his idea of a San Jose court was a new one for the Santa Clara County bar and community leaders. Many citizens in the town had difficulty understanding the division of work loads between the state and the federal courts. Explaining why a federal court should hold sessions in San Jose was a confusing proposition. Although no local group opposed the San Jose court, with so many other pressing concerns about developing the San Jose area, they found it hard to get excited about whether or not the northern district court should sit in the city. Against such opposition, and with such lukewarm support, H.R. 2701 was a lost cause. As Beresford expected, the bill languished in committee and died a quiet death with the expiration of the Eighty-first Congress. The advantage of retrospect allows us to see the extent Beresford was looking to the future, while others looked to the past. All of his arguments for H.R. 2701 were premised on the belief that the San Jose region's development would eventually necessitate a local federal court. Although many valley attorneys were not ready for a federal court, the only way to get them ready was to give them the opportunity for experience in federal proceedings. A local federal court would provide this.

Beresford did not accept the defeat of H.R. 2701. He would continue his labors for a San Jose court even if others would not share this dream. There were side benefits of his work for a local federal court which were of interest to him. As a relative newcomer to the Santa Clara County Bar Association, he was chairman of the Federal Court Committee and had the responsibility to speak for the association on federal court issues. This gave him an opportunity to make contact with those active in promoting the development of the central coast region. It had the indirect effect of building him a political base which could be used to make his dream for San Jose come true and advance his own ambitions.

But it was clear that opponents of a federal court in San Jose would have no difficulty fighting off the attempts of this lone attorney. Beresford would have to create a committed set of allies, both inside the San Jose bar and outside it, to prevail. The northern district court remained in San Francisco. The Santa Clara County Federal Court Committee remained dormant, with Beresford its chairman and most active worker and supporter. Until enthusiasm for a local federal court could take root, it seemed the committee hibernated. It would take time to reverse the opposition of all three branches of government. It would do no good to struggle, not until the prospect of success improved — a period which came to exceed a decade.

# 8

# The Unified Strategy

*Joseph Franaszek*

Members of the Santa Clara County Bar Association considered attorney Russell V. Roessler a solid, dependable lawyer. They found him a man of considerable enthusiasm, hope, and determination — as well as having a love of the local community. Roessler had come to Santa Clara County in 1939 from South Bend, Washington to attend San Jose State College's program on law enforcement. After service as a Marine Corps officer in World War II, he continued on in the central coast area of California. He graduated from Stanford Law School in 1948 and came to consider the Santa Clara valley his home. It was not long before he became an active figure in the local bar and a dynamic, energetic practitioner in the region's courts.

In 1963, his colleagues selected him as president of the Santa Clara County Bar Association. Things were still run as they had always been. The president called the shots for the organization and appointed the committees and those who would chair the committees. This was not a burdensome task; it involved finding those in the organization who displayed ability as well as interest in the mission of a particular committee. As had become tradition with a long line of bar association presidents reaching back some fifteen years, Roessler reappointed Bob Beresford chairman of the Santa Clara County Federal Court Committee. He also appointed as committee members those indicated on a short list submitted by Beresford.

When he assumed the presidency of the county bar, Roessler may not have anticipated how much time and attention he would soon give to the Federal Court Committee. He might not have expected that he would break with tradition and chair the committee himself when Beresford was appointed to the bench in 1964. Something happened to Russ Roessler pushing him to the forefront of the struggle for a San Jose federal court. Recalled Roessler, "There isn't any question about it that Bob Beresford's enthusiasm

*Russell V. Roessler. In 1964, as president of the Santa Clara County Bar Association, Roessler began what would be twenty years of effort to secure a federal court presence in San Jose. This and all subsequent photographs by Ira Nowinski were taken in 1984.*

rubbed off on me while I was president of the bar association." Although Roessler's practice was of a local nature, he soon wanted to see the federal district court in San Jose and he became a "heavy pusher" for this project.[1] So it was with many other members of the Santa Clara County bar. Beresford's fifteen years of work for the San Jose federal court had prepared them to consider 1963 as the year for the northern district court to come to San Jose. With the central coast region developing so dramatically, both economically and socially, it seemed getting a federal court was only a question of time.

Not long after Roessler joined the crusade for a central coast federal court, he and Beresford attended the annual meeting of the California State Bar Association in San Francisco in September 1963. A major theme for the bar meeting was to pay tribute to the Supreme Court of the United States and its Chief Justice Earl Warren, who had suffered some extreme political attacks. It was with considerable interest that Beresford and Roessler filed into the darkened auditorium to hear the chief justice address the membership. Smiling, he told the members how good it was to be home in California. He reminisced about his appointment to the Supreme Court. But soon he was down to business.

He told the California State bar that the controversy affecting the courts was attributable to the turbulent "times in which we are living." The judiciary, he implied,

*Chief Justice Earl Warren at the 1963 convention of the California State bar. To Warren's right are Governor Edmund G. Brown and Chief Justice Phil S. Gibson of the California Supreme Court. (Courtesy The Bancroft Library.)*

should not step back from the requirements of the law because of this. In tumultuous times of change, there was a dual concern: not merely protecting rights, but also administering the courts to protect these rights.

This administration of the courts Warren called "one of our most pressing and difficult problems." Merely increasing the number of judges was not the answer. A new approach was needed. "We cannot afford a nostalgic look backwards to the conditions and practices which were in vogue a generation ago, or in any other past era," the chief justice declared.[2]

Beresford and Roessler must have wondered if Chief Justice Warren could possibly help in their attempt to get a federal court in San Jose. Would he see that confining the northern district court to San Francisco to the exclusion of San Jose was based on a nostalgic view of the Bay Area — that it was the San Jose area, not San Francisco, which was so alive with people, industry, and progress? Would he recognize that the people of the central coast were entitled to accessible federal justice? Beresford and Roessler would have the opportunity to find out the next night.

The chief justice was a tireless worker. In the grandeur of what he called his "marble mausoleum," the Supreme Court Building, he professed to be homesick for his native state. It would be difficult to believe that such a man was not aware of the phenomenal growth and development of the Santa Clara valley.

The national news media had begun to describe the prospects for the area. A *Business Week* article on San Jose announced to the nation that "San Jose discovers how it feels to be rich: a once-sleepy area of the Santa Clara valley . . . is now one of the nation's fastest-growing regions — with a young, well paid, and free-spending population."[3]

The prediction of a bright future which Bob Beresford and Russ Roessler had heard so much about after the war was now a reality. The valley no longer depended upon seasonal canning and harvesting. It now had a "diversified industrial economy heavily weighted with electronics, aerospace and other science-based business." Since the 1950s its population had risen 188 percent. The magazine pointed to startling statistics showing that the residents were "big earners and big spenders . . . They splurge on swimming pools, boats and hi-fi equipment; and though they rarely see snow in their benign climate they buy skis . . . and drive 200 miles to Sierra resorts." Food sales of $1,233 per household ranked among the ten highest areas of the nation. Personal income at 1.9 billion dollars in 1961 had quadrupled since 1950. One fifth of the area residents' federal tax returns indicated personal income exceeding $10,000, leading all other metropolitan areas of the United States. The magazine indicated that wealth was not the only resource of the area; the residents were patrons of the arts and cultural activities.

Only ten years previously, much of the population had been migratory — following harvests from job to job. But now the population, technically educated and skilled, expected the area to grow and to rival San Francisco in its attractions. The writers concluded that San Jose "is no longer the tail on anybody's kite."[4]

From these tremendous changes, one might infer a considerable transformation of the area's legal needs. The region's new industries needed a legal community responsive to their situation. In addition, growth and diversification brought people to the area who were more aware of their federal rights. On the whole, they were better educated and intended to remain in the community permanently. They understood the importance of a local federal court, especially in the 1960s when the federal judiciary was playing an active role in protecting citizens' rights.

Beresford was determined to speak to Chief Justice Warren about a San Jose federal court. His opportunity would come during a reception for Warren the next day. Beresford was one of hundreds of attorneys attending, but unlike many there, Beresford had been active in the central coast region mobilizing expressions of support for the chief justice and his Court. As chairman of the Santa Clara County Bar Association Federal Court Committee, he had pushed through a resolution supporting the chief justice and the Supreme Court.

Beresford's meeting with Chief Justice Warren was rather quick, but greatly exceeded the exchange of handshakes given other lawyers at the reception. Beresford suggested to Warren the inadequacy of the two district courts in the state to the federal judicial needs of the times. The chief justice listened carefully, but ventured no opinion. Earl Warren was known as a cautious, prudent man. "He moves slowly, studying each step," one associate described him. " 'Let's pick this thing up by the four corners and take a look at it' he used to say when a new problem came along." The chief justice did not alter this approach for Beresford. He was friendly, courteous, and noncommittal. But he urged Beresford to send him more information.[5]

Shortly after the end of the bar association meeting, Beresford sent Warren a letter, enclosing copies of a Santa Clara County Bar Association report on the San Jose federal court proposal. In his letter, Beresford argued, "The people of this great area are being deprived of some of the important benefits of federal justice." This must have suggested a type of malapportionment to Warren, one of the justices who had joined in *Baker v. Carr* to protect citizens' equal voting rights. But Beresford stepped back from this. The real problem was the lawyers who, "because of their unfamiliarity with federal courts are failing to give sufficient attention to federal law when advising their clients. Most of the fourteen percent of the civil cases arising from these counties . . . were handled by San Francisco lawyers."[6]

Beresford received a friendly reply. Inviting Beresford to visit with him whenever he was in Washington, Warren was judiciously neutral on California redistricting. Apparently Warren was awaiting the United States Judicial Conference's study of the problem of California judicial redistricting. But the chief justice had picked the thing up — perhaps by its four corners — and was taking a look at it. The chief justice would hear a lot more about California redistricting in the next year or two. But whether he would support the proponents of a San Jose court was unknown. It would be awhile before anybody knew.

In talking with Chief Justice Warren, Beresford acted consistently with a strategy he developed years before, consciously or unconsciously. The strategy involved speaking with the various players in the political process: legislators, bureaucrats, judges, and representatives of the media and special interest groups. He attempted to win the sympathy, if not the support, of each. It was a slow, building process and would take time.

A major part of this strategy, since the expiration of the Eighty-first Congress in 1949, was education. Beresford attempted to inform those who would ultimately be affected by the presence of a federal court in San Jose — the residents of Santa Clara County. But into the 1960s, his activities diversified. Since 1949 he had regularly attended the chamber of commerce meetings where, among other things, he discussed the San Jose federal court with all who would listen. It was there that he eventually convinced Congressman Charles Gubser to introduce a bill to bring the area a federal court. He talked with newly appointed northern district federal judges about the needs of the central coast area for a federal court. He worked for the appointment of a Santa Clara County resident to the northern district court, so that there would be at least one voice on the bench sensitive to the needs of the central coast community. Through a growing friendship with local editors and reporters, Beresford secured their interest in the federal court issue. Beresford explained the actions of his committee to reporters. Local television stations and newspapers ran editorials on the need for a local federal court presence. Inspired by Beresford's reasoning, they used his arguments. Readers or listeners were told that while they may never have noticed the absence of a federal court, "Justice is like insurance. People tend to ignore it as long as they don't need it." The implication was clear. The federal court might not be a life or death question for anyone in the area now, but it could mean the presence or absence of justice when such was needed in the future.[7] The media called for a local federal court just as they called for development of the region's roads, schools, and industrial base.

But changing the perception of the court in San Jose was a slow, painstaking process. Beresford was no longer shocked by the woeful ignorance and fear many in the legal community had of the federal courts. He relished telling of a local attorney who reacted to Beresford's plans for a local federal court with shocked, "Oh, federal court! I've never been in that court, and I wouldn't dare go." Amused by this, Beresford would remark, "Now here was a man who had served on the Board of Governors of the

[California] State bar, had the largest . . . [firm] . . . in town . . . lots of litigation — and yet he had a completely negative reaction to the federal court. You'd think he was talking about the International Court of Justice in the Hague."[8]

Unfortunately, there was little Beresford could do to reassure those of this temperament. Some, even though very successful practitioners, did not welcome the federal court's new and unknown challenge. They were comfortable with the way things had always been and saw little reason to invite a change that might affect the nature of their prospering practices. Many of the active backers of the federal court in San Jose were attorneys of skill and ability who had not established their practice firmly in the county. The prospect of court practice in a local United States District Court would give these less established attorneys a possible legal specialty unhindered by competition with the traditional and well-known firms that, at least initially, were not as vitally concerned with federal practice.

The growing general interest in a local federal court in the 1960s invigorated those fighting for it. No longer defensive on their own home ground, nor having to explain themselves extensively, the advocates of a San Jose court took a more aggressive attitude toward achieving their goal. This caused them to be overconfident. In 1961, Beresford prevailed on Congressman Charles Gubser to introduce a bill, not for the northern district court to hold a session in San Jose, but for an entirely new district to be created for the central coast counties. This was a dramatic change from Beresford's past efforts for a local federal court presence. But the growing interest in a San Jose court lead him to believe, "We were going strong in '61. That was when we came out with the 'Central Coast District.' By that time we said the heck with it; we were big enough, the heck with having a division or court sessions, we wanted a district." Instead of asking for a politically realistic goal, he asked for everything. Beresford's confidence was apparent to all. One attorney watching his activities found Beresford to be "a whirlwind" and such a force that "San Jose in 1962 and 1963 really carried the ball" among the advocates of redistricting California.[9]

But this confidence did not survive in Washington. 1961 marked the reemergence of legislative activity on the subject of a San Jose federal court. That year, three different proposals for new California judicial districts had been introduced, seeking to establish district court at San Diego, Sacramento, and San Jose. H.R. 9051 by Congressman Charles Gubser of the Santa Clara region encompassed the proposal for the San Jose federal court.

The House Committee on the Judiciary considered these bills in 1962. The reception of the bill by the subcommittee hearing it, and especially by the subcommittee chairman, Emanuel Celler, was no more encouraging to San Jose proponents than it had been during the consideration of H.R. 2701 in 1949. The years had made a difference in the interest expressed by those in the central coast area about acquiring an accessible federal forum. But what could they get?

A subcommittee of the House Committee on the Judiciary considered H.R. 9051 on February 28, 1962. Testimony on the inadequacy of present judicial districts in California came entirely from California congressmen. The subcommittee had heard these arguments many times before, by proponents of a San Diego district, a Sacramento district, or an Oakland district. San Jose was the recent entrant in the race for a district.

Congressman Gubser testified for his bill. His was the last appearance of the day. To the few who remained past 5:00 P.M. to hear him, Gubser expressed his general agreement with previous speakers. "It is wrong for us to continue to look upon San Francisco

*Congressman Charles S. Gubser in 1964. Throughout the 1960s and early 1970s Congressman Gubser played an active role in efforts to establish a federal court in San Jose. (Courtesy San Jose Mercury News.)*

as the only area in which court should be held" in northern California, he declared. The central coast area had experienced such a rapid growth, it deserved "better court service."

But Chairman Celler was impatient and had little humor for this argument. After all, it was late in the day. "You want to create a new district?" he asked. Almost apologetically, Gubser replied in the affirmative. But noting Celler's grim visage, Gubser offered that if Celler did not want to give San Jose a district, "another purpose of this bill is to focus attention upon the problem [of a federal court presence in San Jose] . . . if the committee policy is against forming new districts, then . . . the very least my area is entitled to" is an authorization for the northern district court to sit in San Jose. Celler cut through the argument, asking "You are interested that a court be held in those four [central coast] counties?" Gubser affirmed this. Then Celler curtly told him, "You don't need a new district for that."[10]

Apparently, the strategy of asking for more than one expected or assumed to be politically expedient backfired. Celler had never liked the idea of new federal judicial districts in California when his committee considered such proposals during the 1950s.

The Santa Clara County bar's flexibility on the question of a San Jose district allowed Celler to dismiss their cause as frivolous. Santa Clara County would like a new judicial district; if not that, then at least authorization for the district court to sit in the central coast counties. Celler found these requests in the alternative to indicate a lack of real desire for a district. If they just wanted a court division or session of court in San Jose, why bother his subcommittee with the issue of providing them with a new district?

Another part of the problem was to be able to cite some hard statistics supporting the creation of a San Jose court. Population statistics were interesting, but did not really indicate the number of federal cases that would arise in any area. Gathering data on the actual number of federal court cases from the central coast area would take a long effort, but it could not be ignored if they were to prove the need for a local federal court on the basis of the traditional indicators.

The effort to collect this data started with requests to the northern district court for statistics. In 1959, the Santa Clara County Bar Association requested that Chief Judge Louis Goodman survey civil cases of the northern district for that year. Goodman's survey disclosed that over 10.6 percent of the district's civil cases originated in Monterey, San Benito, Santa Cruz, San Mateo, and Santa Clara counties. According to judicial administration statisticians, this should be a sufficient work load to occupy 70 percent of a federal district judge's time.

In June 1961, Beresford's committee requested that Goodman update the 1959 survey. But gathering such information had required an inspection of all civil case filings for the southern division of the northern district. In 1961, the district court lacked the personnel to complete such a study. Judge Goodman suggested that if the Santa Clara bar wanted such information, they should come to San Francisco and inspect the files themselves.

Accordingly, the county bar hired a third-year University of Santa Clara law student to study the civil case files for fiscal year 1961. The results indicated an increase in central coast filings in the northern district from 10.6 percent in the 1958-1959 survey to 14 percent in the 1961-1962 survey. Now more than enough cases existed to support at least one federal judge.

But statistics were not enough. Ninth Circuit Chief Judge Richard Chambers was fond of telling about his effort to use court statistics to get a new judgeship for the district court in Arizona. It was not caseload statistics that told him a judge was needed: "Just watching the moving vans unload in Arizona, I came to the conclusion that Arizona needed three federal judges." He did not have the "conventional statistics at that time for a third judge, and I was generally laughed at." By 1959, when he managed to get the appropriate statistics, he still could not get a judge for the district. Only the right statistics, combined with the skillful use of politics, finally produced a third judge for the district.[11]

The bar's statistical findings helped form the factual basis of reports by the Federal Court Committee on the need for a central coast area federal court. Armed with these statistics, the county bar presented its arguments to a variety of forums, especially the California State bar, the judges, judicial administrators, and, of course, Congress.

The California State Bar Association was the major forum for proponents of a central coast federal court. In many respects, the state bar was dominated by the San Francisco and Los Angeles bars, both opponents of proposals to redistrict the federal courts in California. Presentations before such a forum could not have much hope of success, but they served an important purpose of distributing data and arguments about the federal courts in California. The repeated expression of concern by county bar associations like that of Santa Clara alerted the larger county bar organizations that there was a problem, and that it was one they could not simply ignore.

Under such pressure, the state bar became less adamant in its opposition to the northern district court sitting in San Jose. The board of governors instructed the state bar's Federal Court Committee to make a study of the federal court needs of the central coast counties, but the committee did nothing on this instruction for at least a year. In the end, it refused to recommend even a division for San Jose.

The important benefit of state bar meetings was the opportunity they offered Beresford to talk with other county bar representatives also concerned about the availability of federal justice in their areas. He found allies for this struggle against the big city bar associations. The San Diego Bar Association had long pursued proposals in Congress allowing the area to secede from the Southern District of California and to create a San Diego federal district court. By mid-1962 they had made substantial progress in their efforts. They had succeeded in getting Emanuel Celler's commitment that he would allow a bill through his subcommittee providing for a new federal district court in California. But the California congressional delegation would have to tell him where this new district should be. Should it be in San Diego, Sacramento, Oakland, or — possibly — San Jose? A committee of five California congressmen was selected by their colleagues to investigate the issue. This committee asked the state bar for its preferences. The California State Bar Association's Federal Court Committee considered the question on May 23, 1962. The lineup of votes in that committee among redistricting proponents made it essentially a choice between San Diego or Sacramento.

The battle for allies began, with the San Diego bar's committee issuing a report for the California State bar meeting. The report argued that San Diego should have the district. The San Diego Bar Association tried to gain support from San Jose and Oakland delegates by calling for a division of the northern district court to be established at San Jose and at Oakland. The head of the San Diego committee contacted a prominent Palo Alto lawyer, David Friedenrich, a member of Beresford's Federal Court Committee, about this idea for a central coast division "with a judge sitting in San Jose from time to time to see how business develops" and with an eye to creating a district if court business eventually warranted it.[12]

At the May 23 State Bar Federal Court Committee meeting it appeared that San Jose was a swing vote. After a full morning of testimony, a vote was taken which rejected the San Diego district and by a one-vote majority supported one at Sacramento. After this result was announced, San Jose switched its vote to San Diego, leaving the committee evenly divided. Had the committee chairman permitted the San Jose switch, the tie would have left the committee with no recommendations as to where the new district should be. But the chairman did not permit the vote change.

The board of governors met two days later to consider the committee's recommendation of a Sacramento district. They rejected it entirely and directed that the California congressmen be told that "there is no demonstrated need for any new federal judicial district in California."[13]

The lesson in this vote came forcefully to those who supported federal court redistricting in California. No one would ever see an alteration in the two federal judicial districts — the northern district and the southern district — unless redistricting proponents stopped fighting one another. They should negotiate a common plan. Recalled Russ Roessler, who was instrumental in building this consensus: "Everybody was going their separate ways. There was a consensus reached that this was the wrong approach — that if San Diego, Sacramento, and Santa Clara put their heads together we could accomplish a lot more for our respective causes . . . that was really the thing that got us off the ground, because we knew we were always going to be opposed by Los Angeles and San Francisco . . . and we had to do something to overcome that."[14]

Sherwood Roberts, Chairman of the San Diego Federal Court Committee, took the first steps to develop this unity. Inviting delegations from the bar associations of Sacramento, Fresno, and Santa Clara counties, he proposed a Sunday meeting in Sacramento for the delegations to work out a common strategy. They hoped it could be forwarded to the five-man congressional committee as an alternative to the state bar opposition to new districts in California.

Sacramento County Bar Association President Frank K. Richardson, who later became a distinguished associate justice of the California Supreme Court, hosted the meeting in his Sacramento office. The San Diego delegation of three was headed by Roberts. The San Jose delegation consisted of Roessler, president of the Santa Clara County bar, and Beresford for that bar's Federal Court Committee. Sacramento was represented by its President Richardson and its Federal Court Committee chairman William Lally. The meeting was cordial but with a considerable amount of hard bargaining. The result was a unanimous agreement. It was not just a gentlemen's agreement; each delegation bound its respective bar associations.

The agreement was set forth in a letter sent to Congressman B.F. Sisk, chairman of the committee that would recommend to Chairman Celler where a new district should be. The Sacramento conference told Sisk that the Northern District and Southern District of California were insufficient despite the state bar's findings. Instead, three additional districts were needed — one in Sacramento, one in San Diego, and one in San Jose. But, if three districts could not be secured at once, the Sacramento district should be established first. This should be followed by San Diego, and finally, by San Jose. However, pending creation of the latter two districts, Congress should create a new division to the northern district which would include the four central coast counties, with court sitting in San Jose.

Agreement in Sacramento that Sunday was one thing; ratification of the agreement by the local bar associations was quite another. The San Diego bar especially criticized its delegates for not insisting that the first priority for a district go to San Diego and not to Sacramento. "Personally," complained Sherwood Roberts, "I have caught brickbats" for letting Sacramento have the district first. But the Santa Clara County Bar Association quickly ratified the Sacramento agreement. Yet there were still elements of uncertainty and distrust among the bar associations participating in the agreement. While Santa Clara County Bar Association President Russ Roessler was delighted with the agreement, he sought additional assurances from the Sacramento Bar Association "that your people will continue to fight for establishment of the central coast district after your district and the San Diego district are established."[15]

The purpose of the Sacramento meeting had been to give the congressional delegation some indication of where a judicial district should be created in California if Chairman Celler allowed California only one new federal judicial district. It failed to accomplish this. Congressman Sisk informed Chairman Celler that the California delegation refused to choose which section of the state was to constitute the new district. The delegation insisted that California receive more than one new judicial district. The delegation completely disregarded the results of the Sacramento meeting, as well as the results of the California State Bar Association's Board of Governors meeting. The failure to tell Celler where the new district would be doomed any chance of redistricting the state for that year.

But there was a benefit of the Sacramento meeting which would last for years — a growing commitment to a unified strategy for getting new federal district courts in the state. Part of this was reflected in the increased communications between the county bars with interests in new federal judicial districts. Bob Beresford would write to Sherwood Roberts of the San Diego bar about the development of their strategy for gaining such districts; and vice versa. The separate bar associations of Santa Clara, San Diego, and Sacramento began to think as one about how to redistrict the state. Recalled one Sacramento member, "San Diego and San Jose said it looks like you've got the best chance, so we'll go for . . . you having the district. But we want it understood that you aren't going to abandon us." Although considerable inducements would be offered to break their unity, they "were all able to stand together." It reminded one participant of "some of the frontier movies, when they could stand back to back and fight, they could hold off quite a herd of people circling around trying to massacre them."[16]

In 1949, Bob Beresford's federal court proposal had made little progress because of the unanimous opposition by various individuals and organizations deeply involved in the administration of the judiciary. During the years since 1949, Beresford's attempts to find allies among those concerned with judicial administration met with mixed success. But in 1964, when Beresford went on the bench and Roessler took over leadership of the Federal Court Committee, Roessler enlarged the successes initially achieved by Beresford.

Beresford's contact with the northern district judges had been cordial, but most were San Franciscans, and he found no advocate among them. Beresford was more successful in finding a supporter in Sherrill Halbert, the northern district judge sitting at Sacramento. The Sacramento Bar Association had sponsored proposals to leave the northern district and form its own central district of California. This northern district judge serving in Sacramento was sympathetic to the proposal. He could easily see the need to separate the Sacramento court from the dominance of San Francisco.

Initially, Judge Sherrill Halbert had stood cautiously with the northern district judges on the San Jose court question. But when the San Francisco judges refused to compromise in the face of growing and united lobbying for redistricting by county bar associations, Halbert came to the aid of the insurgents. Judge Halbert's counsel was so helpful that the Santa Clara bar included him as an honoree at a bar dinner. Eventually, Halbert would write to Beresford suggesting strategies the Santa Clara County Federal Court Committee might consider. The judge assured Beresford that he would lobby the Sacramento area congressmen for a federal court in San Jose.[17]

As helpful as Judge Halbert was, to find a supporter among the northern district judges in San Francisco would be even better. When it seemed there was no prospect of making a convert of anyone in San Francisco, Beresford's attention turned to placing someone on the northern district bench who could understand the needs of the central coast region. The easiest way to break the unanimous opposition of the San Francisco judges to the needs of the central coast counties would be to insure new placements on that bench who appreciated San Jose's needs for a court.

This possibility arose whenever a vacancy opened on the northern district bench. Possible nominees would search for supporters to contact the attorney general and support their nomination. Occasionally a San Francisco attorney seeking a federal judgeship would write to Beresford expressing support for the idea of a session of the court in San Jose. The hope of such a writer was to win an endorsement.

Beresford thought the Santa Clara bar should not support court nominees who, out of desperation, requested endorsement in exchange for support of a session of the court in San Jose. If the San Jose court were ever to be won, what was needed was a judge who truly believed in such a court. Any judge sitting in San Jose must not feel out of place or that San Francisco would be a better place to sit. So the committee labored on for appointment of a sympathetic voice on the northern district bench. As early as June 1961, the Santa Clara County bar recommended that a central coast resident be appointed to the northern district court.

Six months later, the County Bar Association was more specific. It called on President Kennedy to appoint Superior Court Judge Robert F. Peckham to the federal bench when the 1961 Omnibus Judgeship Bill passed Congress. In making this recommendation, the County Bar Association had determined that "there would not be much chance in securing a new federal court district for this area . . . [but there was] . . . a good chance that a federal district judge would be appointed from this area and that such appointee would probably sit in San Jose on a regular basis." Judge Peckham was considered the only central coast resident who "has a chance to receive the appointment."[18]

Peckham's nomination was seriously considered by the Kennedy administration. Peckham, a Democrat, had been endorsed by all the bar associations of the central coast. However, he was eliminated after Republican criticism in Congress that the administration was appointing only Democrats to the omnibus judgeship vacancies. Instead, a San Francisco Republican with liberal credentials, Stanley Weigel, was selected. Bob Beresford, a Republican, deplored this last-minute elimination of Peckham and remained convinced that "the central coast counties will never have an adequate voice in federal court operations until they are represented on the federal bench."[19]

Although there was no sympathetic voice for San Jose on the federal district bench in San Francisco, Beresford found a helpful hand on the Ninth Circuit Court of Appeals in Chief Judge Richard Chambers. Chambers's careful counsel, his balanced arguments about the prospects and difficulties of a San Jose court, and his deep insight into judicial politics were of inestimable value to Beresford and the federal court committee.

# 9

# Through the Congressional Maze

*Joseph Franaszek*

February 15, 1964 found Congressman Don Edwards on his way to meet with Chief Justice Earl Warren at the Supreme Court. Edwards had served in the House for over a year now, and on the House Committee on the Judiciary only a few months. He was becoming a seasoned Washington veteran, but in all probability shared that quiet, implicit respect so many individuals have when they pass the dignified and stately white marble building in which the Court sits. One is inclined to pass the structure quietly, as if the slightest noise would disturb the deliberations of the justices. The structure lends dignity and grace to its corner of Capitol Hill. It suggests the judiciary's idealized tradition of independence from the tensions and struggles which occur in the congressional buildings only a block or two away.

In the public's mind, the Supreme Court Building's apparent remoteness from the controversies flaring around the Capitol was reassuring. The Court often considered questions of great political significance, yet without seeming to dip into partisan struggles. The Court's building maintained that illusion of distance and separation from the main business of the Hill — politics. It was believed that the justices shunned much of Washington's confusing, excited whirl. Their dealings with members of Congress always seemed at arm's length, although invariably courteous.

The chief justice was keenly aware of his duty to express some views on legislation affecting judicial administration. But it was the Administrative Office of the United States Courts whose voice was more easily heard in the halls of Congress. Perhaps pressures of a heavy work load and tradition influenced the justices to steer clear of politics. They appeared aloof from the political scramble, but like many impressions held about the institutions of the Capitol, this had elements of truth and illusion. Members of the Court often touched upon politics, but they did so judiciously.

*Congressman Don Edwards in 1984. It was through Congressman Edwards's skillful efforts that a bill authorizing federal court in San Jose passed Congress. (Photograph by Ira Nowinski.)*

Edwards had consulted no one when he arranged to meet Chief Justice Warren, but he received the benefit of good advice once the meeting was scheduled. Ninth Circuit Chief Judge Richard Chambers continued to pass on bits of advice on matters of judicial administration. In preparation for the meeting, Chambers told Edwards that Warren probably was sympathetic to the proposal for a San Jose federal court. This sympathy, suggested Chambers, would be strengthened if Edwards could emphasize some of the congressional factors behind his proposal.

Undoubtedly Edwards had heard much about Earl Warren. At least he must have known the frequently confirmed public view of the chief justice as a big, friendly man with a good sense of the political world. Edwards probably recalled that during Warren's term as governor of California, he seemed a born administrator who got the bureaucray moving through use of his warm, unforbidding demeanor. Yet like many involved in politics, Warren was said to be a loner — both personally and politically. He followed his own path when he could.

Edwards sought the meeting with the chief justice to advise him about legislation concerning the organization of the district courts in California and providing for more judgeships there. Edwards's advisors suggested he meet the chief justice before March 18, 1965, so that any favorable results of the meeting might influence the March United States Judicial Conference. If Warren could be convinced to buck decades of precedent and tradition which opposed creation of new districts or court administrative divisions,

111

Edwards might get more support for his bill from the judiciary. The chief justice chaired the Judicial Conference as the administrative leader of the third branch of government. Realizing this, Russ Roessler suggested to Edwards that since the chief justice was "from California and acutely aware of the tremendous growth, your plan to see him . . . should be exceedingly helpful in encouraging the Judicial Conference to request an omnibus [judgeship and court redistricting] bill in the first half of the current [congressional] session." Surely, if the chief justice and the judges of the Judicial Conference moved the judiciary's lobbying arm — the Administrative Office of the Courts — to seek omnibus legislation, it would help Edwards's efforts to redistrict the state. Roessler counseled Edwards to "tell the chief justice . . . that your bill will again have the near unanimous support of both the Democratic and Republican delegations to the House . . . it will move him to weigh very heavily the request for an omnibus bill now."[1]

When Don Edwards entered the Supreme Court Building he was conducted to the chief justice's chambers. The chief justice had a small staff, much smaller than a congressman's: a secretary, a messenger, and two or three law clerks. But Warren did have quiet, hushed quarters unlike the noisy and crowded congressional offices Edwards was used to.

Soon the genial and friendly justice emerged to greet his visitor. With a beaming smile and moving quickly to shake hands, he exchanged pleasantries with his guest while ushering him into chambers. The two men settled down in the paneled room. The walls of the room were shelved with law books and law reporters. By Warren's desk was a red leather chair. From it he could catch a pleasant view of the Jefferson Building of the Library of Congress. On the wall above him hung a portrait of a melancholy, brooding Abraham Lincoln. Warren's chambers appeared a place for contemplation. In that room the two Californians could discuss calmly issues which had produced few moments of quiet reflection for their colleagues of the California bench and bar.

His discussion with the chief justice seemed to move rapidly. Warren probed whether Ninth Circuit Chief Judge Chambers supported the bill; he did. But Edwards had to inform Warren that the northern district judges, many of them close friends of the chief justice from his days as governor, opposed it. Warren was concerned about the effect an omnibus bill — one providing for more judges across the whole nation — might have on Edwards's H.R. 4534 which concerned new districts and divisions in California only. Edwards was confident an omnibus bill which provided for more California districts and district judges would increase the prospect of H.R. 4534 receiving approval. Warren expressed a guarded approval of Edwards's bill. He did so not because he favored further division of the prevailing geographical spread of the courts. Rather, he found the unique problems of the recent decade of California growth should not be ignored. He could recall that as a freshman at the University of California, he had heard Lord James Bryce predict that California someday would number over fifty million inhabitants. As governor, Warren had often declared that California should plan for a population of twenty million. He told those working with him that, "We have to plan for a whole new city of ten thousand every Monday morning," so phenomenal was the state's growth.[2]

He realized as governor that the newcomers to the state would need schools, roads, hospitals, water. Now, as chief justice of the United States, he understood that his expectations as governor had been accurate: the population was nearing twenty million. And these people would now need federal legal facilities — indeed, they were demanding such facilities. Surely California deserved to be an exception to the general rule that no new court divisions should be created.

As a result of the meeting, Warren could offer little more than to ask that Edwards keep him, as well as the Administrative Office of the Courts, informed of the bill's progress. As chief justice he would act indirectly to foster the progress of the California court bill.

The meeting was most encouraging for San Jose court proponents. But the support of the chief justice could not be easily used to win new supporters in Congress immediately. Edwards was warned about this by Judge Chambers, who had watched Warren's politics for quite some time. "His support will be rather deft but of course is a big asset," concluded Chambers. Apparently Warren's political style and his conception of his role as chief justice would make it difficult to use his support as a weapon. His support meant he would do what was possible to move the judiciary's administration to give Edwards's bill a fair chance.[3]

This was all that could be expected from Chief Justice Warren right now. Few of his close associates ever found Warren to be a crusader. Rather he was a carefully cautious administrater. "I'm a slow walker," the chief justice once explained, as he quoted Lincoln, but "I never walk backwards." Warren's cautious support of Edwards's bill meant he would not walk backwards and keep California in its present situation. The people of the state — of San Diego, of Sacramento, of Oakland, and of San Jose — must receive better federal court access. But it was well known that while it took Warren long to reach a decision, once he had listened to both sides of the argument and determined his stand, he could not be "easily budged." It seemed after Edwards's meeting with him, that the chief justice had taken his stand with those who favored redistricting the federal courts in California.[4]

Edwards could take a large degree of satisfaction in the meeting, not only because of its results, but because it indicated the extent to which his activities during the past two years had given him a stature not usual for a second-term congressman. His neighbors in the Santa Clara valley found him charismatic, with a well-measured and balanced disposition. Edwards made it a point to listen to all his constituents. He had been born and raised in San Jose, was a member of an old San Jose family that owned the region's leading title insurance company, and attended Stanford University and its law school. Shortly before the war he served as an FBI agent and during it he served as a naval intelligence and gunnery officer. After the war, he was president of a major title company in the valley. He was then a Republican and served as president of the California Young Republicans in 1950.

But Edwards later found himself more interested in the Democratic party and made a run for his first public office: the Democratic party nomination for Congress in the 1962 elections. These were the first elections after the reapportionment of 1960. Population growth in the Santa Clara valley and nearby regions had necessitated cutting up the area's old congressional district. In this process, Santa Clara County was attached to southern Alameda County, forming the Ninth Congressional District. It was a safely Democratic district and Edwards intended to represent it.

As a candidate for Congress he first became involved in the California court redistricting controversy. The Santa Clara County Bar Association resolved on June 11, 1962, to ask all congressional candidates to pledge in writing to support every element of the program to bring a federal court to the central coast area. The response the bar received to this request indicated that Edwards's commitment to a San Jose court was a strong one, perhaps because of his experience as an attorney in the area. Early in the congressional race, Edwards indicated informally that he would work to get a federal

*Congressman Emanuel Celler in the 1960s. During the 1960s Congressman Celler chaired both the House Committee on the Judiciary and the subcommittee which heard bills authorizing federal court in San Jose. (Courtesy Jane Celler.)*

court in the area. But unlike "virtually all" of the candidates for congress who supported that goal, "Don took it seriously."[5]

After his successful election campaign in 1962, Edwards went to Washington for his first term. There he received a letter from Bob Beresford concerning the effort to bring a federal court to the central coast counties. Beresford thought that immediate action on the San Jose court would be possible, and that it would be easy to maintain the struggle on a bipartisan basis, and minimize the opposition from those outside the California delegation.[6]

As for the federal judiciary, Beresford warned that "all of the federal judges in San Francisco seem to be more or less opposed to our objective. A similar feeling seems to exist [among the judges] in Los Angeles." However, "you will find a different attitude . . . on the part of federal judges who are sitting outside of these two centers of political and economic power." In general, "big city federal judges seem to place greater emphasis on the claimed economies of court operations in centrally administered districts." Their colleagues in the smaller districts are "more sensitive to the importance of bringing federal justice to the people outside of the major population centers."

Initially, Beresford found Ninth Circuit Chief Judge Richard Chambers neutral on the San Jose court issue; he appeared to have "deferred to the views of the majority of his judges." Yet if the San Jose project made headway, Beresford predicted that Chambers "will not veto our project, as did . . . his predecessors."[7]

Beresford concluded his letter by discussing the results of the meeting of the Santa Clara, Sacramento, and San Diego county bars at Frank Richardson's Sacramento office in June 1962. Beresford emphasized the unity these county bars found when they urged, unsuccessfully, that the California congressional delegation agree with Celler on California getting at least one new judicial district.

Don Edwards promptly took up the problem of the San Jose court during his first weeks in the House. He found the California delegation again facing the question where the new judicial district would be because Chairman Celler was determined to give the state only one new judicial district. Beresford then urged Edwards to introduce his own legislation, even before a unified California approach was adopted. That would enable Edwards to press for passage of a San Jose court bill if the statewide bill should get blocked. At least San Jose would get its division, even if no one got a district. Others followed this same tactic. By March 1963, three bills had been introduced to establish a northern district court division at San Jose. Another three were introduced for a new San Diego judicial district.

In mid-April, the California House delegation began working out details for a unified bill. Initially a proposal to establish a new district at Sacramento and one at San Diego, as well as add a new Oakland division to the northern district made headway. Since the proposal left out San Jose, Edwards refused to support it. The proposals might multiply if the California delegation failed to adopt a common proposal.

Efforts started again for a unified delegation approach, but differences persisted. By June more than seven statewide redistricting bills had been introduced. Four bills provided for new districts at San Diego and Sacramento, as well as a division in the northern district at Oakland and at San Jose. But three bills excluded San Jose, apparently because East Bay congressmen feared that Chairman Celler would not allow statutory divisions to be created at both Oakland and at San Jose. They felt their local bar association would not want to risk this prospect, and consequently, tried to exclude San Jose from the very beginning.

If this were not enough of a problem, Edwards found the strategy for redistricting more difficult than anticipated. Part of that strategy involved having congressmen introduce identical bills providing for statewide redistricting. But Edwards found that all agreed "the important thing is to get the four districts [San Diego, Sacramento, San Francisco, and Los Angeles]. Then the divisions fall into place." But unless these divisions could be settled, there was no prospect of any progress. Chairman Celler would allow the state only one new district. The California representatives could agree that four districts were needed, but they could not agree about what should be done if four districts were not forthcoming.[8]

These affairs remained locked in place in 1963. Celler had declared California would get no more than one district. The California delegation insisted upon more than one district because they could not select the area of the state which would receive that one district. Part of their concern was that if they received only one district from Celler, they would be unable to gain any more in succeeding years.

This deadlock did not lack for hopeful news. On November 1, 1963, the Santa Clara County Bar Association and labor and business organizations gathered to celebrate at a banquet honoring Congressman Don Edwards. The occasion was Edwards's recent appointment to the House Committee on the Judiciary. At last a San Jose court proponent had a vote and voice on the committee that had bottled up redistricting proposals in previous years.[9]

Edwards's previous assignments had been to Veterans' Affairs and the Post Office and Civil Service Committees. Each was far removed from an issue of great interest to him:

securing social and individual justice for all Americans. So his new assignment was particularly gratifying to him. In addition, a seat on the Committee on the Judiciary "was coveted almost as much as a run for reelection unopposed." Invariably the committee turned away applicants; it was a choice and prestigious panel. Recalled one member, "Members were eager to deal with the great and difficult issues of national moment. We were writing history, and many wanted a hand in the writing."[10]

Now Edwards had gained a prominent hand in writing the history of the northern district court on the central coast. He started on it quickly, preparing a bill that would do more than redistrict the federal courts in California. The bill would create new districts in San Diego and Sacramento; it would create divisions of the northern district at Oakland and at San Jose. To attract support for the bill from the Los Angeles judges, he added two new judgeships to the Southern District of California. Two new judgeships for the northern district were also added so that one new appointee could handle the San Jose division and the other the Oakland division. To insure the Northern District judges would not pretermit, or disregard, the sessions in San Jose or Oakland, Edwards included a provision designating San Jose and Oakland as official stations for at least one judge in the district. It was hoped no San Francisco judge would have to sit in San Jose or Oakland. A new judge, especially if selected from the legal community of the new divisions, would have more sympathy with the development of a court sitting outside of San Francisco.

Finally, Edwards incorporated in his bill several technical corrections suggested to him by Chief Judge Chambers. After the bill was reviewed by Beresford, Roessler, Judge Chambers, and by members of the California congressional delegation in the House, Edwards introduced it on January 7, 1964, as H.R. 9567.

The next step would be to see whether he could overcome the divisions in the California delegation that stalled the movement for redistricting in 1963. Russ Roessler wrote to Edwards about the possible success of a strategy similar to that used in 1963. Roessler argued it would be "extremely helpful" to have others in the California delegation introduce bills identical to H.R. 9567. He believed that faced with this show of support for the same redistricting plan, Chairman Celler would no longer insist the state get only one new district. Edwards agreed with the general idea, but doubted Celler's opposition to more than one district would so easily vanish. Instead of twisting arms to get other members to introduce identical bills, he merely asked them to sign a letter addressed to Chairman Celler. The letter informed Celler that "the California Democratic delegation supports H.R. 9567 . . . we feel that the reforms as provided in this legislation are long overdue."[11]

The letter gained signatures quickly, simply because it did not require the staff time and research that a bill would, but would have much the same impact. Edwards worked with Congressman Pat Martin of California, a Republican and also a member of the House Committee on the Judiciary, to gather Republican signatures for a bill Martin would introduce. This would be the Republican version of H.R. 9567.

Edwards started gathering signatures in January. By March, thirteen of California's fifteen Republican congressman and all of the state's twenty-two Democratic congressmen had signed the letter. This made a grand total of thirty-five out of the thirty-seven-member delegation (there was one vacancy in the delegation that year). Celler received the Democratic letter on February 28; the Republican letter was sent on March 12. In response, Celler announced March 25 hearings on the California redistricting bills.

The joint letter had another effect which was not completely expected. On March 16 and 17, 1964, the United States Judicial Conference turned its attention to the measures creating new court districts and divisions in California. The conference had "for many years opposed the creation of additional judicial districts," but it now recognized that California "has a unique problem because of the large geographic area it embraces and its rapidly expanding population and continuing economic development." The conference determined that it would not adhere "to the policy it has consistently followed," yet it declined to support any particular bill on court redistricting because of "insufficient information on the subject." Why this change? Ninth Circuit Chief Judge Chambers felt that Don Edwards's joint letter in support of H.R. 9567 had compelled the conference to embrace what seemed to be inevitable.[12]

During this period, the Southern District of California judges considered the various redistricting bills. In the past they had opposed splitting up the southern district because no plans had been made to replace the two judges who would be lost in the division of the district between Los Angeles and San Diego. But H.R. 9567 added two new judgeships to the Los Angeles district after San Diego left the southern district. The southern district judges could support Edwards's redistricting bill. But they refused to express an opinion on the provisions to establish a division of the northern district court in San Jose.

Edwards prepared for the Committee on the Judiciary hearing by solidifying support for his bill. He wrote a letter to his California colleagues with extensive data and arguments, urging them to make their interest in the bill's progress known. Shortly before the hearing, Edwards sent letters to the six Democratic members on the subcommittee that would consider the bill. He emphasized the great support within the California House delegation for the bill.

Despite the support expressed for H.R. 9567, Chairman Celler presented the California delegation with difficult choices for the 1964 session. Edwards was advised by House Committee on the Judiciary Chief Counsel William Foley that Chairman Celler would be more accommodating to the idea of new districts in California this time around. However, there was "absolutely no chance" of obtaining the new judgeships H.R. 9567 established. Additionally, Celler was willing to have the subcommittee report an amended bill establishing the new districts at Sacramento and San Diego but not the new divisions at San Jose and Oakland. Instead of creating a court division of the northern district at San Jose, it would only authorize the court to sit in that city.[13]

This concession was really none at all. If the northern district court were only *authorized* and not *required* to sit in San Jose, the judges might choose not to sit there. Also, without the new judgeships H.R. 9567 provided, most of the federal judiciary, including Chief Judge Chambers, could not support the measure. The judges believed that the increase in the places court must sit and the new cases that might be filed because of better availability of the federal court would necessitate an increase in the number of judges for the state. Edwards would lose their support if he broke faith with the judges. The additional judgeship provision had won for his legislation the support of the Los Angeles district judges and the Ninth Circuit Judicial Council. It was a necessary feature of a unified approach to redistricting the federal courts of California.

An executive session of the subcommittee allowed Edwards to probe what options he had. He found the subcommittee unwilling to report H.R. 9567 because it created four additional district judges for the state. But the bill would not be satisfactory to Edwards or to the California congressional delegation unless additional judges were included. So Edwards left the bill stuck in the subcommittee. He could go no further with it in the

1964 session. Leaving it there would at least maintain the united California support for redistricting. He might have more success in the 1965 session.

Edwards reported to Russ Roessler that he was not discouraged with the results; they had made splendid progress that session. "I honestly expect success in the Eighty-ninth Congress . . . I will, my reelection assumed, start work immediately in January 1965. That should give plenty of time to bring the matter to a successful conclusion."[14]

Edwards was handily elected by his district and in January 1965, started revising the statewide federal court redistricting bill. He added a section increasing the number of new judgeships to eight, as requested by Judge Chambers, instead of the four requested in 1964. He hoped this would give the California delegation room to bargain, without risking loss of support if the number of judgeships were reduced in the subcommittee. After securing approval from Roessler, Edwards introduced H.R. 4534 on February 8, 1965.

Another joint letter by the California delegation was drawn up and quickly signed. This time twenty-two Democrats and eleven Republicans affixed their names to the letter. The one new member of the California Democratic delegation, Congressman Phil Burton of San Francisco, did not support the redistricting bill; the measure was too strongly opposed by the federal district judges sitting in his city. But by March, the joint letter had gained thirty-three signatures of the thirty-seven-person delegation. This continued support would be invaluable in pushing H.R. 4534 through the legislative maze.

That February found Edwards once more at the Supreme Court to discuss court redistricting with the chief justice. Later he had meetings with other judges of influence in matters of judicial administration. Among them was Judge John Biggs, chairman of the Judicial Conference Committee on Court Administration. Judge Biggs's committee would review the redistricting bills and recommend appropriate action to the conference. After reviewing Edwards's legislation, Biggs ventured his opinion that the Committee on Court Administration would approve its provisions for new districts and divisions. But Judge Biggs felt that four new judgeships were enough; eight would be rather excessive.

The director of the Administrative Office of the United States Courts, Warren Olney, also a Californian, told Edwards that the Judicial Conference traditionally opposed redistricting bills as well as measures that required court to be held in new cities. But the chief justice's concern about the California situation had altered this traditional view. The Administrative Office now understood that the situation in California was entirely different than in the rest of the nation. As the major lobbying arm of the judiciary, the Administrative Office would disregard its usual stand on the question of redistricting. If the Judicial Conference came out for redistricting the California courts, the Administrative Office would be ready to press it before Congress.[15]

Edwards's conferences were later reflected in definite action. Judge Biggs's committee approved of H.R. 4534's provisions for two new districts, but recommended several modifications, including that San Jose and Oakland be designated as places of holding court, not as statutory divisions of the northern district court. The committee also came out for four new judgeships for California: two for northern California and two for southern California. The Judicial Conference approved this report after supportive remarks by the chief justice during the March meeting of that year.

But there was a problem in the conference's endorsement of H.R. 4534 as far as Don Edwards was concerned. San Jose insisted on some assurance that the northern district court would actually hold sessions at San Jose for the central coast area. Mere authorization to do so was insufficient. Edwards was ready to press his bill through the House Committee on the Judiciary, accepting the conference's support for the new districts but fighting for statutory divisions at San Jose and at Oakland. This would reject the Judicial Conference's suggestion that those cities merely be designated as places where the northern district court could hear cases if it so desired.

The conference directed that the Administrative Office draft an omnibus judgeship bill. This bill was to create additional court of appeals judgeships and thirty-one additional district judgeships (including the four Edwards wanted for California). The omnibus bill would provide for two new districts in California but it would only authorize, not require, that court meet in San Jose and Oakland. The Administrative Office submitted a draft of this omnibus legislation to Senator Olin Johnston, chairman of the Senate Judiciary Subcommittee on Improvements in Judicial Machinery on March 26, 1965; a week later, the omnibus bill was introduced to Congress by the senator and designated S. 1666.

The Judicial Conference's action, as incorporated in the Senate bill did not meet with the approval of the Santa Clara County Bar Association. Mere authorization did not insure that the court would actually sit in San Jose. Russ Roessler discussed this aspect of the bill with Chief Judge Chambers. Chambers understood and made arrangements to satisfy Roessler's objections. The conference was reluctant to order that the northern district *must* meet in San Jose. But this did not mean that the conference objected to court sessions in San Jose. Chambers searched for a way to satisfy the conference's desire for maximum judicial flexibility, yet insure that the northern district court would satisfy the needs of the central coast counties. It was a touchy problem but Chambers soon worked out an arrangement.

Edwards still intended to push his H.R. 4534 in the House but he found that the subcommittee handling his bill was apparently too busy with voting rights legislation to consider court redistricting. Consulting with Congressman Celler about S. 1666, Edwards said that there were "serious errors" in the Senate legislation. Celler advised Edwards that he should continue his efforts to have H.R. 4534 reported favorably by Celler's subcommittee and by the House. It was wise advice. There was a strong possibility of a lengthy civil rights dispute developing over a section of the omnibus bill that attempted to alleviate the Fifth Circuit Court of Appeals' backlog of civil right cases.

It appeared that a lengthy, humid summer would end long before S. 1666 got anywhere, but without having held any hearings on the measure, the Senate Committee on the Judiciary reported it to the Senate floor. The full Senate now faced the questions of whether new judgeships should be added to the federal bench, whether California should get two new districts, and whether the northern district court should be authorized to sit in Oakland and San Jose. Senators briefly debated portions of the bill concerning the circuit courts, but no difficulties were expressed on the California redistricting provisions. The desire to pass the measure without a civil rights battle aided in rapid passage. The Senate did not deliberate long: S. 1666 passed the Senate on June 30, 1965.

When the Senate sent S. 1666 to the House, it was referred to the House Committee on the Judiciary. Don Edwards, after conferring with Russ Roessler, changed his strategy and made his primary push for S. 1666 rather than for H.R. 4534. Edwards would not insist that the House include a statutorily mandated court division for San Jose. Instead he would accept S. 1666 which incorporated the Judicial Conference's modifications of H.R. 4534. After the Senate passage of S. 1666, Chairman Celler's H.R. 9168, the

House version of the Senate bill, embodying all the elements of S. 1666, became the focus of attention for those involved in the battle over federal court redistricting.

The pressures of considering the legislation of President Johnson's Great Society in mid-1965 made the prospects for House passage of the bill bleak. By late August, Edwards discussed possible scheduling of the bill with Chairman Celler. Celler told him that the House Committee on the Judiciary would not have time to consider the bill. However, he assured Edwards that the legislation would be taken up by the committee during the first weeks of the second session beginning on January 3, 1966. Celler's subcommittee planned hearings on S. 1666 during eight days in September, because "there was very little in the nature of a hearing in [the Senate] prior to the passage of its bill."[16]

The *New York Times* compared Celler's move to the precipitous Senate consideration in a brief headline: "House Holds Up Bill for 44 New Judges." Chairman Celler insisted his committee must examine "absolute need for the additional judges in each of the circuit and district courts" before it would provide more judgeships. The Judicial Conference's recommendations would not be blindly accepted by Chairman Celler.[17]

For more than two years, Don Edwards had labored to get a California redistricting proposal to this point. The hearing in Celler's subcommittee must have been anticlimatic to say the least. It was not well attended. Often Chairman Celler was the only committee member there. It frequently appeared that while the hearing continued, the chairman transacted other business from the dais, consulting in hushed tones with his chief counsel, conferring with other staff members, or talking with visitors who followed him to the hearing.

The hearing's first few days covered testimony by judges on S. 1666. Then on September 7 and 8, members of the California congressional delegation had their opportunity. The first congressman to testify on California federal court redistricting, B.F. Sisk, criticized the California judges who opposed redistricting. He had been chairman of the California delegation committee on court redistricting in 1962. He could recall the judges' highhandedness when he asked the state bar for its recommendation on where to put a new California judicial district. Sisk told the subcommittee, "I am not too concerned about a little inconvenience on the part of a judge. I think sometimes when you consider their salaries, the fact that they have life tenure, and that their retirement benefits are good, I am inclined to think the judges should be a little more willing to avail themselves to the needs and to serve the needs of the people as other public servants are supposed to do."[18]

The next day, Don Edwards came before the committee. The hearing room was familiar to him. Yet he may have felt a bit out of place down at the witnesses' table, rather than up at the dais. Edwards's testimony indicated the general support for court redistricting among the California House delegation. He dwelt upon the difference between his H.R. 4534 and the Judicial Conference's revisions as embodied in S. 1666. Edwards stated a willingness to accept the conference's recommendation: the provision creating a court division in San Jose be eliminated from H.R. 4534. He said he recognized the conference's argument that "divisions made by [court] rule are a more efficient way to proceed. I am willing to accept the judgment of those who are far better acquainted with this problem than I am and would not argue strongly for the inclusion of the statutory divisions."[19]

The committee's concern during much of the hearing seemed focused upon the creation of new judgeships rather than on whether the California federal courts should be redistricted or whether San Jose should receive a court division. Edwards thought "the questions raised [were] only mildly hostile and I hope I am not deluding myself in being quite hopeful."[20]

The committee hearings demonstrated the difference several years had made in the acceptability of the idea of redistricting California's federal courts. Redistricting in California now had the support of thirty-three of the thirty-seven-person California congressional delegation, the support of the Ninth Circuit, of the United States Judicial Conference, and of the judges of the Southern District of California. Only fifteen years previously, Congressman Anderson's bill for a San Jose court session (H.R. 2701) had been opposed by all groups involved in judicial administration, by various California congressmen, by the courts, and it had only lukewarm support by those in the Santa Clara valley area. The diligent efforts of Beresford and Roessler, the adroit leadership of Edwards in Congress, and the potent support of Warren and Chambers in the judiciary had changed the balance of political forces completely. Only the San Francisco district judges stood out in opposition, but not as actively as they once had. In fact, they seemed to mount no more than a letter writing campaign against the bill.

The gap between the last day of hearings on S. 1666 and the beginning of the new congressional session was a period in which some factor could interfere with S. 1666's progress. By mid-October, Edwards felt that "the cards seem to be being held close to the vest" as far as Celler's next action on the bill. The director of the Administrative Office of the Courts wrote Edwards that the success of S. 1666 may depend on the action of the Justice Department. In the month previous to the subcommittee hearings, the deputy attorney general stated the department's approval of the judgeship provisions of S. 1666. But the department opposed the California redistricting provisions although not with any vigor. The attorney general did not send anyone before the subcommittee to express opposition. This indicated the department's opposition was rather soft.

Faced with the united stand of the California congressional delegation and the Judicial Conference in favor of redistricting, and the rather weak opposition by the Department of Justice, Celler could not afford to keep S. 1666 bottled up for long. In late January 1966, his subcommittee reported out S. 1666 to the full House Committee on the Judiciary. The bill went before that committee, also chaired by Celler, on February 3. One amendment was introduced by Congressman James C. Corman of Los Angeles for three judgeships to be added to the Southern District of California instead of two. The committee seemed unexcited about accepting this amendment. Celler, on a voice vote, ruled it had failed. But when Edwards requested the vote be taken by a show of hands, the Corman amendment passed eight to seven.

During the debate, Celler expressed some reservations about the Sacramento district the bill would create. He feared there would not be enough work for the judges there. Edwards countered by showing a large map of the state with the most recent population figures in the eastern district (Sacramento). After this demonstration of how dramatically the population had risen since Sutter's Fort was built, Celler was quieted. But for this one dispute, the two new districts for California and the authorization to hold court in San Jose and Oakland passed without debate.

A month later, S. 1666 came to the floor of the House. Debate there was uneventful. No organized opposition to its passage arose; no amendments were proposed. Don Edwards knew the battle for California redistricting had been won long before the House vote. Consequently he did not change vacation plans he had made for the first week of March, when he initially thought the bill would be on the president's desk. Learning the bill was scheduled for his vacation period, he checked with Chairman

Celler to see if his presence was needed. Assured he need not change his plans, Edwards prepared a statement to be printed in the *Congressional Record* for the measure and left for a long-deserved and hard-earned rest. While he was traveling, the House passed the bill; the Senate concurred in the House amendments on March 8. Ten days later the president signed the bill and it became public law (P.L. 89-372).

As Congressman Edwards took his leave of the House, he could indulge in a singular feeling of satisfaction. The central coast area would be able to have its federal court; he had tested his legislative skill in maneuvering complex legislation through the capitol maze; he had proven his effectiveness as a legislator. But he would soon discover that some of these thoughts were premature. The dance of legislation had a profusion of false steps. He would find on his return that the dance was not quite done.

But his labor of four years' duration earned many thanks. Hopeful souls wanted to introduce him as a candidate for senator or governor. And still others declared he had been the spearhead of the California delegation for S. 1666. But Edwards knew better than to accept all this praise. He found that the "dedicated sustenance and counsel" of those in California — and especially in San Diego, Sacramento, and San Jose — accounted for much of the success in meeting the judicial needs of a transforming state.[21]

# 10

## Judicious Approval

*Joseph Franaszek*

There was no more room for procrastination or quibbling. The many small actions began to add up and indicate a trend that could not be easily reversed. The United States Judicial Conference was to begin a debate on H.R. 4534 during its mid-March 1965 meeting. Should the delegates exempt California from the ironclad rule against creating new judicial districts, and endorse H.R. 4534? That Congress might pass such a measure appeared inevitable. But a "bloody" debate, full of "open ugliness" on the question seemed likely. It could be averted only if some definite leadership brought the delegates to their senses. Yet, as the anxious session commenced, there seemed not the slightest indication that such leadership would be exercised.[1]

Viewing this situation with his keen political insight and from the vantage point of one who had seen the dispute somewhere before, Ninth Circuit Chief Judge Richard Chambers must have reflected on how much a letter by thirty-four of the thirty-seven-person California congressional delegation meant. Would the conference endorse redistricting the state as the California congressmen advised? By doing so they would avoid opposing a determined delegation. Would the conference stick to broad, decades-old principles against new districts and permit no deviations? This could put them in an ugly, and probably losing battle.

Chief Judge Chambers was a tough and resilient man who had learned the uses of a multitude of political techniques. Among his talents was skill in timing and planning, and he was a hardened realist. He had overseen some of the many small actions that slowly eroded a mountain, bringing the conference to reconsider its long-standing policy on redistricting. He appeared to reduce this issue to one which could be settled in the ordinary give and take of politics. He indicated that redistricting for California was necessary because of the state's unusual accelerated development: making an exception there would not open the door to exceptions elsewhere.

Chief Judge Richard Chambers of the United States Court of Appeals for the Ninth Circuit in the mid-1970s. Judge Chambers's efforts helped win United States Judicial Conference approval for holding federal court in San Jose. (Photograph by Ray Manley, Tucson; courtesy Judge Richard Chambers.)

Judge Chambers assumed his seat as the United States Judicial Conference met in the Supreme Court's large East Conference Room. One of the most striking features of the room is its stateliness. This quality is reflected in an old portrait of Chief Justice John Marshall that hangs at the head of the room, above a dark fireplace, radiating its calm, unsurprised, careful spirit over the room's occupants. Rembrandt Peale painted Marshall's portrait during the chief's seventy-ninth year, when one year remained to

Marshall's life. Peale depicted the justice as a man whose years pressed upon him, yet the seeming darkness coming upon Marshall was overcome in the painting by a bright, contrasting, background light, suggesting the light of Marshall's legacy to the nation.

Marshall's calm visage looked out on the Judicial Conference's delegates, many of them from states and courts with names he never imagined. His dark eyes seemed to follow those who glanced at his portrait and might have given a strange feeling of solemnity, for it seemed as if he followed the proceedings with no little interest.

Marshall was not the only chief justice whose portrait watched the proceedings. Others observed silently from their distant portals along the walls and lent a sedate atmosphere. The highly polished wood paneling, separated by square wooden columns every few feet, gave an impression of quiet stability. The carpeting continued this motif. The square arrangement of tables for the meeting filled the center of the room. This configuration seated no more than twenty-five judges with convenience, and normally the meeting had more than that number of attendees. Name placards marked the spot where each judge sat in a black upholstered chair.

Chief Justice Warren focused the conference's attention on H.R. 4534 with a brief story: "When I was a boy in California, there were a million people in California, and now, gentlemen, how many are there?" The answer was, of course, nearly sixteen million. The chief justice used this answer to describe the changes occurring there since he was governor. The state's economic growth and population increases were phenomenal. He argued that the old pattern of judicial districting no longer fit. California should not be penalized in its access to federal judicial services because of its unusual history.

The implication of Warren's argument was unsettling to some delegates. The chief justice was hinting that the conference reverse itself. The conference subscribed to the axiom that centrally administered district courts, with a concentration of judges, were a most efficient way to handle a growing caseload. In a shocked manner, one of the judges asked: "Chief, do you mean that this conference, after twenty-five years without deviation from being opposed to the creation of more districts and divisions is now changing that policy so that we will have divisions in every little way station?" Chief Justice Warren replied with calm and careful reasoning: "I do not recommend the divisions," he stated deliberately. At least, he said, he could not accept the idea of Congress establishing a division in San Jose through legislation. But this did not mean that the judiciary should not establish, on its own initiative, a division there through the local court rules. "How can you say that Alameda and Contra Costa counties are way stations when they have a million people and San Francisco only has 800,000; and how can you call San Jose and Santa Clara County way stations when they have 1,250,000 people?" challenged the chief. "Now, they aren't way stations, are they?" Apparently nothing but silence answered this question.[2]

A delegate felt the exchange set the pattern for the meeting. The chief had given the conference a direction to follow, and follow it the delegates did. A participant observed that when "the old boy said it was necessary, the conference was not inclined to contradict him."[3]

The conference's reaction to H.R. 4534 was especially fortunate. Chairman Celler had delayed final consideration of the bill by his subcommittee pending a report of the Judicial Conference's determinations. The conference now had its report, recommending a certain number of judgeships be requested from Congress, and therefore directed the Administrative Office of the United States Courts to seek a sponsor for an omnibus judgeship bill. This bill was to include much of H.R. 4534, especially the sections providing for redistricting of California federal courts. The conference's omnibus bill did not go as far as Judge Chambers (or the Santa Clara County Bar Association) had wished. Accordingly, Chambers voted against the proposal at the conference. But the conference followed Chief Justice Warren's lead and ratified the report of its Committee on Court Administration which had recommended endorsement of H.R. 4534 with certain modifications. The committee did not recommend to the conference that statutory divisions of the northern district court be created at San Jose and at Oakland. Instead, the committee urged Congress to authorize the northern district court to hold hearings in those cities, but not require regular sessions in those places. Finally, instead of the eight new California federal judgeships provided in H.R. 4534, the committee recommended four.

An air of uncertainty about the committee's recommendations initially pervaded the conference. Quite a few members had considered H.R. 4534 a radical departure from good judicial administrative practices. Wanting "the whole [bill] wiped out," they believed that legislation should incorporate the prevailing view of efficient court administration. The administration of courts should be centralized: there should be one large district for California, not two or four.[4]

But more realistic heads prevailed. Judge John Biggs, chairman of the Committee on Court Administration, expressed the view that one large district for California "might have been desirable" from an administrative perspective. But the task facing the committee was not to find what was theoretically best; rather "the question was whether or not [one big district in California] was feasible." The California congressional delegation's letter urging more judicial districts for the state, not fewer, clearly indicated that one big district was not politically feasible. The conference should consent to "fractionating" the existing two federal judicial districts of the state into four.[5]

This confusion over whether to capitulate to political necessity or to uphold the prevailing theory of efficient judicial administration was left to the conference to resolve. The chief justice set the meeting's tone: practicalities should come before some vague, unproven, and, in California's case, perhaps unworkable principle of court administration. Finding California an exception to the policy against new districts did not open the way for another exception to be made. The conference did not accept Judge Chambers's arguments completely, nor did it go beyond Warren's recommendation. It refused to support a statutory division for San Jose. Visions of "some congressman securing a statute that would direct one judge be stationed [in a statutorily created division] at his little old hometown in Podunk," haunted the delegates. The conference preferred that the mechanisms of judicial administration create a division without congressional interference. This way, Podunk would have no precedent to appeal to in its arguments for its own federal judge, but the expanding municipality of Santa Clara County could get its long-sought federal district judge.[6]

Undoubtedly it was with some satisfaction that Judge Chambers reported these United States Judicial Conference results to Congressman Edwards and to Beresford and Roessler in San Jose. Nearly two years had elapsed since Chambers had first indicated he could easily live with the redistricting of the courts and with a court in San Jose. Now, his efforts had paid off. The United States Judicial Conference now agreed with the proposal for court to sit in San Jose and for the California federal courts to be redistricted. Through all of this effort to secure redistricting, Chambers had been much like the Sierra guides of old California: these guides had traveled the Sierra, charted the passes, viewed rough terrain as well as more passable, and advised those crossing the mountains of their choices and the consequences they faced. As a modern-day version of this guide, Chambers had traveled with the redistricting proponents, giving them some indication of what to expect next and how to best cope with what developed. He did this while maintaining a certain detached perspective on the whole controversy.

His involvement in United States District Court redistricting in California started as early as 1961. That year marked his sixth year on the United States Court of Appeals bench. Previous to his appointment by President Eisenhower, he practiced law in Tucson; his activities in 1961 took him far from the problems of his home base. Initially he worked for legislation providing San Diego an extra federal courtroom so that three judges of the Southern District of California could try cases there simultaneously. In 1961 he maintained a reserved attitude towards congressional legislation designed to establish a federal judicial district there (as well as an Oakland division of the northern district court). But of more interest to him was securing an increased number of judges on the district courts in California. He probably did not support redistricting when he first became chief judge of the Ninth Circuit, yet he found himself using many of the arguments developed by redistricting proponents to support his requests for new judgeships. His primary interest was always to obtain judgeships for California. As to new districts or divisions, initially he found it difficult to support them because Congress was always after the judiciary to keep expenditures to a minimum. He could not see how this could be done with new administrative units being created.

In the same year that he became chief judge, Chambers met Bob Beresford, chairman of the Santa Clara County Bar Association Federal Court Committee at a California State bar meeting at Los Angeles. As Beresford recalled their conversation, Chambers was noncommittal about a San Jose court but seemed "mildly receptive to the idea of serving" the San Jose area with a federal court presence. But Beresford's continual activities in the state bar, in working with Congressman Charles Gubser on H.R. 9051 to establish a new judicial district in the central coast counties, attracted Chambers's attention.[7]

The Ninth Circuit Judicial Council had repeatedly opposed the innovations Beresford advocated. As early as June 1954, in response to a congressional measure for a northern district court division in Oakland and an entirely new judicial district in San Diego, the council reacted strongly against the measure because it was "unnecessary" if not "too costly." When the United States Judicial Conference considered the same issue, it concurred. After all, the Ninth Circuit was merely holding to the letter and spirit of a 1948 United States Judicial Conference policy opposing the creation of any new districts.[8]

Proponents of a San Diego court attempted to overturn this 1948 policy by contacting the conference's delegates. But this attempt at open politics failed miserably. Rather than reverse their policy, the conference in 1955 specifically approved of the Ninth Circuit Judicial Council's findings that neither the Oakland nor the San Diego measures should pass Congress.

But the repeated demands from regions of California for redistricting the federal courts compelled the conference to study "whether the creation of any additional divisions of judicial districts ought to be opposed." In March 1956, the conference's Committee on Court Administration reported that opposition to redistricting was the only proper course. New divisions within districts involved "new court quarters with attendant expense." A more flexible, less costly, and administratively sound approach would be for the district judges or the Ninth Circuit Council to take "judicious action" to meet the "asserted needs" which gave rise to the claim for new divisions. But in 1957, the Ninth Circuit Judicial Council's response to this suggestion was to deny the need for any new districts in California. In so doing, the council noted that costs and judicial statistics indicated the new district in San Diego would be unduly expensive and inefficient.[9]

However, pressure mounted when more California redistricting proposals were introduced in Congress in 1961. The judiciary then hoped Congress would increase the number of federal judges to handle ever-increasing caseloads. In an attempt to utilize whatever allies they could find among those calling for redistricting, the judiciary found itself trying to soft-pedal its opposition to new districts or divisions and to emphasize new judgeships as a way to handle a mounting caseload.

Like his colleagues, Chambers went to great lengths to emphasize the need for new judgeships, yet he was silent on new divisions and districts for California. But during 1961, the United States Judicial Conference faced the question of additional districts and divisions for California again. Considering its 1948 and 1955 findings against such administrative units, the conference maintained its policy of disapproving the various proposals for the creation of additional districts and new divisions in existing judicial districts. No new districts had been created since 1928 in the nation, declared the conference, because of "the disadvantages normally accruing with the creation of a new district: over-compartmentalization and uneconomic operation."[10]

Chambers probably realized the issue of new California districts and divisions was not a passing phenomenon. The issue was continually raised, had gained congressional support, and had ultimately stumbled due to the disagreements of the redistricting proponents. But in 1962, Chambers might have paid particular attention to the redistricting proponents' efforts to unify their approach as they pushed the California congressional delegation to tell Chairman Celler where at least one new district should be located. Clearly, the demands for new judicial administrative units, since 1948, indicated that the current concentration of the federal courts in Los Angeles and San Francisco left deeply felt needs unfulfilled. The demographic makeup of California since World War II might have given rise to these needs. Chambers, as far as can be determined, believed in the theory of having a minimum of district courts. Yet, faced with the realities of California's unique development, he was more than willing to have theory take second place. To some it was clear that demands for local and accessible federal district courts would continue. It was especially clear to Chief Judge Chambers that throwing theory at the problem would not stem the demands. He could recall grappling with these same court theorists when they refused to admit that Arizona's federal courts needed more judges. Anyone who counted moving vans along the streets and viewed the swift development of once primitive western communities could see the need.

As Chambers became involved in the redistricting controversy he adopted an entirely different attitude from that of preceding circuit chief judges. For instance, during January 1963, the California State Bar Association's Federal Court Committee began hearings on the needs for a federal court in the central coast counties. The committee chairman invited Chief Judge Chambers to attend. Although Chambers did not attend because of pressing business in Los Angeles, he did not avoid expressing his views on the question — to the state bar, to Bob Beresford, and even to Chief Judge Harris of the northern district court. He reminded them that "the Judicial Conference of the United States is opposed to further fractionating of the judicial districts." The Ninth Circuit Judicial Council endorsed this policy, as did the northern district judges. "Therefore,"

Chambers wrote the state bar, "I could not very well . . . advocate the creation of a new division in San Jose."[11]

But Chambers did not stop with these official constraints. He went on to indicate his real view of the situation. "Personally, I have no dedicated opposition to either the proposed Oakland or the San Jose division," he wrote. "I think such fractionating would cost some more money (how much is arguable), and that the cost is the real issue." This statement indicates his independence and suggests the growing effectiveness of redistricting proponents in demonstrating their needs.[12]

In June 1963, the Ninth Circuit Judicial Council again considered congressional measures on court redistricting. Instead of taking a position consistent with that held by the United States Judicial Conference and its own previous resolutions, the council remained neutral on the pending redistricting bills. It claimed it had insufficient information with which to assess the impact of the measures. The Ninth Circuit's determination had considerable effect at the United States Judicial Conference's mid-September 1963 session. Instead of reiterating its view against new districts, the conference postponed deciding the issue: it would await the Ninth Circuit's position before considering California court redistricting.

The Ninth Circuit Council took six months to reach a new position on redistricting California's federal courts. On December 11, 1963, the council found that new districts at Sacramento and San Diego "appear to be warranted at the present time, provided, however, that two additional judgeships are added to the new central [Los Angeles] district." The council found that the population, businesses, and geographic situation of those regions, as well as the fact that court facilities already existed there, supported this plea for new districts. It was willing to support the new districts provided the state also received new federal judges to relieve mounting court congestion.

But their concession to the proponents of redistricting was balanced by a refusal to endorse the entire redistricting package. "From the standpoint of efficiency and service," the council argued, "there is not present justification for creating divisions of the northern district at either Oakland or San Jose. If, however, either or both such divisions are created, it should only be on condition that an additional district judgeship be added to the northern district for each such additional division created." The council found that the relative proximity of Oakland and San Jose to San Francisco's large federal court building, and the lack of any available facilities for holding court in those two cities, made the proposed divisions there inadvisable. In addition, the judges of the northern district were unwilling to trade a court in San Jose and Oakland for new judges to sit in San Francisco.[13]

Chambers dissented from the council's findings against the San Jose division. Unlike his colleagues, he found "considerable merit to the proposal for the San Jose division and that the only argument which is a substantial one against it is cost: the cost of new facilities and the cost of manpower."[14] But others disagreed. Chambers had once remarked to a northern district judge that the district court could afford to have divisions outside San Francisco, "that San Jose and Oakland [divisions] weren't immoral." To which the northern district judge dryly observed, "I don't know about that." But for many judges there was a willingness to bend; compromising on the repeated demands for redistricting was the way to end these demands. The Circuit Council compromised by granting what the most active redistricting proponents — those for Sacramento and San Diego — demanded. These areas had the least opposition from the district judges.

But to Oakland, which had fallen silent since 1961, and to San Jose which became active in 1961 after eleven years' dormancy, the council refused to support divisions. The San Francisco judges vehement opposition to the new divisions tended to outweigh the activities of the San Jose and Oakland proponents. For instance, during the council meeting, Judge Oliver Carter of the northern district presented his colleagues' arguments and "talked extensively. He began by saying that his basic belief was that California should be one judicial district. Basically, . . . he was opposed to all new divisions and districts. Then he went on to present a long argument about why the Eastern [Sacramento] District of California would be a good idea." Like Carter, many judges refused to believe that redistricting was an efficient tool of judicial administration, but quite a few found that politically it was best to accede to some of the demands for redistricting.[15]

How the judges evaluated the politics of the situation depended on who had bothered them. Judge Chambers tended to oppose an Oakland division but to support one in San Jose. "Perhaps it is only because no one from Oakland had been trying to sell me anything lately," he explained, "but my inclination now is to say that there is virtually no justification for Oakland. As to the other three, [San Diego, Sacramento, and San Jose] the argument against is cost. Of the three for which there is considerable to be said, my inclination is to say that the strongest case is for the eastern [Sacramento] district, the second is the San Jose division and the third is the San Diego district." Because Oakland had dropped its agitation for its own division, Chambers found no political reason to support a division there.[16]

A further indication of the political nature of the council's decision can be seen in Judge Chambers's attempt to explain it to the San Jose proponents. When he sent the council's resolutions to Bob Beresford, Chambers told him he would not like it, but he cautioned: "Please wait until you get the [council's] resolution before you go clear through the ceiling. I think that it is to your advantage that our council has finally 'given in' on something. Actually I was quite surprised that the council went as far as it did."[17]

Although disappointed in the decision, Beresford was quick to insure that the council's resolution would not disrupt the California delegation's unanimity on the California redistricting question. Beresford had to make sure all would fight for San Jose's division, just as San Jose would fight for the other county bar associations' districts.

The resolution indicated that the circuit judges were unwilling to stand against the strong political movements for new districts in California. The council would not uphold an amorphous principle of judicial administrative efficiency in this instance. But on the question of new court divisions, it did not bend, because proponents of the court divisions were not yet strong enough.

Although San Jose's case had been rejected, Judge Chambers felt "the dike has been breached, and that surprised me. That is quite important to San Jose."[18] Now the question was whether the trickle from the dike could become a flood. Many uncontrolled factors would determine that, but Judge Chambers made special efforts to help the flood along, consulting frequently with those for and against the redistricting proposal. For instance, as early as November 1963, he carefully studied Edwards's H.R. 6847 and indirectly suggested corrections to various inadvertent technical difficulties in the bill that might detract from its effectiveness. He advised Edwards as to the timing for the introduction of revised statewide reorganization bills. Edwards used this advice in 1964 when he introduced H.R. 9567. The bill provided for two new districts in the state, a division at Oakland, and another at San Jose.

The United States Judicial Conference met on March 16 and 17, 1964. H.R. 9567 had been introduced by Congressman Edwards and thirty-five of thirty-eight California congressmen had signed Edwards's joint letter supporting the bill. It was understood that Chief Judge Chambers would "carry the ball" at the conference for the redistricting proponents. Better still, he would report the Ninth Circuit's December 11, 1963, decision to support the creation of districts at San Diego and Sacramento. It was hoped he would speak in favor of a court division at San Jose. The conference did not endorse H.R. 9567, but it did disregard its traditional deference to the principle of no new judicial districts. It recognized that reorganization was necessary, and it discussed the various bills to create new districts and divisions in California. The conference directed its Committee on Court Administration to consider the redistricting bills further and to recommend specific action. Probably this came about because of the united congressional support indicated by Edwards's letter. Judge Chambers had made sure those attending the conference learned the letter's contents; it was a potent argument in support of court redistricting.[19]

But H.R. 9567 never moved from the House Committee on the Judiciary. Chairman Celler offered its proponents the new districts and divisions they desired, but he refused to have the committee consider the new judgeships. Edwards refused this offer because accepting it would cause the redistricting alliance to unravel.

All of this maneuvering indicated to those in the Judicial Conference that if they hoped to gain the additional judgeships, they would have to take some active steps. They could not rely on Congress alone: an active push for more judgeships must come from the judiciary. Accordingly, in September 1964, the United States Judicial Conference authorized its committees to consider drafting an omnibus judgeship bill for the 1965 session of Congress. The conference members hoped to make a regular practice, every four years, of assessing the use and needs for judicial manpower in the nation. Because the last omnibus judgeship bill had passed in 1961, the next appropriate time for that assessment was 1965.

Despite the conference's intention to have an omnibus bill introduced, Chambers worked with Don Edwards to include provisions for new California judgeships in his new redistricting bill for the Eighty-ninth Congress. Russ Roessler, drafting the Santa Clara County bar's suggestions on Edwards's proposed bill, consulted with Chief Judge Chambers about the measure. Chambers urged that Edwards increase the number of California judgeships that his bill would create. This would provide a way to endrun the Judicial Conference which was thinking of only a modest omnibus judgeship bill. Edwards's bill could provide a means of getting more judgeships for San Francisco and Los Angeles than the Judicial Conference wanted to provide.

These suggestions were placed in Edwards's bill, H.R. 4534. The Judicial Conference endorsed this measure, except that it cut the number of judgeships from eight to four and it disapproved of creating statutory divisions at Oakland and San Jose. The Ninth Circuit representatives at the conference — one of whom was Judge Chambers — were the only ones to vote against the conference's recommendation because of the cut of new California judgeships.

Although he voted against the recommendation on H.R. 4534, Chambers was firmly committed to its goals. He became a major force in keeping the redistricting proponents united behind the Judicial Conference's plan. On Don Edwards's suggestion, Russ Roessler discussed with Chambers the results of the meeting and the steps that redistricting proponents should pursue, but it soon became clear that the redistricting coalition was disintegrating. The northern district judges' strong resistance to every sug-

131

gestion that San Jose deserved a federal court presence, helped build doubts among the Santa Clara County bar's Federal Court Committee that the San Francisco judges would ever voluntarily sit in San Jose. Having Congress establish a court division at San Jose seemed the only way to insure that the court would actually sit on the central coast.

The conference rejected this view. Having a law specify that court meet in San Jose was too inflexible. Creation of a division through the district court's rules would have the same effect, but if the San Jose area declined in the future the court would not be forced to hold inefficient sessions there. The court could then alter the location of its sessions merely by changing the rules. It was probably clear to Chambers that the same feature that made the rules division attractive to members of the judiciary — its flexibility — was the very reason the redistricting proponents would reject that approach. If the district judges could easily establish a session at San Jose, they could just as easily abolish one. San Jose's years of efforts for a federal court left the redistricting proponents distrustful. The proponents felt that only by eliminating the judges' discretion to sit in San Jose, would the northern district come to the central coast.

As if recognizing the difficulty, Edwards's bill attempted an alternative way of establishing a statutory division. At the suggestion of Judge Chambers, his H.R. 9567 of 1964 and H.R. 4534 of 1965 provided that at least one judge of the northern district would be stationed at San Jose. But the Judicial Conference objected to this and found it unnecessary. The Ninth Circuit Council had the power to fix the residence of district judges. If San Jose needed a resident district judge, the council could use its administrative authority and discretion to place one there as "the public interest and the nature of the business of the court so require."[20]

Russ Roessler told Chief Judge Chambers that his committee would have difficulty supporting Senator Johnston's S. 1666, incorporating the Judicial Conference's recommendations on H.R. 4534. The bill did not establish a division in San Jose, nor did it station a judge there, so the Santa Clara County bar could not support it. Chambers understood this position, but saw that the assurance that the San Jose redistricting advocates required could destroy the unanimity of the California House delegation on redistricting, and on more judgeships for the state. Loss of unanimity would doom any hope for redistricting the state or acquiring additional judgeships.

Judge Chambers acted swiftly and imaginatively to extinguish this "little flare-up." He contacted the Administrative Office of the United States Courts, which prepared reports of the conference's meetings. He explained the difficulties the Santa Clara County Federal Court Committee had with the Judicial Conference's positions on California redistricting as it was worded. As Judge Chambers understood it, the conference acted to preserve the discretion of the judiciary in the administration of the courts. But the conference's elimination of statutory divisions did not signify a national judicial policy that there be no division at San Jose or Oakland. Precisely the reverse: the conference favored a federal court presence in those cities. Such divisions should be established through flexible, judicial administrative mechanisms, not by permanently carving such divisions on the northern district through congressional legislation. Indeed, the Ninth Circuit Council decided a law establishing a San Jose division was unnecessary because the council could fix the residence of a district judge. All Chambers need do was have the Judicial Conference's minutes make it clear that the conference recommended the Ninth Circuit Council station a northern district judge in San Jose.

Judge Chambers arranged that the minutes be adjusted to explicitly satisfy the Federal Court Committee's concerns. He would have the minutes state that the conference approved H.R. 4534, excepting the bill's provisions for a statutory division and legislative designation of the judges' stations. In return for the passage of such modified legislation by Congress, the conference recommended to the Ninth Circuit Judicial Council that "action be taken to designate one or more judges to reside and have their official stations at Oakland and at San Jose." Chambers submitted the proposed wording to Chief Justice Warren. The chief justice approved. The minutes were altered to express more fully the actions of the conference and to allay the fears of Roessler and Beresford.[21]

The conference's record attempted to reconcile the irreconcilable. San Jose proponents objected to the latitude the northern district judges would have under the conference's plan. After their long struggle with the San Francisco judges, they could not accept what the conference tried to preserve: the judges' ability to exercise their judicial administrative discretion. Congress could authorize the district court to sit in San Jose. The Ninth Circuit Council could insure that a district judge was attached to that city. If the council failed in this, it transgressed national judicial policy. All this was clear. But it was also clear that the conference had no mechanism to enforce its decisions. Rarely was policy so specific and centered on the needs of one location. But, argued one scholar, the conference set the policy it did on the San Jose court only to prevent Congress from doing so. The Ninth Circuit Council would have to decide if the nature of court business at San Jose and the public's interest made it necessary that a northern district judge reside in San Jose or be stationed there.[22]

Judge Chambers's solution to San Jose's objections was not satisfactory, at least formally. The Santa Clara County Bar Association Federal Court Committee never endorsed the Judicial Conference's action, but they did not actively oppose it. Ultimately they preferred H.R. 4534, but they would accept S. 1666 (the bill encompassing the conference's recommendations) when it passed the Senate. Despite the faults of the Senate legislation, it was acceptable because San Jose's congressman, Don Edwards, would play a key role in selecting the new northern district judges provided for by the bill. One would probably be the judge who would sit in San Jose.

## 11

# The Reaction in San Francisco

*Joseph Franaszek*

The dark, blocklike structure at 450 Golden Gate Avenue had been a long time in planning, a long time in the execution, and a dreadfully long time overdue. While less ornate than the district court's old quarters at Seventh and Mission streets, it was a decided improvement. At various times in their old building, the judges coped with a minimum of space, increasing noises from street traffic, and the troubles of a slowly deteriorating neighborhood. The newer, more utilitarian quarters in a twenty-story structure marked more than a change in atmosphere. To some, such as the district's chief judge, George B. Harris, the building was a landmark to one of the busiest judicial districts in the nation, the Northern District of California. It signified a growing court, maturing and adjusting to the demands of the times.

It was planned to accommodate the needs of the court far into the future. Chief Judge Harris's predecessor as chief judge, Louis Goodman, and his colleague, Judge Oliver Carter, had for seven years planned and supervised.the building's architects and the General Services Administration before the new courthouse opened. The structure would house courtrooms, chambers, and necessary supporting facilities and offices for almost double the number of judges the court had when construction had started. Chief Judge Harris declared with obvious pride that with its thirteen courtrooms, the new courthouse had "all essential facilities . . . to meet the needs of federal court business in the Northern District of California for many years to come."[1]

In this respect, the building was a physical embodiment of the judges' expectations for their district. They expected an increased use of federal tribunals; this was reflected in doubling the number of district judges the new building could house. They expected the federal court's leadership in protecting constitutional rights against the shifting currents of politics to continue; perhaps the new courtrooms, located far above the noise of

*Chief Judge George B. Harris of the United States District Court, Northern District of California, about 1960. As chief judge, Judge Harris voiced the opposition of the San Francisco judges to holding federal court in San Jose. (Courtesy Archives, United States District Court for the Northern District of California.)*

the streets and the occasional crowd of protesters in the federal plaza below reflected this attitude. They expected the court to modernize its procedures and practices for more efficient handling of a growing caseload; the new courtrooms' utilitarian design, with a simple yet not severe style, reflected this determination.

Of course, not all of these expectations were realized in the manner the judges contemplated. Chief Judge Harris had watched the development of each with an administrator's careful eye. Yet, by 1970, he considered setting aside this burden and adopting senior status. Then he could complete many other projects of a non-legal nature which, for years, had been beyond the limits of his time. There could be a certain reluctance to do this. After nearly a quarter century as a judge, it might be difficult to imagine oneself not under the pressures that had become so usual. It was a change that would take some getting used to. Although, perhaps not as much as getting used to the role as a federal judge had taken. Chief Judge Harris had served as a municipal court judge, yet it had taken him time to transcend a slight tinge of self-consciousness in his chambers at the old federal courthouse during his first years on the northern district court. It was a self-consciousness that one must advance a great judicial legacy, going back to the first northern district judge, Ogden Hoffman, in the California of the gold rush. The self-consciousness was rooted in the almost impossible expectations of the bar and of the people for flawless performance as a judge. It involved extensive demands on one's time, energies and efforts. It was all this that the judge had adjusted to in the late 1940 after his appointment to the federal bench.

Yet he had a wide range of non-legal concerns. He was a man with a great fascination for the arts — literature, music, and especially theater — which nearly equaled his love for the law. From these non-legal concerns, it is possible he gained an intuitive appreciation of his role in the legal system as a federal judge. There were those who saw in his concern for the arts some motivation for his behavior as a judge. After all, the successful actor transformed the flat words of the dramatic script into a living character — just as a judge used the impersonal principles of the law as an active force in resolving the disputes brought into court.

Those serving as judges served as symbols in America. To the public, they came to represent the possibility of a fair, impartial, reasonable, and fair forum for the resolution of disputes, quite apart from the disreputable and unequal world of politics. Judges were expected to reflect a judicious dignity, a careful impartiality, and a rational interest in advancing the spirit of the law. They did this by trying to separate themselves from the self-interested concerns of common men.[2] Yet this expectation of judicial behavior overlooked the fact that it was not merely legal skill that brings judges to the bench, but often a lifetime of serving in distinctly non-judicious roles — as legislators or politicians.

The duty to operate the northern district court necessarily involved the judges in activities that transcended their symbolic roles. Besides the duty to decide cases, they also had the duty to administer the court. For Chief Judge Harris, this presented a further burden. He had been chief judge of the district since 1961 and consequently served as chief administrator for the court. In this position, he represented the district court in consultation with his colleagues.

Harris enjoyed his role as administrator, but as the 1960s unfolded, he faced a troubling administrative problem that involved serious political questions. The difficulty involved a matter which Harris and his colleagues feared could disrupt the efficient administration of the district. The bar associations of counties which rarely appeared in the federal court — the bars of the four central coast counties in the northern district — were seeking congressional legislation requiring the northern district court to sit in those central coast counties. It was Harris's duty as chief judge to represent the almost-unanimous beliefs of the district judges, and to a lesser extent his own views: he must act to defeat such plans. In so doing, he would be compelled to abandon, for short moments, his public and symbolic role as a neutral and fair nondisputant. He would have to intrude into the political process to maintain what the judges believed was the efficiency of the northern district court.[3]

A lithe, medium-sized man, whose hair swept back from his forehead, crowning a dignified countenance, Harris had served on the federal bench since 1946. To observers he was a handsome, determined, sometimes controversial man. He appeared a stern judge, not merely because he, indeed, was. It was an image he carefully fostered. Observers noted the dramatic force in photographs taken of Chief Judge Harris. Even the routine FBI photos, snapped by agents more expert in unflattering criminal portraiture, did not mute this dramatic quality. His pictures could not fail to convey the impression of a forthright, determined judge.

Had George Bernard Harris been born a hundred years previous to August 16, 1901, he might have gone into the theater. Undoubtedly, he had the capacity to be one of the

West Coast's great actors. It was an era when actors could make substantial fortunes entertaining entrepreneurs and miners who escaped to San Francisco to trade their gold for relief from the monotony of their struggle for riches. In this atmosphere, he might have found what the theater did not present to him in the 1920s — the prospect for financial security and prominence. Or he might have derived satisfaction as a Christian Brother or Jesuit priest. He had a pervading interest in the intellectual challenges of his religion. Probably he would have been particularly interested in navigating the administrative mazes of the centuries-old church bureaucracy.

But as his life was, he chose the law. It was a means of challenging himself intellectually while supporting himself, and his other interests, financially. Early in his youth, he rejected the priesthood, despite the earnest encouragement of his teachers at Sacred Heart College. He did not feel he "had the moral distinction" for the task and feared the possibility of spending countless years being "farmed out to some [remote] area [to] conduct the parish duties of a catechism class." Yet he never lost his devotion to the church and later the Pope would honor him with an appointment as a knight in the Catholic church.[4]

It took him much longer to decide against a career in the theater. It "was always crowding everything else out of my life," he admitted, but he felt he could achieve only a "minor degree of success" in that profession. But even as an attorney and as a judge, the theater played a major role in his life. He wrote several plays, joined the Actor's Workshop, prepared skits, arranged musicals, and acted in plays at the Bohemian Club. As chairman of the board of the Actor's Workshop, he negotiated the financing for repertory performances in San Francisco.

He claimed he always wanted to be a lawyer, ever since he could remember. Law offered the prospect of getting to "know everything about everybody, and without being pretentious." It provided a chance to become a scholar, a gentleman, and to do well financially all at the same time.[5] Law provided a satisfying mixture of those things which most interested him. Like a priest, an attorney must have a strong devotion to ideals. Like work in the theater, trial work involved a strong element of drama and creativeness. But law was a more secure path towards prominence.

If he had not achieved the prominence he desired in 1946 when President Truman appointed him a United States district judge, or when he dominated the nation's front pages in *United States v. Harry Bridges,* then becoming chief judge of the northern district court must have given him a singular feeling of accomplishment. He considered it a recognition of his capacity as a judge and of the length of his labors for the court. Yet, the law always had an element of insecurity and the prospect of failure. Even near the end of his active life of accomplishment, he fondly and perhaps teasingly recalled his childhood chores, such as mopping and cleaning the stables of his family's drayage business. That humble and arduous duty at the stables, and not his service to the law, he considered "in the nice part" of his life.[6]

Perhaps this element of insecurity, which he tried to avoid in his choices through life, was reflected in his attitude towards politics. As chief judge, he could not avoid politics; his leadership position gave him important responsibilities in the politics of court administration. Generally, he found that issues of court administration greatly interested him. He enjoyed the responsibility immensely because of its constant challenge. Yet, such questions often had an undercurrent of politics. In the McCarthy era, he had seen even a routine judicial question of bail for alleged communists become a hot political question in the northern district. Later, he watched the intrusion of partisan politics against the northern district judges appointed by Democratic presidents.

He professed a low opinion of most politics, yet he could not escape it. He appeared to minimize his role in partisan political life. He explained his participation in politics as one of taking "the citizen's viewpoint of what is good for the country and what is bad." He attempted to paint his political participation with a light brush, acting as if it were of little consequence to him. "I could win or lose without too much anguish," he declared. Rather than exhaust himself in politics, he would "rather go down and see a good show." When he did dip into politics, he insisted it was of a different nature than the usual. In his type of politics, "great friendships" developed and there were "clean fights" handled on very high planes, with "no mud slinging."

He appeared reluctant to acknowledge the role of politics in his life. Publicly, he attributed the credit for bringing him to the bench to circumstance, providence, destiny, and fate. He avoided discussing the politics of his placement on the federal bench, stating that to discuss it would be time-consuming, that he had "no comment" and that he did not want to pass judgment on the politics involved because it was another field of endeavor from his — the law.[7]

One issue of court administration inextricably linked with politics was the issue of the central coast counties of the northern district's jurisdiction. The question that kept arising at bar meetings, in Congress, and in various judicial conferences involved whether a new district or division should be formed of these counties. The issue arose at a time when Chief Judge Harris and the northern district judges felt a need for relief from their incessant work to meet the demands of the court's calendar. Judge Harris suspected these pressures took a terrible toll on the judges. He believed that his predecessor as chief judge, Louis Goodman, had been under such a terrible load in his work on the bench that it hastened his demise in 1961.[8]

The court undertook to promptly dispose of its cases despite a chronic shortage of judges. Throughout much of the 1960s the northern district court, among the large metropolitan districts, had the smallest number of judges on the bench. However, the volume of work accomplished was astounding. For instance, a study for fiscal year 1967 revealed that each judge terminated a total of 343 civil and criminal cases, the second-highest total of the ten largest metropolitan United States District Courts. In terms of the number of protracted cases (such as antitrust cases), the northern district totaled almost 67 such cases per judge. This exceeded all other districts in the nation that year. In addition, the median time per civil case in the northern district was a modest fourteen months from issue to trial, third best among the ten largest metropolitan district courts. Chief Judge Harris was proud of this record of judicial productivity, especially because it was accomplished with the court short by one judge and with another seriously ill and incapacitated.[9]

The northern district judges searched for ways to cope with their expanding caseload. They pursued several solutions. They intended to supplement their industry in handling cases with all of the innovations, inventions, and ingenuity suggested by a modern scientific approach to the problem of court overload. But the methods the court would use to control its docket would take a final form only at the end of the decade.[10]

Chief Judge Harris believed that the major difficulty had been that he and his colleagues had expended "years of inactivity in the area of getting [new] judges" for the district. Most judges, he explained, were specialized in acquiring new judgeships for their districts at the slightest hint of the calendar overcrowding, but not so the northern district's judges. No reforms in court procedure could compensate for the definite need for more judges to hear cases in the district.[11]

Getting new judgeships was a sticky problem. The creation of judgeships involved more than a simple demonstration of need. It also required political pressure on Congress. However, at the same time he and others in the judiciary pressed, with some success, to increase the number of district judgeships in California, the proponents of court redistricting had made considerable headway. After several years pursuing their causes independently, representatives of the bar associations of San Jose, Sacramento, San Diego, and Fresno had united on a proposal to increase the number of judges as well as reorganize the boundaries of the present California districts.

Although they did not directly express their position, it soon became clear that the northern district judges favored new judgeships. But they opposed any efforts to alter the administration of their district by reorganizing its divisions because this would result in a requirement that court be held in a city other than San Francisco. At first, the judges made their opposition known on an informal basis. But over the years since 1948, as proponents of redistricting gained allies, the judges made more formal presentations of their opposition.

As early as June 1962, Judges Oliver J. Carter and Albert C. Wollenberg appeared before the San Francisco Bar Association Legislative Committee to express the northern district judges' views on hearing cases outside San Francisco. The Legislative Committee needed little deliberation to decide to support the judges' arguments that such a requirement would "tend to impair the flexibility and efficiency" of the court. The committee reported that the principal need of the court was not to sit in any of the central coast counties, but to have the present judicial vacancies filled promptly. Under the influence of the San Francisco Bar Association, the California State bar adopted this view completely.[12]

But in time, the San Francisco Bar Association's influence diminished on the issue of holding federal court exclusively in San Francisco. By April 1964, the state bar's Federal Court Committee for the Northern Section approved the creation of a division for the central coast counties within the northern district, "with the understanding that there would be [an] additional judge appointed" to care for the new division. The committee's action came despite Judge Alfonso J. Zirpoli's report against such a plan. Judge Zirpoli spoke for the northern district judges in opposing such an arrangement. The committee's recommendation was not adopted by the state bar. Rather, the committee was instructed to study further the question of holding court outside of San Francisco, as well as the need for additional judgeships.[13]

The San Francisco Bar Association's eight-member Special Committee on Federal Courts supported the state bar by releasing a study of the proposed central coast counties court. The study quoted Chief Judge Harris's opposition to a San Jose court plan. The new fourteen-million-dollar Federal Courthouse in San Francisco and the increased cost of providing federal facilities and personnel for courts in other cities would be prohibitive, argued Harris. Added to the cost factor was an assumption reflected in the committee's finding that a "centralized multiple judge court is best for the efficient administration of justice, particularly for the San Francisco Bay Area." However, the committee did no more than state this axiom, it produced no evidence to support it except the suggestion that the city was the "most sensibly located hub" of the area, with rapid transportation readily available. The committee specifically cited a letter written by Chief Judge Harris. In it, he argued that holding court outside San Francisco was "both uneconomical and unwise." Not only would it affect the administration of justice with varying court rules for attorneys in the area, but it would cause confusion as to the geographical jurisdiction of the courts. He expected the result of the court sitting outside

San Francisco would be a reduction in the uniformity and harmony in the decisions at the trial court level, as well as a decreased specialization and interaction between the area's district judges.[14]

The resolutions against court sitting outside of San Francisco left proponents of redistricting with one enduring conviction: that the resolutions were a "San Francisco decision" demonstrating the powers of the San Francisco judges and the city bar. The Santa Clara County Bar Association found that a "small group of lawyers and judges in San Francisco oppose this federal court in San Jose for self-serving reasons and pride." One northern district judge who sat in Sacramento warned Bob Beresford that the San Francisco federal judges wanted to stop the proposal for court outside of San Francisco and that they had determined that the San Francisco Bar Association would make the best case against the proposal in lobbying Congress and the state bar. This suspicion was reinforced by the perception that the San Francisco lawyers benefited by keeping the federal court from San Jose. After all, the San Francisco attorneys would lose federal court referral work from the central coast counties if the court were to hear cases in those counties. Circuit Chief Judge Richard Chambers warned that the "strongest opposition" to the San Jose court would come not only from the northern district judges in the city, but also from the San Francisco newspapers and the San Francisco lawyers.[15]

The opposition mounted by Chief Judge Harris as advocate for the San Francisco judges' views played an important part. No doubt he shared his colleagues' feelings that San Francisco was the center of the northern district universe, and he expressed this feeling both formally and informally. Yet his efforts against the San Jose measure lacked what some of his colleagues displayed: the conviction that sitting in San Jose would be ruinous to the court. Harris did all he could conveniently do to defeat the proposal. Letters, telephone calls, and conferences in chambers were his weapons. It was left to other judges to represent the court in situations were there was the possibility of confronting the opposition directly. Other judges appeared before the bar to argue against the San Jose proposal — not Harris. To proponents of the San Jose court, the chief judge's actions indicated an opposition not as inflexible as displayed by some of the other judges. They considered Harris more neutral and vaguely sympathetic of the needs expressed by San Jose court proponents. Even now, proponents recollect the vigorous opposition of some of the judges, but do not recall anything of the sort on the part of Chief Judge Harris.[16] Some suggest that his detached concern was a way of encouraging negotiation between the judges and proponents of a San Jose court. It could also have been that his benign stand was a cover for some greater plan to frustrate the movement for a federal court to be located in San Jose.

By 1965, the northern district judges' position reached a turning point. Their past tactics to defeat efforts to have their court sit outside San Francisco had been based on two beliefs: (1) maintaining the support of the San Francisco Bar Association was sufficient to influence the state bar (and through it, the state congressional delegation); and (2) the views of local district judges on issues of local court administration would be accorded deference by Congress and by the various administrative bodies of the judicial branch. Neither of these factors proved true in 1965. The increasing expertise that redistricting proponents had gained in the political process as well as the changes in the national political climate reduced the influence of the district judges on the issue of court redistricting.

After defeats in their efforts to secure ready access to a federal forum in San Jose prior to 1963, the Santa Clara County bar united with other county bars in California with similar concerns and agreed on one common federal court redistricting plan for the entire state. The plan tied the prospect of obtaining new federal judgeships in existing districts to an alteration of the district boundaries. The plan helped the redistricting proponents' proposal win endorsement from a majority of the California congressional delegation. Additionally, it provided the state's non-metropolitan bar associations with more leverage over the powerful municipal bars of San Francisco and Los Angeles.

The United States Judicial Conference was more willing to make its own independent policy judgments that might affect the local district courts, even though each district was not directly represented at the conference. This came at a time when the protection of civil rights in district courts of the southern states was accorded great attention. The conference occasionally directed administrative action at which the local district courts might balk. Holding northern district court proceedings outside San Francisco did not directly involve a civil rights issue. But the resources, time, personnel, and expertise the conference and its staff had gained in the southern civil rights struggle were now used to evaluate the need for changes in the district courts, including the northern district court. The committees and the conference would no longer simply defer to the district judges in reaching a position on legislation affecting particular districts.

Consequently, the conference was willing to take action affecting the northern district of California although the district's judges might resist. Another aspect of the conference's growing expertise was a preference to administer the court system internally, rather than defer to Congress. The conference preferred that Congress leave the internal organization of a district to the judiciary; as a result, it approved congressional legislation regarding judgeships and redistricting in California but suggested that Congress not legislatively create a division for that court at San Jose. Instead, to retain the support of the Santa Clara County bar, the conference reached an understanding with the Ninth Circuit's chief judge that his Circuit Council would mandate that the northern district judges establish a rule division south of San Francisco.

S. 1666, an omnibus judgeship bill which also reorganized California's federal courts, was introduced by Senator Olin Johnston of South Carolina on April 1, 1965, at the request of the Administrative Office of the United States Courts. The Administrative Office incorporated in this legislation the United States Judicial Conference's recommendations on the San Jose court. However seventeen days later, Olin Johnston died, leaving his bill stalled and leaving vacant his chairmanship of the Senate subcommittee which would debate the measure: the Subcommittee on Improvements in Judicial Machinery. Yet, nearly two months later, the full Senate Judiciary Committee unexpectedly passed S. 1666. No hearing had been held on the bill. Even experienced Capitol watchers were surprised by its swift progress through the Senate since Senator Johnston's death.

Movement on the bill continued to be swift in the upper chamber under the leadership of the subcommittee's new chairman, Senator Joseph Tydings of Maryland. Before Tydings brought S. 1666 to the Senate floor for consideration, California's senators Thomas H. Kuchel and George Murphy ignored the California State bar's request that they oppose the measure. Because the senators would do nothing to stop the bill, the state bar acquiesced in its inevitable passage.

S. 1666 passed the Senate on June 30 with no objections expressed to its provisions on the San Jose court. Indeed, the measure passed the Senate on a quick and simple voice vote. In this scramble to get on the bandwagon for its passage, no one was left standing up for the northern district judges. Consequently, no opposition to S. 1666 was

*Judges of the United States District Court for the Northern District of California in the late 1960s. From left to right are Judges Albert C. Wollenberg, Lloyd H. Burke, William T. Sweigert, Alfonso J. Zirpoli, and Robert F. Peckham. (Courtesy Judge Robert F. Peckham.)*

reflected in the bill's legislative history. Reading the Senate record of its passage, no one could imagine that anyone opposed the San Jose portion of the bill.[17]

With the bill's passage, the San Francisco judges faced a difficult choice. The developments in Congress, in the bar, and in the judiciary had isolated the northern district judges from a meaningful role in the debate over legislation affecting their district. To regain some leverage, the judges considered their involvement in politics. Their choice was to become more active in presenting their views. With Senate passage of legislation which might force the court to sit in San Jose, the judges would have to find some way to stop the measure as it went for a hearing in the House of Representatives.

For Chief Judge Harris, stopping the bill was probably a difficult, distasteful duty. Not only did he claim to have a constitutional dislike of politics, but he was forced to enter a controversy the district judges appeared to be losing. In addition, stopping the bill in the House involved going before the public with their opposition. This rubbed against the judges' concept of their role in the government. It was their misfortune that the continued and exhaustive efforts of the San Jose court proponents had transformed an issue of court administration into something much broader. It had now become an issue of geographical politics, pitting older, more established urban areas against the younger and still rising outlying areas. To oppose the San Jose court publicly would mark the judges as partisans of the urban areas in the political dispute between regions in the district.

It was a situation in which the judges were forced to bend their concepts of the proper conduct for a judge. One northern district judge admitted: "Had we wanted to become politically involved, we could have gone to congressional committees earlier with statistics, or appeared before the Judicial Conference. But this was a political matter we viewed with distaste."[18] The judges had a distinct reluctance to attempt to lobby the Congress publicly on a legislative issue.

Yet even this reluctance was rooted in politics: it shielded the judges from any close examination of their views. It was not inappropriate that the judges speak out on the issue of where court should sit. But the judges politicked sparingly because of a suspicion about politics and a belief that they had no role in the political world. Explained a northern district judge, his colleagues had "a great reluctance to enter into public debate" because "judges have no forum. They feel they can't communicate. Their motives are suspect." Consequently, the "courts because they are courts are terribly disadvantaged" in going before the public on legislative matters.[19] To preserve the public perception of their role in government as one of inherent authority and unquestioned reasonableness, the judges were circumspect and calculated in their use of political tools.

The judges' reaction to the Senate's passage of S. 1666 was well measured and vigorous. The reaction caught proponents of the San Jose court off guard. "I thought perhaps the passage of the bill by the Senate would put San Francisco [federal judges] to rest, but apparently it did not," exclaimed Russ Roessler. Far from resting, the judges seemed madly awakened by the bill's passage. The day S. 1666 passed the Senate, Chief Judge Harris sent a letter to Emanuel Celler. Celler's subcommittee would consider the bill on the House side. The chief judge made an effort to stop the bill, even though he could no longer be discreet in doing so. Harris's letter of June 30, initially drafted by Judge William T. Sweigert, was cosigned by his colleagues. The letter discussed several reasons why S. 1666 should not be passed by the House. The judges' resentment about the entire matter was apparent. "Whatever the source of the pressure for this legislation may be," they warned Congressman Celler, "we find it difficult to understand how anyone . . . would be willing to impose this legislation on our court." Because Chairman Celler had introduced a House version of S. 1666, the judges modified this criticism slightly by suggesting that one not "aware of our local situation" might not appreciate the "obvious enormity" of the problem that the bill created for the northern district court.[20]

The judges framed their arguments on the view that the politics of a self-interested group was interfering with the discretion judges normally exercised in administering their own district court. The judges felt eminently able to make decisions as to where the court should hear cases, and San Jose was not one of those places. They argued the reasonableness of their decision at considerable length, but it was a gloss to two unstated but strongly implied arguments which would not escape Celler's attention. The bill, they claimed, threatened to disrupt the independence of district judges to administer their district without the interference of various "pressures" which played so strong a role in the political process. To allow those pressures to succeed would be to force the judges into politics to maintain the independence of their administrative decisions: an administrative process would be transformed into a political one.

But even if local court administration should be subject to such political pressures, the question remained how such a change in the local court rules should be undertaken.

The judges objected to the substance and the form of S. 1666. They felt it would rob them of the opportunity for a hearing into why they administered their district as they did.

The judges correctly claimed that S. 1666 was the result of a report adopted by the Judicial Conference in March 1965, which agreed that if statutory divisions and residence requirements for judges sitting at San Jose were removed from Congressman Edwards's bill on court organization, the conference would administratively accomplish Edwards's goal of a court division located in San Jose. Upon enactment of the legislation, the conference would request the Ninth Circuit Council to "administratively designate judges of our district to reside and have their official stations . . . at San Jose." The judges pointed out that this conference report "was approved despite the fact that the judges of the Northern District of California have constantly taken the position that no such changes are needed or even administratively tolerable."[21]

Part of the judges' letter implied that administration of the local court was becoming political. Decisions on court administration would be based on political pressures rather than on sound administrative discretion. In addition, the Judicial Conference intended to direct the administrative policies of the northern district without consulting the local judges. In part, this was because the northern district judges were not directly represented on the United States Judicial Conference, which purported to direct a revision in the northern district's rules; the only district judge from the Ninth Circuit on the Judicial Conference was from Oregon. No one seemed interested in the district judges' view. "No notice of this resolution [by the conference for a San Jose rules division] was ever given to the district — none whatever. There was no chance for us to appear" to contest the resolution, complained Judge Carter.[22]

In short, the judges were excluded from their rightful role in debating the matter of a San Jose court. They were left to engage in the type of politics employed by proponents of the San Jose court. It was judicial administration by politics, not policy. All of this, the judges implied was a somewhat irregular manner of court administration and one that lacked proper authority. The judges did not dispute the authority of Congress to make what they regarded as an unwise decision, nor their duty to obey it. But they did dispute the authority of the Ninth Circuit Judicial Council to compel the district judges to manage the district court in an "unworkable and demoralizing" manner.[23]

Chief Judge Harris and his colleagues bolstered their case against the form of judicial administration underlying S. 1666 with a lengthy discussion of the inadvisability of the understanding reached by the Judicial Conference. Referring especially to the March 25, 1965, report of the San Francisco Bar Association, they indicated there was "neither need nor justification for the northern district to hold court at . . . San Jose." The judges charged that hearing cases outside San Francisco would be costly, amounting to over 1.2 million dollars, excluding expenses for United States attorneys, clerks, marshals, and other supporting personnel. This was a considerable expense in an effort to reduce the commute time and costs incurred by San Jose attorneys in a one-hour train ride to San Francisco. "A check by the clerk of our court . . . reveals that out of 519 cases filed during the first quarter of this year, there were only 31 cases in which any attorney of record was located in any of" the four central coast counties, the judges argued. "We are certain," they claimed, that based on these facts, "it would take decades, if not centuries, to equate net savings of minutes or cents, if any, for a few lawyers with the huge, unnecessary outlay of federal money that will be required" if the court were to sit in San Jose.[24] This argument ignored the real possibility that litigants from the central coast area were compelled to undergo the burden and inconvenience of taking their cases to San Francisco firms rather than using local firms. Because the court itself was located in faraway San Francisco, that city's bar would be looked to before the local bar.

Yet there was another argument. Court at San Jose would "result in an unworkable and demoralizing fractionation of the business of our court, with its long-established San Francisco headquarters. . . . There are bound to be difficult and unnecessary problems concerning administration, uniform rules and policy, and efficient utilization of judicial manpower, not to mention the vexing problem of venue of actions as between the proposed . . . practically adjacent city courts" of San Jose and San Francisco.

Given these factors, the judges indicated they would not compromise. It was more than just judicial work load that formed the basis of their objections to sitting in San Jose, and therefore, their position against the San Jose court "stands, regardless of how many additional judges the Congress sees fit to provide for our district."[25]

The judges did not simply ask the defeat of S. 1666. Rather, their strategy was slyly political. They asked Chairman Celler to allow them "to have a full and meaningful opportunity" to make their case before the Judicial Conference. Because the conference's resolution formed the basis for S. 1666, the judges wanted the chance to present their arguments to the conference before its resolution "with respect to the holding of federal court and judicial residence at San Jose . . . may become the predicate of congressional enactment." They were asking for two things. First, that Congress delay to provide the judges an opportunity to air their views in a nonpolitical context. Their second purpose probably was more political. Within the California legal community there were rumors that since 1962, the chief counsel of the House Committee on the Judiciary, William Foley, and Chairman Celler were "very angry" with Ninth Circuit Chief Judge Richard Chambers. Chambers had opposed Celler's 1962 bill, H.R. 6690, which allowed some of the district court judges to sit on circuit councils. At that time, the circuit judicial councils included only the appellate judges, even though they considered administrative problems of the district courts. The bill received the approval of the United States Judicial Conference, unanimous approval by the House Committee on the Judiciary and by the House of Representatives. It also passed the Senate Committee on the Judiciary without objection. But the bill never emerged from the Senate. Chambers's Ninth Circuit Council came out against the bill and he waged "an active campaign at random among the members of the Congress, including an organized effort of letters and telephone calls" in order to defeat it. One consequence of this was that hard feelings arose between congressional leaders and Chief Judge Chambers. Senator Olin D. Johnston and Congressman Emanuel Celler lost some of their prestige as effective leaders when Chambers managed the defeat of their bill. Feelings were especially hard between Chairman Celler and Chief Judge Chambers. One circuit judge noted that it was the Ninth Circuit and Chief Judge Chambers who were "particularly strenuous in opposing [H.R. 6690], when they themselves had suggested it in the first place." Celler never referred to the disagreement or anger he felt towards Chambers. Chambers only said of it, "I wouldn't attempt to explain Mr. Celler."[26]

Aside from this tension, there were rumors that Celler was seeking some way to scuttle S. 1666. Bob Beresford heard that "Congressman Celler is personally hostile to the new districts in California. It was . . . suggested that Mr. Celler was receptive to the intervention of the Department of Justice, as a ground for inaction" on bills establishing a San Jose court.[27]

Judge Harris and his colleagues' letter to Congressman Celler was politically astute.

They complained of lack of participation in decisions regarding administration of their district, a matter which Celler had tried to remedy in 1962 and 1963. The problem was simple: the district judges had no representation in deciding matters vitally affecting the administration of their district. Their arguments implied that had they been represented and had they been allowed to present the facts on the San Jose court question to the Judicial Conference, those groups would not have decided as they did. This was an issue on which Celler was especially sensitive and interested.

To defeat S. 1666, the northern district judges did not ask for a direct vote against the measure. Instead, they asked only for delay so that they could make their case. Rumors had it that Celler was not anxious to see the San Jose measure make headway in Congress. In the years previous to 1965, Celler had taken actions that did not enhance the likelihood of such bills passing his committee. He accepted S. 1666 as a viable measure only after it had so unexpectedly passed the Senate.

The San Francisco judges asked for time to present their case to the appropriate judicial meetings. This would allow them to explore other means of opposing S. 1666 and to build an opposition to the measure. Emanuel Celler's reply to Chief Judge Harris's letter is not known, but Celler did take actions which, in effect, acceded to the judge's request. Celler delayed hearings on the bill. Eventually he had his subcommittee schedule the bill for hearings after the Eighty-eighth Congress had adjourned.[28]

But Celler had other reasons to delay hearings: he could not afford to spend time on the San Jose bill. His committee struggled with reapportionment bills and new immigration measures. So the San Francisco judges had the time for the hearings they requested. Beginning that July 1965, the judges could choose between several forums for presenting their views against the San Jose court. They could urge the Justice Department to join them in opposition. The department could be an especially useful ally. Celler was rumored to be awaiting Justice Department opposition as an excuse for tying up S. 1666.[29] The judges could also try to add the Ninth Circuit Judicial Conference to the ranks of opponents to S. 1666. Another possibility was to appear before the House Committee on the Judiciary to present their case directly. Finally, the judges had the opportunity they explicitly requested. They had the chance to go before the United States Judicial Conference in Washington, D.C. that August to seek changes in the conference's resolution supporting court in San Jose.

So there came a delay in the progress of S. 1666 through Congress. But the judges probably did not realize the extent of that delay. Chairman Celler revealed his plans for a hearing on the measure only in August — more than a month after the judges had sent their letter to him. Prior to that time, the bill was merely "pending" in his subcommittee, but not scheduled for hearings.

After the letter to Celler, Judge Harris sent the attorney general a similar letter. He requested that the Department of Justice oppose the provisions of S. 1666 concerning the northern district court in San Jose. The response to this letter must have been disappointing. A month after the department received Harris's letter, the attorney general responded that the department "normally defer[s] to the views" of the United States Judicial Conference and would not generally depart from this tendency.[30] Because the conference supported S. 1666, it seemed likely that the department would fall in line and not enter the battle against the San Jose portion of the bill.

Eventually, the Justice Department decided to come out in opposition to the bill. But the attorney general opposed only that section creating new districts in California and did not take a position concerning the northern district court sitting in San Jose. When the Department of Justice position was announced, Harris asked the department to reexamine the San Jose provisions in the bill. Surely the department would oppose the "wasteful and administratively intolerable" requirements these provisions would impose. Writing to Attorney General Nicholas deB. Katzenbach, Harris urged the department to at least request "that the provision for redistricting be amended out of the bill pending presentation of the matter to the United States Judicial Conference for further consideration."[31]

But this appeal had rather hopeless prospects. United States Attorney Cecil Poole in San Francisco had filed reports with the department on the evils on the San Jose proposal. But these reports and the judges' opposition did not move the department to take active steps. The department would not alter its position to include objections to court sitting at San Jose. Worse still in the judges' view, the department did not emphasize its opposition to the parts of S. 1666 with which the attorney general had difficulties. It was clear the department would offer no pretext for Chairman Celler to delay consideration of S. 1666, or to prevent its passage.

Although the attorney general offered the judges no assistance, Russ Roessler suspected the judges would win allies elsewhere: the mid-July Ninth Circuit Judicial Conference. This conference was composed of the Ninth Circuit's circuit and district judges and attorney-representatives from each district. Unlike the Circuit Judicial Council (composed only of the circuit judges), the conference was merely advisory. The *council*, not the *conference*, had the authority to overview operations of the districts.

The San Francisco judges attended the conference. During its sessions, Chief Circuit Judge Chambers openly discussed his expectation that with passage of S. 1666, the northern district court would hear cases in San Jose. But there was no debate or dispute on this matter. None of the northern district judges present expressed their strong views on this issue. The judges refused to make their case to the Circuit Conference because they believed the meeting an inappropriate place to do so. As Judge Chambers explained: "In the Circuit Judicial Conference, there are three lawyers per judge. There is a definite tendency to eschew matters that only concern a portion of the circuit. Phoenix lawyers or Las Vegas lawyers going to the Circuit Judicial Conference feel they should keep their noses out of a local problem." Whether the northern district court went to San Jose was considered a local problem.[32]

Northern District Judge Oliver Carter explained his colleagues' acquiescence at the Circuit Conference with a similar explanation. It would be rather unseemly for the judges to wash their judicial laundry in front of the attorneys attending the sessions. Besides, the judges felt that "going before the conference would have produced debate with no result." The conference had no power, only the Judicial Council did. In this view, Judge Carter was technically correct but politically wrong. If the San Francisco judges hoped to impress on Chairman Celler the degree of opposition to the San Jose court, an adverse decision from the Circuit Conference could be helpful. But they wanted to avoid the open politics used by San Jose court proponents. They wanted to end the problem of sessions in San Jose finally, and with one swift stroke. The prospect of a long and loud public dispute (and the distinct possibility of losing the contest) was understandably unattractive to them.[33]

The judges' refusal to employ open politics was apparent after Celler scheduled subcommittee hearings on S. 1666. Congressman James C. Corman of California, a member of Celler's subcommittee, invited Harris to testify on the bill. In all probability this was an indirect invitation by Celler himself, since the chairman, not the subcommittee members, had the responsibility to arrange for witnesses' testimony. In August Celler announced his intention to hold hearings on S. 1666, after the close of the congressional session in September. But Corman's invitation to Harris dated from late July. Corman understood that Celler would hold the hearings on an unspecified date. While there is no clear evidence of Corman's intent, his letter appears to be a feeler — an attempt to see if Harris would press his opposition to the bill.

Harris declined to testify. "Our preoccupation in disposing of a very lengthy trial calendar precludes us from a personal appearance," the Judge wrote. But this refusal to testify did not mean the judges' position went unnoted at the subcommittee's hearing. Their letter to Celler was referred to by other witnesses. In addition, Celler included a copy of Harris's letter in the hearing record.[34]

Probably the failure of the northern district judges to testify was a result of their reluctance to openly air judicial disputes. The need to "reduce the intensity of the intra-judicial fighting" was foremost in the minds of many judges. In all probability, Judge Chambers had expressed a need for such discretion.[35]

Celler's timing of the hearing on S. 1666 gave the San Francisco judges one advantage. They had requested a delay until they could bring their case before the United States Judicial Conference. The conference allowed nonmember district judges to make presentations and to participate in debates on the issues directly affecting their districts: precisely the opportunity for which they had argued. The conference would meet in Washington, D.C. on September 22 and 23, 1965 — a week before the hearings Celler had scheduled on S. 1666. Had the San Francisco judges made their position — especially the intensity of their opposition to sitting in San Jose — clear, the conference might have reconsidered its position or might have withdrawn its support for S. 1666 pending further study. Such an action would have doomed the chances of the San Jose portion of S. 1666 passing Celler's subcommittee before the end of the congressional session.[36]

The United States Judicial Conference met that September, discussed S. 1666, and revised several of its previous recommendations to Congress on the bill. These revisions did not touch on the issue of San Jose. The conference never reconsidered the San Jose dispute because none of the San Francisco judges appeared. Apparently they made no effort to have their objections considered.[37]

The failure to present their case to the United States Judicial Conference — although it was precisely for the reason of presenting their case there that they had asked Chairman Celler to delay House action on S. 1666 — doomed any hope that Celler would directly act to satisfy the judges' objections to the bill. Perhaps the northern district court's calendar was so crowded as to forbid an appearance by a judge before the conference or before the subcommittee. But, given all the time and effort Harris and other San Francisco judges had devoted to behind-the-scenes lobbying on S. 1666, this was unlikely.

A one-day appearance before the subcommittee of the House Committee on the Judiciary or the Judicial Conference, even including the preparation time, could have been much more effective than all the letters Harris had written over three months. The failure to pursue the opportunity he had asked for was probably due to a belief that his pleading would be futile. For one thing, United States Supreme Court Chief Justice Earl Warren of California had, at the March meeting of the Judicial Conference, seemed against them. Indeed, Harris later received a copy of a letter the chief justice had written to Lemuel H. Matthews, president of the Bar Association of San Francisco. Warren told

Matthews that "California is such a large state, both geographically and population-wise, that the [United States Judicial] Conference decided it could not reasonably insist" on the organization of the federal courts that had prevailed there for so long.[38] The chief justice had approved of Judge Chambers's view that the Ninth Circuit Council have the northern district establish a rules division at San Jose. The San Jose proponents had gathered the united support of California congressmen of both political parties for the movement of the court to San Jose. The prospect of reversing the Judicial Conference's prior resolution probably seemed remote. Harris might have been unwilling to place himself in a position of losing this battle in public.

Judge Harris and his colleagues failed to take the opportunities they had to argue for the defeat of S. 1666 at the Circuit Conference, the United States Judicial Conference, and the House Committee on the Judiciary. As reluctant as they seemed, they were quite adept at finding allies to do battle for them. San Francisco Congressman Phil Burton was one such ally. Burton was serving his second term in the House, but was already known as a skillful legislator. His district office was located in the same building as the district court. Burton knew many of the judges quite well. For example, he counted Judge Oliver Carter as a personal friend; Carter had been state Democratic party chairman when Burton began his active involvement in politics years before.

Representing San Francisco's interests, Burton advanced the judges' arguments that they should not be compelled by the Circuit Council to hold court in San Jose. But, the ever-realistic Burton recognized that he "couldn't stop the bill" establishing the San Jose court. Indeed, he was inclined to vote for it "because I think we need more judges."[39]

The San Francisco judges tipped off Burton to a peculiar aspect of S. 1666's provisions on San Jose. There was no statutory guarantee that a judge would in fact sit in San Jose. As far as could be determined from the legislative language, the northern district court still had the discretion to determine if the volume of business warranted sending a judge to sit in San Jose. The only assurance the San Jose court proponents had that a court would be established there was their faith in Chief Judge Chambers. His political guarantee that the Circuit Council would direct the district court to sit in that city, supported by the political assurances of the United States Judicial Conference, were all that proponents had actually won after fifteen years of struggle. Mere authorization by Congress that the northern district judges could sit in San Jose would leave the judges free to decide this issue. Only in the light of its legislative history could S. 1666 be interpreted as mandating establishment of a court in San Jose. But an attempt would be made to alter this legislative history. So skillfully would the San Francisco judges be in this attempt that proponents of S. 1666 did not realize anything had happened to their bill until after it had passed the House.

Congressman Don Edwards could be justifiably proud of the results of this three years of labor for a San Jose court. S. 1666 seemed to be irretrievably on its way to passage. Accordingly, after consulting with Chairman Celler, Edwards scheduled the first of March for a brief break from his congressional duties. He would not be in Washington on the day S. 1666 would be debated on the House floor. But few could find any reason to doubt the establishment of a San Jose court with the eventual passage of S. 1666.

On his return, Edwards found that the San Francisco judges had struck in a most unexpected way. This was made clear to him when he reviewed the *Congressional Record* report of House passage of S. 1666. He found the debate in the House and his speech on the bill, which as was common practice, he had submitted for inclusion in the debates before he left Washington. His statement indicated the growth experienced by San Jose, the city's need for a federal court, and the fact that S. 1666 was designed to provide a judge for San Jose. "I was born in San Jose," the *Record* for March 2, 1966 had him telling the House. "I remember when the country was dotted with fruit trees. [But] now the industrial giants of the nation have huge plants . . . in Santa Clara." The area needed a court nearby to service the needs of these industries as well as the needs of the new communities. Accordingly, Edwards told the House, he was "most pleased that [S. 1666] provides for a resident federal judge in San Jose."

Edwards continued to read the *Congressional Record*'s version of the debate. He noted that Chairman Celler, who was managing the bill through the House, next allowed Congressman Phil Burton to make a statement. Burton asked the Speaker of the House for permission to revise and extend his remarks on the bill. This was readily granted. Then a most unusual thing occurred. Burton turned to Chairman Celler and said, "Mr. Chairman, I have a series of questions to pose in order that the intent of the Congress may be clarified." In effect, Burton was saying he was going to address how the courts should interpret the legislation which the House would pass. Burton asked Chairman Celler a series of six questions on the bill, all of which Celler answered with a simple yes. Burton's questions and Celler's answers undermined the careful compromise the United States Judicial Conference had reached. It seemed to erase the understanding Edwards, Chambers, and the United States Judicial Conference had that if Congress refrained from establishing a statutory court division at San Jose, then the Ninth Circuit Judicial Council would have the northern district court make a rules division there.

According to the *Congressional Record*, Burton asked Chairman Celler if the bill's intent was not to compel the judges of the northern district "to reside and hold their official stations at Oakland and San Jose [and that they would go to those cities] only upon independent investigation and finding that the public interest and the business of that court so requires." Celler affirmed this. Then Burton asked if "the mere authorization of the Northern District Court of California to sit in Oakland and San Jose does not carry with it a requirement that the court sit in these places?" Celler affirmed that it did not. This was followed by further questions by Burton and answers by Celler.

At the conclusion of the debate, the Speaker moved the House to a voice vote on the bill. As members voted, the Speaker declared that the bill had passed. But a dissatisfied member required that a roll call vote be taken. The results of this vote were 371 members for S. 1666, 23 against, and 39 not voting. Phil Burton voted for the measure. Don Edwards was recorded as not voting because he was not on the floor at the time of the vote.[40]

Burton's brief questions to Celler could have a devastating effect on the effort for a San Jose court. Essentially, Burton had asked the chairman of the committee that passed the bill to explain the legislation's intent. As such, this printed exchange of six questions and Celler's simple yes answer to each represented not just Burton's views on the bill, but became a statement of the collective understanding of the House before it passed the measure. This would be an important tool for understanding the bill's meaning.

There was one thing wrong with Burton's questions to Celler. They were not actually raised during the House debate. According to Congressmen George Miller and Jeffery Cohelan who were on the House floor during the debate, Burton had simply asked to extend his remarks. He never questioned Celler. Apparently, Burton later submitted the series of questions and Celler's answers as his remarks to be inserted into the *Congressional Record*'s version of the House debate. Therefore no member of the House had a chance to differ with the interpretation of S. 1666's impact. This attempt to rewrite the bill's legislative history without allowing an opportunity for San Jose court proponents to respond became known as "Burton's colloquy."

It was a masterful maneuver. How was it devised? The available evidence, while confused on this issue, suggests that the northern district judges were at the root of it. *San Francisco Examiner* reporter Tom Hall wrote that the strategy evolved "after a hasty meeting [of Burton] with the judges" of the northern district. Their purpose was to challenge the obvious "intent of the United States Judicial Conference [which] recommended to the Ninth Judicial Council . . . that when the bill was passed it make sure that judges be designated to reside and have their official stations at Oakland and San Jose."[41]

Some San Jose court proponents differed with this account. They suspected that Burton's "curve" was pitched on a more deliberate basis. They believed that the fact that the colloquy could appear at all showed that the House Committee on the Judiciary's Chairman Celler and Chief Counsel William Foley were never for the bill despite their earnest professions of support. Congressman Miller went to see Chief Counsel Foley after Miller discovered the colloquy in the *Congressional Record*. Foley told him that he allowed Burton to insert the colloquy to "save your bill" from defeat and that he was sure that Congressman Conway (from southern California and a member of the committee) had told Don Edwards of the colloquy and that Edwards approved. In addition, Foley asserted that although Chairman Celler had approved the colloquy, the chairman had not seen Burton's prefatory lines to it. These lines, as printed in the *Record,* stated that the questions Burton asked of Celler were posed "in order that the intent of the Congress may be clarified." But even were this the case, Burton's colloquy would have remained in the *Record* of the proceedings as the legislative intent.

But how did Burton develop the questions? Some believed that Northern District Judge Stanley Weigel was in Washington a few days before the March 2 debates in the House on the bill and proposed the colloquy's questions to Burton. In all probability, however, Burton's colloquy was neither a hastily arranged affair, nor solely the product of Judge Weigel's travels. In mid-January 1966, Northern District Judge William Sweigert phoned Congressman Burton to discuss the imminent passage of S. 1666 by the House Committee on the Judiciary. The judge repeated arguments from the judges' June 30, 1965, letter to Chairman Celler, especially its assertion that the Circuit Council had no power to impose the San Jose court on the northern district judges. The possibility of incorporating this assertion into the bill's legislative history was considered.

Congressman Burton asked "the judges to prepare as a personal favor . . . a statement . . . to clarify administrative problems and jurisdiction concerning the new places of holding court." The judges responded quickly. They considered how to best alter the bill's legislative history so that it avoided the problems they foresaw their district would suffer if a San Jose court were established with a full-time federal judge. They decided to propose a series of four questions "to be propounded by" Burton on the House floor. Judge Harris sent these questions, each on a separate sheet of paper, to Burton on January 27. He also enclosed a copy of the judges' June 30, 1965, letter opposing the bill.[42]

When he received these materials, Burton went to see Chairman Celler. Apparently, they discussed the tactic of the colloquy and its effect on the bill. Eventually, the questions were expanded from the four that the judges had suggested to six. The four questions the judges proposed were used without any substantial revision. The two added questions were to clarify the power of the northern district court to determine for itself where and when it would hold court. Chairman Celler consented to use of the colloquy.

151

The use of the six questions with his simple answer of yes to each "was clearly all right with Celler," claimed Burton.[43]

Given the existence of Burton's colloquy, the San Jose proponents were faced with the problem of reestablishing the proper legislative history for the bill. S. 1666 was premised on an idea that did not appear in its statutory language. Congress would not statutorily establish a division in that city, but the judiciary would use its own procedures to set up a rules division there. The understanding was clearly expressed in the existing committee hearings on the bill. As part of its legislative history, it would be interpreted with the statute and would compel the northern district court to sit in San Jose.

But Burton's colloquy touched on all the informal political arrangements designed to insure a judge would actually sit in San Jose. The colloquy negated all these political arrangements and left full discretion with the district judges as to whether they would sit in San Jose or not. The colloquy would have S. 1666 maintain the status quo, except that it allowed the judges to sit in San Jose if they so desired.

The assistance rendered by the San Francisco judges in the preparation of the colloquy indicated their political skill. They kept away from all situations where they would have to defend their views, yet they remained a potent force in the political process. They presented formidable opposition to the establishment of a San Jose court by their indirect methods of resistance. They objected not just to what they believed an ill-considered booster movement to bring the court to San Jose. Their objection was much broader: they objected to the Circuit Council directing the district judges in the administration of their court. Burton's colloquy was intended to suggest that Congress did not in fact support the court being forced to San Jose.

It took a considerable amount of work to undo the damage inflicted by the colloquy. After reading the colloquy, Chief Circuit Judge Richard Chambers wrote to Judge Harris with evidence he obtained from congressmen who had been on the House floor when the vote was taken on S. 1666. These congressmen wrote that Burton's colloquy did not in fact occur. Chambers then wrote to Harris, asking if any House member except Burton and Celler knew the contents of the colloquy before the vote was taken. He warned Harris that "two members of the House who were present . . . have told me they have no recollection of the actual colloquy between Mr. Burton and Mr. Celler and their first knowledge of it was on March 3 when they read the *Congressional Record* of March 2."[44] The implication was that if the colloquy never occurred on the House floor, the House would not have known of the Burton-Celler interpretation of the legislation's meaning before the vote on the bill. Thus, it could not be part of the House's understanding of the bill's purpose.

Apparently Judge Harris did not deny the obvious. Judge Chambers made the details of the transactions leading up to the passage to S. 1666 by the House, including Burton's colloquy, clear to the members of the United States Judicial Conference and judges on the Ninth Circuit Council. This would block anyone from citing the colloquy as an expression of congressional intent in passing S. 1666. The San Francisco judges had been outmaneuvered. But it would be premature to say that they were beaten.

While the judges were not able to eliminate the understanding that the Judicial Conference and the Circuit Council had about the legislation, they could still use their discretion in interpreting the legislation. The guarantees of Chief Circuit Judge Chambers and the Judicial Conference "were only as strong as the political power which could be brought behind them under a challenge by the sitting district judges in San Francisco," commented one observer.[45] The judges apparently never challenged that power directly. But indirectly they mounted a strong resistance against this attempt to bypass the ability of district judges to administer their district in the manner they deemed most efficient.

# 12

# The Court That Would Not Die

*Joseph Franaszek*

On November 15, 1966, the *San Jose Post-Record* reported an event long awaited by some and of considerable interest to many others. The editor reported that on November 10, "the induction of the first judge into the newly-created San Jose branch of the United States District Court" took place amidst "an impressive array of legal luminaries." Numerous friends and colleagues had crammed into the Santa Clara County Board of Supervisors' chambers to see the induction. By 4:30 that Thursday afternoon, all the judges of the United States District Court for the Northern District of California sat *en banc* as their chief judge conducted the impressive ceremony. The Ninth Circuit United States Court of Appeals judges, under the leadership of their chief judge, Richard Chambers, attended as well. So did a large contingent from the California Supreme Court and the First District of California Court of Appeals. Practically all the judges of Santa Clara County, and many judges from the other central coast counties were there, including Judge Robert Beresford, who had struggled for so long to bring about this moment. Never in the history of the region had so many judges gathered in one place at one time. Peckham, a "member of a long-time and well-known local legal family and one of the favorite jurists of the area" could take much satisfaction in this demonstration of respect.[1]

It was a well planned occasion. Chief Judge Chambers had been especially concerned about the ceremony. When Santa Clara County Federal Court Committee Chairman Russ Roessler checked with him about the San Jose location for the ceremony, Roessler asked whether the room was a satisfactory place for Judge Peckham's induction. Chambers felt the room was excellent but warned Roessler to make sure the room was equipped with "bench chairs that look like bench chairs."[2]. The northern district court should have no grounds for finding fault with this new site.

*Chief Judge George B. Harris swearing in new United States District Court Judge Robert F. Peckham, November 15, 1966. (Courtesy Judge Robert F. Peckham.)*

The induction ceremony had a long history — going back to the time of the northern district's first judge, Ogden Hoffman, who had taken the oath of office in San Francisco in 1851. Hoffman was the last federal judge to hear federal court in San Jose. He discarded the practice in 1853 because of lack of business. But in 1966, after a lapse of over a hundred years, the practice of holding court in San Jose was to be restored.

The chief judge of the northern district court, George B. Harris, led the ceremony. Harris had the clerk of court read Peckham's commission from President Lyndon B. Johnson. Immediately following this, the chief judge and the federal judge designee stood before a long bank of curtains. The men raised their hands. A photographer's camera flashed as Harris asked Peckham to swear to faithfully execute the office of district judge and protect the Constitution of the United States. A slight smile appeared on Peckham's face as he answered and Harris seemed to glance back with knowing pleasure.

Now the tributes began. Chief Judge Harris set the tone when he told spectators that "Judge Peckham comes to us as a professional in every sense of the word" having manifested in his career, "a compelling fashion to do justice." California Supreme Court Justice Phil Gibson echoed this, telling the audience that the new district judge had been a Stanford Law School classmate of Gibson's wife. He and his wife found Bob

Peckham to have "common sense and courage and an intuitive feeling . . . for justice," clearly important qualities to find in a judge.[3]

The president of the Santa Clara County Bar Association, David Adams, continued this train of thought and outlined the history of the ceremony. He recalled that "some eighteen years ago, in 1948, when I was a partner with Bob Beresford . . . Bob said to me . . . 'Dave, what we need in San Jose is a federal district court.' Bob was not one to have an idea and do nothing about it," Adams told the amused audience. He explained the hard work Beresford started and that Russ Roessler continued. Roessler's efforts finally culminated in the legislation to bring the court to San Jose.

But a problem existed, declared Adams. The northern district judges would find Bob Peckham to be not only a hard-working judge, but "one who will endear himself to them with his attractive, human qualities." Adams seemed to stop just a moment to size up his audience. "Our only fear," he suggested with a smile, "is that the San Francisco judges will become so fond of Judge Peckham that they will keep him in San Francisco."[4] The audience chuckled at this remark. They recalled the considerable agitation of the local bar over the rather abbreviated schedule the San Francisco judges made for Judge Peckham to hear cases in San Jose. Instead of a federal court meeting full-time central coast counties as had been expected with the passage of S. 1666, the plans for the San Jose court did the opposite. Judge Peckham would hear only transferred cases in San Jose. The district court administration made no concerted effort for permanent chambers for Peckham's court in the South Bay because Peckham would be there so infrequently. It was intended that his station be San Francisco. Any federal cases Judge Peckham scheduled for hearing in San Jose, he would hear on the fifth floor of the Santa Clara County Superior Court Building, where he had served as presiding judge just recently.

The spectators listened intently as three speakers addressed them on the importance of the event. All three speakers had played crucial roles in bringing about the ceremony. Judge Robert Beresford introduced the judges of the Ninth Circuit Court of Appeals to the audience. Then, attorney Russ Roessler, who had led the Santa Clara County Bar Association's effort for a San Jose court, commented on the long wait that the community had been through before it was recognized as a place where the northern district court should sit. This recognition was a result of the "joint efforts of our total community led by the bar, but with the solid support of business, labor, local government, press media, and our congressmen."[5] Eventually, Congressman Don Edwards, who handled much of the Washington strategy to get the San Jose court, got his say. He made some brief comments about the role of the legislature in the administration of the courts.

There now passed a long succession of speakers. Perhaps not a few in the audience looked forward to the reception to follow the ceremony. Then they could talk with friends and associates, recalling some of the past struggles to get the federal court to San Jose and the bright promises of this court for the future of the region. But one last speaker remained before the ceremony's end: United States District Court Judge Robert F. Peckham.

Before he introduced their neighbor, now a new federal judge, Chief Judge Harris reminded his listeners that "a person doesn't undergo any biological change merely because he happens to be elevated to the [federal] bench." The chief judge stepped aside and the new district judge stepped forward. Then, in his usual, self-possessed tone, Judge Peckham looked to the past and to his services on the "vital and harmonious" Santa Clara County Superior Court, perhaps foreshadowing a wish that his service on the United States District Court would equal that experience. He saw that his service as a United States judge in San Jose would give the "young and competent" bar of the area an opportunity for "increasing experience in the federal court."[6] This would take time, but it was inevitable.

As Judge Peckham looked out on all his friends and neighbors of so many years, and across to the new associates he would join on the district court bench, he may have indulged for a moment in his avocation of historical speculation. He probably did not escape the vague feeling that it had not been a straight path to his present position. As early as 1962, the Santa Clara County Bar Association had unanimously recommended him to President Kennedy for a district court vacancy. The Monterey County, Santa Cruz County, Palo Alto, and Sunnyvale bars had eagerly joined in this recommendation. The Kennedy administration had carefully considered his nomination, but in light of Republican pressure that not all of Kennedy's nominees under the 1961 Omnibus Judgeship bill be Democrats, had instead appointed the well-respected Stanley Weigel, a San Francisco Republican with liberal credentials.[7]

Consequently, when S. 1666 became law in March 1966, the bar took great interest in who might assume the new seats in the northern district. The proponents of the central coast court believed that the judge for that area must be sympathetic and sensitive to the region's needs. The central coast region expected to play a major role in the selection of the judge to sit in San Jose. California's two United States senators were Republican. The Democratic president was unlikely to ask them for advice on the judicial appointment. But the House delegation had numerous Democratic members from the northern district area, and it was likely the administration would heed their recommendations. Because Congressmen Don Edwards of San Jose and George Miller of Oakland had played leadership roles in the battle to bring the court to San Jose and Oakland, their suggestions would carry considerable weight.

The Santa Clara County Bar Association resolved that a judge or practicing attorney from the central coast should receive the new judgeship in San Jose. Don Edwards anticipated this action and settled on Santa Clara County Superior Court Judge Robert Peckham. Edwards was on the California House Democratic subcommittee to determine who should be the nominee. The four other members of the subcommittee also represented parts of the northern district. The subcommittee had early on determined that the northern district judge for Oakland should be an attorney of that city; and the judge for the central coast should be one of the judges of Santa Clara County.[8]

Judge Peckham was especially suited for the federal bench. The Peckham family had been among the earliest to settle in the San Jose area. They also provided the early leadership of the region's legal life. The founder of the Peckham line in California and the man for whom Robert Peckham had been named, had come West by sea from Rhode Island in 1846. He was considered one of the wittiest and most versatile practitioners of the law. His namesake a hundred years later did not differ from him in those respects. But where the founder had no formal education, his namesake received both undergraduate and legal education from Stanford University. The founder explored the world as a sailor, a merchant, a railroad official, a lumberjack, a judge, a farmer, and a mill operator. His namesake explored the world in a different way, through steady application of the law.[9]

After private practice in the Santa Clara area in the 1940s, he joined the staff of the United States attorney for the Northern District of California. His uncle, I.M. Peckham, had served as United States attorney, before the Roosevelt years. Soon after his thirtieth birthday, Robert Peckham became chief assistant-in-charge of that office's criminal division. He was respected as a fair but tough prosecutor. During his tenure as chief of the criminal division, he successfully prosecuted several important income tax evasion cases.

Robert Peckham's great-grandfather delivered a speech in San Jose in 1864 supporting Republican President Lincoln's reelection. The younger Peckham had different party loyalties. He was active in the Democratic party, serving at various times as state president of the Young Democrats, vice-chairman of the California Democratic Central Committee, and chairman of the county's Democratic Central Committee.[10]

In his private practice, he was a member of a law firm that had among its clients several labor unions. But by 1956 he wearied of the commute to San Francisco and installed himself in the Santa Clara County office of the firm. He preferred trial work and concentrated on eminent domain cases. In 1957, he was elected to the first board of trustees for the newly created Foothill Community College District; served in that position until his appointment to the bench. During his tenure on the board, the college's basic operations were established. Its first president — Calvin Flint, a nationally noted community college educator — was chosen; a two-campus site was designated and acquired for the college; architects were selected; and classes commenced. At the time of his resignation from the board, Peckham was serving as its president.

In 1959, Governor Edmund G. (Pat) Brown appointed him to a vacancy in the Santa Clara County Superior Court bench. Brown's judgment was ratified twice by the voters when they reelected Peckham to the judgeship without opposition. During his seven years in that position, he served two terms as presiding judge.

Before assuming his duties as judge, Peckham avoided being identified with any one faction of the Democratic party. In part, this was a function of his personality. He was noted for his moderation, well before he became a judge. When he had "played an active part in local Democratic party politics," he was noted for "exerting a beneficial moderating influence."[11]

Peckham's judicial role merely emphasized this natural tendency towards balance and moderation. Peckham had "served a thorough apprenticeship in the work of the federal courts" as an assistant United States attorney and as part-time United States commissioner in San Jose. His judgeship on the superior court had trained him in the ways of the judiciary. With this training and with his natural inclinations, he was ready to serve the people of the central coast in a new capacity.

In April 1966, a California Democratic delegation subcommittee met in Washington, D.C. to recommend to the president nominees for the northern district court. Although the subcommittee considered the legal skill and liberal credentials of possible nominees, whether the nominee lived in the central coast counties was a prime factor.

The subcommittee considered how the judgeship to be filled was created. It let those who worked to create the new judgeships play key roles in filling them. Congressman Miller indicated that Edwards had done most of the work to get the new judges so that court could sit in San Jose and Oakland, and Edwards was thus entitled to recommend an appointee.[12] The delegation agreed that Edwards's nominee should be recommended to the president.

Deputy Attorney General Ramsey Clark, who screened nominees to the federal bench, soon received word of the House Democratic delegation's decision for Peckham. Clark hoped to proceed on the appointment expeditiously. This would gratify San Jose court proponents, who hoped a judge would be sitting in San Jose before the year's end. He submitted Judge Peckham's name to the Federal Judiciary Committee of the Ameri-

Judge Robert F. Peckham and San Jose area Congressman Don Edwards in Washington in October 1966. This picture was taken during the confirmation hearings on Judge Peckham's nomination as the new judge for the United States District Court, Northern District of California. (Courtesy Judge Robert F. Peckham.)

can Bar Association and that committee promptly recommended approval of Peckham's nomination.

It was at a meeting with California Supreme Court Chief Justice Roger Traynor in San Francisco in early September that Peckham learned the good news. "The phones began to ring" and it was learned that President Johnson had submitted his name to the Senate as the next northern district court judge.[13]

Senate confirmation came more than a month later, after a trip to Washington to appear before the Senate Committee on the Judiciary. On October 5, at its 10:30 A.M. session, Judge Peckham was introduced to the committee by California's United States Senator George Murphy. Ewing Haas, a legislative aide to California's United States Senator Thomas Kuchel, read to the committee a warm letter of endorsement from the senator who was out of Washington. An amiable and short hearing ensued.

But the Senate hearing formed only part of this memorable trip. Judge Peckham and Congressman Edwards visited later with Chief Justice Warren. Warren was gratified with Peckham's nomination, but wondered about the bitterness with which the San Francisco judges greeted the success of S. 1666. "My friends on the [northern district] court in San Francisco are really put out with me," exclaimed Warren. "They may not forgive me for having supported S. 1666."[14]

But the feelings of the San Francisco judges were far from Judge Peckham's mind as he and Don Edwards talked at the Rayburn House Office Building. They stepped outside of a terrace facing the Capitol. A brisk wind from the West whipped the Capitol's flag straight out; in the distance, masses of clouds dominated the sky. The trees, not yet shedding their richly tinted leaves, seemed blurred because of the wind's action. The two Californians contemplated what the future promised both for them and for their community. Peckham extended his right hand to Edwards, with a genial and concentrated smile. The day had gone well. Edwards grinned back, knowing that it would not be long before his district would have its own United States district judge. The two men seemed unruffled by the brisk wind. It was calm for them, although turbulent elsewhere.

On September 12, 1966, the *San Jose Mercury* ran an editorial on Peckham's appointment, pointing to its advantages to the central coast region. It brought a "respectable and knowledgeable jurist who can be expected to do an excellent job" to the northern district court. Also, it could "almost certainly ensure establishment of a federal court in San Jose on a permanent basis." The *Palo Alto Times* of September 10 and the *San Jose Post-Record* of September 13 stated similar views.

In the mythology of American political science, a major struggle for one who becomes a United States district judge is the winning of that judgeship. What comes after is merely a process of keeping order in the court. Judge Peckham would have been particularly lucky had this been the case. As he came to the district court bench, he found himself facing several sensitive problems.

He had to balance multifaceted loyalties. He naturally wished to conform to the standards of the court and the expectations of his fellow district judges. But the other district judges' expectations encompassed not merely attitudes towards the disposition of one's caseload. They demanded that one uphold the dignity of the district court and have a loyalty to the court as an institution. Conforming to these norms would enable Judge Peckham to work harmoniously with his colleagues. But his San Francisco colleagues appeared to have one standard that Judge Peckham could not accept: the opinion that hearing court in San Jose on a frequent or regular basis permitted the San Jose judge to evade his rightful work load. For many of the San Francisco judges, hearing court in San Jose on a sustained basis was not in the best interest of the northern district court.

Judge Peckham could not accept this. He had a deep and abiding commitment to having the district court sit in San Jose, a commitment born of years of practicing law in the central coast area and sitting on the Santa Clara County bench. Many of the proponents of the San Jose court were his close friends. He realized that his name had been advanced by the San Jose court proponents because of his natural understanding for the region's needs. It would be unseemly to become a San Francisco chauvinist when he assumed the federal bench.

But the expectations of his district court colleagues often contradicted those of his valley neighbors. His colleagues on the district bench had not acquiesced to the San Jose court. They believed it would result in inequalities in the judges' work loads. They feared the growth of forum shopping by attorneys who would try to take their cases to San Jose. If this happened, the new judge would spend considerable time in San Jose hearing cases transferred there for the convenience of the parties. But Judge Peckham shared the San Jose proponents' conviction that the passage of S. 1666 necessitated the opportunity to make federal proceedings available to the people of the area. He should serve the central coast region, to the extent it needed such service, first. As time or events allowed, San Francisco should receive the remainder of Peckham's time . . . not the other way around.

Clearly, the passage of S. 1666 and Peckham's elevation to the district court bench did not put an end to the struggle for a San Jose court. It just changed the nature of that struggle, and to some extent, the actors in that struggle.

When the bill establishing Peckham's judgeship was signed by President Johnson, Ninth Circuit Chief Judge Richard Chambers celebrated its passage with some reflections on the politics of the judiciary. He recognized the range of future difficulties. He warned that the struggle was not over and that the only real change after the passage of S. 1666 was that a different set of people was then on the short end. For the moment, these people happened to be the San Francisco judges rather than the San Jose court proponents. This situation could soon reverse. Yet despite that danger, Chambers considered it "remarkable to get [the San Jose court proposal] through without more blood-letting." He did not yet counsel any active steps in the continuing war for a San Jose court. He tried to calm the growing fear that the San Francisco judges would not arrange for the central coast court in good faith. The judge suggested the San Jose court proponents await, not anticipate, the actions of the district court. "The function of the Judicial Council is supervisory," he maintained when some suggested the Ninth Circuit Judicial Council force the northern district court to immediately open operations in San Jose. The Circuit Council would interfere only if the district court disobeyed the resolutions of the United States Judicial Conference.

Initially, Chief Judge Chambers expected no problems in implementing the spirit of the Judicial Conference's understandings about San Jose. After all, establishing a court division by its rules in San Jose "was a matter of basic integrity" for the northern district court, given the position of the United States Judicial Conference on the matter. The important thing was to give the northern district judges time to adjust to S. 1666 and to take the necessary actions. "Popping off" about what the judges should do would be of minimal benefit.

Yet a question persisted for San Jose court proponents while the San Francisco judges remained silent on what would happen next. Even if Congress had authorized them to hold court in San Jose, could the judges of the northern district "attempt to sabotage San Jose"? Admittedly, the United States Judicial Conference allowed the judges considerable leeway in establishing a rules division at San Jose. Chambers had a simple answer to this concern. The San Jose proponents would be no worse off than they would have been under the legislation Don Edwards had introduced in which Congress established a division by statute in San Jose. "Keep in mind," he counseled Bob Beresford, "the same attempt [by the northern district judges] could have been made under the bill as introduced by Mr. Edwards in the first place. The chances of failure or success would have been about the same." With either statutory divisions or rule divisions, Beresford and his allies would have to fight to establish the local complements of the court — the probation office, the United States Attorney's office, and United States Marshal's office.

In short, the burden was still on San Jose. There was nothing that could easily correct the way the northern district judges administered their court. Passage of a law creating a court division had frequently been ineffective in establishing a federal court presence. The only way to make the San Jose court work was to demonstrate to the San Francisco judges that it was needed. "The absence of much actual or potential business" in the San Jose court would kill it, no matter how the rules of the court or legislation tried to lock it in.

161

It appeared that the northern district judges planned to put the San Jose court at a distinct disadvantage. Chambers warned Russ Roessler that some of the judges intended to start the San Jose court on the day Congress authorized the court to sit in San Jose. They would send a judge to San Jose "without staff [and other necessary resources] to prove that [the San Jose] court wasn't needed." But other San Francisco judges seemed uncharacteristically friendly to San Jose. Chief Judge Chambers concluded this was no change of heart, but indicated "that the judges of the San Francisco division intend to swamp the . . . San Jose division with love — in reverse." By smothering the San Jose court with lavish facilities and resources, the judges would demonstrate in a year or two that the San Jose court was an inefficient use of district funds. All expected that in the first few years of San Jose court, case filings would be low. Area attorneys were only beginning to learn about and use the district court.[15]

Chambers steered a careful course. He counseled against open fighting with the San Francisco judges until the San Jose court had taken root. His strategy was to keep the San Francisco judges from battling with San Jose court proponents. He believed that, with time, even the San Francisco judges would not deny the need to serve the central coast. To battle out the San Jose court question in 1966 would not only put Judge Peckham at a distinct disadvantage, it would risk uprooting the San Jose court before it was firmly established.

So Chambers bent over backwards to defuse controversy. For example, he interpreted deliberately hostile actions by the San Francisco judges as complying with S. 1666 and the United States Judicial Conference understanding on the San Jose court. This interpretation discouraged any San Jose effort to grapple directly with the judges.

Responding to the passage of S. 1666, the northern district judges formulated a new rule — Rule Two — allowing for a San Jose court. Unanimously adopted by the district judges as meeting "the intendments" of S. 1666, the rule provided that "all proceedings . . . for which venue lies in this northern district . . . shall be commenced and prosecuted at San Francisco." Proponents of the San Jose court wondered how cases would get to San Jose. The rule stated that cases must be transferred there. Civil cases could be transferred to San Jose if a judge found "that the convenience of parties and witnesses, in the interests of justice will be served" by such a transfer. Criminal cases required similar showing.[16]

Prior to this rule, Chambers had urged a different course. He had encouraged the judges to establish a court division in San Jose by using their rules. Chambers felt this was what the United States Judicial Conference resolution leading to the introduction of S. 1666 mandated. Apparently the judges reacted to this suggestion with considerable agitation. Chambers was taken aback. "If the letter of your judges . . . to me on the subject of 'rule divisions' [for San Jose and Oakland] had been written to me from Fresno or Sacramento," he wrote Judge Harris after a particularly sharp exchange, "I would regard it as explainable by the summer heat." Chambers reiterated his position that making a "rule division" was fundamentally a symbolic action and did not "amount to very much unless those making the rules are dedicated to making something out of the division." Yet this begged the question of whether the district judges were complying with the spirit of S. 1666 and the United States Judicial Conference report for a San Jose rules division.

Chief Judge Chambers avoided any dispute with the San Francisco judges about whether their Rule Two created a rules division (as the United States Judicial Conference expected, or was merely a transfer rule (as the district judges characterized their action). He simply told the judges to call it what they wished and that he would call it what he wished. He was willing to find that the northern district court had fulfilled its obligations regarding the San Jose court if the following elements were in the rules: (1) some designation of a territory, (2) a place for holding court in that territory, and (3) some rule "about what will be done with (1) and (2)." Because Rule Two did "provide for holding of some court at Oakland and San Jose . . . I expect to continue to refer to Oakland and San Jose as 'rule divisions' unless one of your number is prepared to enjoin me," he told the northern district judges.

Rule Two was consistent with the United States Judicial Conference understanding that a rules division would be established at San Jose, Chambers concluded, provided the judges allowed for a vigorous court there. Yet Rule Two was ill-advised and petty. "You are obviously going to get a San Jose judge and an Oakland judge within this fiscal year . . . you had no duty to take any notice . . . of those men [until] both qualify," he wrote Harris. But, Chambers told them, "I would have thought it better to at least per-mit [the San Jose judge and Oakland judge] to express their community viewpoints before acting [on Rule Two]. If I were Judge Peckham," concluded Chambers, "I would wonder why you were scared."[17]

Those whom Judge Peckham might wonder were scared were not at all unified on the San Jose court after S. 1666 passed the Congress. During the debates over adoption of S. 1666, the northern district judges maintained a unified opposition to sitting in San Jose. They warned they would not give any effect to the United States Judicial Conference expectation that the Ninth Circuit Council compel their court to sit in San Jose. They believed that only the district court had the power to administer the district and that it had the discretion to do this in the manner it found most efficient. The district judges believed the Ninth Circuit Council had no authority to direct the district court to sit in San Jose. Accordingly, the United States Judicial Conference resolution on the San Jose court was to be considered a mere recommendation. The conference could not bring the court to San Jose when the plain words of S. 1666 itself were silent on this proposition.

The judges were not alone in this view of the district court's powers. They received letters from attorneys on the controversies surrounding S. 1666, expressing alarm that "there seems to be considerable agitation to place some sort of supervision over our federal independent judiciary and to subject them to discipline by a super-disciplinary organization . . . within the judiciary. . . . " Allowing this would absolutely destroy the independence of the courts, according to these supporters. The district courts owed "their strength to their independence and freedom from fear of supervision by lawyers or by political groups."[18] This argument directly applied to the San Jose matter. Permit-ting a San Jose interest group, or the Ninth Circuit Council, to force the judges to sit in San Jose against their better judgment was a step towards weakening the district court's judicial independence.

The northern district judges fully explicated this view in a letter to Chambers ex-plaining their recently adopted Rule Two. The judges considered their duty unaltered by S. 1666. They must use the court's manpower, recently enlarged by the addition of two judges, one of whom would be Judge Peckham, "to provide for the fairest and most effective administration of justice in the cases within our jurisdiction." Only if a suitably heavy work load existed in San Jose would they allow a judge to hold court outside of San Francisco. To act differently risked wasting judicial manpower, the judges warned. "Whatever might be the countervailing pressures, political or otherwise," they would not "position any judge of our court (who would not want it anyway) to carry any less than his fair share of the work load." The judges emphasized that it was not a distain for San Jose but rather getting "our job done effectively and soundly" that dictated their Rule Two.[19]

After this firm statement of the power and right of judges to administer the district as they determined best, disagreements persisted among the northern district judges about the most effective utilization of judicial resources in the long run. This disagreement concerned whether the district court should permit the San Jose court a chance to prove itself.

Available sources indicate that the majority of the judges — Sweigert, Wollenberg, and Zirpoli agreed with Judge Weigel. Weigel argued in a July 7, 1966, letter to Harris that S. 1666 required no alteration in the operation of the northern district as to the location of court sessions. To reach this conclusion, he identified several crucial questions S. 1666 raised and answered each question in turn.

The first question was whether the bill required "that the official station or residence or regular assignment of any federal judge be in . . . San Jose or that there be United States courthouses and supporting judicial personnel" in San Jose. He found nothing in the language of the bill requiring this. The bill's history, including the United States Judicial Conference recommendation that no statutory division be created in San Jose, left the matter up to the northern district court. Any congressional intent that the court hold sessions in San Jose was merely in the nature of a suggestion, which the court was free to disregard. Weigel cited Burton's colloquy as support for this argument.

But what of the "understanding" between the United States Judicial Conference and "one or more interested members of the federal Congress" asked Judge Weigel. Did Congressman Don Edwards have a clear understanding from the conference that a rule division would be created in San Jose? Judge Weigel thought this question was irrelevant. He thought it would be improper "to substitute the product of an unofficial . . . understanding for the plain words of a statute." If directions for creating a rule division were not in S. 1666, the district court could not be compelled to create such a division.

Assuming the northern district court was free to decide whether sessions should be held in San Jose, then what standards should govern the issue? The only standard the judge found was that of "the public interest in the fair and effective administration of justice." Given that standard, the "purely political considerations" he found behind the effort for a San Jose court should be given no weight. Judge Weigel concluded that the evidence available in July 1966 indicated no "solid reason, in terms of public interest, for requiring that any judge . . . be officially stationed in . . . San Jose." All he could give was a resounding "NO!" It was important for the court to resist unequivocally pressures "which seem . . . political in nature, for stationing judges in Oakland and San Jose and for the waste of public funds which would attend provision of courthouses and personnel." The court's first duty was to further the fair and effective administration of justice. It should have no part in providing San Jose boosters with a federal judge and forum for their own political gratification.[20]

Judge Oliver Carter appeared to advocate a different position. He felt a session of the court should be held in San Jose beginning in 1967 and acted to arrange for such a session.[21] This was not entirely surprising: Chief Judge Chambers had once recommended him to the San Jose court proponents as a northern district judge who might support their efforts. However, Judge Carter joined his colleagues in opposition to moving the court from San Francisco. But his opposition never seemed unyielding. He was sensitive to the political nature of the determination of where court would sit. Once S. 1666 passed Congress, he felt it best to compromise on the continual demands of San Jose for a federal court presence.[22]

Accordingly, he urged the court to go to San Jose. It should provide the necessary court facilities and permit that region to demonstrate its need for the district court. If the court was not used, the Judicial Conference would not prevent terminating its session there.

The northern district court judges adopted a position on the San Jose court that was a compromise between the Weigel and Carter positions. Judge Harris secured this agreement, which was incorporated in the court's Rule Two. Like the Weigel position, the rule looked towards actual demonstrations of need for the court in San Jose. Court could sit there only as the work load in the region required. Where it was equally convenient for central coast parties to come to San Francisco as to go to San Jose, court would be held in San Francisco. But where it was shown that a hearing in San Jose was convenient to the parties, then the case could be heard there. Like the Carter view, it allowed for hearings in San Jose, and if the demand arose, would permit extensive use of court hearings there.[23]

The district judges insisted their Rule Two created no rules division in San Jose. They would never create a rules division there. All central coast cases would have to be filed in San Francisco. Behind Rule Two was a recognition of the difficult political background of the San Jose court and a refusal to bend completely to the pressures of those politics.

The judges felt compelled to maintain their publicly unified stand on the San Jose court. Therefore, they adopted Rule Two before Judge Peckham joined the court. In adopting the rule, the court hoped to indicate it would not submit to intense political pressures. It vindicated the court's concern about maintaining a fair and equitable division of the caseload. And in 1967, the judges maintained this fair division would not allow a judge much time in San Jose.

The proponents of the San Jose court were divided too. After the March 1966 approval of S. 1666 by Congress, many San Jose proponents had a forgive and forget attitude toward the district judges. But there were persuasive arguments to continue their militancy, especially after they discovered Burton's colloquy. A former northern district court judge (and now, as a result of S. 1666, an eastern district judge), assured Bob Beresford that insiders were "fully aware of the fact that this whole thing [Burton's colloquy] is as phony as a three dollar bill." The judge suggested Beresford "get one of your local newspapers to run a story or editorial on the subject, setting forth the facts, and then have Congressman Edwards put this story or editorial in the Congressional Record. . . . That ought to set the record straight." Beresford considered it, but he realized that the San Jose court proponents must learn to live with the San Francisco judges. The goal of the central coast bars should be directed towards the long-range prospects and developing "a happy relationship with" the judges to "help them adjust to the inevitable."[24]

Accordingly, the frustrating effort of trying to reach some informal accommodation and understanding with the San Francisco judges continued. The possibility of getting Superior Court Judge Robert Peckham on the district court bench was considered good. Although Peckham supported the San Jose court, he had substantial San Francisco support. Some expected that with Peckham's placement on the bench, the central coast bar's requests would not be received with quiet disdain.

Ultimately, as Russ Roessler explained in a television interview on September 16,

165

# Federal Court: A Snag

The decision of Chief Judge George B. Harris of the Federal District Court in San Francisco that San Jose shall have only circuit-rider federal justice is arbitrary and unwarranted

In addition it is contrary to the sense, if not the precise letter, of the legislation authorizing federal courts in San Jose, Oakland and other California cities.

Judge Harris for no discernible reason has determined that San Jose, Oakland and Eureka shall see a federal judge, dispatched by Judge Harris in San Francisco, only once every three months or so. This amounts to a denial of justice to the millions of Northern Californians who must file their actions in San Francisco—or else.

For several years, San Jose and the Central Coast area have provided an increasing volume of litigation in the Federal Court. The volume has grown to such proportions that Congress this year decided San Jose, among other cities, should have its own court. The nomination of a San Jose jurist, Superior Judge Robert F. Peckham, to the federal bench is evidence that the executive branch of the federal government concurred with the legislative in this judgment.

Now Judge Harris is attempting to frustrate the will of the Congress and the Executive branch of the government. His arbitrary and capricious efforts will be resisted.

*A San Jose commentary on Chief Judge George B. Harris's announcement of Rule Two, limiting federal court presence in San Jose. This editorial appeared in the* San Jose Mercury *on September 17, 1966. (Courtesy* San Jose Mercury News.*)*

1966, the test for a San Jose court would be its use. Citing the government agencies and the substantial firms of the valley, Roessler ventured to say that as soon as the court holds regular sessions in San Jose, it would "be busier than some of the other courts in California."[25] San Jose proponents felt that given a fair test, the San Francisco judges could not help but become converts to a San Jose court.

But the news of Rule Two convinced many San Jose court proponents that there would be no easy accommodation with the San Francisco judges. On September 17, 1966, the day after Rule Two was announced, a *San Jose Mercury* editorial blamed it all on Chief Judge Harris. The editorial claimed that the rule gave San Jose "only circuit-rider federal justice." The paper called the rule "contrary to the sense, if not the precise letter, of the legislation authorizing federal courts in San Jose, Oakland, and other California cities." The *Mercury* considered the "once every three months or so" sessions of the court in San Jose under Rule Two to be "a denial of justice to the millions of Californians who must file their actions in San Francisco, or else." The paper warned that the judges' continued opposition to the San Jose court, which "frustrate[d] the will of the Congress and the executive branch of the government," would be resisted vigorously.

# Who's On First?

"Don't worry, I'll cover all of the bases from here."

*Another commentary on Judge Harris's announcement of Rule Two. This cartoon appeared in the* San Jose News *on September 19, 1966. (Courtesy* San Jose Mercury News.)

One prominent San Jose attorney, Robert Morgan, wrote Judge Harris enclosing the *Mercury* editorial and confessed, "I cannot understand why the judges in San Francisco so stubbornly resist the legitimate request of lawyers and citizens of this county to have a federal court." The central coast prevailed over San Francisco's opposition in Congress. But now "to have that congressional authority frustrated by a private, clandestine, non-public decision by rule is certainly bitterly received." He warned that "you should know that there is a genuine bitterness in this community and that the Bar Association [of Santa Clara County] will not stop in endeavoring to be treated fairly and avoid domination by San Francisco interests in our legitimate requests."[26]

But not all reaction to Rule Two was negative. A Santa Clara County assistant district attorney wrote supporting Judge Harris and Rule Two, saying: "outlying courts are in some instances extremely inefficient and costly when compared with a centrally located court." He thought Rule Two struck a fine balance between the convenience of litigants and the costs to the public. "One of the common remarks heard in our county with respect to the possibility of a full-time federal judge" was "what on earth will he do all day, every day?" He urged the San Francisco judges to continue their resistance to the San Jose court, declaring "you certainly have the support of more than one lawyer in this county."[27]

The public reaction appeared to be against the San Francisco judges. The *San Jose News* ran a political cartoon on September 19, featuring a crusty Judge Harris in baseball uniform, standing on a pitcher's mound labeled "San Francisco." His back was turned to spectators and to two bases — one labeled "Oakland" and the other "San Jose." Another worried player pointed towards the San Jose base, apparently asking "Who's on first?" Player Harris told him, "Don't worry, I'll cover the bases from here." Harris indicated the pitcher's mound labeled San Francisco on which he stood. The cartoon implied that Harris would cover the needs of San Francisco, Oakland, and San Jose, by keeping all resources in San Francisco.

In an accompanying editorial, the *News* characterized Rule Two as a "rear guard action." It suggested that Harris must have little "grasp of the realities of the situation" if the San Jose area (with population of nearly one million) was entitled to the same circuit-riding treatment that Eureka (with population of twenty-eight thousand) received. The editorial called on the area's congressional representatives to "waste no time in straightening . . . out" the San Francisco judges' lack of compliance with S. 1666. Russ Roessler's reaction was that "the press is taking the hard line, and hopefully it will set the stage for our judge [Peckham]."[28]

Roessler wrote Bob Beresford that Rule Two need not be too upsetting. Judge Chambers probably convinced Roessler of this. "Initially," Roessler noted, "a San Jose judge can't keep busy until 10:00 A.M. on his civil business from the area. Alone, this would prove (falsely) that the San Francisco judges are right." Because twenty percent of the northern district's crimes arose in the San Jose area, Roessler was prepared to fight so that San Jose criminal cases would be heard in San Jose. Getting a full-time court in the area would require continued and careful work. It also depended "on how tough" Judge Peckham would be. The San Francisco judges could not stop Judge Peckham from making San Jose his first priority in holding court. "A San Jose judge will not be impeached for saying he is going to do his work in San Jose." Therefore, the focus should be on the business of the San Jose court. If Judge Peckham had cases to hear in San Jose, nothing could stop him from hearing them there. In addition, if the San Jose court had enough cases, the San Francisco judges might not object to Judge Peckham spending more and more time there.[29]

The only real assurance that San Jose would keep and develop its federal court was Judge Peckham. Judge Peckham concurred in Roessler's moderate views that it would be a slow process convincing the San Francisco judges of a San Jose court's usefulness. Soon after his nomination to the northern district bench, Peckham expressed his determination to "meet with my colleagues and discuss with them the problems and needs of this [central coast] area."[30]

He was well suited to the task before him. He was noted by those practicing in his court to be patient with everyone as well as courteous to their feelings. Even facing the most extreme provocations, he rarely displayed anger or even irritation. Most who dealt with him for any period of time came away with the impression that he carefully considered the arguments presented and refused to act from mere impulse or inclination. Russ Roessler commented that Judge Peckham "isn't the type of man who loses his patience."[31]

But Judge Peckham eventually did lose his patience. Those who knew him received a shock nearly three years after his appointment to the bench. The district court issued a "General Order of the Court Re: Rules of Practice, Assignment Plan and Inventory, Accounting and Reporting System." In it, the judges approved the report of their Rules

Committee switching the court from the master calendar system to the individual assignment system. The order was signed by Chief Judge Harris and all the northern district judges but one: Judge Peckham. Some dispute had occurred at the court and one judge refused to consent to the court's new direction.

Attorneys aware of daily life at the court could guess the cause for this disagreement: Judge Peckham was dissatisfied with the court's handling of the San Jose session. Yet many did not expect the judge to come to such an open disagreement with his colleagues. Judge Peckham had been the moderate voice on the district bench — one seeking compromise and accommodation. His dissent from the order could not be ignored. The court's rules had remained substantially the same since 1955, but with the growth of court filings, the judges considered revisions to help cope with the drastic increase in the weight and complexity of the cases they heard.

A long series of meeting began in 1966 with the August draft revisions of the court's rules; a second version was discussed in 1967. A third version, incorporating the change to the single assignment system was discussed in March 1969. Finally, at a meeting on June 5, 1969, rule changes were aired and evaluated. At each meeting he attended, Judge Peckham dissented on the court's handling of the San Jose rule.

Judge Peckham's first year on the federal bench set the pattern of his activities to encourage central coast attorneys to use the San Jose court and to convince the San Francisco judges of the central coast's need for a federal forum. During the first month of his judgeship, but before the first session of the district court in San Jose on January 16, 1967, he wrote to the bar associations of the central coast informing them of the need to transfer cases to San Jose under Rule Two. He took particular pains to talk with local legal newspapers on the requirements of the rule. He made it clear that the success of the court depended on attorneys taking "the initiative to obtain the transfer to the San Jose calendar."[32]

Early in his judgeship, he explored possible changes to Rule Two. He reported to Russ Roessler on December 23, 1966, that he was studying the civil rules of all United States District Courts which sat in several cities within their district. He also advanced Roessler's suggestion that the twenty percent of the northern district's criminal business originating from the San Jose area be arraigned and tried there. He worked to entrench the San Jose court with proposals for rules on the selection of jurors for trials at San Jose. With this rule, jury trials could be transferred to San Jose. In addition, with such a rule the court would be forced to appoint a jury commissioner for San Jose (as permitted by statute for any place designated for jury trials).[33]

But these earnest — and Judge Peckham felt, reasonable — suggestions were not adopted. Three years after the court opened in San Jose there was still no jury commissioner for the area. Nor was there a clerk's office (although space was provided for such an office by Santa Clara County). All actions still had to be filed in San Francisco and go to a hearing before a judge in San Francisco (where a party could move for transfer to San Jose).

It was clear to Judge Peckham soon after he opened his court in San Jose that his colleagues were no more favorably disposed to a federal court presence on the central coast that they had been before S. 1666 passed Congress. Accordingly, on May 22, 1967, the judge sent a memorandum to his colleagues stating his discontent with plans to continue the operation of rules which gave the San Jose court second-class status. His colleagues had heard Peckham's discontent on this issue. Now they received a closely reasoned argument.

Judge Peckham suggested Rule Two be revised. All civil and criminal cases arising on the central coast should be filed and tried in San Jose. He also suggested that the northern district court post notices in the San Jose legal newspaper, so that area attorneys could be apprised of the court's activities. Pretrial statements filed in the court should set forth the county of residence of each party or where the subject of the action occurred. This would permit the court to gather statistics on the number of cases from the central coast counties.[34]

The northern district judges did not respond to his arguments. Something more pressing was on their minds. Although S. 1666 had provided two additional judgeships, by 1967 the president had appointed only one — Judge Peckham. With the blossoming of President Johnson's Great Society, the passage of civil rights legislation, and a growing public discontent over foreign military involvement, the federal courts experienced an avalanche of new litigation. In 1967, the northern district judges faced a backlog of 1,398 cases. This put the court behind 4,194 trial days. Even if the court's eight judges heard trial on only the backlogged cases every day (including weekends and holidays), it would take them more than a year and a half to erase the backlog. But then they would face a new backlog of cases filed during that time.

Judge Chambers teased the judges about this problem. He was not unsympathetic: he had tried to get the northern district court three new judgeships during the struggle surrounding S. 1666. He received no help from the northern district judges then. Instead, they had opposed him, declaring they would prefer to do without any new judges rather than have the San Jose court. Judge Chambers, noting much of the backlog was composed of protracted antitrust cases, proposed a simple solution: extend the requirement that cases from the central coast be filed and heard at San Francisco (and not at San Jose unless the convenience of parties was proven). The northern district should extend a similar restriction to the antitrust cases. He wrote to Judge Harris saying, "if you would put all antitrust cases in Eureka, they would file some place else but San Francisco and life would be much easier for you."[35] Chamber's implication was clear. If the northern district judges wanted to reduce use of the court, why not place the San Francisco attorneys and clients under the same inconveniences and burdens central coast attorneys and clients faced? Except for this dig at Rule Two, Judge Chambers was silent about the problems of the San Jose court.

Having done all they could to sink S. 1666, the San Francisco judges now tried to cope with their heavy duties. One method was to keep Judge Peckham in San Francisco as much as possible. Rule Two forced all San Jose cases to be tried in San Francisco unless a party confronted the trial judge with the claim of extreme inconvenience in coming there.

The judges hoped to reduce their backlog by making sure each judge carried his fair load. To insure this, they wanted to change the assignment of cases so that the efforts of each judge could be carefully monitored and adjusted. This involved changing the case assignment system from one based on a master calendar to one based on individual assignments. With the individual assignment system it would be eminently clear whether any judge was not pulling an appropriate share of the work. It would also lead to a more efficient system of trial in the court. The change from the master calendar assignment system to an individual assignment system would produce a substantial improvement in the court's disposition of cases. The master calendar system was ineffective because "every case is in effect nobody's responsibility." For the same case, motions could be heard by one judge, pretrial conferences by another, and the trial conducted by still another: "a masterpiece of judicial nonresponsibility, duplication of judicial effort and resultant inefficiency."[36] The individual calendar system would make judges more accountable for dispatching their caseloads, and a larger number of settlements were expected as counsel learned earlier exactly which judge would handle their case.

Judge Peckham favored a switch to the individual assignment system to promote productivity and efficiency. He believed this system would allow more court sessions in San Jose. But in the adoption of the new rules, he refused to consent to continuing the central coast's second-class status. He had been voted down once on the San Jose court receiving equal status. The judge believed this refusal hindered the development of cases from the central coast area. He believed the issue of Rule Two should not be a point of "bitterness or divisiveness" between himself and his colleagues. He would dissent from his colleagues' views in the best tradition of the federal bench. With renewed arguments, new data on federal court use in San Jose and his growing expertise as a federal judge, he would present the concerns of the central coast bars.

The judge found a compelling duty to insure that court in San Jose would eventually come to its full promise. This feeling was fueled by his perspective on the court. The San Francisco judges, looking at the present case filings from the central coast, declared the statistics proved there was no need for a separate court in San Jose. Judge Peckham and the San Jose court proponents rejected this measure of court use. They knew the business was there, but it was either being handled by San Francisco attorneys or the disputes were not going to the federal court at all. They looked to a future when the local bar had gained experience in federal court and the area's litigation had expanded . . . as surely it must. It would not happen immediately — perhaps not in a decade — but they had no doubt it would happen if the San Jose court was not stifled. Judge Peckham's duty was to prevent the strangulation of the San Jose court.

Informally, to colleagues who lent willing ears, Judge Peckham discussed the prospects and needs of the central coast. Formally, whenever the judges voted on Rule Two as they revised the court's rules, Judge Peckham made clear his dissent. For instance, in September 1967, as the court's Rules Committee circulated a revision of proposed court rules, Judge Peckham renewed his objection to Rule Two. Writing his colleagues, who apparently wished he would finish his role as the San Jose representative, he noted "no one is more anxious that I to come to a resolution of the problem. I certainly do not look forward to months and years of dispute, friction, and misunderstanding among the bench and persistent complaints from the bar and the community from which I come." He did not intend to let the "unworkable and unrealistic" Rule Two go unchallenged. He told them that the "thinking of the past" regarding San Jose's federal court must be reexamined. He advocated that civil and criminal cases from the area automatically be filed and heard in San Jose. A branch of the clerk's office should be opened there. In short, the San Jose court should receive equal treatment. But Judge Peckham won no converts to his position.[37]

More than a year after Judge Peckham's second attempt to revise Rule Two, Russ Roessler sent him the September 1968 Report by the Santa Clara County Bar Association's Federal Court Committee. That bar had joined the San Francisco Federal Bar Association to study the northern district's local rules. The Santa Clara bar proposed Rule Two be changed to incorporate Judge Peckham's suggestions on case filings and hearings in San Jose. But the Federal Bar Association in San Francisco rejected this. Yet their rejection was not as vigorous as their opposition to the San Jose court had been in the past. There was strong sympathy and understanding of the San Jose court proponents' position, but the San Francisco federal practitioners were reluctant to go against "what they felt was a majority attitude of the San Francisco federal court." The report emphasized that the struggle for the San Jose court must be won among the judges. "Judge Peckham must of necessity carry the laboring oar [in revising Rule Two] and we are hopeful that his patience and understanding will be rewarded by a realistic Rule Two."[38]

All this while, the northern district court's Rules Committee continued revising the rules. On March 11, 1969, the committee asked the judges for suggestions on the final draft of the revised rules. Judge Peckham's reaction was not what they were looking for. He indicated that the "individual assignment system [proposed by the Rules Committee] in my judgment is a great step forward" because of "its accommodation and adaptability to the operation of the San Jose court." He then urged his colleagues not to readopt Rule Two, now renumbered as Rule Seven. Peckham warned that if the court included the rule in its final draft, it would force him to "respectfully disagree with the division of business within the northern district" encompassed by that rule.[39]

On August 7, 1969, the judges refused to amend Rule Seven. Judge Peckham warned them again of his problems with the rule: "I wish to emphasize that my dissent is only from the provisions relating to the division of business with respect to the San Jose court." He did not disagree with "the long overdue departure from the master calendar system or the other provisions of the [new] rules." In his dissent, he noted the failure of the rules just adopted to create a rules division at San Jose. The individual assignment system he believed was "a great step forward" but the court's reluctance to allow for an operating San Jose court appeared to be several steps backward.[40]

Although disagreeing with Judge Peckham's position, both Chief Judge Harris and Judge Zirpoli were concerned by their colleague's assertion that Rule Seven did not "carry out the spirit of the 1966 legislation [S. 1666] and resolutions of the United States Judicial Conference" regarding court in San Jose. Harris and Zirpoli believed Rule Seven was restrictive as a matter of necessity and not with any intent to strangle the San Jose court. The seeming restriction on the San Jose court was necessary for equitably apportioning the court's work load between the judges. Indeed, this concern with equitable work load was a major reason for the individual assignment system. Some of the judges believed they could not very well clamp down with this new assignment system but allow Judge Peckham a way to avoid it with a less restrictive rule on court business in San Jose. But Judge Peckham argued that this would not be the effect of such a change. He proposed a mechanism to balance out the cases, so that the weight of his cases in San Jose and San Francisco would equal the weight of the cases assigned to a judge sitting only in San Francisco.

Judge Peckham had refused to consent to his colleagues' court rules dividing the business of the court between the judges. When judges of a district could not agree on rules regarding the division of business before the court, Congress directed that the Circuit Judicial Council "make the necessary orders" to settle the dispute.[41] On September 5, 1969, the judges held a meeting designed to head off the possibility of the Ninth Circuit Judicial Council making such orders. There was a hope, a faint hope, that the division on the court would end. Neither Judge Peckham nor the other judges had yet cut off the possibility of a compromise, but years had passed without any signs of one. By 1969 it was clear there were few remaining opportunities to consider the rules regarding San Jose. The new local rules had been adopted in a final form. The issue of revising the rules would, in the future, be closed off for all practical purposes. This left Judge Peckham with no choice but to appeal to the Circuit Council.

Recognizing this last chance for compromise on the court, both Chief Judge Harris and Judge Zirpoli urged their San Jose colleague to once again propose how he would change the new rules. Within a week, Judge Peckham submitted a draft to the judges. Judge Peckham's suggestions could be a surprise to no one. They would clearly lead to a sustained federal court presence on the central coast. Yet they were also designed to allow considerable flexibility "to the problems inherent with a branch operation court" and for adjusting caseloads to insure equitable apportionment of cases between judges. He assured Harris that under these revisions to the rules, he would not have difficulty pulling his "fair share of the load at San Francisco" as well as remain the judge for San Jose.[42]

After receiving Judge Peckham's suggestions, Judge Harris called on his colleagues to attend a September 5 meeting. The results were no different than before. Several of the judges may have been tired of all the clamor over San Jose because they failed to attend. After discussion, Judge Harris proposed tabling Judge Peckham's proposals until the next week. He believed this would "allow time for further consideration and a full attendance by the court."[43]

But their debate that next week was to no avail. As he had proposed for over three years, Judge Peckham argued that civil and criminal cases arising from the central coast area be tried in San Jose. But many San Jose litigants used San Francisco lawyers to present their federal case. Should these firms have to travel to San Jose? This inconvenience for the large San Francisco firms posed no problems for Judge Peckham given the inconvenience Rule Seven imposed on central coast firms. Let the San Francisco firms appear in San Jose for their clients and move for transfer to San Francisco if it is convenient to the parties. After all, this was simply what San Jose attorneys had to do with their cases in the federal courts.

In addition, Judge Peckham explained that a San Jose judge's work load could easily be monitored. Merely give the San Jose judge a pro rata share of the court's San Francisco business. When a San Jose case was filed, the San Jose judge should hear it and an equivalent case that the San Jose judge was expected to hear in San Francisco would be moved over to a full-time San Francisco judge.

Judge Peckham won no converts at that meeting — at least none who would stand with him for an operational San Jose court. His colleagues considered his proposals, but they refused to vote on them. Judge Peckham was convinced after these meetings that most of the judges were sympathetic with his position. "A majority of the court does not object to the proposals," he told Judge Chambers. However, no change on the rules could be expected because "an adamant minority of at least two . . . cannot agree" to depart from the position held by the district court for decades. Their harsh opposition to changes in Rule Seven made their colleagues reluctant to depart from the rules just adopted.[44]

No reconciliation appeared possible now. On one side was Judge Peckham, committed to court rules that would not inhibit the growth of the San Jose court. On the other were his colleagues who believed any concession to increased use of the San Jose facilities would be costly and not improve the district's use of judicial manpower. Judge Peckham realized his colleagues would never be excited about the San Jose court. There were only varying degrees of disapproval. It ranged from the dark frowns of Judges

Sweigert and Weigel (who believed this trouble over a San José court was simply the result of political pressures which the court should resist to the utmost), to the calmer but still immovable disapproval of Judges Zirpoli and Levin, (who were convinced that holding court in San Jose would not contribute to the administration of justice in the northern district), to the quietly reluctant visages of Chief Judge Harris and Judges Carter, Wollenberg, and Burke (who believed the issue to be "mostly for convenience of the lawyer").[45]

The future of the San Jose court seemed bleak; the rule was strangling the San Jose court. It made transfer of cases from San Francisco to San Jose rare as well as difficult. For instance, one San Jose attorney received only cold stares from a San Francisco judge when he moved for transferring a case to San Jose. Most motions to transfer to San Jose "were denied just routinely," explained Russ Roessler. As word of this got around, attorneys stopped making such motions. "It's not a way to get off on a real good first step with a judge. Particularly if . . . you want the case transferred to San Jose and he says no and you are forced to try the case in San Francisco — now you've got to live with that judge through the trial . . . it's just very poor strategy."[46]

If Judge Peckham did nothing, the San Jose court would meet an early death under Rule Seven. Central coast litigants and their attorneys could not reasonably be expected to incur the expenses of litigating in San Francisco. Nor could the district court reasonably expect Santa Clara County to continue providing facilities for the federal court at one dollar a year. The Santa Clara County Superior Courts were growing with the area's expanding population. The county would soon want to use the top floor of their court building for its own courts rather than for a federal district court which spent its time trying to choke off use by restrictive rules.

Since the judges terminated their discussion of Judge Peckham's proposed revisions to Rule Seven without a vote, they left him with only one course of action: to request that the Ninth Circuit Judicial Council consider ordering a division of business in the northern district which would allow for the San Jose court's development. Judge Peckham believed this required the council to direct the district court to allow certain cases arising from the central coast region to be heard automatically in San Jose. It would also involve fixing Judge Peckham's official residence at San Jose rather than at San Francisco as well as opening full-time district court offices (such as the clerk's office) at San Jose. Judge Peckham submitted a memorandum to the Ninth Circuit Judicial Council requesting a rule change.[47]

His colleagues were not about to let his appeal go uncontested. At their earliest opportunity they met to consider what to do. Judge Peckham, knowing their purpose, did not attend the meeting. The judges decided to present a reply to Judge Peckham's memorandum to the council. Chief Judge Harris would present the views of the judges in this controversy once again.

Judge Harris's memorandum to the council on behalf of the judges was sent nearly a month and a half after Judge Peckham's appeal. The chief judge's memorandum disputed that the Circuit Council could force the northern district court to San Jose. The issue of the San Jose court, he argued, was not a disagreement between the judges over the division of business. Rather, it was merely a disagreement over venue in the district. The Circuit Council, he reminded them, had no power or authority to issue orders regarding venue. Judge Harris attempted to show that changing Rule Seven would be unwise and the changes proposed by Judge Peckham would further neither the fair nor efficient administration of justice in the district.[48]

Judge Peckham's appeal to the Circuit Council reported that on the date of his dissent, only thirty-six civil cases and thirty-four criminal cases were pending at San Jose. Most of these cases were there because of Judge Peckham's efforts. Of the thirty-six civil cases, ten had been sent there by Judge Peckham's order; the other twenty-six by order of the district's remaining six judges. In the thirty-four criminal cases, thirty were selective service cases ordered to San Jose by Judge Peckham when he served as selective service calendar judge. This calendar of business was meager, just as it had been during the court's first year in San Jose. During that first year in 1967, Judge Peckham held only twenty-nine trial days of court on the central coast. The rest of his time he sat in San Francisco.[49]

These disappointing figures contrasted sharply with the growth of the San Jose region. For instance, the northern district's criminal filing (excluding selective service cases) in 1970 was nearly 600 cases. Seventy-three of these cases came from the central coast region. This was 12.3 percent of the district's total criminal (non-selective service) case filing. Yet something was surely wrong when the San Jose judge had only four of these non-selective service criminal cases to hear; the remaining sixty-nine cases from the central coast region were being retained in San Francisco. Surely more cases from the region could be heard at San Jose. The central coast area had nearly one and a half million residents; they were served by nearly 1,500 attorneys. In addition, it was clear that over one-quarter of the district's bankruptcy filings came from the area. All of these factors led Judge Peckham to conclude that the San Jose court "has not been allowed to develop fully under the restrictive intradistrict venue rule."[50] Judge Peckham found the meager number of cases before the San Jose court to be compelling evidence that Rule Seven effectively stifled business from the area. Absent that rule, the region would have a more substantial involvement in the federal court.

In his response to Judge Peckham's appeal to the Circuit Council, Judge Harris argued that the small use of the San Jose court to date was evidence there was no real need for it. He explained that in the three years the district court sat at San Jose, nearly 6,700 criminal and civil cases had been filed. But only thirty-four motions were made during those three years under Rule Two (later Rule Seven) for transfer to San Jose (and all but three of those motions were granted). These facts alone demonstrated the severe "paucity of interest of litigants and lawyers in federally litigating in San Jose" declared Judge Harris. Indeed, in the three months previous to Judge Peckham's appeal, nearly 900 cases had been filed in the district court. But "in only thirty-two of these cases did any attorney" of the central coast counties "appear of record for any party." Judge Harris argued that the thirty-six civil cases and thirty-four criminal cases pending before Judge Peckham at San Jose — a grand total of seventy — were only 2.5 percent of the northern district court's total number of cases pending. This minor portion of the district's business should not divert scarce money and manpower to the central coast area. "The time may come," admitted Judge Harris, when a revision to Rule Seven "would be justified in terms of demonstrated need; but it is certainly not at hand."[51]

Having received these arguments on Rule Seven, Judge Chambers prepared to present them to the Ninth Circuit Judicial Council. He delayed any immediate deliberations on this matter by the overburdened council. He also tried to defuse this controversy. For instance, he wrote to the judges about possibly obtaining an extra district judge under a bill making its way through Congress. This new judge should blunt the objections of the San Francisco judges to more sustained business in San Jose. With an extra judge, Chambers reasoned, the northern district judges should be less worried

175

about the perceived inefficiencies of sending a judge to San Jose. But Judge Harris wrote back to Chambers saying that their opposition to revising Rule Seven remained the "position . . . of every judge of this district, saving only Bob Peckham."[52]

It took the Ninth Circuit Council nearly six months to consider Judge Peckham's appeal. As the date for its deliberations approached, Judge Chambers wrote the district court for additional facts on the handling of San Jose cases. To supply the information Judge Chambers requested, Judge Harris assigned the court's deputy clerk to work with Judge Peckham's law clerk, Lionel Allan (now a leading Silicon Valley corporate lawyer), in reviewing and counting the cases from the central coast region.

By late spring of 1970, it was clear there would be no backing down by either side. In response to Chambers's hints that the district court should amend Rule Seven, Harris declared that the court "has not modified its rules regarding San Jose . . . " indeed, "further experience with Rule Seven shows it to be a good rule."[53]

The Circuit Council met on June 11, 1970, to discuss the problem of the northern district, the San Jose court, and Judge Peckham's objections to Rule Seven. The results of their deliberations were quickly reported to the judges. Few had any illusions about the likely result. Recalled one northern district judge: "Judge Richard H. Chambers was the chief circuit judge . . . and when he was chief judge, he was pretty much the council. If he was in favor of it [the San Jose court], they were in favor of it." Indeed, placed in the position of having to settle disputes between judges, undoubtedly the council members were "happy to have [Chambers] do it."[54]

And so Chambers did. He wrote to Judge Harris that "we are all convinced that your present apportionment [of cases between San Jose and San Francisco] is not carrying out the implications of the mandate of the Judicial Conference of the United States with respect to . . . San Jose." The Judicial Conference had expected that "cases arising out of the geographical area surrounding San Jose . . . should be handled at San Jose," not San Francisco. However, because the Ninth Circuit Judicial Council had difficulty defining exactly when a civil case "arose" from the central coast area, the members of the council "have in mind" that "the federal crimes . . . supposedly committed in Santa Clara, San Benito, Monterey, and Santa Cruz counties should be handled at San Jose." It was hoped that the northern district judges, having allowed for the development of criminal case filings in San Jose, would also amend their rules, with time, to include civil cases. In any event, the council intended to reserve for later consideration the question of automatic civil filings at San Jose.[55]

The council was not yet exercising its authority to make orders on the division of business in a district where the judges disagreed. It had unanimously voted that Chambers submit the council's thinking to Harris, thus giving the northern district judges a face-saving way out of their stringent opposition to the San Jose court. Chambers, writing for the council, had simply indicated what the council would order done if the northern district judges did not do it themselves. The council's suggestions on handling criminal cases from the central coast at San Jose should be accepted or rejected by the district judges. Judge Chambers left to speculation what the council would do if the suggestions were not promptly adopted. "You may be assured that this is not the kind of work that we personally like," concluded Judge Chambers in transmitting this information to the northern district judges.[56]

The northern district judges immediately considered their next steps. Every judge must "make every effort to attend" a meeting on June 22 to consider the Ninth Circuit Judicial Council's action, even if it meant putting off the start of afternoon sessions of court.[57] The results of their meeting were not immediately apparent. They appeared to delay in responding to Judge Chambers's letter. Perhaps this delay was a result of their distress over facing the question — and disagreements — of a San Jose court once again. Or the delay may have been a result of difficulties drafting the order the Circuit Council wanted: that central coast criminal cases be heard in San Jose. The most persuasive reason for the delay, however, was a recent change in the court's administration. On June 1 — before the Circuit Council had considered the San Jose court dispute — Judge Harris dictated a letter to his secretary, addressed to President Richard M. Nixon. The judge assured the president that "it has been a great privilege to serve the United States government." However, "having attained the age of sixty-eight years on August 16, 1969, it is my honor to advise you that I hereby elect to retain my office, but retire from regular active service [as a judge] effective at the close of business on Friday, July 31, 1970."[58]

So, the northern district court would have a new chief judge: Judge Oliver J. Carter. But in this switch of chief judges, the reply to Judge Chambers's letter reporting the Circuit Council deliberations on the San Jose court lingered. Chambers had asked the district judges to inform him whether they would accept the council's suggestions before July 6.

But as that date approached, no reply had been sent Chambers. Chambers's letter sat on Judge Harris's desk. But there was some indication that the court's reply would be left to the new chief judge — Oliver Carter.

Apparently, the northern district chief judge designate sent word to Chambers that the district court would implement the council's suggestion. Central coast criminal cases would be tried in San Jose. An order was drafted to this effect and was circulated among the judges. They worked under a deadline of the end of July. The order amended Rule Seven by specifying that when the "offense charged is alleged to have occurred in Monterey, San Benito, Santa Clara, or Santa Cruz" it would go to the court at San Jose for a hearing. Apparently the judges did not resist the spirit of the Circuit Council's suggestions, but they did not go beyond those suggestions to allow for easier transfer of civil cases to the San Jose court. The final version of the amended rule was approved after the judges had worked over the rule change informally and all were ready to sign it.[59]

On July 31, 1970, the northern district court issued its long awaited — and by some, long dreaded — order. It was signed by all the northern district judges, even those who had strenuously resisted the movement of the court to San Jose. At the head of the judges' signatures was that of Chief Judge George B. Harris. This was the last time his name would appear on a court document as chief judge of the northern district court. What his thoughts were as he signed the order, Harris never revealed. He was not the first judge to sign the order; Judge Carter, who had coordinated the drafting of the revised rule, was the first. But it is difficult not to believe that when the order was presented to Judge Harris for his signature on his last day as chief judge of the district, he reflected momentarily on the course of the San Jose court controversy.

It had been such a minor irritation when he assumed the chief judgeship a decade ago; it had become a major source of division between his colleagues on the bench recently. In the early years of his chief judgeship, Judge Harris believed holding court outside of San Francisco would not simplify the administration of the court. The proposal seemed wasteful and inefficient. He feared it would be expensive, confusing, and would diminish the prominence of the northern district court. He presented this view for the judges of his court, even though over the years, a certain ambivalence grew on him. By the time Congress passed S. 1666 allowing the San Jose court, some observers felt Judge Harris was reconciled to the idea of holding court there. Judge Peckham felt that his chief judge consistently tried to find some accommodation between colleagues who were vehemently opposed to a San Jose court and the new San Jose judge.[60] But, as chief judge, Harris was committed to advance the views of his judges in their resistance to the court's movement towards San Jose. In playing this role, he earned the distain of many in the central coast bars.

The judge probably felt this reaction simply indicated how good an actor he was. His actions for the judges of his court may not have matched his personal views. To be sure, he would have preferred not having the court in San Jose. But he did not think it necessary to make too much out of this issue. Indeed, at times he seemed to be vaguely sympathetic to the needs expressed by the San Jose court proponents. But his script was written for him by his court. It was his duty to act it as best he could. He had not lost his touch for the dramatic: he was still a superb actor after all.

But now his involvement in the San Jose dispute drew to a close. He had set down his chief judgeship. The court had finally adopted a rule that allowed some development of its San Jose branch. Some unity could be restored to the judges of the court. Perhaps he recalled with some amusement one of his last newspaper interviews as chief judge of the district. Given soon after he had announced he would leave that office, and published on June 2, 1970, the interview was with a reporter from the *San Francisco Chronicle,* a paper that consistently supported the judges in their battle against the San Jose court. The reporter reviewed the details of Harris's long career in the judiciary and turned to Harris's accomplishments as chief judge. Harris confided that during his administration of the district, there were many innovations "which may be regarded as noteworthy." He then gave examples. The first was his effort (in collaboration with Alfonso J. Zirpoli) to design a system for representation of the indigent in the federal district court. Long concerned with the sorry position of those unable to afford defense counsel, Harris labored continuously for mechanisms to fill this deficiency in the court system. He mentioned the change from the master calendar system to the individual assignment system as another accomplishment. Then he turned his attention to another innovation during his chief judgeship which corrected a severe deficiency. Perhaps he smiled as he told of this achievement. It was the "establishment of United States District Courts in San Jose and Oakland" which he regarded as another major achievement and innovation of the court under his administration. The people of these areas would not be without access to a federal court in their bright and challenging future.

# 13

## An Equal Partner

*Joseph Franaszek*

Nearly ten years after the dedication of the first, albeit temporary United States District Courthouse complex in San Jose, another cornerstone for the northern district court's history was placed. This cornerstone would not be evident to the numerous people who passed the temporary courthouse, nor would it be visible to anyone strolling by the new courthouse under construction. Yet it was there — and the process of laying it had occupied years of effort. This effort had come from the central coast area's four United States district judges; from Russ Roessler; and from the San Jose Federal Court Advisory Committee, which he chaired for over twelve years. Judge Robert Beresford's dream back in 1948 and Congressman Don Edwards's constant efforts in Washington were now yielding a big payoff for the residents of the central coast counties.

The cornerstone was a new rule adopted by the judges of the United States District Court for the Northern District of California. After seventeen years of effort by proponents of a San Jose court, there would, as of May 1, 1983, be a full-time federal court presence in San Jose. Members of the local bar associations and of the district court gathered at the temporary federal court facilities on Taylor Street on March 30 to celebrate this change. They gathered in Judge William A. Ingram's cramped courtroom to recount the struggles of the past and their dreams for the future.

The courtroom was packed by the time Chief Judge Robert F. Peckham stepped forward to address the crowd. From the courtroom podium, Judge Peckham announced what most of his listeners already knew but were waiting to hear again: "The judges of the Northern District of California agreed to amend the court's local rules insofar as they affect" the San Jose court. No longer would a motion to transfer be necessary for civil cases to be heard in San Jose. Instead, all central coast civil cases would be filed and heard in San Jose as a matter of course.

179

United States District Court Judge Robert F. Peckham. In 1983, Chief Judge Peckham announced the northern district court's establishment of mandatory venue in San Jose for civil cases arising in the central coast counties. This action gave the area its first full-fledged federal district court. (Photograph by Ira Nowinski.)

The new rule meant there would be an immediate and significant increase in the caseload for the northern district court located at San Jose. To handle the expected increase of cases, Judge William A. Ingram would sit in San Jose full time and his colleague, Judge Robert P. Aguilar would join him, full time if necessary. Judge Spencer Williams and Chief Judge Peckham would also come to San Jose to take up any overload in the San Jose calendar's demands.

Judge Peckham went on to recount the history of San Jose in the northern district. He explained that originally, San Jose, like San Francisco, was a place for United States District Court hearings. But the northern district's first judge, Ogden Hoffman, convened the court in San Jose twice, once in 1852 and again in 1853. Due to lack of business, he found holding court in San Jose an "empty formality." At Hoffman's request, Congress eliminated it as a place for holding court. But "over 100 years later," declared the judge, "our own congressman, Don Edwards, initiated legislation again designating San Jose as a place for holding court." Chief Judge Peckham told of the effort to get a courthouse built and how, in 1970, "mandatory criminal venue was placed in San Jose" for offenses committed in the counties of Santa Clara, San Benito, Santa Cruz, and Monterey. With the addition of mandatory venue in civil cases, the San Jose court will have become an equal part of the northern district and "convening the United States District Court in San Jose will no longer be the 'empty formality' that annoyed Judge Hoffman 125 years ago."[1]

The applause seemed to reverberate off the thin walls of the courtroom which Chief Circuit Judge Chambers had once described as adequate only for Tom Thumb. The chief judge of the northern district looked around at his listeners, smiled in appreciation, and made his way back to his seat next to Judge Ingram and his models of the new courthouse.

There would be few other events of this sort. Soon, the court would sit at its permanent quarters in San Jose and would have gained equal status with the rest of the northern district. People might someday ask: "Didn't we always have a federal court here in San Jose?" so much would the court become a part of the community. It would no longer be considered an outpost.

What might the observer have seen upon entering Judge Ingram's courtroom at this point? The cramped room had a rather makeshift appearance; it was not designed with an eye towards space or emphasizing the dignity of the court. Opposite the entrance door and to the right was what passed for a bench — its distinguishing characteristics being its bulky shape and the fact that it was raised. Behind the bench and to its right stood the national flag. The bright colors of the jurors and spectators' chairs seemed a bit out of place. But the yellow carpet managed to lighten the claustrophobic feeling one might easily get in this windowless room.

The observer would soon notice that Judge Peckham had just resumed his chair. He had come a long way since his appeal of Rule Seven to the Ninth Circuit Council in 1970. He enlarged his expertise in presiding at trials and now chaired the National Conference of Federal Trial Judges. He explored the new and growing role for the trial judge: insuring efficient justice. In 1976, when Judge Oliver J. Carter retired to senior status, Judge Peckham was elevated by his colleagues to the chief judgeship. There is some irony in the fact that this position of the court had passed into the hands of one so committed to facilitating the growth of the court in San Jose. Only twenty years before, Louis Goodman, a strong opponent of San Jose's claim to a federal court, had occupied the position of chief judge. It then passed to George B. Harris who represented his colleagues' views opposing the central coast court. Finally, after the northern district was forced to allow mandatory criminal venue at San Jose, Judge Oliver Carter became chief judge. Carter acted to facilitate the court's growth in the central coast counties and was especially concerned with getting appropriate quarters for the court in San Jose. But on Carter's leaving active status, the court's lone dissenter against efforts to minimize the growth of the San Jose court became chief judge. Judge Peckham now was in the position from which he quietly, gently, but effectively moved the court to provide for the central coast area.

The next speaker was Congressman Don Edwards. The San Jose court had initially been one of his major concerns. He learned the "dance of legislation" through this issue. These lessons were very useful to him as he gained leadership positions in the House of Representatives as the fourth ranking Democrat on the House Judiciary Committee and as chair of its Civil and Constitutional Rights Subcommittee.

But before Edwards reached the microphone, the observer's eyes might have been diverted a moment down the front row of jury seats to one from which a rather small, intensely active man watched. It was Judge Robert Beresford, now in what he considered retirement. But retirement was a word only. He was still active in promoting dreams: improving the local court's ability to render justice, or obviating the need to resolve disputes in court in the first place. These ideas might seem unattainable to some, but then in 1948 Beresford's idea of a federal court in San Jose was only a dream too.

But it was coming ever-closer to reality today. Beresford was an active member of the American Bar Association's Section on Special Courts and a member of the Committee on Alternate Dispute Resolution. He still served on the San Jose Federal Court Advisory Committee and was a director for the northern district court's historical society.

It might have been hard for Judge Beresford to contemplate how San Jose got from the developing town it was in 1948 to the sprawling community it was today. He and the town seemed to grow and mature together, as if linked in an odyssey. He might have recalled a sign that he often passed in the beginning of this odyssey. In 1948 it was painted on the side of the Knights of Columbus building. It advertised motor oil and pictured a road leading through a wide expanse of forested mountains and calm, placid valleys. The sign announced that "IT TAKES EXTRA QUALITY TO GO FARTHER." And Beresford had gone farther — farther from New York than he ever imagined and further than his colleagues in the Santa Clara County bar to build for the time when a federal court could sit in San Jose. It was a path of continual struggle. It is clear that he had the type of persistence and ability — that extra quality — required for the task.

Looking to the back row of the jury bench, the observer might have seen an individual who looked on the proceedings with a calm sense of satisfaction. This was Russ Roessler. For twenty years he had led the local bars in their efforts to secure full-time federal justice. Yet in his law practice he had minimal experience with the northern district court. As a senior partner of his law firm, he engaged in the general civil and trial practice of the superior courts. Most of his specialties — negligence, corporate, insurance, tax, and family law — rarely brought him into the United States District Court. Why did he labor so for the court? The answer was remarkably simple. Roessler was committed to the development of the Santa Clara valley. He could see no reason that the area should not have an equal opportunity before the federal court. It was not self-interest, but a commitment to San Jose's development that moved him on.

When Judge Peckham had pursued a change to Rule Seven, he invariably reported his progress to Russ Roessler. The judge knew that Roessler could be depended on when something had to be done. During Peckham's early years on the federal bench, the Santa Clara Bar Association's Federal Court Committee, chaired by Roessler, was still active. The committee itself did not always meet formally, but Roessler continued the efforts to secure a full-time federal court presence.

"The committee's principal effort has been in connection with the court rules," reported Roessler to the board of the Bar Association in 1969, "and primarily that rule having to do with venue." He attempted to present a liberal San Jose venue rule to the court. His proposal to the Federal Bar Association in San Francisco was rejected, but he had the satisfaction of noting "a strong sympathy and understanding . . . of our position but a reluctance to go contra to what they felt was a majority attitude of the San Francisco federal court." Roessler had done what he could for a change in the venue rules on the bar level. Roessler was also actively pressing the California congressional delegation members to have any newly appointed United States attorney "make an unequivocal promise to establish an office of the United States attorney in San Jose as one of his first orders of business."[2] Other than this, Roessler and the committee watched and waited for Judge Peckham to achieve the necessary rule change.

By June 1970, Judge Peckham was becoming concerned about the future of San Jose court. Negotiations over his dissent from the northern district court's rules were continuing, the results uncertain. In addition, the Santa Clara Superior Court, which so gra-

*The San Jose Federal Court Advisory Committee. Standing, left to right, are Anthony J. Trepel, Lionel M. Allan, Douglas H. Pendleton, and Edward P. Davis, Jr. Sitting, left to right, are W. Robert Morgan, Russell V. Roessler, and Lewis Fenton. The Advisory Committee played a crucial role in building a federal court presence in San Jose. (Photograph by Ira Nowinski.)*

ciously lent court facilities to the federal court for one dollar a year, would have difficulty doing so when the lease expired in 1972. There was a current of opinion that wondered how long the county taxpayers would have to support federal court facilities. Judge Peckham knew something must be done to unify support for the central coast federal court. In June 1970, he spoke with Russ Roessler on the telephone. Something was needed to unify the people of the central coast counties behind their federal court and its needs. He proposed forming "an advisory committee for the United States District Court at San Jose." As Russ Roessler recalled, their main concern was to show everyone "we are still alive down here" and that "if we could secure community support from the four counties and make a strong push for a building, it would be sufficient to stave off the [Santa Clara County] Board of Supervisors if they had any idea about pushing the court somewhere else" when the federal court's lease expired.[3]

The major and most urgent task for the Advisory Committee would be to secure "the construction of a new United States Courthouse at San Jose." Judge Carter was trying to develop the space requirement estimates for such a building and the perilous position of the court's lease made it necessary that the courthouse project be expedited by Congress and the General Services Administration (GSA). The committee should also work for the "establishment of an office of the United States attorney" because so far the new United States attorney in San Francisco had done little for permanent operations of his

*Louis Oneal, another member of the San Jose Federal Court Advisory Committee between W. Robert Morgan and Russell V. Roessler. (Photograph by Ira Nowinski.)*

office in San Jose. Other projects involved "a contract . . . with respect to the use of the jail facilities for the detention of defendants pending trial; education of the bar of the four counties with respect to the present and proposed venue provisions, and the establishment and operation of a panel of attorneys to represent indigent defendants."[4]

The membership would "be appointed by the judge assigned to the district court at San Jose." Judge Peckham asked Roessler to serve as chairman; he accepted. The presidents of the four central coast county bar associations would be members, as would those who had been active in the battle for passage of S. 1666. A criterion for membership seemed to be that one have "an intimate familiarity with the San Jose court and . . . be of immeasurable assistance" in accomplishing the committee's goals. Under this standard, two local law school professors became members, as did one of the judge's former law clerks.[5]

Initially, Judge Peckham planned to have the committee's first meeting on June 27, 1970. But with the news that the Circuit Council had asked the northern district to alter Rule Seven to allow for mandatory venue in San Jose criminal cases, he thought it wiser to wait so that the committee could know what revisions of the venue provisions had been made. The first meeting, to be held in San Juan Bautista, was put off until September 26, 1970.

As reported by Lon Allan, the committee's secretary, the meeting had an impressive list of guests. These included the district's Chief Judge Oliver Carter, who reported on plans for construction of a San Jose courthouse; United States Attorney James Browning, who reported on prospects for his office in San Jose, and Federal Defender James

*The San Jose Federal Court Advisory Committee: Edwin Jones, Jr. (Photograph by Ira Nowinski.)*

*The San Jose Federal Court Advisory Committee: Austen D. Warburton. (Courtesy Mr. Warburton.)*

Hewitt, who discussed the need for an indigent defendant panel under the 1964 Criminal Justice Act.

Subcommittees were appointed. The five subcommittees included one concerned with securing a temporary and permanent San Jose court building, a subcommittee to find qualified members to serve as counsel for indigent defendants, a subcomittee to consider how to publicize the local rules with respect to the transfer of civil business to San Jose and the mandatory venue of criminal cases. Also created was a subcommittee to consider the possible problems the soon-to-be-appointed federal magistrate might find in performing his duties in San Jose. A fifth subcommittee was formed to act as liaison with the clerk's office in establishing a branch at San Jose.[6]

These subcommittees soon produced results. By the 1971 meeting of the Advisory Committee, many of its projects had been accomplished. For instance, the subcommittee to find counsel for indigents quickly formed an Indigent Panel and disbanded. With the passage of the Criminal Justice Act Amendments of 1970, the federal defender in San Francisco could promise that "As the caseload in San Jose increases, a full-time staff member could maintain offices to provide full services" to the San Jose court. The new magistrate system began its functions on the central coast: Nordin Blacker was appointed U.S. magistrate for Santa Clara County and Francis Carr was appointed for Monterey County. The system was designed to ease the burden of district judges by providing a magistrate to assist the court in hearing certain pretrial matters, arraignments, misdemeanor criminal cases, and writs of habeas corpus. Blacker was initially appointed as a part-time magistrate, but the scope of duties under the mandatory criminal venue rule for San Jose expanded his job to a full-time one during its first month. The provision of a full-time magistrate for San Jose seemed to answer the purpose for which the subcommittee on magistrates had been formed. The subcommittee to act as liaison with clerk's office had to wait for the plans concerning where the court would sit when its lease with the county expired. Once this was settled, plans could go forward. Long forgotten were the proposals that Judge Peckham's courtroom deputy act for the clerk's office in San Jose. With criminal venue now automatic in San Jose, such a proposal did not look reasonable. Unfortunately, the subcommittee on the United States Attorney's office for San Jose was less successful. It was unable to convince United States Attorney Browning to assign some of his San Francisco staff and resources to San Jose. However, Browning was willing to open the United States Attorney's office there when Congress provided funds for additional assistant United States attorneys. So the future of this proposal depended upon an increase in his staff and budget.[7]

But by the 1971 Advisory Committee meeting, one major item was unfinished business and would remain unfinished for over a decade. This concerned the work of the subcommittee charged with securing congressional authorization to plan and erect a United States Courthouse and Federal Building at San Jose. The *San Jose News* identified the significance of the Advisory Committee's activities in an editorial of October 13, 1970. It noted the committee had representatives from each of the four central coast counties and was "coordinating a campaign for a federal building in San Jose." The paper identified the strong case for such a building, stating that the counties "provide twelve percent of all the cases handled by the federal court." The paper admitted that Judge Peckham sat in San Jose "from time to time" but undoubtedly "many cases originating from this four-county area still are heard in San Francisco. This means the principals, lawyers, and witnesses must make the long round trip to conduct their business." This situation placed the growing federal bar in San Jose in the position of "operating out of a car trunk," while San Francisco lawyers had easy access to their nearby offices. The editorial concluded that the San Jose Federal Court Advisory Committee "deserves broad community support" for the building of a local federal courthouse and building.

The struggle for adequate federal court facilities was under way. It would be the major struggle for the Advisory Committee, one that would take twelve long years. The second meeting of the Federal Court Advisory Committee was held on June 12, 1971, soon after the long-expected notification by the chairman of the Santa Clara County Board of Supervisors that the "expanding superior court facilities" in the county forced it to refuse to "continue to furnish facilities for the federal court." The committee had a jump on this problem, but little did they anticipate the years it would take to get the necessary facilities. They heard reports on the subcommittee's considerable progress. The committee passed a resolution calling for congressional legislation authorizing funds for a permanent courthouse and federal office complex, sufficient to the counties' needs over the "next several decades" and that until that structure was complete, Congress make appropriations for "temporary accommodation" of the court and its adjunct offices in San Jose.[8]

And so its work would go on — for years. Each year the committee met and considered its progress. The committee's membership expanded as the court acquired a firmer foundation in the community. During the fall of 1971, the Santa Clara Bar Association adopted a resolution on the construction of temporary United States court facilities which the Advisory Committee had arranged to be placed near the intersection of Taylor Street and Guadalupe Parkway. The association urged that the facility, which had been cut back by GSA for lack of funds, be expanded to provide for the United States Attorney's and Marshal's offices. The resolution was signed by Robert P. Aguilar, president of the association. Aguilar attended the January 5, 1972, meeting of the Advisory Committee as the Bar Association's delegate. The committee's business that year was to meet with Congressman Don Edwards to discuss the progress of the court and to plan for its temporary and permanent facilities. Also attending this meeting was the newest addition to the northern district bench, Judge Spencer Williams of the San Jose area. Like Peckham, Williams eagerly encouraged the Advisory Committee's work.[9]

But the committee's actions did not alleviate many of the burdens on Russ Roessler. His role was that of intermediary. He was a natural for it: he got along easily with politicians of any political stripe. He patiently, but realistically, dealt with numerous bureaucrats. And he smoothed the way for a unified stand by the Advisory Committee on the large tasks ahead. He suggested to United States Senator George Murphy that in considering the appointment of a Republican United States attorney for the northern district with the incoming Nixon administration, he consider a candidate's views on opening a United States Attorney's office in San Jose. "Only in this manner," wrote Roessler, "will the court in San Jose serve the public" as intended when S. 1666 passed Congress. Roessler also took on the cumbersome government agencies. He bird-dogged GSA to prepare the necessary studies for building the San Jose courthouse. Finding that agency's response to his urgings cryptic to say the least, he concluded that: "we had, perhaps, better use our congressmen's and United States senators' assistance in making certain that the central office of the General Services Administration gives the San Jose courthouse . . . the priority it is entitled." He quickly implemented this strategy. At his insistence, Congressmen Don Edwards and Charles Gubser, and Senators John Tunney and Alan Cranston began to emphasize the need for federal facilities in San Jose. This soon got results, even in the face of mounting confusion and governmental paralysis over the Watergate scandal. But with time and numerous urgings, GSA's progress made Edwards "think that things are about as good as they can be with regard to our top priority for early construction of the building." Little did either expect that despite "top priority," nearly ten years would pass before the building would formally open.[10]

But as Roessler well realized as he sat in the jury box of the temporary courtroom listening to the announcement of the change in the San Jose venue rule, his years of effort had paid off. The new courthouse was going up. The district court finally accepted the central coast region as an equal partner. Little had he expected when he arrived in San Jose in 1938 that he would play such a major role for the San Jose community. He had begun to develop his practice in the Santa Clara valley at precisely the time Bob Beresford arrived in San Jose from the East Coast. Roessler's activities to improve the administration of justice in the Santa Clara valley rapidly won him a place on the Santa Clara County Bar Association's Board of Trustees. From then on, his service to the bar was diverse; but his major priority was always the federal court in San Jose. This devotion was well acknowledged. For instance, Congressman Don Edwards, writing to him in 1974, noted the fact that the federal court building project was finally underway and said that this "is in large measure due to your hard work and interest."[11]

One of the many letters Roessler received about the progress of the court building aptly summed up Roessler's work for the court. The correspondent penned in at the bottom margin of the text with a felt pen the suggestion: "The Roessler Bldg?" This merely emphasized the belief that no matter what the building was formally named, it would always be the Roessler Building. Roessler admitted himself that when he walked by the new building and saw "it being utilized, you recall all the time you spent on it and devoted to get it. And you feel it was well worth the twenty years. It certainly was well worth the struggling to make federal facilities and the federal courts available to the people here."[12] It would not matter what the building was formally named, to those who knew the building's history it would always be "Russ Roessler's Building."

But this new and still unnamed building was going up on the date of the rules change ceremony at the temporary courthouse. Congressman Don Edwards would be the next speaker at this event, and as he stood at the microphone he quickly sized up his audience before beginning to speak extemporaneously, as was his custom. It was a friendly gathering. He glanced for a moment towards the jury box and seemed to study briefly the curious jury assembled there.

In the jury box, to the right of Edwards's vacant seat, was United States District Judge Robert P. Aguilar. Aguilar was a friend of long standing — long before the San Jose court controversy of 1966. The judge gazed steadily at the congressman. The look on his face might have been one that would meet a litigant in his court during a lighter moment: bemused eyes looking through dark-rimmed glasses, a firm, confident shadow of a smile. Aguilar was the most recent addition to the northern district court from the central coast area. With his induction to the bench in the summer of 1980, the central coast region supplied one-third of the federal district court's judges.

Aguilar's fifty-year journey to the northern district court bench suggests, in a rough manner, a paradigm for the development of the court itself. The court had grown where few persons, even those living there, initially expected a federal court could exist and develop. Yet through the commitment and hard work of a few individuals, long tradition was broken and a singular institution — the federal court in San Jose — was given birth. It was similar with Judge Robert P. Aguilar. Born in a large family of eleven children of immigrant parents, he struggled to help the family survive the dismal last years of the Great Depression. When his parents first emigrated from Mexico to the United States, they worked picking fruit in California. This was migrant labor. But the elder Aguilar, a man who taught himself seven languages although he never attended school nor learned to write, eventually found employment as a lumberman — and later as a steelworker. His ambition to better his position impressed itself on his children. But, in spite of his advances, for many years, his salary did not match the needs of his family. There seemed to be a continual necessity for the children to work and bring in supplemental income. But this did not eclipse the importance of a sound education. Accordingly, young Robert applied himself to school by day and in any other time available, he took up various jobs, such as delivering newspapers or breads for the local bakery.

This pattern of constant effort to advance to a better position continued in the young man long after high school. Soon after he graduated from the University of California, Berkeley, he entered Hastings College of Law. He financed this education by work — any work. Frequently it was necessary to leave the academic program to earn more money to pay the bills. Thus, his undergraduate career found him serving as a mail carrier, a laborer, and an insurance claims examiner. He sandwiched law school between work as a liquor warehouseman and as a stock clerk in San Francisco.[13]

He persisted in his studies, graduated from Hastings in 1959, and was admitted to the bar in 1960. One might think that having labored so long to enter the law profession,

*United States District Court Judge Robert P. Aguilar. Appointed to the federal bench in 1980, Judge Aguilar worked with Judges Peckham, Williams, and Ingram to establish the San Jose federal court as an equal partner to that in San Francisco. (Photograph by Ira Nowinski.)*

he would wait a week or so to catch his breath. He had gone a long way from delivering bread for the local baker. But on June 22, 1960, the day he was sworn into the California bar, he appeared in the San Jose Superior Court before Judge Marshall Hall to represent a client in a probate matter. This would be the beginning of nearly twenty years as a general practitioner in the Santa Clara valley.[14]

His labors to reach this point suggest much about the man. His education and professional credentials were much like those of his fellow practitioners in the valley. Indeed, he had authored for the *Hastings Law Journal* a probing analysis of the problems encountered in enforcing desegregation decisions. Like many of his colleagues in 1960, he was a newcomer with boundless faith in the possibilities of the region. But there was a distinct difference separating him from his professional colleagues. He had confronted the world of barriers — education, money, time — and had prevailed over them. Unlike many of his profession, he knew the tedium of the delivery man on the route, and he knew the strain of the manual laborer under the day's hot sun. He was a man of two American worlds — the world of the disadvantaged as well as the world of the advantaged. This left him with a sensitive understanding of the powerful and the powerless who would come before his court and a conviction to do what the law dictates and what humanity demands.

Like Bob Beresford and Russ Roessler before him, Aguilar was convinced San Jose was "a good community in which to start practice." An additional inducement was the experience of his older brothers Jess, who both practiced law in the Santa Clara valley, and Charles, who later entered practice in the San Joaquin valley. Robert joined Elva Soper, to whom he was then married, to form the firm of Aguilar & Aguilar. There he handled a wide variety of cases, a few of which were in the federal courts. With time, he developed strength in criminal defense work. This occurred during the exciting days in which Earl Warren's Supreme Court attempted its civil rights inroads.[15]

He served the community as a judge *pro tempore* and as a juvenile court referee. He participated on a variety of boards and commissions concerned with juvenile delinquency and the problem of drug abuse. He sharpened his skills as a conciliator by acting as an arbitrator in the neighborhood small claims court for the San Jose-Milpitas judicial district, in which was located the bulk of the region's Mexican-American community. In addition, he continued in academic study and analysis of the law. For instance, he coauthored an article on uninsured motorist coverage, as well as one on property agreements between spouses in California.[16]

His capacity for work helped him advance in the local bar. He was president of the Santa Clara County Bar Association in 1972. He served in the local criminal trial lawyers association and was a member of the San Jose Federal Court Advisory Committee. In all of these activities he was motivated by a desire to better society while attempting to achieve and strive for a better position in that society.

If there is one quality Judge Aguilar possesses which comes across immediately, it is his sense of confidence. It is a well-placed confidence in his understanding of the law, of people, and of his skill in dealing with these. It is a confidence born of his years of struggle to advance in school, in the bar, and finally, in the district court. He is not afraid to make mistakes if they are unavoidable. As one attorney described this quality: "he exudes judicial confidence from the bench without being overbearing." Another marveled that "he's got a lot of guts . . . . He follows the dictates of his own conscience and integrity and does what he thinks is right. He seems to approach each case on its own terms, not trying to evaluate issues as if a higher court were also a party to the case; he is not terrified that some higher court might reverse him."

It may be that this ease in handling matters renders him a controversial figure in the Northern District of California. There are many vexing questions that arise as legal issues in the district. Characteristically, the judge does not retreat from these issues; he confronts them. He learns from controversy in which he is placed. Accordingly, he finds time to review his often negative "fan mail" for constructive comments and criticisms. His "fans" often react with outrage and disappointment at his tendency to read the protections of the bill of rights broadly and his inclination to exercise his discretion with a utilitarian sensitivity.

But even those disappointed with the judge's decisions are pleased by his professionalism and efficiency. Parties in his court feel they can get "a very fair shake from him" in their trial and are often "pleased to have him as the trial judge," because he is such "a very fair trial judge." Respect for his judicial ability does not come automatically. It comes from long exposure and testing of a judge's qualities. With Aguilar, the bar found he "obviously reads everything" filed and "always seems well prepared when he takes the bench, plus he rules promptly. He seems to be on top of everything." Many recognize Aguilar's deep commitment "to do his job as a judge." One attorney admired the judge's tendency to reach decisions promptly. Even if he does not have written opinion at hand, the judge will "take a recess and draw one up quickly so you don't have to wait for weeks."

Aguilar probed for ways to exercise his judicial discretion to do some good, to make the northern district a better place. This often meant searching for untraditional solutions and incurring the wrath of those more steeped in tradition. For instance, when he ordered a tax evader with nearly .5 million dollars of unreported income (allegedly from the illicit drug trade) to work as a computer instructor for the probation department, and to purchase $10,000 worth of equipment as part of his sentence, some found it "unconscionable." Yet for Aguilar, it was a question of having the punishment do some good.

While this order may have often been untraditional, it was motivated by a goal with considerable tradition: trying to make the defendant a "productive member of the community." It is "senseless to get productive individuals put in prison when they can do much more good overall out working in their various skills," explained the judge. With crowded prisons, it simply "costs too much" in terms of taxpayers' money and lost productivity for the community to impose a sentence with minimal effectiveness. It is perhaps a unique, utilitarian view of the justice system. Yet it is characteristic of the flexibility of this judge. He does, however, readily impose imprisonment where the defendant "constitutes a threat to the community and is involved in serious acts of criminality extending over a long period of time that are apt to repeated, as opposed to a one-shot situation such as a tax evader."[17]

Judge Aguilar was the first Mexican-American President Jimmy Carter appointed to the federal bench. He viewed his appointment, like that of other minority individuals, as significant in providing role models for minority youths. In his efforts to gain an education, to learn a profession, and to become an active citizen, he had no role model. Perhaps this accounts, in part, for that inner sense of confidence so characteristic of him and of the central coast region today. Reporters sing the praises of "self-made" people who have the confidence to achieve. Aguilar undeniably exudes this quality. So too, the early San Jose court proponents, who struggled against hopeless odds to bring the northern district court to San Jose.[18]

His confidence stems from a natural pride in all that he has achieved so far. This was most evident in October 1982, when he presided over the naturalization of his father. "It [was] the first time that a federal judge has sworn in his own father, to my knowledge," ventured the judge.[19] The hallmark of his confidence is the conviction that something can be done to improve and change things. It is in this spirit that the judge has encouraged the growth of the San Jose court. He admits this is easy today because of the previous work of those who dreamed of a federal court in San Jose. Nearly three years after his appointment to the bench, he joined with his colleagues on the northern district bench from San Jose to untie the last vestiges of San Francisco "provincialism" by voting for mandatory civil venue of central coast cases in San Jose. With the expected increase in business with mandatory civil venue in San Jose, he looks forward to the day when there will be not only a demand for one full-time judge in San Jose — Judge Ingram — but two — Judges Ingram and Aguilar.[20]

Sitting in the first row of the jury box, next to Judge Aguilar and Judge Beresford, was United States District Judge Spencer Williams. Judge Aguilar's rise to the bench has been interpreted as a paradigm of the San Jose court's history: in him is seen the area's vibrant growth, the striving to develop a new America, the building for the future, and the longing for something — anything — better than the status quo. Judge Williams's strivings incorporate a different aspect of this general theme. In Williams's struggles

191

United States District Court Judge Spencer Williams. Judge Williams worked with Judge William A. Ingram to build a full-time federal judgeship in San Jose through the transfer of relevant cases to the San Jose court. (Photograph by Ira Nowinski.)

leading to the district court bench, one sees intense political activity in which he tried to advance a new vision of government's role in California.

Williams graduated from the University of California, Los Angeles, receiving his undergraduate degree there in 1943. He then served in the navy's Pacific theaters. With the end of World War II, he returned to San Francisco and entered Hastings College of Law. A year later, he transferred to Boalt Hall of the University of California, Berkeley, and received his law degree in 1948. During the next year he was admitted to the California State bar.

Williams started his career in the law by affiliating with a San Jose law firm that had opened only three years earlier — the firm of Beresford & Adams. Under the supervision of Bob Beresford and his partner Dave Adams, Williams learned the ins and outs of local practice. He also participated in the firm's case, *Western Well Drilling Co. v. United States* which Bob Beresford presented in federal district court in San Francisco. Williams joined Beresford in his long drives to San Francisco to present the case and well knew that there were few attorneys in San Jose's legal community with any experience with the federal courts who could offer advice on the finer points of federal practice. Since the implementation of the federal rules of practice, federal procedure heavily emphasized motion practice in the courts; it was dissimilar from much practice in the state courts which focused on disposing cases at trial. The lack of federal court facilities in San Jose and its effect on the local bar brought Beresford to propose a Federal

Court Committee of the Santa Clara County Bar Association. Could Williams have possibly realized then what impact this effort Beresford was starting would have on his career?

Williams was associated with Beresford's office only briefly. In November 1949, he left to work in the office of the County Counsel of Santa Clara County. Soon after, he spent two years working at the Pentagon, then returned to the office of county counsel. It was a position in which he would be active in all phases of local government. In 1955, he was appointed county counsel, responsible for providing legal counsel to the various agencies of the county government. This office suited his interests: he had responsibility in litigation, in offering legal advice, and in representing the county and its agencies before the legislature. So extensive was his experience in these activities, that he stood as candidate for the state assembly in 1954, but his race for this position was unsuccessful. He remained in this position until 1967 when success in politics drew him to statewide service.

Williams's expertise and experience, his magnetism as a speaker, and his critical assessment of the enforcement of the law in California made him a key contender for the office of the attorney general of California. Besides being the top law-enforcement position in the state, this was considered a stepping stone to the governorship. News of the possibility that Williams would run for attorney general received attention in the state newspapers as early as the summer of 1965, when Williams jockeyed for the position on the Republican ticket.

In 1966, as Republican nominee for state attorney general, on a ticket that would send Ronald Reagan to the governor's office, Williams carried forward an issue that would become prominent in the late sixties. This was a concern he developed in 1963 as president of both the California District Attorneys Association and the National Association of County Civil Attorneys. The issue involved the perception that American society was suffering from an excess of crime and violence. Williams declared that if there was a "war on crime," the army of law enforcement was without a leader. He called for direct and positive action, not ineffective studies.[21]

Williams won the Republican primary contest on June 8, 1966. He was seen as a member of Ronald Reagan's "big team" that would reform and redirect the state government. Williams began to describe how he would do this in law enforcement. He emphasized the need for stiffer penalties for persons using guns in crimes, with possibly a mandatory sentence. He also paid attention to institutional reform and the plight of prisoners. For instance, he urged that college-level training be offered to inmates in state prison.[22] However, he narrowly lost the November election to Thomas Lynch, a former district attorney of San Francisco.

This loss only intensified his role in state politics and government. The new governor, impressed with Williams's managerial abilities and clarity of vision, appointed him administrator of California's health and welfare agency and the youth and adult corrections agencies; these agencies were consolidated a few weeks later as the Human Relations Agency. Williams was sworn into this position on Governor Reagan's cabinet on January 4, 1967; he would serve until 1970.[23]

He was the chief executive officer of an agency that had responsibilities for the health and welfare of Californians. Williams kept a major goal in view: to gain acceptance of Governor Reagan's economy program in the way the department was administered. Thus, only two weeks after his appointment, Williams announced changes in the state medicare program to save 30 million dollars. His activities won him appointment as one of three secretaries of state agencies to oversee the operations of all of California's agencies and report on them to the governor.

One of the larger battles Williams would fight was to cutback the State Department of Mental Hygiene. He moved a measure through the legislature against the opposition of an entrenched bureaucracy. A difficulty soon arose concerning the constitutionality of the cuts, and within two weeks of the cuts, a state judge in Sacramento issued a temporary restraining order against Williams. By the time the court ruled that the cuts were illegal, most were in effect and had to be reversed.[24]

But in his second year administering the programs of Governor Reagan, the rumor was that the new Nixon administration was interested in stealing Williams. They wanted Williams to take a position in the Federal Department of Health, Education and Welfare. At the same time, Williams appeared to be moving in a different direction. He seemed to have his eye on the attorney general's spot for 1970. Yet, polls found him trailing in the push for the Republican nomination. He continued to campaign throughout the state. Eventually, this contest came to occupy most of his time and he resigned his position in the State Department Human of Relations. He became affiliated with the Sacramento law firm of Evans, Jackson & Kennedy and with the San Jose law firm of Rankin, Oneal, Center, Luckhardt, Bonney, Marlais & Lund. His best dreams were not realized: in the primary that June, he lost to Evelle Younger.[25]

Williams's strong leadership in administering the state's social welfare programs, the public health and health care agencies, corrections, and youth authority did have an important effect on California. He had overseen an agency of some 48,000 persons, operating in each county in the state with a budget exceeding some 3.5 billion dollars. During this period, the governor had utilized Williams's expertise by appointing him to various councils and commissions, especially to those dealing with the justice system.

His private practice of law in Sacramento and San Jose was short-lived. In early July 1971, he was nominated as judge for the Northern District of California. Later that month, he received the consent of the Senate, enabling the United States attorney general to send him a commission as district judge. He was sworn into office in San Jose on August 13, 1971. This was the second induction ceremony by the northern district court of a judge appointed from the San Jose region. As a judge, he rose quickly to prominence. In 1978, he began service as an officer in the Ninth Circuit District Judges Association, becoming president in 1981. The national Federal Judges Association chose him as their president in 1980.

Roessler and Aguilar, Williams and Beresford, in the jury box made for a rather unusual jury panel — even in the Santa Clara valley. On finishing his remarks, Don Edwards joined them. The ceremony's last speaker, Judge William A. Ingram, started to offer his comments to the audience on the design and construction of the new United States Courthouse in downtown San Jose. Having listened to his three colleagues on the district bench and Congressman Don Edwards speak on the struggle to get the court to San Jose and keep it there, Ingram rose to make his remarks. He avoided using the amplification system and instead stood in the middle of the courtroom between defense and prosecution's tables to describe the court's future quarters. He used several artists' "impressions" of the design for the new building. As he stopped during his presentation to show the architectural portraits to the audience, it is likely he wished the building's construction had been as easy and effortless as it was to impress his watchers with the 34 million dollar structure rising from a deep pit in downtown San Jose.

Since his 1976 induction to the district court, one problem after another plagued the building. These problems ranged from the plans for courtroom size to the number of courtrooms that would be built to accommodate the central coast's litigants until the twenty-first century. As he described the permanent building, it may have struck Judge Ingram that the new building would present a marked contrast to the building in which he now spoke. The temporary court complex seemed barely sufficient. This was not merely a result of overcrowding, especially during complex, multiparty trials. He recalled one trial over which he had presided in this courtroom. No sooner had the trial started than the courtroom filled with exhibits necessary to understand the testimony to be given. It got so crowded that normal court functions ground to a halt at times. Merely taking testimony from a witness was a complicated exercise. A witness could not approach the stand directly, but had to leave the courtroom, go into the clerk's office by a back door, and enter Judge Ingram's reception room. From there, the witness had to pass through Judge Ingram's chambers and eventually return to the courtroom via the same door that the judge used to enter the courtroom.

It took a while to get used to the peculiarities of the room in which Judge Ingram had presided for eight years. He could vividly recall the first jury trial case he heard in this courtroom. During that trial, which involved the Trading with the Enemy Act, he used a substitute court reporter to take the trial record. Unfortunately, when the furnace for the building went on, it made a horrible noise. This noise was so disconcerting to the substitute court reporter that he failed to report much of the trial. The defendants were convicted of shipping silicon chips — marked as refrigerator parts — to the Soviet Union by way of Zurich. The case went to the Ninth Circuit Court on appeal; that court was particularly interested in the testimony of an expert witness who had been on the stand for three days. The court reporter's transcript had only two pages devoted to these three days of testimony. Accordingly, the court of appeals asked Judge Ingram and the attorneys to try to reconstruct the transcript. This was impossible to do adequately, and the court of appeals had to set aside the verdict.[26]

These deficiencies were disturbing inconveniences. But at times the courtroom's shortcomings presented a threat to life and safety of the public. This trouble was first discovered by Judge Spencer Williams. The temporary court facility had no holding cell for criminal defendants; they were kept in the jury room. The prisoners were to use the plumbing facilities for the jury room. One prisoner broke through the ceiling of the restroom, climbed on to the roof of the temporary courthouse and made an escape.[27]

In 1978, Judge Ingram's court was disturbed by a more dramatic escape. On that occasion, the courtroom was "packed" with attorneys, law enforcement officials, and citizens. The courtroom was "in a state of confusion. It was filled to capacity in the public seating area with others standing on the edges of the room and near the doors."[28]

The defendant was to be sentenced for robbing a savings and loan association. Judge Ingram had a reputation as a "strict, but not harsh" sentencer, giving rather stiff sentences for confrontational crimes like bank robbery. The judge himself admitted that he had given "severe sentences in confrontation-type crimes . . . that in retrospect might have been a little on the high side." The reason was his assessment of whether the defendant's rehabilitation was possible. He believed that in most bank robberies, rehabilitation was not possible and so "the factor of retribution becomes an important one" in sentencing. "As far as I'm concerned," he admitted, it ought to be "pure punishment."[29]

And so it seemed to be this day. The defendant and his attorney stood at the courtroom's podium facing the bench. The judge pronounced a sentence of sixteen years. When he had finished, the defendant stepped closer to his attorney. It seemed he wanted to consult on the sentence. "Within approximately five seconds," estimated one observer, the defendant threw the attorney to the floor and "bulldozed" his way past a United States marshal at the right of the bench. He ran by the right side of the defense counsel's table, struggling between the chairs of the table and the wall of the courtroom. One probation officer attempted to tackle the defendant, grabbing him around the waist. But his grip loosened and he fell to the floor as the defendant passed the courtroom's railing. A United States marshal reached over the railing and gripped the defendant for a brief second. His hold was also broken. Pursuit by others was delayed as the probation officer who initially tried to restrain the defendant fell over his chair, creating a bottleneck near the courtroom's entrance. The defendant quickly merged with the spectators at the court's doorway. He was out of the courtroom and outside the court complex within fifteen seconds after Judge Ingram's sentence. One spectator enthused by the escapee's tactics, yelled: "Go . . . Go." And so the defendant did, through the parking lot, later escaping to San Francisco in his wife's car. The incident availed him little because he was recaptured the next day in the city.[30]

The cause of the escape's temporary success was not the mad attempts of surprised officials to tackle the defendant; rather it was the inadequate courtroom. It was hard enough to keep some defendants in properly designed ones. This escape from the temporary United States District Courthouse reminded Judge Ingram of a client he had represented in 1960 who made an effort to escape from the county municipal court. This client, a rancher sentenced to ninety days in jail for violating city fire hazard ordinances, left the municipal courtroom with Ingram and a bailiff. As Ingram discussed the jail sentence, his client quickly muttered to the surprised attorney: "I'd rather die." He then dived headlong over the third floor banister at the Hall of Justice. Rather than die, he landed virtually unhurt on the marble floor thirty feet below, his fall partly broken by a stairwell projection.[31]

This was only one of a long list of experiences Judge Ingram could tell of his practice of the law. It was a practice enabling him to continually refine his legal skill and expertise and one that would help make him a highly-respected judge. His expertise was readily recognized. Thus, a client was to write him before his appointment to the bench in 1969: "If Clarence Darrow were still around he would be proud to [be] called the 'Bill Ingram' of the midwest." This admiration for Ingram's skill and character brought colleagues to write then-Governor Reagan that Ingram "would be among the most exceptionally qualified persons" to become a judge. Ingram's appointment would be considered "a favor to the people of Santa Clara County."[32]

The man about whom all this was written was born in Jeffersonville, Indiana, in 1924. His undergraduate education was at both Stanford University and the University of California. In 1943, in the midst of World War II, he joined the Marine Corps as a corporal. But with the end of the war, he returned briefly to Stanford to finish his undergraduate degree and then entered the University of Louisville School of Law. He expected to join an uncle in law practice in Kentucky after his graduation.

Instead, graduating in 1950, he returned to California to work at a labor law firm in San Francisco representing employer's causes. He resided in Palo Alto and was active in the Palo Alto Republican Assembly as well as in the California Young Republicans. In September 1955, he gained appointment as a deputy district attorney for Santa Clara County. He handled a variety of criminal prosecutions and learned the finer points of plea bargaining. He worked out of the San Jose Courthouse, as did the other deputy dis-

*United States District Court Judge William A. Ingram. During the early 1980s, Judge Ingram became the first northern district judge to sit predominately in San Jose. (Photograph by Ira Nowinski.)*

trict attorneys. Toward the end of his tenure there, Ingram pioneered the fractionation of court-related offices. Selected to head the Palo Alto-Mountain View District Attorney's office, he was on duty at the two city police stations, working closely with law enforcement agencies.

From his stations in Palo Alto and Mountain View, he handled criminal cases in the municipal courts of the cities. He believed that fractionation of the District Attorney's office was "bound to work out successfully," if for no other reason than it helped one gain a more complete picture of the offense before trial. Ingram labored away in his small office in the Palo Alto police building adjoining the municipal courtroom and at the Mountain View station. On December 1, 1957, he resigned his post as deputy district attorney to join the Rankin, Oneal law firm in San Jose. The county's district attorney was chagrined to lose this most "outstanding deputy in our department" to a private firm.[33]

Ingram remained with this firm for twelve years. Here he became one of the region's experts in medical malpractice. In addition, during some of this time, he served as a judge *pro tempore* of the Superior Court of Santa Clara. His other activities covered a whole range of causes; he represented a high school teacher who was released from employment for being "too strict"; the San Jose Chamber of Commerce in hearings concerning a proposed deep water port for San Jose; and the Southern Pacific Railroad in all manner of actions. He represented the Santa Clara County Medical Society in connection with its medical malpractice cases. He was also active in partisan politics, serving, for instance, as Republican Party chairman for Santa Clara County in 1962.[34]

On July 29, 1969, the *San Jose Mercury* reported Ingram to be a "front runner" for a vacancy on the municipal court. His candidacy won "wide support within the northern Santa Clara County legal profession." Other reports surfaced that "GOP chiefs tag Ingram for bench." Yet, this was a bit of a setback: Ingram initially had been interested in a superior court judgeship that the legislature was considering creating. Since the measure did not go through, the only position open to him was on the municipal court. Ingram soon expressed interest in that appointment and it was not long before he received it. A year and a half later, on April 1, 1971, Governor Reagan named Ingram to the superior court bench. The governor based this appointment on Ingram's "excellent record" as a municipal judge. Hearing of the appointment, Ingram quipped: "I hope it's not an April Fool's joke."[35] It was far from that. Ingram's style of presiding on the bench soon emerged. This style was a winning one. In a poll of the Santa Clara County bar, Ingram received the highest ratings as a judge of the superior court. Ingram's attitude was that what is important is "not where a guy rates, but in what he can do to improve himself."[36]

This open-minded attitude and willingness to learn account for his appointment to the northern district court. The appointment was part of "a package deal whereby two Republicans and one Democrat" would be nominated by President Ford to fill three vacancies on the federal court. The deal was reached by a Democratic-controlled Senate Judiciary Committee which refused to clear any nomination by President Ford before the November 1976 presidential election. But the "two for one" deal was "politically palatable" to the committee's Democrats and they approved Ingram for the bench. Thus, at the end of May 1976, President Ford had nominated Ingram to succeed Judge Alfonso J. Zirpoli who had taken senior status in September 1975.[37]

The need to protect the San Jose court was also a factor in the selection of Ingram. Judge Peckham realized that when Chief Judge Oliver Carter took senior status, Peckham would become the northern district chief judge. This presented a problem because as chief judge it would be difficult to station himself in San Jose and run the district at a distance from the San Francisco Court Building where most of the district's judges were located. He was considering this problem when he learned of the "two for one" deal from Congressman Pete McCloskey. Because California had no United States senators of the president's party, it fell to the Republican congressmen of the northern district to suggest possible nominees. Peckham suggested William Ingram as a judge with the requisite experience, judicial temperament, and commitment to preserving the federal court in San Jose. The northern district Republican House delegation committee agreed and presented Ingram's name to the president. The president nominated Ingram along with William W Schwarzer of San Francisco, and Cecil Poole.[38]

Ingram's confirmation by the Senate followed in July. On receiving his commission from the attorney general, he traveled to San Francisco to be sworn in as judge: he wanted to begin his work immediately. His formal induction to the court came that fall in the Santa Clara Board of Supervisors' chambers, where Judge Peckham and Judge Williams had been inducted earlier.

Judge Ingram would bring to the northern district court more than the "frequent smile and seeming relaxed air" that some cynical souls in San Francisco expected. Rather, he would bring his concern that "no lawyer will ever leave my courtroom, nor will his client, feeling that they have been ill used." The judge was determined to "provide a forum for any person who has business there to feel that no matter whether I'm right or wrong, or whether they agree or don't agree, at least they'll feel that they had a right to present everything that they wanted to present."[39] And part of making justice accessible to everyone was to make sure it was also available to the citizens of the central coast counties.

Ingram's elevation to the district court brought praise from those who had watched him on the county bench: "It would be difficult to find anyone more qualified by training, experience, and temperament for the post." One radio commentator extolled Ingram's "personal warmth and compassion for people," stating his confidence that "Bill Ingram will make an outstanding federal district court judge because first of all he is a fine man." But the commentator found one problem in Ingram's appointment to the federal district court. This problem was that "Santa Clara County is losing him to the feds [at] the federal district court bench in San Francisco." He was confident that Ingram's talents would soon bring San Francisco to lose the judge too, to some "still higher courts."[40] As Judge Ingram's appointment turned out, Santa Clara County did not lose him for long. Indeed, Ingram's persistence in advancing the San Jose court would end the part-time federal justice for the central coast region. Ingram would become the first full-time federal judge to preside in the central coast counties.

Before coming to the northern district bench, Ingram did not know much about the operation or the problems of the federal court in San Jose. As a municipal and superior court judge, he had little direct contact with the federal court or its judges. He recalled that with his heavy court schedule, he "took almost no interest," in the federal court and "just had no knowledge" of the San Jose court's affairs. There was no "particular interplay between" the two court systems on a professional level. Although Ingram did recall seeing Judge Peckham occasionally "on the street," other than that "I wouldn't have known he was here."[41]

But with his placement on the northern district court, Ingram was also made a member of the San Jose Federal Court Advisory Committee. In discussions with now-Chief Judge Robert Peckham, he learned the history and long struggle for the federal court in San Jose. Ingram became committed to seeing that the court would survive and grow on the central coast. One way of doing this would be to change the civil venue rules regarding the San Jose court. In 1970, the rule was changed to allow automatic venue of criminal cases in the area; but civil cases still had to be filed and transferred from San Francisco to San Jose.

Ingram recalled that at one meeting of the Advisory Committee, "there was a real ground swell of feeling that civil cases should be tried" in San Jose without having to move for transfer of those cases there. The current transfer rule was choking off the natural caseload that one could expect for San Jose, so the Advisory Committee considered possible strategies to revise that rule. The committee members could recite a list of judges who routinely would refuse motions for transfer, thinking that they might otherwise open the door for forum shopping which would damage the administration of justice in the district.[42]

Many ideas were proposed on how San Jose could get around the necessity for a civil case to be transferred. This included an insistence by some members that the region's congressmen introduce a bill that would create a division at San Jose or at least would direct that civil cases arising in the central coast area be tried in San Jose. But the committee decided to "hold back" on directly challenging the venue rule. Faith was placed in the San Jose judges on the court to assess when a court vote to change the civil venue rule might pass. Judge Ingram recalled that at almost every meeting, the Advisory Committee discussed whether the time was right. But the years passed with the judges informing the committee that the San Francisco judges had not yet changed their opinions with regard to the civil venue rule.[43]

This did not deter Judge Ingram from implementing his own strategy to bring full-time federal justice to San Jose. Three judges from the San Jose area now sat on the northern district court. If the criminal cases automatically heard in San Jose were divided between them, no judge would spend much time at the court facilities on the central coast. But if Judge Ingram assumed the San Jose cases heard by his northern district colleagues, he might have a sufficient number of cases to keep busy in San Jose full time.

During his first year on the federal bench, Ingram sat more often in San Francisco than in San Jose. This was in spite of the transfer of Judge Peckham's San Jose cases to Ingram, necessitated by Peckham's reduced caseload on becoming chief judge. So Ingram undertook a "concerted effort" with Judges Peckham and Williams to get cases heard in San Jose. Every case these judges got in San Francisco that had any substantial connection with San Jose, whether it arose there or not, they transferred to be heard in San Jose. To aid in the building of a full-time federal judgeship for San Jose, Williams transferred any civil case with a central coast connection to Judge Ingram's calendar in San Jose. In return, Ingram transferred to Williams an equivalent San Francisco case on his calendar. Judge Williams continued to call his criminal calendar in San Jose because this insured a rapid resolution of these controversies.

Ingram's determination to sit in San Jose produced a slow change. During his first three years on the court, he spent more time in San Francisco than in San Jose. But by 1980, the number of San Jose cases he acquired rose and he split his time evenly between the two cities. Then the judge felt confident enough to test how well San Francisco attorneys liked being treated as the San Jose attorneys had been treated in San Francisco for years. In the spirit of "turn about is fair play" Judge Ingram started calling his San Francisco calendar down in San Jose. This caused a certain amount of friction with the San Francisco bar, but it quickly dissipated. Many of the larger firms of the city were locating branch offices in San Jose. If San Francisco judges could require San Jose litigants to appear in their court to transfer a case to San Jose, there was no reason a San Jose judge could not require San Francisco litigants to do likewise. The last year Ingram split his trials between San Francisco and San Jose was 1982. That year he was in San Jose for over eight months and in San Francisco for the remainder.[44]

Taking all the San Jose cases he could get, Judge Ingram spent more and more time in San Jose, even though the court's rules on San Jose venue had not changed. Without any change in the rules, he effectively arranged what the San Francisco judges had avoided doing since 1966 — placing a full-time federal judge in San Jose. Some of the other judges might not have liked this development, but they could do little about it. To a degree, it appeared Judge Ingram's success in becoming the federal judge for the central coast obviated any immediate need for a venue rule change. Although such a change would increase the number of cases at San Jose to their proper and natural level, the northern district judges from the San Jose area still "did not think it was [an] appropriate" time to ask the court to change the rules. But as he sat in San Jose almost on a full-time basis now, it was becoming apparent that the court there would become a full-time one despite the court rules hindering this. As Judge Ingram's constant sitting there

*The four judges of the San Jose federal court. From left to right are Judges William A. Ingram, Spencer Williams, Robert F. Peckham, and Robert P. Aguilar. (Photograph by Ira Nowinski.)*

became known, other judges were more inclined to grant motions for transfer to San Jose.

All of these developments compelled Judge Ingram to consider whether the time had come for civil cases from the central coast area to be filed and heard at San Jose. He started to speak with each of his colleagues about changing the rule and discovered the opposition was not as strong as first imagined. With Robert Aguilar now on the northern district bench, of the twelve active judges, one third were from the San Jose area. Each of these four judges was a strong proponent of a full-time federal court on the central coast; only three more judges would have to be found to support a change in the civil venue rule. Ingram suspected this might not be too difficult. The San Francisco judges were beginning to face a new reality: the General Services Administration had already begun construction of the 34 million dollar court facility in San Jose. It would be a sad commentary on the court if the judges did not allow the building to be fully utilized. In addition, many of the judges who had been ardent opponents of the San Jose court from the days when Bob Beresford, Russ Roessler, and Don Edwards battled for a San Jose court bill had either left the court or adopted senior status. Of the court which, in 1966, adopted the restrictive venue Rule Two — the original rule requiring transfer to San Jose of both civil and criminal cases — Judges Harris, Burke, and Zirpoli were now senior judges and could not vote on the rules. Judges Wollenberg and Sweigert had died. Judge Renfrew had resigned.

This did not mean there was no opposition to a rule change. The strongest reasons

*The judges of the United States District Court for the Northern District of California,
November 1984. Clockwise from the left rear are Judges Samuel Conti, Charles A. Legge,
Stanley A. Weigel, Lloyd H. Burke, Robert F. Peckham, Robert H. Schnacke, Robert P. Aguilar,*

Spencer Williams, John P. Vukasin, Jr., Eugene F. Lynch, William A. Ingram, William W Schwarzer, Alfonso J. Zirpoli, William H. Orrick, Marilyn Hall Patel, and Thelton E. Henderson. (Photograph by Ira Nowinski.)

against the change were important ones. Some judges feared that giving the San Jose court a full and equal status with San Francisco would lead to a clique of judges who would hear cases full-time in San Jose, refraining from any San Francisco activities of the court. There would be a true fragmentation of the court and the court's efficiency would be irreparably damaged. With one court in San Francisco and another in San Jose, there would no longer be the collegiality that characterized the northern district's bench and made it a premier court on which to serve. There was a fear of dissolving into a divided district, on the order of the Eastern District of California, where it was believed that the judges were divided between Sacramento and Fresno. The eastern district judges had frequent troubles administering their district with one voice and with a balanced hand. A Fresno judge might consider himself an eastern district judge in name only, inclined to consider only the problems of his court in Fresno and not the problems of the entire district. There was also the fear that Judge Harris had originally raised about a court divided between two cities: with fewer judges at each courthouse in a fractionated district, the interchange of new ideas and professional observations between the judges would slow to a trickle. The court and its ability to adjust to changed times would suffer.

Despite these fears, the judges from the San Jose area felt strongly that giving the court on the central coast equal status would outweigh these disadvantages by a large measure. They drafted a revision to the venue rule to eliminate the need to transfer civil cases from San Francisco to San Jose. The San Jose judges had discussed a possible version for this new rule with their San Francisco colleagues. They found a general lack of excitement by some, and resignation by others concerning the prospect of a rule change to allow liberal venue at San Jose.

The judges gathered on January 18, 1983, to consider the San Jose venue change rule. After some general conversation about the effect and reason for the rule, a general consensus emerged: "It's inevitable!" This decided — nearly seventeen years after Congress allowed the court to meet in San Jose — the judges set May 1, 1983, for the rule to be implemented. Then San Jose would, at last, become an equal partner in the northern district with San Francisco.

The effect of this rule change was dramatic. On the day the rule change became effective, Judge Ingram had only 75 civil cases in San Jose. A year later, this figure would rise to nearly 600 cases. And the numbers kept rising. In 1984, the San Jose court drew as many as 65 or 70 civil cases a month. This was a marked contrast to the caseload for the San Jose court when Ingram had first come on the court. In 1976, only 13 civil cases were pending before Judge Ingram in San Jose. This figure rose to 26 by 1977. The criminal load was similar. In 1976, he had 28 criminal cases to hear involving some 37 defendants. In 1977, this rose to 54 cases involving 69 defendants. These figures appear miniscule compared to the filings in San Jose after the venue rule change in 1983. During the first year of the rule's operation, the San Jose court had 736 civil cases and 128 criminal cases filed to be heard there.[45]

The dramatic increase in San Jose filings had another impact: the area would need more than one full-time federal judge. During the venue rule's first year of operation, when a San Francisco judge averaged 378 civil case filings per year, the San Jose judge almost doubled this figure with 749 civil case filings per year. Similarly, where the San Francisco judge averaged nearly 50 criminal cases per year, his colleague in San Jose averaged 98 criminal cases per year. This made necessary the assignment of more than one judge to the San Jose Courthouse. Accordingly, Judge Robert P. Aguilar readily joined Judge Ingram to hear cases in San Jose.

Those gathered at the venue rule change ceremony that bright morning in March 1983 at the San Jose temporary courthouse could not yet know these figures on the San Jose court's use, but few would have been surprised by them. Most expected this meeting to be the last gathering of the San Jose court proponents before the court found its final home in downtown San Jose. The group might meet like this once more — at the dedication of the new court building — and then, with the San Jose court an equal partner in the northern district, each would go their separate ways in the history of the United States District Court for the Northern District of California.

But there remained one thing uniting them. It was a characteristic indispensable to the thirty-four-year struggle for a court in San Jose — it was a quality called faith.

It was faith in the development of a modest town of San Jose, that Bob Beresford had adopted in place of New York, that propelled him on the path to finding an accessible federal forum for the community as early as 1948. Russ Roessler's faith in the central coast bar and in the expansion of the Santa Clara valley into the Silicon Valley prevented him from slowing or dropping his struggle for a local federal court. Similarly, Don Edwards's faith that he, a newcomer to Congress, could maneuver an unprecedented proposal to divide the district, through the maze of Washington politics, contributed to his advance in Congress and his ability to further the interests of the San Jose court. It was the faith of Judge Richard Chambers that the San Jose court proponents were going somewhere that brought him to enlist in their ranks and to encourage an administration of justice that would be equal rather than merely efficient. Finally, it was Robert Peckham's faith that made him stand up for the San Jose court against all of his colleagues on the northern district court . . . a faith that, in the end, the court in San Jose could not fail.

Former Chief Judge George B. Harris and his colleagues on the northern district bench had lacked this faith. Having lived and struggled to rise to the northern district court in San Francisco, they had little reason to reassess their view of San Francisco as the center of the northern district's universe.

Judge Richard Chambers once predicted the court at San Jose would become "a very busy place," and declared: "On this, I shall be vindicated." A day later, Chambers put himself on the line — so strong was his faith in the central coast region and its need for a court. "I know you are not a betting man," Chambers told Harris, so he challenged Harris to "inquire of Stan Weigel if he wants to bet" on whether the San Jose court would ever have enough cases to support itself. Apparently Harris replied that this was no bet — even Harris entered this contest. He and Weigel, another northern district judge and San Jose court opponent could accept Chambers's challenge. This acceptance did not faze Chambers, and he dryly told Harris, "I would be glad to take your money as well as Stan's."[46]

In 1983, years after Harris and Chambers exchanged challenges, the central coast counties — Santa Clara, San Benito, Santa Cruz, and Monterey — achieved equal status as part of the Northern District of California. This is one bet that Chambers surely won.

# Part 3

## An End to the Odyssey— A Home in the Central Coast Counties

The people of the central coast counties might not have been much aware of the struggle for their federal court and courthouse, yet, over the years, they would benefit from it. Others would benefit daily: the wandering life could now change to one with the stability of a home. There would be no more long hours in the car, no more using the car trunk as an office, more simplified interaction with other federal offices, and generally better treatment.

The first chapter of this part provides a view of the concerns faced and overcome in getting the courthouse designed and built. Written by Michael Griffith, historian and archivist for the United States District Court, Northern District of California, it is a behind-the-scenes look at the structure that now holds the court and its adjunct offices.

The other chapters are also from insiders' perspectives, from those whose offices have been directly affected by the plans for a courthouse and federal building. Santa Clara County Superior Court Judge Mark Thomas, Jr. and United States Magistrate Nordin F. Blacker provide an account of the commissioners and magistrates of the central coast counties, concluding with a discussion of Magistrate Blacker's present duties as part-time magistrate. A graduate of the University of Southern California Law School, Magistrate Blacker also practices law in San Jose, specializing in family law matters. A native of San Jose, Judge Thomas graduated from Stanford and Santa Clara Law School. He served as a Marine Corps platoon leader in the Korean conflict. In addition to his duties as a judge, he writes a weekly column in *The Independent Advocate,* a San Jose legal newspaper.

First appointed as a referee in bankruptcy in 1965, Bankruptcy Judge Warren C. Moore is well qualified to describe the San Jose bankruptcy court, past and present. In his chapters, one sees the changes in the bankruptcy system as well as how the caseload has grown in San Jose over the years.

An office whose work load has undergone perhaps an even more dramatic alteration in recent years is the United States Clerk's office. The chapter describing how this office and its staff have changed over the years is written by Michael Griffith.

Paul M. Chandler, a United States probation officer from 1956 to 1982 and former national president of the Federal Probation Officers Association, has written a history of the United States Probation office in San Jose. The chapter describes the establishment of the office in San Jose and traces its development and alteration over the past two decades.

Another office which has undergone considerable change since its opening in San Jose is that of the Federal Public Defender. Describing that office is Assistant Federal Public Defender Patricia V. Trumbull, who has been in the San Jose office since 1978. A graduate of Georgetown Law School, Ms. Trumbull clerked for United States District Court Judge Spencer Williams prior to joining the Federal Public Defender's office in 1975.

The final chapter of this part is by Michael Griffith and by Donald B. Ayer. Mr. Griffith first gives an overview of the United States Attorney's office and the machinations involved in getting a full-time branch office in San Jose approved. Mr. Ayer, a graduate of Harvard Law School and former law clerk to Supreme Court Justice William Rehnquist, then fills in the details. Now United States attorney for the Eastern District of California, he shares his firsthand experience as an assistant United States attorney, first making the long odyssey to San Jose, and then as the first assistant United States attorney in San Jose full time. The chapter and this part concludes with Mr. Griffith's description of the United States Marshal's office, integral to the functions now performed in San Jose and to the safety and well being of the court's judges.

# 14

# The United States Courthouse and Federal Building

*Michael Griffith*

Standing before the frame of girders, Judge William Ingram began his speech to the crowd, composed primarily of prominent political figures from the central coast counties. They knew that the ceremony, marking the topping off, or completion, of the steel framework for the new United States Courthouse and Federal Building in San Jose would be a special occasion for the San Jose federal judges, who had long held court in vastly inferior facilities.

In his remarks, the judge did not hide his feelings about the impending change. Reflecting on his current facilities, he likened them to being "lost in the wilderness." In contrast, the new building would be like a "palace." [1]

While the word "palace" was a misnomer for the new building, the use of "wilderness" was apt. Although in 1966 proponents of a San Jose federal court secured a law authorizing a federal court presence in the city, for years they lacked a facility worthy of the court. Only through the efforts of a great many individuals was such a building obtained.

During this struggle, the court made do in temporary quarters. At first, the Santa Clara County Board of Supervisors provided free facilities in the new Superior Court Building in downtown San Jose, but the supervisors ended that agreement in 1973. From that date until 1984, when the new building opened, the court sat in two portable modular buildings placed on a city-owned site near the intersection of West Taylor and Guadalupe Parkway.

In 1966, San Jose court supporters probably did not feel they were venturing on a wilderness journey. Rather, they likely regarded the acquisition of temporary quarters in the Superior Court Building as a great triumph. Only later would the years in the temporary facilities seem part of a wearying journey toward an acceptable courthouse.

*United States District Court Judge William A. Ingram speaking at the topping-off ceremony for the new United States Courthouse and Federal Building, August 26, 1982. (Photograph by Marci Severson.)*

The acquisition of the superior court housing for the new federal court formed part of the overall campaign to persuade Congress to permit federal court sessions in the city. Sharing the belief that San Jose deserved a federal court, the Santa Clara County Board of Supervisors, composed of Sam Della Maggiore, Charles Quinn, Ralph H. Mehrkens, Sig Sanchez, and Martin J. Spangler, made clear its willingness to provide temporary facilities well before the passage of any law allowing a federal judge to sit in San Jose. Writing to Congressman Don Edwards in late 1965, Chair of the Board Sig Sanchez noted that the supervisors had informed the congressman of their willingness to provide such facilities "on several occasions" and repeated the offer, specifying five years at one dollar per year. This offer helped persuade recalcitrant congressmen to approve the San Jose court provision, since the board proposal would significantly reduce costs associated with the change.[2]

With this offer, the physical move of the court to San Jose proved a simple matter. In late March or early April 1966, Judge Oliver J. Carter, then the northern district judge in charge of space questions, wrote the various court offices asking their space needs for San Jose. In early November, Judge Carter and Judge Robert F. Peckham, then presiding judge of the superior court but soon to be sitting in San Jose as a federal judge, visited the building and approved the offer of courtroom thirteen on the fifth floor. The

Government Services Administration (GSA) executed the lease with the county of Santa Clara in time for Judge Peckham to open federal court in San Jose in January 1967. [3]

Facilities for other court offices took longer: until December 1967. Even with space ready, most court offices refused to move on the ground that demand did not justify a permanent presence in San Jose.

Initially San Jose court supporters did not campaign for a permanent building. They realized that it would take some time for court business to build in San Jose, and until that time, proposals for a new facility would have no chance. In a December 1968 letter to Russ Roessler, head of the Santa Clara County Bar Association's Federal Court Committee, Judge Peckham noted that his colleague Judge Oliver J. Carter had encouraged him to put the planning in motion for a courthouse and federal building. In addition, he wrote that Judge Albert C. Wollenberg in his capacity as the Ninth Circuit district judge representative to the United States Judicial Conference had learned about the number of localities throughout the country making plans for new courthouses and federal buildings. After consulting on these matters, area Congressman Don Edwards contacted GSA in Washington, D.C. to urge a study be made of the need for such a building. [4]

Within three months, GSA was making such a study. In late February 1969, the Washington-based Administrative Office for all federal courts contacted Judge Carter. In their letter, they included the data they proposed giving GSA about court needs in San Jose in response to the GSA inquiry, and they asked for the necessary approval from the district judges and from the Ninth Circuit Judicial Council, the federal court administrative body within the circuit. [5]

Between this letter and the court's submission of data, however, the standing of the San Jose court changed dramatically. When the Administrative Office wrote to the northern district, cases were heard in San Jose only if a judge transferred them there, something that was not obligatory. Probably because of the limited jurisdiction of the court, the Administrative Office's proposal called for only one courtroom and allocated reserve space, to be used by other agencies until needed by the court, for only one more.

In September 1969, though, Judge Peckham protested the division of business between the court in San Francisco and in San Jose, and in mid-1970, under pressure from the Ninth Circuit Judicial Council, the northern district judges made it mandatory to hear criminal cases in San Jose if they arose in the central coast area. With this change in status, the need for a larger courthouse was quite evident since the San Jose court would necessarily hear many more cases than it had before.

In asking court officials to assess the adequacies of the Administrative Office's proposal, Judge Carter requested that they plan for the future, not just for the present, and he noted that "San Jose and Santa Clara County have been rapidly growing areas" and that "both . . . will probably be the most heavily populated in the Bay Area within [twenty years]." The judge also pointed out that the northern district judges would be requesting two courtrooms be built immediately and space for two others kept in reserve, twice as much as originally indicated. [6]

The courthouse finally proposed by the northern district judges significantly exceeded that suggested by the Administrative Office. Instead of two courtrooms, the judges called for five, two immediately and three as reserve space. Instead of a 2,030 square-foot clerk's office, the district asked for one of 7,925, including reserve space; and instead of space for two referees in bankruptcy, the new plan called for larger quarters for three.

The Superior Court Building in San Jose. From 1967 through 1972, the United States District Court sat in this building. (Photograph by Scott Chandler.)

Altogether, where the old plan had been for 23,610 square feet, the new one was for 59,039, including reserve space, only 6,629 square feet smaller than the courthouse ultimately built.[7]

With the expanded venue to include all criminal cases, there also came an important change in the campaign for a permanent courthouse. At the time of the rule change, Judge Peckham proposed to Russ Roessler and other court supporters that a San Jose Federal Court Advisory Committee be formed of attorneys from the central coast counties. It was envisioned that the committee would provide advice and leadership on a variety of problems that would confront the area's newly expanded federal court. And so, the struggle for a permanent courthouse moved to another level. As a means through which bar opinion could be obtained, the committee aided the judges and local congressmen in making their plans. As a separate group whose members had important contacts of their own, the group helped broaden the base of active support for the new courthouse. And as an energetic and independent participant in the struggle, the committee helped increase pressure for action.

Carefully organized to involve all those concerned with the federal courts in the central coast counties, the committee had a diverse membership. It included the presidents of the bar associations of Santa Clara, San Benito, Santa Cruz, and Monterey counties. It also included the chair of the federal practice section of the Santa Clara County Bar Association, the president of the Santa Clara County Barristers, and the president of the San Jose chapter of the Federal Bar Association. To round out the membership, there were three additional attorneys from Santa Clara county, two from Monterey county, and one from Santa Cruz county. Also serving were all attorneys from the area who had been delegates to the Ninth Circuit Judicial Conference, the United States magistrates from Monterey and Santa Clara counties, the referees in bankruptcy, and representatives from the law schools at Stanford University and at the University of Santa Clara.

In particular, the building subcommittee played an important role. From the first Advisory Committee meeting, Austen Warburton and Edwin Jones served as joint chairs of the subcommittee. They, along with Lionel Allan, the Advisory Committee's secretary, and, of course, Russ Roessler, the chairman, played especially important roles in the campaigns which followed.[8]

Shortly after the building subcommittee was organized, Judge Carter transmitted the northern district court's expanded courtroom proposal to Washington. On November 2, the Administrative Office accepted the judges' new figures for the proposed courthouse. On November 10, Judge Carter wrote Judge Chambers, chief judge of the Ninth Circuit Court of Appeals, seeking the required approval of the Ninth Circuit Judicial Council for the figures, and the council formally granted the authorization.[9]

Judge Carter, chairman of the court's building committee, although committed to his San Francisco colleagues to oppose the expansion of venue for the San Jose court, was enormously helpful to the proponents of the permanent San Jose courthouse by unqualifiedly giving the northern district court's approval to the project. "Without the authorization of the district court, the courthouse project would have been dead in its tracks. It was Judge Carter who alone spoke for the court on building matters and gave its blessing for an adequate courthouse in San Jose. Having come from Redding, in Shasta County, he had an innate empathy with outlanders and understood their aspirations," Chief Judge Peckham has observed. Carter had succeeded his father in the state senate of California when the latter became an associate justice of the California Supreme Court and was California Democratic party chairman in 1948 when President Truman carried California.[10]

During this same period, the building subcommittee was not idle. Without waiting for GSA to take action, they began meetings with San Jose city planners to discuss possible building sites. By early February 1971, the city and subcommittee identified five possible sites, three in downtown and two in the Civic Center area, with the city preferring one of the former locations.[11]

After the building proposal went from the Administrative Office to GSA, court proponents sought to shepherd it through that agency. On December 2, 1970, the building subcommittee met with Judges Peckham and Carter to discuss strategy and thereafter contacted area congressmen. Word from area congressmen quickly indicated to the building proponents that they had a long road ahead of them. In describing their meeting with GSA, Congressman Edwards noted that they had been unable to secure a commitment as to when GSA would draw up a courthouse proposal, and Congressman Charles Gubser called the meeting "not encouraging." Writing to Austen Warburton two months later, Congressman Gubser advised him not to worry about site difficulties because "right now, our principal problem is getting the federal building authorized."[12]

*The temporary Federal Building and United States Courthouse on West Taylor Street in San Jose. This view shows the judges' parking area on the northeast side of the courthouse building. (Photograph by Ira Nowinski.)*

In May 1971, however, a new crisis confronted court supporters, and it turned their attention from the permanent courthouse for over two years. In that month, Santa Clara County announced its intention of not renewing the five-year lease the federal court had for space in the Superior Court Building. Since the lease ran out in January 1972, the court and its supporters faced the problem of finding new space during the next six months.

The Santa Clara County Board of Supervisors acted for a number of reasons. As Judge Peckham and Russ Roessler had seen would happen, the expansion of the county superior court created a need for the borrowed space. At the same time, the supervisors felt that without a push from them, the federal government would never act. There also was a feeling that the county should not be subsidizing the national government in a way Judge Peckham described as "revenue sharing in reverse."[13]

The Advisory Committee acted quickly to rally support for both a temporary and a permanent solution, contacting congressmen and senators. Despite these efforts no quick solution was found for the problem.

Ultimately, though, a solution was contrived. Judge Peckham knew that temporary federal court buildings at San Diego would no longer be used with completion of that city's new federal building and courthouse. Judge Peckham and Judge Spencer Williams, who had joined the court in 1971 and was a strong supporter of the San Jose court, went to San Diego to see if these could be taken apart, brought to San Jose, and reconstructed. At the same time, the city of San Jose, wishing to retain the court, agreed to lease a site near the intersection of West Taylor and Guadalupe for five years, with a five year

*A view of the northwest front of the temporary Federal Building and United States Courthouse
showing the boardwalk along the courthouse section of the complex. The probation office
occupied the federal building located to the right of the stairs in the foreground. (Photograph by
Ira Nowinski.)*

renewal possible. The county also allowed the court extensive additional time until the
new facilities were ready, and in January 1973, the court moved into its new quarters.
Judge Peckham, not wanting to impose further upon his former colleagues on the superior court moved the federal court to a vacant superior court in the North Santa Clara
County Office Building in Palo Alto for the months of November and December 1972.
When the San Diego buildings became unavailable to San Jose, GSA ordered new portable modules with redwood siding.[14]

On June 12, 1973, the new buildings had their formal dedication. Speaking before a
crowd of local "judicial, legal and government leaders," Judges Carter, Peckham, and
Williams made brief remarks after the welcome delivered by Russ Roessler, and Congressman Edwards then delivered the main address. Despite their pleasure at the court's
having finally secured a home of its own, all the speakers expressed a wish to move forward with securing a permanent building. Indeed, in his speech at the dedication, Congressman Edwards told the crowd that he had already called GSA in Washington and
had been "assured that we have a high priority."[15]

Federal building advocates soon followed up Congressman Edwards's initial conversation with GSA. By early October, having heard no news, Russ Roessler contacted the
San Francisco branch of GSA to inquire about schedules. In his letter, he noted that in a
June meeting with Edwards, GSA officials in Washington had promised to send out letters initiating the planning process in the "very near future," to complete a preliminary
study in three months, and to send a building proposal to the Office of Management and

Budget (OMB) in six months. OMB would study the proposal and, it was hoped, approve it and send it to Congress.

GSA's response to the Roessler letter indicated the need for continual work. According to the San Francisco regional administrator, GSA had identified a "need" for a San Jose federal building and it was "one of our priority projects for construction [by 1977]." However, the official noted, the project had to be judged "nationwide based on the comparative urgency of need and an equitable distribution."[16]

Although neutral in tone, the letter disturbed Roessler. Basically, it made no promises and, in fact, held out the possibility that the building might not even be authorized, much less built, through 1977. The neutrality seemed to indicate that GSA felt no particular enthusiasm or sense of urgency about the building. Writing to Judge Peckham, Roessler concluded that "we had, perhaps, better use our congressmens' and United States senators' assistance" if GSA was to give the courthouse and federal building "the priority to which it is entitled."[17]

Working with congressmen and senators did lead to some progress. In late February 1974, Congressman Gubser requested from GSA a report on federal space needs in San Jose. About the same time, Congressman Edwards urged the agency to make "a definite and clear commitment" for "this badly needed facility." Edwards also helped arrange a meeting between GSA and two San Jose city council members, James Self and Susanne Wilson, visiting Washington in March. At that meeting, GSA announced that a feasibility study would be undertaken as a further step in the planning of a proposed courthouse and federal building.[18]

Even with the promise of a feasibility study, the proponents of a San Jose courthouse and federal building did not relax their efforts. They feared that a promise in March might mean nothing in September. Within two weeks of the meeting between GSA and the San Jose city council members, Russ Roessler began setting up a meeting among California Senators Alan Cranston and John Tunney and local advocates of the building; his efforts gained additional commitments from Senators Cranston and Tunney.[19]

The process continued throughout 1974. Continually the congressmen contacted GSA. Continually Russ Roessler and the congressmen corresponded, and San Jose officials involved themselves. In late May, GSA announced a field survey would be carried out for the new courthouse and building. In mid-August, GSA's San Francisco office announced that its planned development report would be completed within a month.

By late September, Russ Roessler's main concern was not that GSA finish its report but that the building be assigned a reasonably high priority. Writing to both Gubser and Edwards, he asked each who in GSA "if it is GSA" would make the recommendation and who locally would be "most effective" in persuading GSA and the administration. Roessler's concern, although warranted by past events, proved groundless. The project had advanced far enough and had sufficient support that there no longer was any possibility of it dying in GSA. As Edwards noted in his reply to Roessler's letter, "things are about as good as they can be" although "it would certainly do no harm" for appropriate individuals to "drop Jerry Ford a line." [20]

Early 1975 saw the end of the first stage of the struggle for a permanent courthouse and federal building . On February 11, GSA formally submitted its prospectus for a federal building and courthouse in San Jose to OMB. Upon approval by that office, it would go to the public works committees of the House and Senate.[21]

At this point, proponents of the San Jose courthouse and federal building probably

*Congressman Norm Mineta of San Jose. It was through Congressman Mineta's persistence and dedication that funding was secured for a new United States Courthouse and Federal Building in San Jose. (Photograph by Ira Nowinski.)*

remained apprehensive. Experience had taught them that gaining a new building would be a difficult process and one that required careful attention all along the way. Although they hoped the proposal would sail through OMB and then through Congress, they remained concerned.

As events would show, their concern was highly warranted. After having moved out of GSA during early 1975, the plans for the San Jose courthouse and federal building came to a dead stop in OMB. As became an almost standard policy from the mid-1970s on, OMB refused to forward proposals for new federal buildings to Congress. For the remainder of Ford's presidency, OMB held onto the San Jose proposal, and no progress at all was made during the rest of 1975 or during 1976.[22]

By early 1977, proponents of the court no longer wished to wait for OMB action. At this point, Congressman Norm Mineta stepped in and began the series of actions which ultimately led to passage of an appropriation for the new building. A graduate of the University of California at Berkeley, Mineta became a respected San Jose insurance broker and civic leader. After establishing himself as a popular and able mayor of San Jose, Mineta entered Congress in 1974. In 1977, he became chair of the Public Buildings and Grounds Subcommittee of the House Committee on Public Works and Transportation, a powerful position from which to act, since that subcommittee recommended whether or not to construct new federal buildings.

Mineta first moved to circumvent OMB. Under a provision of the 1959 Public Buildings Act, his subcommittee could require GSA to make a report on federal space needs in an area. If GSA stated construction was needed and if the subcommittee and the full committee approved, then the construction was authorized by the House. Unlike with other projects, a full vote of the House was not required. Of course, after authorization, an appropriation still had to be obtained if the approved project actually were to be built.

Frequently consulting with his colleagues, Mineta quickly managed to gain a request for a GSA report. Not surprisingly, GSA reported that San Jose did need a federal building (although had they stated the contrary that would have been the end of the process). Upon Mineta's urging, both the subcommittee and the full committee then approved the building.

Obtaining an appropriation for the building proved more time consuming. Mineta had to do an enormous amount of legwork consulting with colleagues on the House Committee on Appropriations. By carefully outlining the need for the building, however, the congressman eventually secured the approval he sought and then easily gained a favorable vote from the House as a whole.

In the Senate, of course, other persons carried the load. However, Mineta also kept close watch over the Senate proceedings, and at one point he appeared before the Senate Committee on Appropriations to testify to the need for the building.

In early 1978, Mineta's efforts finally bore fruit. After a prolonged House-Senate dispute over wholly unrelated matters, Congress approved the Supplemental Appropriations Act of 1978, which contained, among many larger appropriations, 34 million dollars for a San Jose courthouse and federal building.[23]

Passage of the Supplemental Appropriations Act concluded the decade-long quest for a courthouse and federal building in San Jose. Involving the judges, the bar, the local press, and San Jose officials, the movement reflected the widespread belief that San Jose deserved better. With the continued support of the area congressmen and the backing of California's senators, the building finally won authorization.

And yet, for at least some of the participants, the struggle had not ended. Having won authorization for a building, long-time advocates of a federal court for San Jose faced the new problem of turning the appropriation into a suitable courthouse. In particular, court supporters soon found themselves engaged in a heated struggle over the size of courtrooms in the new building.

The struggle over courtroom size had its roots in a study carried on under the auspices of Chief Justice Warren E. Burger. In 1971, the chief justice sponsored creation of an ad hoc Committee on Court Facilities and Design to look into ways of making courtrooms more efficient, more economical, and more secure.

Although little noticed by supporters of the San Jose court in 1972, the guidelines adopted by the committee laid the groundwork for the struggle that followed in 1978. Among other things, the committee proposed and the Judicial Conference, the overall administrative body of the federal courts, agreed, that courtrooms in new courthouses should range from 1,120 square feet (28 feet by 40 feet) to 1,496 square feet (34 feet by 44 feet). The conference also approved the construction of "one or more" large ceremonial courtrooms "for unusual purposes, such as multiparty cases" and "where need is demonstrated." These courtrooms were to be 2,400 square feet (40 feet by 60 feet). In later publications, the sense of the conference was understood to be that at least one large courtroom would be built in each new courthouse. According to the conference, the number of each size of courtroom would be set by the Judicial Council of the appropriate circuit after consultation with the district court judges affected.[24]

It was not over the guidelines themselves, however, but over the interpretation to be given them that the struggle centered. For the San Jose judges, who included Judge William A. Ingram since 1976, the conference resolution presented not ironclad rules but rather signposts to be used in requesting courtroom space in new buildings. However, for the chief justice, the conference resolution constituted a commitment to the sizes indicated and to smaller courtrooms in general. Indeed, the chief justice apparently believed the conference had mandated a standard courtroom size of 1,100 square feet, although the resolution itself only set size ranges and noted the situations in which larger courtrooms could be requested. For the San Jose judges the literal application of the guidelines threatened to severely harm the courthouse for which they had so long worked. Rather than gaining a new, suitable home for the court, they would have poor facilities "for fifty years or more."[25]

Partly as a result of the strong differences in outlook, the struggle over courtroom size was long. Before its resolution it would involve a wide range of people, and its conclusion would decisively alter the courtroom size guidelines for the nation.

The struggle began in December 1977, when Judge Peckham, by then chief judge of the northern district, learned from Jay Solomon, the Washington head of GSA, that the chief justice had a "firm commitment" to 1,100 square foot courtrooms. Starting in late February 1978, the judges showed a sense of urgency, because the head of GSA pledged to have the courthouse and federal building planned, designed, and built in two and one-half years, a period described by one judge as "astonishingly short." Given this commitment, the judges felt a new need to move quickly on the courtroom size issue if they were not to be confronted with a fait accompli.[26]

Initially the judges' efforts centered on gathering information necessary to make an informed presentation to GSA and to other interested parties and on building community support for their struggle. On March 11, Judge Peckham addressed the regular meeting of the San Jose Federal Court Advisory Committee on the issues and found himself "very encouraged from the response." To provide input into the design process, the group resolved that the county bar association presidents of the areas served by the court would appoint a committee of fifteen after consultation with the judges. The judges also met with Congressman Mineta on March 28, and presumably covered the question of courtroom size.[27]

At least initially, events seemed to be moving in the judges' favor. On March 23, the Santa Clara County Bar Association recommended that there be five courtrooms in the new courthouse, with three finished immediately, two of 2,400 square feet and one of at least 1,800. During March, the judges also discussed the April presentation of their case to the Judicial Council. Overall, they must have felt confident that they had a strong case. Besides the Santa Clara County Bar Association resolution, they could point to the size of other courtrooms in the area, including 1,900 square foot superior court facilities in San Jose, and to the large number of multiparty cases filed in San Jose, exactly the sort of cases which would rapidly overwhelm the capacity of a small courtroom.[28]

After the initial victories, however, events began to flow in a different direction. In mid-April the Circuit Council approved the judges' request for the larger courtrooms and increased the total number of courtrooms to eight, with five as reserve. About a week after the Administrative Office received the Circuit Council's resolution, it wrote back to Circuit Executive William B. Luck, pointing out that the 2,250 square foot courtrooms were "at variance" with the Judicial Conference's October 1972 resolution and that the Administrative Office lacked authority to deviate from the guidelines there set down. But the judges did not shy away from their commitment to a workable court at the first sign of opposition. Consulting with Circuit Chief Judge James R. Browning and with former Chief Judge Richard Chambers, they decided simply to ask for three 2,400 square foot courtrooms rather than one at 2,400 and two at 2,250, and in July, the Judicial Council agreed to their proposal. By this action they adhered to the guidelines set down and at the same time obtained courtrooms adequate for the cases they anticipated hearing.[29]

The judges' commitment to large courtrooms was strengthened by an event one month later. On July 31, a just sentenced bank robber successfully fled from one of the tiny temporary San Jose courtrooms. Pivoting "like a quarterback" he "shot out of the courtroom" while the crush of spectators, court officials, and tables made it impossible for the marshals to mount an effective pursuit. His temporarily successful escape provided further evidence of the "woeful foolhardiness" of building small courtrooms, in which adequate security could not be provided. [30]

Perhaps not surprisingly the judges' initial action on the courtroom size issue did not end the struggle, but rather intensified it. In early August, Judge Chambers, then in Washington, learned that while the Administrative Office had not disapproved the Circuit Council request for three courtrooms, GSA had. According to GSA, they could not build more than one large courtroom in a new courthouse without justification, a stand supported by the chief justice, according to Jay Solomon, the head of GSA.[31]

With the defeat of their first efforts, the San Jose judges had to begin again to secure courtrooms of a reasonable size. Moreover, with the invocation of the chief justice on the other side, the struggle clearly had become a weightier matter. Basically, however, the judges followed the same steps they had earlier. Acting on Judge Chambers's suggestions, they sought to indicate the liabilities of the smaller courtrooms while building support for the larger ones. In particular, they had the question investigated whether the small courtrooms would violate San Jose ordinances with respect to occupancy of public rooms, but the results were inconclusive. At the same time, they consulted with area Congressmen Don Edwards and Norm Mineta about means of changing GSA's outlook.[32]

As before, Circuit Council action lay at the center of what had to be done. In the Administrative Office's understanding, justification for the three 2,400 square foot courtrooms should come from the council, presumably to be forwarded to GSA. Such a justification had to reflect need either based on projected case loads or on "other unusual purposes."[33]

However, before the San Jose judges could prepare such a justification, the dispute reached its highest levels with the direct intervention of the chief justice on the side of small courtrooms. Writing in late August to Chief Judge Browning, the chief justice noted that there appeared to be some resistance to the 1972 conference action, which he interpreted as fixing the standard courtroom at 1,100 square feet. "It is our collective obligation," he asserted "to see that the conference action is implemented."[34]

In a memorandum to Chief Judge Browning, Judge Peckham outlined considerations that had always motivated the judges in their efforts to achieve larger courtrooms. Among other things, he noted that the San Jose area had a heavy load of "complex multiparty" litigation, a result of the growth of Silicon Valley. In addition, he pointed out how little spectator room there would be even in 1,500 square foot courtrooms, the other alternative the Judicial Conference's 1972 resolution seemed to allow. Of course, he also mentioned the question of safety in light of the recent escape from San Jose.

The judge probably also had available letters sent to Judge Ingram about the temporary courtrooms. During early September, counsel from three separate firms, all involved in a patent case in San Jose, wrote to the judge to point out the inadequacies of the current courtrooms (1,100 square feet in size) and to urge that the permanent building have larger ones. An attorney summed up the prevailing views when he condemned the temporary courtrooms as "not only too small, but much too small."[35]

Any lingering optimism the San Jose judges may have felt about a solution surely dissipated in mid-October. During that month, they received copies of a September 29 letter from the chief justice to the president in which the chief justice indicated the possibilities of significant savings in new courtroom costs "with the support of the executive branch." Describing the Judicial Conference resolution of 1972, the chief justice noted that some judges, "once secure in office," might press for larger courtrooms unless "prior to their appointment the attorney general urges each new district judge not to." The chief justice also noted that "a positive directive" to GSA would be "equally important to achieve this objective." It was, in the words of one district judge, a "very interesting" letter and one which was "in many respects shocking."[36]

Perhaps fittingly, the solution to the courtroom controversy came not from the judiciary but from the executive branch with which the chief justice had corresponded. Writing in early January 1979 to Jay Solomon at GSA, Attorney General Griffin Bell described the problems of crowding and security the Department of Justice anticipated with courtrooms of 1,100 or 1,500 square feet. After noting that "the adverse effects" might not be outweighed by "the savings," he recommended that all courthouses have one 2,400 square foot courtroom, that "multijudge, large metropolitan cities" have "at least two" and that "the majority of the courtrooms should be approximately 1,800 square feet."[37]

With that letter, the chief justice decided to abandon the fight. Noting that it was a matter "over which we have no jurisdiction," he took satisfaction in that even the attorney general's proposed standards would "save very substantial amounts" over the courtrooms of the past, and he decided to " 'acquiesce' and move on to other problems."[38]

Even so, the San Jose judges did not get all of what they wanted. On February 14, 1979, the head of GSA issued a new directive embodying the chief justice's decision, and under its guidelines, the San Jose courthouse received one courtroom at 2,400 square feet and two at 1,800. Although they felt unhappy with the allocation, preferring two courtrooms of 2,400 square feet, the judges did not vigorously press the matter.[39]

The courtroom guidelines, however, was not the only area from which threats emerged to the existence of a usable building. By allowing inflation to reduce the value of the appropriation, disputes over site acquisition threatened to drastically shrink the size of the building. Only by the continued efforts of Congressman Norm Mineta was the damage limited in its scope.

To a large extent, the dispute originated in events wholly unconnected with the San Jose courthouse. In mid and late 1978, a series of purchasing scandals rocked GSA, and the investigations made sensational national news. In consequence, GSA officials everywhere began examining with extreme care what would otherwise have been routine transactions.[40]

*A courtroom in the temporary Federal Building and United States Courthouse. Taken from the public seating, this picture helps make clear the inadequacies of the 1,100 square foot courtrooms. (Courtesy Judge Robert F. Peckham.)*

Nonetheless the site acquisition went well at first. Even before the appropriation passed for the courthouse, Congressman Mineta, the head of GSA, and San Jose officials surveyed sites in that city, and they quickly agreed on a list. In Washington, the formal site selection process proceeded quickly, and on February 21, 1978, GSA announced the selection of the block bounded by First, Second, Paseo de San Antonio, and San Carlos as the site of the new courthouse and federal building.

Once the process shifted from selection to negotiations over price, progress halted. City officials offered what they believed a fair price for the site and one that paralleled the estimates presented by the appraisers hired by GSA. However, GSA officials held out for a price similar to that granted a hotel developer who had negotiated purchase of a nearby site from the city, and they found unconvincing city officials' contention that the situations differed in significant ways.

Primarily it was the good offices of Congressman Mineta that kept the negotiations moving, even if at a slow pace. Phoning, remonstrating, and cajoling the different parties, the congressman spent long hours to make sure the two sides at least continued talking to each other. Because of the congressman's efforts, damage caused by the delays was kept relatively limited. Although the failure to reach final agreement until January 7, 1980 did harm the building, the principal loss was that of a full-scale basement, rather than of significant office space. [41]

*The start of construction on the new United States Courthouse and Federal Building. Taken March 24, 1982, this shot looks north across the site from South First Street. (Courtesy San Jose Mercury News.)*

The ending of the difficulties over courtroom size and site purchase marked a sort of turning point for the building. After the resolution of these two problems, no major threats to the structure emerged. However, that change did not mean the remaining process went easily for those involved with the new building. Rather, as is perhaps inherent in any large project requiring coordination among many groups, delays, snafus, and other frustrations, major and minor, marred construction from its start to its finish. Of the many problems that emerged, two stand out. Due to errors of GSA and the architect, the issue over courtroom size issue emerged again, and ironically, the San Jose judges finally received something closer to what they originally requested. In addition, a struggle over the size of bankruptcy court facilities continued well into construction until it received an outcome relatively satisfactory to the bankruptcy judges.

The courtroom size issue reemerged in 1982 at about the time of the topping-off ceremony. Although the details of the story are complicated, the main points can be easily summarized. Through planning errors by the building architects, which went undetected by GSA, the judges suddenly found themselves confronted with having one courtroom of 2,240 square feet and two of 1,500. Not surprisingly, the judges felt outraged, having undergone a protracted struggle to obtain larger facilities. The consequence was a study of how the error could be rectified. It turned out to be simpler to build two courtrooms of 2,400 square feet (with one of about 1,800) than to restore the original and now mangled design.[42]

The struggle over space for the bankruptcy court would take a separate study to tell

*The new United States Courthouse. This view shows the courthouse half of the Courthouse and Federal Building along South First Street. (Photograph by Ira Nowinski.)*

*The new Federal Building. This picture shows the federal building half of the Courthouse and Federal Building complex on the South First Street side. (Photograph by Ira Nowinski.)*

*The new United States Courthouse and Federal Building. This view looks northeast from South First Street through the courtyard. (Photograph by Ira Nowinski.)*

fully, although, again, highlights can be isolated. In many respects, it resembled the dispute over courtroom size with continuing conflicts among the Administrative Office, GSA, and the bankruptcy judges, and it was an even more protracted argument.

From the start of planning for the new building, the two bankruptcy judges, Warren Moore and Seymour Abrahams, worried that in the fights over space, the substantial needs of their expanding court would be ignored. Forced to produce an astonishing number of memoranda, they steadily fought for adequate facilities in the face of attempts to cut space. Basically, those attempts began when GSA released its first space estimates for the new building. Although there had been discussions on bankruptcy space requirements before, they involved no more than the San Jose judges asking for estimates. However, the issue became important immediately when GSA cut the bankruptcy judges' requests by about fifty percent.

In one way, the answer to the bankruptcy problem was simple. GSA based its space estimate on the figures gathered by Judge Carter in 1970, and what was needed was justification for the increase. With such justification, GSA would allot more room. However, the process of providing justification and gaining the space proved a very complicated one. Memoranda and letters went back and forth in enormous numbers. The passage of the Bankruptcy Reform Act of 1978, which altered the duties of the bankruptcy courts, further complicated matters.[43]

To make an involved story simple, the bankruptcy judges ultimately won most of the space they sought. In particular, they received the 1,500 square foot courtrooms they wished instead of the significantly smaller facilities threatened. In addition, they

*The ceremonial courtroom in the new United States Courthouse. This shot shows the bench with the witness box to the right. Between the bench and the attorney's table in the foreground is the area for the courtroom deputy and court reporter. (Photograph by Ira Nowinski.)*

*Another view of the ceremonial courtroom. This shot looks from the area of the witness box toward the back of the courtroom. In the left foreground is the jury box. (Photograph by Ira Nowinski.)*

*Congressmen Don Edwards and Norm Mineta in front of the new United States Courthouse which their efforts in such large measure helped make possible. (Photograph by Ira Nowinski.)*

obtained adequate office and storage space after initial allocations failed to provide any-thing near that necessary. Perhaps most importantly, they won reserve space for two future bankruptcy judges, thus insuring sufficient area for the court to operate in the future.[44]

The rest of the construction was scarcely without problems. Suffice it to say that an enormous number of details, ranging from the wall covering in the courtrooms to the size of the library to the type of courtroom seating, became the foci of often acrimonious disputes. The frequent difficulties led one San Jose judge to conclude that GSA regarded prospective tenants as "enemies."[45]

Ultimately, of course, the acrimony would fade. As the frustrations with the process dissipated, a new pride in what had been accomplished would grow. After all, in place of the temporary courthouse, a substantial new complex had risen. Composed of a five-story courthouse wing and a three-story office building joined by a soaring sunshade over a connecting plaza, the complex gave striking fulfillment to the hopes and aspirations that San Jose court supporters held to for so many years. After their years in the wilder-ness, it indeed provided a home.

# 15

# United States Commissioners and Magistrates

*Mark Thomas, Jr. and Nordin F. Blacker*

In its beginning the new United States of America had need of a judicial system. Within the existing metropolitan centers the presence of well-trained and experienced lawyers made possible an effective creative process. For the furthermost portions of the new frontier, however, the task was more difficult.

Ultimately, within the boundaries of the states, this problem was resolved by establishing a far-flung network of lay judges with the title of justice of the peace. The story of these shopkeepers and farmers who provided a forum for the enforcement of misdemeanor violations and resolution of minor civil disputes is well known. The tale of their federal counterparts, the United States commissioners—an account holding equal fascination and significance—remains to be told.

In 1793 the federal circuit courts were authorized by Congress to appoint "discreet persons learned in the law" entitled "Commissioners" to take bail in criminal matters. Gradually the number of commissioners and the scope of their authority increased, although they were paid on an extremely low, piecework basis. The development of the commissioner system generally paralleled that of the state justices of the peace in that the increased complexity of the law caused the elimination of nonlawyer commissioners and a reduction in the number of part-timers. With the passage of the Federal Magistrates Act of 1968 (effective 1971), a more appropriate remuneration was made available and even the name of the post was changed to magistrate. Further congressional legislation in 1976 and 1979 reemphasized the importance of the office.

The history of the federal commissioner within the four counties of Santa Clara, San Benito, Santa Cruz, and Monterey is perhaps typical of other districts throughout the union, the principal difference being that the first California appointments were not made until 1850.

From the existing records in the federal court in San Francisco and at the federal archives in San Bruno, Court Archivist Michael Griffith has pieced together the list of those who served as commissioners or magistrates and their approximate dates of office. Set forth below, by county, is the schedule of names and dates as well as additional information of interest.

---

### Santa Cruz County

| Commissioner | City | Date Appointed | Date Left Office |
|---|---|---|---|
| E.H. Heacock | Santa Cruz | July 28, 1873 | declined position |
| Roger Conant | Santa Cruz | August 29, 1873 | |

### San Benito County

| Commissioner | City | Date Appointed | Date Left Office |
|---|---|---|---|
| James F. Breen | San Juan | July 13, 1874 | March 3, 1876 |
| W.E. Lovett | Hollister | March 14, 1876 | August 12, 1878 |
| William Lee | Hollister | August 31, 1878 | September 3, 1890 |
| Nash Corwith Briggs | Hollister | September 18, 1890 | 1909? |
| H.W. Scott | Hollister | 1916? | 1926? |
| D.F.H. McPhail | Hollister | 1926? | 1930? |

Breen — Then resident in Monterey, he was appointed a bankruptcy commissioner for Monterey County by Judge Deady on March 18, 1868.

Briggs — The date he left office is uncertain. He was reappointed in 1905 for a four-year term in the last reference located.

Scott — He is listed in 1916 Rules of Practice (earliest in court library); not listed in 1926 version, the next available in the court library.

McPhail — He is listed in 1926 Rules of Practice; not listed in 1930 version, the next available in the court library.

---

In February 1874, James Breen, former county judge of Monterey County, was appointed to a similar position in newly-created San Benito County. Months later he was also appointed commissioner. As a child, Breen had been a member of the Donner party. His family were the first Americans to live in San Juan Bautista. After graduation from Santa Clara University, Breen studied law with a San Francisco law firm. He was later a member of the California Assembly and judge of the San Benito County Superior Court; his great-grandnephew now serves on that same court. Many other Breen descendants still reside in the San Juan Baustista area.

W. E. Lovett had been an assistant United States attorney in San Francisco and was reputed to be the first to open a law office in San Benito County.

Nash Corwith Briggs arrived in Amador County at the age of nineteen. When he reached twenty-one, he completed studies in his father's law office and was admitted to the bar. After practicing law in Alpine County for several years, Briggs came to the Hollister area in 1869 where he was active in the incorporation of the town and of San Benito County. In 1874, Briggs was elected as the county's first district attorney, defeating his commissioner predecessor W. E. Lovett by about 600 votes.

Breen apparently retained his federal position in Monterey County after the change of location of his county judgeship.

Monterey County

| Commissioner | City | Date Appointed | Date Left Office |
|---|---|---|---|
| James F. Breen | Monterey | March 18, 1868 | |
| Edward V. Brown | King City | December 1, 1887 | |
| William Matticks Rogers Parker | Salinas | June 25, 1875 | 1896? |
| George A. Daugherty | Salinas | June 25, 1896 | 1912? |
| Silas W. Mack | Monterey | 1913? | 1940? |
| Henry C. Spurr | Bradley | 1928? | 1930? |
| Joseph Peter Mandl | King City | 1933 | 1936 |
| H.J. King | Salinas | 1940 | 1941 |
| James A. Jeffery | Salinas | September, 1941 | May, 1962 |
| Arthur C. Atteridge | Salinas | June 27, 1962 | February 28, 1963 |
| Henry B. Fulton | Salinas | March 2, 1963 | June 30, 1969 |
| John Andrew Church | Salinas | July 30, 1969 | June 30, 1970 |
| Francis Carr | Monterey | July 1, 1970 | November 9, 1976 |
| Arthur C. Atteridge | Salinas | April 29, 1977 | present |

Breen — He previously served as a United States commissioner in San Benito County.

Parker — The date Parker left office is uncertain. He died in office and Daugherty succeeded him.

Daughtery and Mack — The dates listed are probable dates; they are the beginning dates for which the Records Center lists dockets for these commissioners.

Spurr — He is listed in 1928 Rules of Practice; not listed in 1930 version.

Mandl — These dates are from Amelie Elkinton, Letter to Judge Mark Thomas, Jr., 16 April 1984 based on interview with Mandl, Carmel, California.

King — The dates listed are probable dates; they are the dates for which the Records Center lists dockets for Commissioner King.

Jeffery — The dates listed are approximate dates; they are taken from dates of first and apparently last filings.

Atteridge — The dates listed are probable dates; they are taken from quarterly accounts.

William Matticks Rogers Parker was a Boston native who came to California in 1856. After employment as a surveyor and shopkeeper, Parker took up farming in Castroville in 1862. He was Monterey County clerk from 1865-1867 and served as both clerk and county recorder in 1870-1871. At some point, he must have studied law, because after his service with the county he practiced law in Salinas. His obituary in the *Monterey New Era* of June 27, 1896, referred to him as "United States land commissioner."

George A. Daugherty left his native Ohio in 1884 after graduation from Muskingum College. Upon his arrival in Monterey County, he took any job he could to start. He finally was able to study law under a local attorney and was admitted to the bar. Daugherty developed a major practice and became a principal in title and abstract companies in Monterey County. He served as president of the Board of Education in Salinas and later as mayor of that city.

Silas W. Mack came to Salinas in 1892 where he studied with a local attorney and was admitted to the bar in 1894. He was an organizer and director of the First National Bank of Monterey and the Bank of Carmel. He was also prominent as a Methodist lay religious leader in Pacific Grove.

Joseph Peter Mandl, a graduate of Stanford Law School, practiced law at King City and Salinas. He now resides in Carmel Valley. He was also a justice of the peace and a

*United States District Court
Commissioner James F. Breen.
Commissioner Breen was the first
United States commissioner
appointed in San Benito County.
(Courtesy Judge Mark Thomas, Jr.)*

police court judge in King City. In World War II, Mandl was a judge advocate for the South Pacific Islands.

Harry J. King was a native of Castroville and a nonlawyer. He also served as justice of the peace in Salinas.

James Jefferey, son of the leading hotel proprietor in Salinas, served as justice of the peace and municipal court judge for more than twenty-five years.

The present magistrate in Monterey County, Arthur C. Atteridge, is a graduate of the University of Santa Clara and Hastings College of Law. After his appointment as commissioner, he was appointed by the governor of California to the Board of Supervisors of Monterey County. Atteridge then resigned the commissioner's position because of a California constitutional provision which prohibited a state officer from holding a federal office paying more than $25 per year.

During the tenure of Henry Fulton, the scope of the commissioner's duties enlarged substantially. In addition to the cases of civilians charged with misdemeanor violations on federal reservations and parks, the commissioner acquired jurisdiction of military personnel at Fort Ord and other military bases. Fulton's pay was $2.50 per case unless the defendant appeared in court, when the fee rose to $15 per case; he had a limit of $10,500 per year. Because of the large volume of work, Fulton received his limit by July

United States Commissioner for Monterey County Francis J. Carr being sworn into office by United States District Court Judge Robert F. Peckham on July 2, 1970. (Courtesy Judge Mark Thomas, Jr.)

and worked without pay the balance of the year. A Hastings College graduate, Fulton now resides in North Vancouver, British Columbia.

John Andrew Church, another Hastings law graduate, practices law in Salinas and is active in the labor relations field.

Francis J. Carr was appointed a commissioner in 1970 and became the first magistrate in Monterey County under the new act in 1971. He was a graduate of the University of Santa Clara and the University of California Boalt Hall Law School. Before becoming a commissioner, Carr spent twenty years with the tax department of Pacific Gas and Electric Company and as their Sacramento lobbyist. He also served as director and treasurer of the California State Automobile Association and as treasurer of the California Taxpayers' Association. Carr was a motivating force behind Congressman Norman Mineta's successful efforts to provide congressional legislation for retirement benefits on behalf of commissioners who served prior to the Federal Magistrates Act.

Upon Carr's retirement, Arthur C. Atteridge was appointed as magistrate. He now holds forth in the various areas of federal jurisdiction in Monterey County. A veteran of thirty-five years in private law practice, Atteridge is a former mayor and member of the

*United States Commissioner for Monterey County Arthur C. Atteridge. (Courtesy Judge Mark Thomas, Jr.)*

*United States Commissioner for Monterey County Arthur C. Atteridge. (Courtesy Judge Mark Thomas, Jr.)*

Salinas City Council. His service on the Monterey County Board of Supervisors spanned a period of twelve years.

Santa Clara County's first commissioner, Charles Silent, is remembered chiefly for his contribution to railroading. In 1868, as a newly-admitted attorney, he represented the San Jose and Santa Clara Railroad Company in obtaining a franchise to operate streetcars in San Jose. In 1874 he became president of the narrow gauge railroad between San Jose and Santa Cruz. Later Silent served on the Arizona Supreme Court and practiced law in Los Angeles.

Charles D. Wright was a native of Watertown, New York who came to San Jose when he was six years old. As was the custom, he "read law" in a local law office. He practiced locally for forty years.

Joseph R. Patton graduated from the University of Michigan Law School in 1882. After practicing in San Luis Obispo County he opened his law office in San Jose in 1887.

Born in Fayetteville, Alabama, Calvert T. Bird arrived in San Jose in 1851. He received his education at the Gates San Jose Institute, a school well known at that time. After working as a deputy tax collector he was admitted to the bar in 1882. Bird Avenue in San Jose was named after his father.

William F. James is a Santa Clara County legend. Born in 1875, he lived to the age of ninety-one. He served as a superior court judge of Santa Clara County from 1933-1963,

Santa Clara County

| Commissioner | City | Date Appointed | Date Left Office |
|---|---|---|---|
| Charles Silent | | October 31, 1867 | |
| Wilson W. Hoover | Gilroy | May 1, 1877 | June 27, 1882 |
| Charles Denton Wright | San Jose | July 27, 1875 | |
| James E. Woods | Mayfield - San Jose | August 22, 1879 | July 7, 1887 |
| Joseph R. Patton | San Jose | November 3, 1888 | January 31, 1889 |
| Calvert T. Bird | San Jose | April 2, 1889 | |
| William F. James | San Jose | March 17, 1898 | 1904? |
| vacant | | 1904? | 1929? |
| Elmer D. Jensen | San Jose | 1930? | 1933? |
| Arthur G. Shoup | San Jose | 1933 | 1941 |
| Marshall S. Hall | San Jose | 1941 | 1957 |
| Robert F. Peckham | San Jose | 1957 | October 1, 1959 |
| Gerald Bouchard Hansen | San Jose | November 16, 1959 | 1971 |
| Nordin Blacker | San Jose | 1971 | present |

Silent — He was appointed bankruptcy commissioner.

James — The date listed is the probable year of his leaving office, judging from Clerk's Office correspondence. A newspaper clipping provided by Judge Mark Thomas, Jr. noted that no United States Commissioner sat in Santa Clara County between James's resignation and Jensen's taking the post.

Jensen — According to a newspaper clipping provided by Judge Mark Thomas, Jr., Jensen served three and a half years. Since Shoup had taken office by 1933, Jensen had to have started at least as early as 1929. The 1930 Rules of Practice list Jensen; he could have been appointed earlier. The 1933 Rules do not list him. There are no rules available for 1931 or 1932.

Shoup and Hall — These dates are based on the National Archives and Records Service record shelf list prepared January 16, 1984.

---

joining that court when it had but three judges and leaving when it had seventeen. He was a leader in the juvenile law field. It was said that the severity of Judge James's sentencing could be predicted by the color of suit he wore on the judgment day.

Elmer Jensen was a colorful trial lawyer of the old school, best remembered for his defense of a number of sensational criminal matters including the famous Lamson murder trial of the thirties. He was president of the Santa Clara County Bar Association from 1941 to 1942.

Arthur Shoup came to Santa Clara County from Alaska where he had been a member of the legislature. In San Jose he entered active practice which included representing Southern Pacific Company in claims defense.

Shoup was followed by Marshall Hall who served as commissioner until he was appointed to the Santa Clara County Superior Court in 1957, on which bench he served until his retirement in 1978. Under his leadership as presiding judge, the Santa Clara County Superior Court civil trial calendar became a statewide model of efficiency.

Robert F. Peckham was then appointed as the next commissioner. He served until his appointment to the Santa Clara County Superior Court in 1959. Judge Peckham remained with that court until 1966 when he was appointed to the United States District Court. He later became chief judge of the Northern District of California, and continues in that office.

Gerald Hansen is presently in the active practice of law in San Jose. A graduate of the University of San Francisco law school, Hansen had served in the United States Attor-

*United States Commissioner for Santa Clara County Nordin F. Blacker. (Photograph by Ira Nowinski.)*

ney's office prior to his appointment. He was the last commissioner in Santa Clara County.

With the new federal system came the present magistrate, Nordin Blacker. The following account by Blacker discussing his experiences as magistrate provides an interesting glimpse into the nature of the position.

### United States Magistrate in San Jose

In March 1971, I was selected as the first United States magistrate in San Jose. Not only was I new to the position, the position was new. Fortunately, Richard Goldsmith, the presiding magistrate from the inception of the magistrate's program in the northern district until 1982, when he retired, was extraordinarily helpful. Also, my immediate predecessor, Gerald Hansen, a local attorney and the part-time United States commissioner, was extremely gracious in passing on his own experience.

In 1971 the office of federal magistrate was one of only two part-time judicial positions in the county of Santa Clara, the other being the justice of the peace in Morgan Hill and Gilroy. The justice of the peace position later became a full-time municipal court position. At the time I was appointed, at age thirty-three, I was the youngest judicial officer in Santa Clara County.

In those early days there was virtually no civil business, and the criminal caseload consisted of Moffett Field Naval Air Station military dependents and visitors, and a large number of draft evasion and bank robbery cases. The Moffett Field cases were heard in a makeshift courtroom at Moffett Field. Occasionally a case from the Veterans' Administration facility in Palo Alto would be brought before the magistrate.

No provision was made for magistrate quarters. It was expected that the magistrate's private law office would serve as the magistrate's office as well. The initial appearances on federal charges were handled at the Santa Clara County jail, where the federal prisoners were housed. We used what was then the "drunk tank." As the jail expanded, the "drunk tank" was taken over and there was no convenient place within the jail to conduct the initial appearances. They were then conducted in my private law offices, where they continue to be conducted. As the work load increased and it was necessary to call the master criminal calendar as well as hear occasional civil matters, we began using one of the district court courtrooms when it was not being occupied for the magistrate's regular once per week calendar.

Several years ago the Department of the Navy asked the magistrates to handle not only military dependents and visitors to Moffett Field, but active-duty servicemen charged with petty offenses and misdemeanors. With the advent of full-time United States attorney and public defender services in San Jose, the prosecution and defense of these cases have become more vigorous.

The civil jurisdiction has changed as well. In January 1973, the temporary federal court building was occupied, and a full-time clerk's office established there. Additional judges from the San Jose area were appointed to the federal court: Judge Spencer Williams, Judge William Ingram, and Judge Robert Aguilar. More and more civil cases were being heard here. That fact, along with the expansion of jurisdiction and recent amendments to the Magistrates Act, has meant a greater involvement of the magistrates in civil pretrial motions. Magistrates were also authorized to try civil cases.

In the criminal area, the jurisdiction has also expanded by recent amendments to the Magistrates Act. In addition to the usual magistrate duties involving appointment of counsel, bail, and the like, I have tried all sorts of misdemeanors, both jury and nonjury, and have heard motions ranging from discovery motions to motions to suppress. After the temporary federal building was occupied, I began hearing the master criminal calendar, taking not-guilty pleas and assigning dates for motions and trials before the San Jose United States district judges.

Because of the part-time nature of the job, agents and attorneys have had to catch up with me in various locations. I have issued search warrants and complaints in the hallways of superior courts while on break from some court proceedings, in the lobbies of theaters while attending performances, in parking lots, and at home.

Most of the criminal cases have involved both life's unfortunates and truly dangerous people, but occasionally we have funny moments. We had the case of an individual who impersonated a general; he appeared, pleaded guilty, and was placed on probation. While on probation he could not resist the temptation to play general again, and obtained the use of a Cadillac automobile while posing as a general. One of the references he gave to the Cadillac agency was the federal judge (Williams) who had put him on probation. Another case involved someone being prosecuted for making threats by mail. The defendant was a man who had some serious problems in dealing with women. The case arose out of prosecution in the state courts: the deputy district attorney was a woman, the public defender assigned to him was a woman, and he drew the one woman judge of the Santa Clara County Superior Court.

Recently I was given two additional duties. One is the taking of indictments from the federal grand jury. The other is the swearing in of new citizens. The latter is particularly pleasurable. It is a joyous occasion and has a special meaning for me in that I am administering the very oath my parents took years ago.

# 16

# The San Jose Bankruptcy Court

*Warren C. Moore*

Through the year 1958, bankruptcy cases in San Jose were heard before a visiting jurist. Bernard J. Abrott, who was based in Oakland, conducted court in a room at the San Jose Civic Auditorium on Fridays. A normal calendar would be heard on an afternoon, but if there was a real crush of business, Referee Abrott would be in San Jose morning and afternoon.

The facilities included a long rectangular table seating perhaps twenty persons. Abrott's attire was indistinguishable from that of others in the room except that he and most of the attorneys wore neckties. Seating arrangements were such that strangers had to ask habitués who was whom. The single San Jose trustee was Ralph Williams, a most venerable gentleman. There were trustees also in Santa Cruz, Salinas, and Monterey, but matters from those areas were heard in San Jose. Legal representation of the trustee was by a firm from San Francisco.

The post-World War II boom in the economy of Santa Clara County led the Bankruptcy Division of the Administrative Office of the United States Courts to conclude that the almost inevitable concomitant of a sudden economic boom, a substantial increase in bankruptcies, would justify the appointment of a full-time referee in bankruptcy for San Jose. The Judicial Conference of the United States approved and on January 1, 1959, authorization for San Jose's own bankruptcy court became effective. The appointee as referee was Daniel R. Cowans, a graduate of Boalt Hall of the University of California, Berkeley, who was practicing law in San Jose. The appointment was made by Louis Goodman, chief judge of the United States District Court for the Northern District of California.

There was no federal court building in San Jose. Chief Judge Goodman located space in the old main Post Office Building for the court. It was awhile before the space was

*United States Bankruptcy Judge Daniel R. Cowans. Judge Cowans presided over the first United States Bankruptcy Court in San Jose. (Courtesy Judge Cowans.)*

vacated; in the interim, the court office was situated in a retail boat agency on Lafayette Street in Santa Clara. Cowans was to chose his furnishings from old or spare furniture in the basement of the courthouse in San Francisco. Thus, seating in the first courtroom was on something of a collection of hues and shapes. A certain uniformity existed in that all the chairs were wooden.

The general policy of the Administrative Office to take the bankruptcy court to the populace resulted in conducting court in the chambers of the supervisors of Monterey County in Salinas as well as San Jose. The 800 cases filed with the court in 1959 seemed a considerable load to the court and its clerical staff of three persons. Filings grew and the court staff with it. Before long, the redoubtable Ilse Schwalbe became chief clerk of the bankruptcy court and made known her disapproval of incorrect pleadings.

Space allotted to the bankruptcy system in the Post Office gradually grew with the filings exceeding 2,000 per annum. Once again the Administrative Office persuaded the Judicial Conference to authorize the court's expansion and a second position was created. Chief District Judge George B. Harris appointed Warren C. Moore to the position. Moore, a graduate of Stanford University, had attended the University of Santa Clara Law School, and done graduate work at the University of Grenoble, France and the University of Lausanne, Switzerland.

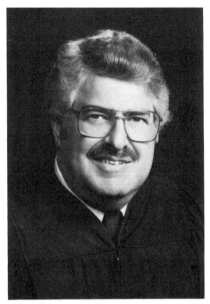 

*The San Jose bankruptcy judges, 1984. To the left is Judge Seymour J. Abrahams; to the right, Judge Warren C. Moore. (Courtesy Judges Abrahams and Moore.)*

The days of the single trustee in San Jose passed into memory. Possibly the best-known attorney for trustees to appear before the court was Alan Parker, who later became chief counsel for the House Committee on the Judiciary in Washington. Parker's interest grew from studying the subject under Referee Cowans who had been his professor of law at Santa Clara University.

Cowans became active in the Seminars for Referees in Bankruptcy. When the title was changed from referee to bankruptcy judge, the title of that organization changed accordingly. Cowans eventually became national president. This took him to Washington where he called upon Congressman Don Edwards of San Jose. Congressman Edwards maintained an active interest in bankruptcy and was most instrumental in obtaining passage of the Bankruptcy Reform Act of 1978.

When national publicity stimulated a considerable interest in increased filings of Chapter XIII wage-earner plans, Duncan Kester of San Jose was made the official Chapter XIII trustee for the territory of the San Jose Bankruptcy Court plus the San Francisco court. In a recent year, forty percent of cases were filings of Chapter XIII in the San Jose court. Marilyn Morgan, currently the president-elect of the Santa Clara County bar, is also a trustee of the court as it is now constituted.

After the successful campaign to bring the federal court to San Jose, the United States District Court joined the federal bankruptcy judges in holding court in San Jose.

In 1974, Seymour J. Abrahams, a Stanford graduate, was appointed to replace Judge Cowans who resigned to return to the practice of law. Judge Abrahams had served as law clerk to the California Supreme Court and as mayor of Los Gatos prior to his appointment. Since that time he was selected to be one of the judges on the Bankruptcy Appellate Panel of the Ninth Circuit.

The Bankruptcy Reform Act of 1978, which became effective October 1, 1979, brought considerable changes. A policy determination of Congress to remove the bankruptcy judge as far from administration as possible has resulted in the administration being handled by the clerk of the bankruptcy court. The present clerk is Paul Karney, Jr. who came from the Administrative Office of the United States Courts. The new law greatly increased the number of cases. A debate rages over whether the flood of cases is due to the provisions of the law, the fact that the country was enduring some very difficult economic times with heavy unemployment, or some other reason. Whatever the cause, the load upon the clerk's office has increased dramatically and is enormous. There were some 3,868 cases in 1974 and 7,361 in 1982. The difference is greater than it appears, since before the new law, husband and wife joint petitions were counted as two cases; now they are counted as one. In addition, the cases themselves produce many more matters within a case than formerly. So, numbers alone cannot tell the full story. The separation of the court from certain procedures has removed meetings of creditors from the judge's calendar. They are instead conducted by a deputy clerk. Including the 500 to 600 such meetings, there are over 2,000 matters placed on the hearing calendar in a month.

Complexities derive from increased activities in business cases. Under the old Chapter XI, the court handled two new filings a month. Now one per day is filed. Furthermore, smaller businesses may and do file under Chapter XIII. The increasingly litigious nature of our society finds its counterpart in the bankruptcy court.

From a date when the staff consisted of nine persons including secretaries and judges, there are presently twenty-four persons on the clerical staff and five on the staffs of the two judges.

# 17

## The United States
## District Court Clerk's Office

*Michael Griffith*

"A Shorter Commute", the newspaper headline read. The article which followed announced the opening of a full time clerk's office for the United States District Court in San Jose. With this opening, the article noted, attorneys would be able to file federal cases in the South Bay city instead of having to travel to San Francisco.[1]

For most citizens, only indirectly involved with the federal courts, the article doubtless seemed another routine announcement. For those long involved in bringing the federal court to San Jose, however, the seemingly ordinary bulletin probably brought a feeling of considerable satisfaction. After many years of trying, they had succeeded in bringing another office of the court to the city.

As with the campaigns to bring the federal court to San Jose and to obtain a permanent building for it, the struggle to obtain a clerk's office involved continuing effort after early discouragement. In contrast to those other stories, though, it was a simpler tale, and the goal was achieved at less cost. /

The first efforts to locate a clerk's office in San Jose came in 1966 shortly after Congress mandated that the northern district sit in that city. In response to the law, Judge Oliver J. Carter, then the northern district judge in charge of such matters, asked various court officers to estimate their space needs for San Jose. Among those he asked was James P. Welsh, then clerk of the court. Welsh called for a clerk's office appropriate to a full-time permanent court. Designed as a long rectangular area, it contained 6,600 square feet of space. As well as the usual office space, it included an extensive storage room for files and an exhibit room.[2]

Not too surprisingly, this office was not built. Probably Welsh's plan embarrassed San Jose court supporters who realized that it would appear extravagant given the anticipated low level of business at the new court. At any rate, in his November 1966 correspondence with the Government Services Administration (GSA), Judge Carter asked for

*James M. Waggener, first divisional office manager of the San Jose clerk's office. This and the following photograph were taken in the clerk's office space in the new United States Courthouse and Federal Building. (Photograph by Ira Nowinski.)*

one room for the clerk's office along with room for growth "when and if it is determined there is need for additional activity and personnel."[3]

Not until late December 1967, did space become available for the clerk's office. During that month, the court was given an unfurnished 195 square foot room in the old Superior Court Building, adjacent to the new building containing Judge Peckham's courtroom and chambers. Presumably, the space was for a one-person operation. Despite this gift, the clerk's office did not open, due to a combination of factors. Unlike the probation office, the San Francisco clerk's office did not have someone already working in the San Jose area who could open the office easily. The suggestion that Judge Peckham's courtroom deputy also serve as clerk was rejected as impractical due to the difficulty that person would have both in maintaining regular office hours and carrying out courtroom responsibilities.[4]

Even with this difficulty, the clerk's office probably would have opened had the northern district judges been sympathetic. However, the staffing problem, when combined with the hostility of most judges to the new court, was sufficient to eliminate the office. That the San Jose court then had a relatively light caseload provided further justification for those opposed to opening a clerk's office.

During 1969 Judge Robert Peckham protested the division of court business between San Francisco and San Jose to the Circuit Council. In 1970, under pressure from the council, the northern district judges mandated that any criminal case arising in the four central coast counties be heard in San Jose. With this requirement, the utility of a local

*Members of the San Jose clerk's office, June 1984. Standing, left to right, are Cynthia Vargas and Esmeralda Garcia. Seated, left to right, are Bernadette Flores and Annabel Sutton. Not pictured were Ronald L. Davis, Gail Gokey, and Linda Monroe. (Photograph by Ira Nowinski.)*

office in which to file papers regarding those cases was obvious. Along with this new need for a clerk's office came increased pressure from the area for its establishment. After the rule change, Judge Peckham formed an Advisory Committee to assist in developing the newly expanded court, and at its first meeting the group appointed a clerk's office subcommittee to help plan that facility.[5]

But despite the obvious need and increased local pressure, no clerk's office was established in San Jose until the court moved into temporary buildings near West Taylor and Guadalupe Parkway in early 1973. It seems likely that the lack of suitable space near the Superior Court Building, where the district court was sitting in 1970, placed an initial obstacle in the way of setting up the office. When the county announced the eviction of the federal court from the Superior Court Building in early 1971, planning the clerk's office became part of planning for the new facility and the drive for a more immediate opening lost its strength.

With the opening of the temporary courthouse, those urging a clerk's office achieved success. Indeed, the opening marked a significant step forward for the San Jose court because district rules required that the office accept papers in civil cases as well as in criminal. As a consequence, attorneys could conduct noncriminal cases in the court much more easily than before, when they had to file in San Francisco.[6]

The opening of the full-time clerk's office in the temporary facility did not, of course, resolve all of the issues regarding the office. Planning for the permanent office continued to form part of the planning for a permanent courthouse in San Jose, as it had since 1970.

In contrast to other parts of the courthouse, however, planning for the new clerk's office proceeded smoothly. As with other offices, there was a considerable expansion of space requested between the first inquiry about space needs in 1968 and the response made after the rule change. However, in contrast to other facilities, there was no struggle over space when planning began in earnest in the late 1970s: the space allocated by the United States Courts Administrative Office in Washington, D.C. proved immediately acceptable to the clerk's office in San Francisco.[7]

Otherwise the story of the clerk's office was one of occasional changes in personnel and of gradual expansion to meet the increase in business at the San Jose court. From two persons in 1973, the office grew to nine in 1984. Initially headed by John Pomeroy, the office was run in succession by Terrence Spink, Ron Davis, and Gail Gokey. In May 1984, the office moved to its new space in the permanent courthouse and Jim Waggener became the first divisional office manager of the San Jose clerk's office. [8] As with the rest of the court offices, after a long journey, the clerk's office anticipated a stable future in a permanent home.

## 18

# The United States
# Probation Office

*Paul M. Chandler*

When prune trees and fruit orchards were giving way to shopping centers and technological facilities during the late 1950s and early 1960s, United States Probation Officer Jack Gildea was traveling from San Francisco to conduct pre-sentence investigations and to provide probation and parole supervision of federal offenders released to the communities of the Santa Clara valley and points beyond. Before him United States Probation Officer Matt Curran had also traveled from his office in San Francisco to bring federal probation and parole services to the primarily agricultural and seashore communities of Santa Clara, San Benito, Santa Cruz, and Monterey counties. Mr. Gildea and Mr. Curran were both fine gentlemen and competent officers whose effectiveness was limited only by the transitory nature of their contacts in the southern reaches of the Northern District of California. In September 1965, as part of a general shift in assignments, United States Probation Officer Paul M. Chandler, a resident of Campbell, was assigned responsibility for the four county area. Although Mr. Chandler continued to travel to San Francisco on a weekly basis to file reports and perform other office duties, essentially he conducted federal probation services in the southern area of the district from his home and automobile. A move had thus been made toward establishing closer and more continuous contact between the probation officer, his clients, and the community.

United States probation officers conduct investigations and complete pre-sentence reports on convicted federal offenders to aid United States district judges in their difficult responsibility of passing judgments. These officers supervise those individuals who are released from the courtroom to the community on probation, providing them with guidance and keeping the court advised as to their progress. United States probation officers also supervise those offenders who are initially sent to prison and who are later released to the community under conditional circumstances such as parole.

*Veteran members of the United States Probation office in San Jose. The staff members pictured here served for many years with the office after its establishment in 1968. From left to right are Robert Coffey, Arthur Honda, supervisor of the San Jose office, Madeline Mascovich, Paul Chandler, and Frank Vasquez. Not pictured is Robbie Thomas. This picture and the one following were taken at the probation office at the temporary Federal Building and Courthouse on West Taylor Street. (Photograph by Ira Nowinski.)*

Since the first salaried federal probation officer was appointed in 1930, the federal probation system has successfully remained sensitive to the needs of individuals and responsive to community concerns and interests. In that tradition, and with a desire to provide the best possible services to the United States District Court being established in San Jose, Chief United States Probation Officer Albert Wahl, early in 1968, expressed his intention to establish a branch office in San Jose. Mr. Chandler, for several months, had already been using desk space and interview facilities made available in the office of Judge Robert F. Peckham's law clerk in the Superior Court Building. Congressman Don Edwards, having a strong interest in the establishment of a federal court in San Jose, was pleased to announce the establishment of the branch United States Probation office in that community on March 4, 1968. The new office was designated as the official duty station for Mr. Chandler and his secretary, Helen Voss. Although Ms. Voss's official duty station was to be San Jose, she continued to split her time between that office and the headquarters office in San Francisco. For that reason, and because Mr. Chandler's duties frequently carried him away from the office, a telephone answering device was installed. It was the first such device to be used in any federal probation office, and probably the first to be used within the federal judiciary.

Under generous provisions of a lease with Santa Clara County, involving only nominal symbolic remuneration, the newly established office was situated in the old Superior Court Building in the county sheriff's former quarters. This historic building with its high ceilings, marbled floors, and oak adornments provided stately surroundings for the first permanent federal court function in Santa Clara County.

Not long after the branch office had been established in San Jose, the workload grew beyond the capabilities of a single officer. For several months federal probation officers Thor Hansen and Donald Faria traveled from San Francisco and Oakland, respectively, to help absorb some of the work, using the San Jose office as a base of operations. Eventually, early in 1970, Doug Dilfer, a native Californian who had entered the federal probation service in Washington, D.C., joined the staff in the Northern District of California and became the second full-time probation officer assigned to San Jose. By the fall of 1971 continued growth and increased caseloads in Monterey and Santa Cruz counties resulted in the establishment of another branch office in Monterey. Mr. Dilfer, assisted by a most capable secretary, Sonja Jackson, assumed responsibility for the Monterey operation. Along with providing more traditional services, the federal probation officer in Monterey County was faced with increasing numbers of juvenile military dependents living in family housing at the Fort Ord Army Base, who were becoming involved in delinquent behavior. Because these juveniles lived on a federal reservation, Monterey County authorities had consistently declined to assume jurisdiction for them.

The problems in dealing effectively with juvenile offenders in the United States District Court, with limited federal resources available in the local community, have been many and have never been fully resolved. Mr. Robert M. Coffey, an experienced federal probation officer with service in Montana and Illinois, replaced Mr. Dilfer in 1971. In the meantime, United States Probation Officer Jean Standage, who had completed the first pre-sentence investigation report for the United States District Court in San Jose, continued to travel to San Jose from San Francisco, to assist with the work load and to work with some women offenders, as needs dictated. She continued to do so until a few months prior to her untimely death due to cancer in 1974. Ms. Standage was one of the finest, most capable officers to serve the federal courts in this district.

Before 1968, federal offenders had typically been bank employees or postal workers guilty of embezzlements; young men taking stolen automobiles across state lines; aliens returning to the United States following deportation; addicts caught stealing government checks; individuals involved in thefts from interstate shipments; midlevel drug dealers; and bank robbers. When the probation office was first established in San Jose in 1968, the United States was fully committed in Vietnam. Resistance to that military action was growing, and many young men who, at the age of eighteen, had registered for the draft without much thought, were reflecting more seriously upon the issues. Increasing numbers of these young men were refusing induction into the military service as an "act of conscience." Since they had not filed timely applications for conscientious objector status with their selective service boards, their refusals to be inducted were clearly in violation of the federal statutes. The criminal calendar of the United States District Court swelled and changed dramatically. These young, idealistic men, most of whom were without any prior record, were faced with potential sentences of five years in prison and fines of $10,000. They represented special challenges to the sentencing process. The courts felt the need to evaluate each case individually on its own merits. The importance of the pre-sentence report was demonstrated, and the probation officer's work load skyrocketed. In a trend that first emerged in the Northern District of California, and later spread throughout the country, more and more of these young men were placed on probation with a special condition that they work two years in some community service. Efforts to establish close contacts with community agencies paid dividends as the resources of the Voluntary Action Center (now the Volunteer Center) were solicited. That organization served as a brokerage helping place these young men in meaningful community work and providing ongoing reports on their services. Community service as a condition of probation is an idea which has since been expanded to other types of offenders. The United States Probation office has continued to work with members of the Volunteer Center; in fact, Mr. Coffey is on its board of directors.

The value of a close relationship between the federal probation office and the local community was demonstrated in an entirely different type of case. Extensive support from local law enforcement officers was vital in the successful prosecution of a case against two sons of a reputed mafia crime boss who had moved into the San Jose area. Charged with collecting debts through extortionate means, they were convicted and sent to prison. Later, while being supervised for subsequent probation terms, they were charged with probation violations. The original trial judge, Robert F. Peckham, by then chief judge in the district, returned to preside over the violation hearings. It became one of the longest violation hearings in the history of the federal probation service and included an unprecedented Saturday court session in San Jose. Probation was revoked and the two were returned to prison.

In time Santa Clara County found it necessary to recall the office space which had been allocated to the federal probation service. In October 1971, the federal probation office was moved to offices off the first floor corridor of the former main Post Office Building on North First Street. These facilities were adjacent to an office which had been established for the assistant United States attorney. The new offices overlooked the Saint James Park across the street and a monument which marked the location where President McKinley had once delivered a speech to the citizens of San Jose. It was in these offices that the probation service would provide a temporary working area for the federal public defender becoming established in San Jose.

In December 1972 the probation service, along with the district court, court clerk, and the federal public defender moved into the temporary federal courthouse at the corner of West Taylor Street and Guadalupe Parkway. Initially, the probation service shared the smaller of the two buildings in the complex with the federal public defender's office. A warm, friendly atmosphere prevailed within this small but important federal complex and all those working with the federal court demonstrated a strong desire to serve the public well. The "temporary" nature of the facility extended to twelve years, a period which for the probation service has been most eventful.

Early in the 1970s Congress, with an interest in improving the effectiveness of community corrections, moved to increase the staff of the federal probation system. This effort to reduce probation and parole caseloads, coupled with continually growing populations, resulted in an expansion of the federal probation staffs in San Jose and Monterey, and eventually in the establishment of another branch office in Santa Cruz. In February 1973, two fine officers from the Santa Clara County Juvenile Probation Department, Art Honda and Frank Vasquez, joined the federal probation staff. Congress had also provided for some paraprofessional positions to be filled primarily by former offenders. Under that program George Thompson, a former drug addict and alcoholic who had successfully changed his life many years earlier, joined the probation office staff in San Jose in 1973. With his ponytail and Fu Manchu beard, Mr. Thompson made a colorful addition to the staff. For several years he enhanced probation and parole supervision through his knowledge of community resources, his street sense, and his rapport with offenders.

The probation staff in Monterey was also expanding. Mr. Dilfer had found it necessary to take extended medical leave and United States Probation Officer Ray Holt, who had entered the federal probation service from Santa Cruz County many years earlier, transferred to Monterey from San Francisco. In 1974 he was joined by Bill Wenger, a particularly capable officer from the county probation service. Together Mr. Holt and Mr. Wenger made an effective probation team. In 1977 the branch office was established in Santa Cruz where large-scale drug violations were abounding. Staffed only briefly by Mr. Dilfer prior to his medical retirement, the Santa Cruz office became the responsibility of Officer Stu Scott. Mr. Scott transferred from San Francisco where he entered the federal probation service from the San Mateo County Probation System.

Establishment of an office in San Jose allowed the federal probation system to develop a valuable relationship with San Jose State University. For several years Mr. Chandler served as a part-time instructor at the university. From time to time, students in the university's sociology and administration of justice departments completed intern programs in the federal probation office. One of these students, Ron Delluome, is now a United States probation officer in Youngstown, Ohio. Another student, Dave Fawkner, entered the federal probation service in San Jose first as a probation officer assistant and eventually as a probation officer. Mr. Fawkner worked very closely with the National Alliance of Business (NAB) in San Jose toward the establishment of an employment development program for former offenders. For two years, while on loan from the federal probation system, he worked with NAB headquarters in Washington, D.C.

Probation officers work under many pressures while gathering extensive information and refining it into meaningful reports to aid the courts in determining appropriate sentences for convicted offenders. Secretaries like Madelyn Robinson, whose friendly manner helps make visitors feel at ease, and Debbie Allen, who came from the United States Parole Commission with considerable knowledge of the federal correctional system, have played an important role in helping to keep the operation moving in a even and steady manner. While performing as a secretary, Beverly Brook (formerly Beverly Boswell) became so interested in the work of a probation officer that she applied for a position as an officer. She met the academic requirements and was appointed to the professional staff. Beverly is now the United States probation officer in the Santa Cruz branch office where she is ably assisted by her own secretary, Linda Norman.

Through the years the United States Probation office in San Jose has been staffed by a number of fine, highly professional probation officers including Marie Henderson, an effective counselor who had previous service with the California Youth Authority and left the federal service for other work; George Mowl who came from the San Mateo County Probation office and eventually moved to the United States probation office in Pittsburgh, Pennsylvania; Joy Valentine, who came from the Santa Clara County Juvenile Probation Department and has since entered private practice as a counselor; Carolyn Poe who entered the federal probation system from the Santa Clara County Adult Probation office and has since left to complete the master of business administration program at the University of Santa Clara; and Fred Casucci, a former naval officer who left the Monterey County Probation office to complete the master of social work program at Tulane University before joining the federal probation staff in San Jose. From the times when Matt Curran and Jack Gildea traveled into the area from San

*The staff of the United States Probation office in San Jose, June 1984. From left to right in the front row are Nancy Kirk, Beverly Boswell Brook, Debbie Allen, and Madeline Mascovich. Left to right in back are David Fawkner, Arthur Honda, Frederick Casucci, Robert Coffey, and Will O'Sullivan. Not present were Sonja Jackson, Linda Norman, Kathy Smath, and William Wenger. (Photograph by Ira Nowinski.)*

Francisco until the more recent times when the staff was joined by Will O'Sullivan, coming from the United States Probation office in Detroit, and Nancy Kirk, joining the staff from Santa Clara County Juvenile Probation office, federal probation officers in this area have continued the tradition of bringing sensitive assistance to individuals restructuring their lives, while being responsive to community concerns for safety and justice. Establishing an office in San Jose has helped maintain those traditions more effectively. Serving on the boards of such valuable community organizations as Pathways, a drug treatment program; Casa Libre, a halfway house; the Volunteer Center; and National Alliance of Business, United States probation officers have become established in the community and a part of the community.

# 19

# The San Jose
# Public Defender's Office

*Patricia V. Trumbull*

The San Jose branch of the Federal Public Defender's office began when James Hewitt, the federal defender for the Northern District of California, sent Frank Ubhaus to San Jose from the San Francisco office in late 1972. At that time the office consisted of only a table and a chair in the United States Probation office in the main Post Office Building, downtown San Jose. After the completion of the new temporary Federal Building and Courthouse, everyone, including the assistant federal defender, moved to the new site.

Frank Ubhaus and Grace Francone, his secretary, occupied the space next to the probation office in the new building. They did not then have a separate entrance, so clients had to enter by way of the probation office. Needless to say, this apparent connection with probation was not the optimum operating environment for a defense office. This situation was quickly remedied when the fire marshal mandated a new front door for the defender's office.

Although appropriate physical identities were then established, a certain unique comraderie among members of the "court family" remained. There are many examples of how this small group worked and suffered together to start and maintain the federal complex. Frank Ubhaus tells of nearly losing his life while trying to help Art Wong and Angel Gonzales of the Government Services Administration cut down an old oak tree in the front yard of the new courthouse. Federal defenders often find themselves out on a limb about to be sawed off but seldom does this analogy become reality.

The federal defender's office has, from its beginning, defended alleged federal law violators who always seemed to have a quality unto themselves. One of Frank Ubhaus's first cases was that of the infamous "Cap'n Crunch," who was accused of fraud by wire. "Cap'n Crunch" allegedly used a whistle from a cereal box to reproduce sounds that

*The San Jose Federal Public Defenders, June 1984. From left to right are Assistant Federal Public Defenders Patricia V. Trumbull, H. David Grunbaum, and Daniel F. Cook. This photograph was taken in the courtyard of the new United States Courthouse and Federal Building. (Photograph by Ira Nowinski.)*

allowed him illegal access to free long-distance telephone lines. His strange genius and case foreshadowed electronics industry crime in the San Jose area.

Frank Ubhaus left the federal defender's office in October 1975 and went into private practice in San Jose. Frank Mangan, from the Federal Defenders of San Diego, Inc., came to take over the San Jose branch office in March 1976. In the interim, assistant federal defenders from San Francisco covered the San Jose office, in a form of circuit riding that was very common to the San Jose operation. San Jose federal defenders have always had to cover the magistrate's court at Fort Ord in Monterey County. The United States Attorney's office did not have a full-time assistant attorney in San Jose until 1978. Until then, assistant attorneys traveled to both San Jose and Monterey from San Francisco. They weren't alone: practicing law out of an automobile was the norm for lawyers and judges alike in San Jose.

The Fort Ord assignment, which has changed little over the years, takes assistant federal defenders south twice a month to represent soldiers and their dependents. Out of the sea of olive green and camouflage come more driving under the influence of alcohol cases than can be imagined anywhere, much less in federal court. Fort Ord has also been the source of a number of violent crimes and murder cases which are relatively rare in the federal courts in California. Over the years, the Fort Ord operation has been affectionately dubbed by defenders as "the law south of the Pajaro" (a river dividing Santa Cruz and Monterey counties).

The San Jose Federal Public Defender's office, June 1984. From left to right are staff members
Patricia B. Ramirez, Tom W. Richardson, and Monica B. Williams. This photograph was taken
in the Federal Public Defender's offices in the new United States Courthouse and Federal
Building. (Photograph by Ira Nowinski.)

The temporary federal complex in San Jose was not just small and folksy at first, it was
not very secure. Over the years beginning with Frank Ubhaus's tenure, defendants and
co-defendants have tried to escape from the makeshift facility. The building has never
had a holding cell and some defendants have quickly discovered that freedom for them
was only a half an inch of tin away. Early in its history, a partially blind man and his
wheelchair-bound co-defendant commandeered the United States marshal's car; fortunately they were returned within the hour by the Santa Clara County Sheriff's
Department. Another adventuresome defendant left by climbing through the ceiling in
the bathroom. He was quickly caught in the field across the street. Frank Mangan lost a
client who leapt out of a crowded courtroom after receiving a sixteen-year sentence for
bank robbery. Another bank robber's escape was quickly foiled when he was tackled by
marshals and probation officers and sprayed by Angel Gonzales from the rooftop with
water from a garden hose. None of these defendants ever went very far for very long and
they all received extended visits to federal prison for their efforts.

When Frank Mangan took over in 1976 the San Jose Federal Public Defender's office
was firmly established. It was still a one-lawyer operation but growing quickly. In the
1974 fiscal year the office opened 130 cases. In the 1983 fiscal year it opened 657 cases.

Regardless of its growth and increased sophistication, things still happened in San Jose
that did not happen in other federal courts. For instance, as Frank Mangan was trying a
bank robbery case before Judge Williams, just a stone's throw away in the parking lot,

the defendant's wife was giving birth aided by a probation office staff member.

In 1978 Frank Mangan left the office, also to practice law in San Jose. Pat Trumbull transferred from San Francisco to replace him. Within six months a second defender position was approved for San Jose and Paul Meltzer from Santa Cruz joined the staff. Two lawyers, a secretary, and a handful of Santa Clara university law students who regularly worked in the office as externs could no longer coexist in the three room office at the courthouse. In 1978 the offices were relocated to the First American Bank Building down the street at the corner of West Taylor and North First Street. This move was symbolic in many ways. There was no doubt that the federal court and its support agencies were here to stay. The probation office had grown so that it needed more space in the courthouse. About the same time the United States Attorney's office established its first permanent office in San Jose. The small pioneer federal court operation was now a thing of the past.

In 1979 Dan Cook replaced Paul Meltzer as the second lawyer in the San Jose office. The third lawyer, David Grunbaum, joined the staff of the federal defender's office in December 1983.

Not only has the caseload grown tremendously but the types of cases continue to be unique and complex. Although hundreds of driving under the influence of alcohol cases are still being handled from Fort Ord and Moffett Naval Air Station, the office must also handle large high technology cases generated by the intensely competitive Silicon Valley. But some things haven't changed. Assistant federal defenders still "ride circuit" and cross the Pajaro twice a month to service the magistrate's court in Fort Ord. Defenders now must also travel to Soledad state prison for parole hearings and to San Francisco to interview clients held in custody in the San Francisco County jail.

As of July 1984, the one lawyer office sharing a table in the probation office in San Jose had grown to three lawyers, one paralegal, and two secretaries. If growth and size are indicators of progress, the federal court complex in San Jose has truly come of age. In many ways, however, the smaller, friendlier, less formal operation will be missed.

# 20

## The United States Attorney's and Marshal's Offices

*Michael Griffith*

In September 1978, the United States attorney first opened a full-time office in San Jose. For most residents of the area, the opening probably went unnoticed. At most, they may have assumed that a slow growth in business at the San Jose federal court had necessitated the change and that it occurred automatically. For San Jose court supporters, however, the opening scarcely constituted a routine event. Rather, it represented the culmination of a long and sometimes frustrating campaign to persuade the United States attorney, stationed in San Francisco, to permanently assign a person or persons to the San Jose court. As was the case with the start of the clerk's office, the opening was an important event in the development of a federal legal presence in San Jose and the central coast counties.

Initially it may have seemed to court supporters that the United States attorney was ready to take such a step. In early November 1966, then United States Attorney Cecil Poole (now a judge of the United States Court of Appeals for the Ninth Circuit) accompanied District Judge Oliver J. Carter and Judge Robert F. Peckham, then presiding judge of the Santa Clara County Superior Court, to San Jose where they inspected space being made available for federal court. As a result of the visit, Judge Carter instructed the Government Services Agency (GSA) to execute a lease for "whatever space is required" by the United States Attorney's office and eventually the space was obtained.[1]

However, whatever impression they may have received from Poole's visit to San Jose, court supporters eventually discovered that he did not intend to station an assistant United States attorney there. Rather, when a case was heard in San Jose, the attorney responsible for it would commute from San Francisco to San Jose. Indeed, Poole never used the space provided "even as an accommodation to his assistants who try cases in San Jose."[2]

*Assistant United States Attorney Joseph M. Burton, head of the San Jose United States Attorney's office, June 1984. This and the following photograph were taken in the United States Attorney's offices in the new United States Courthouse and Federal Building. (Photograph by Ira Nowinski.)*

Overall, Poole seemed uninterested, if not hostile, to San Jose court supporters. He did not go out of his way to help them, by stationing an assistant United States attorney in San Jose as an act of faith in the court and as a service to the area. Beyond that, he was unwilling to provide much guidance on how San Jose court supporters might eventually gain such a permanent office.

Faced with Poole's refusal to act, San Jose court supporters turned to gaining a more sympathetic appointee upon the election of Richard Nixon as president in 1968. Writing to California Senator George Murphy shortly after the election, Russ Roessler, then chair of the Santa Clara County Bar Association's Federal Courts Committee, noted that Mr. Poole had "not been of any real assistance." Speaking for the bar, he urged that the president-elect appoint someone who would "make an unequivocal commitment to establish forthwith an office of the United States attorney in San Jose."[3]

Probably Roessler did not find the reply to his letter particularly encouraging. According to the senator's executive assistant, the senator would be "glad to advise the Justice Department of your recommendation" and that department could then discuss the question "with whoever may become the United States attorney in San Francisco."[4]

Once President Nixon appointed a new United States attorney in San Francisco, there was some change in the situation. The new United States attorney, James L. Browning, Jr., appeared more sympathetic than Poole. Unlike his predecessor, he discussed establishment of a San Jose office and counseled court supporters on steps to take.

*Members of the United States Attorney's office in San Jose, June 1984. From left to right are Joseph M. Burton, Donna Stremmel, Sonja Peterson, Susan Dondershine, Sally Cunningham, Lee Potts, John Mendez, Bernice Lee, Barbara Moore, and Lee Altschuler. Not present were Eric Fisher and Kathy Butler. (Photograph by Ira Nowinski.)*

But little progress was made. According to Browning, budgetary problems tied his hands. Without more funds from the Department of Justice, he simply could not afford to open an office in San Jose.

To some San Jose court supporters, Browning's statements appeared disingenuous. Given that Santa Clara County was providing the space for one dollar per year, they found it difficult to believe that the office could not afford to station one assistant United States attorney in the area. They may also have believed that Browning should have gone to bat more aggressively for whatever funds were necessary.[5]

Even with the rule change of 1970 and with the creation of the San Jose Federal Court Advisory Committee, the situation did not change significantly. The new court rule, brought about by Judge Peckham's protest of the division of court business between San Francisco and San Jose, mandated that all criminal cases arising in the four central coast counties be tried in San Jose. Under the new rule, obviously, the United States attorney would have more cases to try in the San Jose court.

During the same time, the establishment of the San Jose Federal Court Advisory Committee increased pressure for action. Still, Browning continued to argue that he could not act without increased funding. Addressing the first meeting of the San Jose Federal Court Advisory Committee in September 1970, he told them that the "chances" for the office "would be greatly enhanced in the event of the passage of a supplemental appropriations bill."[6]

Even the construction of the new temporary courthouse in San Jose did not bring about the establishment of a United States Attorney's office in the city. Although GSA found funds to construct the portable modular buildings, it pointed out that it could not "guarantee modular space . . . unless justice certifies funds," which, according to Browning, the department was unable to do. As a consequence, there was no United States attorney's office in the new structures when they opened for use in January 1973.[7]

Not until the appointment of Browning's successor, G. William Hunter, did the United States attorney establish an office in San Jose. Regarded as sympathetic to San Jose by proponents of the court, Hunter listened to the urgings of assistant United States attorneys tired of the continual commutes. Applying to the Department of Justice for funds to open an office, he managed to secure the money necessary to rent space and to hire a secretary. He then assigned Assistant United States Attorney Don Ayer to the new office and finally, a San Jose office for the United States attorney came into being.[8]

Don Ayer was reared in the Los Altos area and received his undergraduate education at Stanford. After graduation from Harvard Law School, he was a law clerk to Supreme Court Justice William H. Rehnquist. Ayer's recollections of his tenure as the first full-time assistant United States attorney in San Jose provide us with a sense of that office and its beginning.

It was a welcome day in late September of 1978 when we finally moved into our office on the sixth floor of the American Bank and Trust Building at 675 North First Street, just down West Taylor Street from the Federal Courthouse. I say finally because by then I had spent several months helping to draft requisition proposals and walking the streets of San Jose looking for suitable quarters. I had been with the United States Attorney's office in San Francisco for over a year, and had, for most of that time, been primarily responsible for the San Jose criminal caseload. That meant driving the fifty miles each way from San Francisco two, three, or more times per week, to cover the calendars and trials before Magistrate Blacker and Judges Ingram, Williams, and Chief Judge Peckham. The judges, of course, had been making the trek from their chambers in San Francisco a good deal longer. In the earlier days, they had been served by Bob Carey and Ed Davis, who gave very willingly to me of both their wisdom and experience, and of their shares of the San Jose caseload, shortly after I joined the office in 1977.

And so we — Helen Voss and myself — moved in. She had worked several years earlier in the United States Attorney's office in San Francisco, in the probation offices in San Jose and San Francisco and had moved to San Jose. She had experience in office administration from her work for the Bureau of Prisons, and seemed intrigued by the idea of being secretary and chief of staff in a two-person office starting up from scratch. That was a good thing, since that was certainly what we were doing. At that time, the Justice Department did not recognize the existence of any suppliers of anything west of Washington, D.C. I believe that everything we got, from furniture to pencils, was moved a stick at a time by covered wagon. We spent more months than I can remember using the boxes that the *Federal Reporters* came in as makeshift bookshelves.

Everyone agreed that the San Jose office was a good idea, and it was generally predicted that its presence would cause the caseload to grow. It did. I recall observing in full bloom, however, a bureaucratic conceit (which I have more recently put to good use myself) by which main offices maintain a proper relationship with branch offices. Within the United States Attorney's office, I think the view was widely held that the work in San Jose was not as interesting or as important as the work in San Francisco, because the "big" cases were not there. It always seemed to me that if someone were allowed a respite from the daily flood of bank robberies, alien cases, check forgeries, and gun cases, there might be a major case or two lurking among the one million plus souls inhabiting the central coast counties. This slightly heretical view was borne out first in the narcotics area when, in 1979, the Drug Enforcement Administration Task Force in San Jose made a number of substantial conspiracy cases, including one against an organization headed by Gary Vodak, which at the time was the only Section 848 Continuing Criminal Enterprise case pending in the district.

In handling the high volume caseload which we had we were blessed with the effective assistance of a string of law clerks, all but two of whom came from the law school of the University of Santa Clara. These clerks assumed primary responsibility for the weekly petty offense calendar before Magistrate Blacker, and assisted in the research and writing of motions and appellate briefs. Most of them worked approximately twenty hours per week, in one of the four packing-crate-sized rooms that made up our 600 square foot suite. Ross Nadel, who worked with Ed Davis and myself in the commuting days, has gone on to serve as a law clerk to both a magistrate and a judge of this court, and then as an assistant United States attorney first in Sacramento and now in San Francisco. Donnie Kull, James Lynch, Sara Katz, and Delbert Gee, from Santa Clara, and Bob Amador and Bonnie Gelb Jackson, from Stanford, each made their own substantial contribution as well and have gone on to careers in the private sector.

The work of the office during 1978 and 1979 was as pleasant as anything that I have been involved in. A lot of people were brought through the courthouse on a great variety of major and minor criminal violations. We had our share of trials. We also resolved a lot of cases on terms that seemed reasonable to everyone. It was fun being the legal arm of federal law enforcement south of the San Francisquito, for the last brief period when such a thing was imaginable. There was a certain satisfaction in being able to look down from our self-contained (after awhile we even got a copying machine), if modest, sixth floor corner suite, on the federal court building at the other end of the street.

Much more satisfying, however, was the air of cordiality and respect which seemed to be shared by everyone in the orbit of the courthouse on West Taylor. While we had our moments of tension (during trials primarily), my predominant recollection is of a decency and a pleasantness not often associated with lawyers or their work. The list of people within that orbit — including the judges and their staffs, the magistrate, the clerk's office, the marshal's service, the probation office, and the federal public defender — is a long one, too long to set out fully here. But as I said when I left the office in November 1979, the opportunity to work in such an atmosphere with such a group does not come along often. It was a pleasure to be part of that group.

The United States attorney had been reluctant to put an office in San Jose, but another branch of the Department of Justice was much more willing to establish itself there. Within a year after the reopening of court in San Jose, the United States Marshal's service set up a branch in that city. Despite difficulties in securing adequate space, the marshal's service continued to maintain a San Jose office throughout the 1970s and in 1984 it moved into new quarters in the permanent Courthouse and Federal Building.

At first space proved easy to secure. During November 1966, United States Marshal Edward A. Heslep attended the same meeting with Judges Carter and Peckham as United States Attorney Cecil Poole, and he also inspected possible space for an office. In late 1967, the space became available, and the marshal's service set up its first San Jose office in the old Post Office Building by Saint James Park. Donald Fisher served as the first deputy United States marshal to be permanently stationed in the city.

In 1973, however, when the new temporary federal courthouse opened, the situation of the marshal's service deteriorated. A third modular building had been proposed to house the service, among other agencies, but that portable building was never constructed, presumably due to a lack of funding. With the service having to leave the old Post Office Building, it faced the prospect of having no San Jose office.

Soon, due to the good graces of the clerk of court, a solution of sorts was arranged. Having some space he could spare, the clerk turned over to the marshals a room in the new modular building. Although hardly enough, it was better than nothing. Still, the limited amount of space forced many deputies to operate out of the trunks of their cars rather than from the office space they had a right to expect.

Aside from the constricted office space, the absence of a holding cell provided a considerable difficulty for the service. The marshals had to use one of the jury rooms, none of which was designed for such a task. Virtually all of the attempted escapes from the San Jose temporary courthouse were due to the inadequacy of the holding facilities there.[9]

Despite the obvious need, a holding cell never was built at San Jose. In 1978, pressure for construction of such a cell increased after the escape of a just-sentenced prisoner from Judge Ingram's courtroom, and in early 1979, GSA presented a construction schedule to Judge Ingram. However, the project later was cancelled due to the assumed rapid completion of the permanent courthouse, and so no cell was available until 1984.[10]

From 1967 to 1984, many persons served as deputy marshals in San Jose. After Donald Fisher, the deputy marshals in charge of the San Jose operation were Rudolph Hasty, Ron Hein, James Ledgewood, who served from 1973 to 1978, and Roger Olmanson, who has continued to the present. In addition, James Comerford stands out as a deputy marshal who was long associated with the office.[11]

With the move to the new courthouse in 1984, the marshal's service enjoyed adequate facilities for the first time during its many years in San Jose. For the two deputy marshals permanently stationed in the city and for those assisting them, the change represented a substantial move forward and one which presaged a bright future.

# Part 4

# A Journalist Remembers

From the early history of federal courts in the central coast counties, the story has moved to the protracted struggle for a renewed federal presence and to the federal offices affected. We go now to an overview of the reestablished court's history by Rick Carroll, an award-winning journalist who wrote many of the major stories in the central coast counties in twenty years as a *San Jose Mercury News* reporter and as a *San Francisco Chronicle* correspondent. He was the Bay Area's first journalist to cover the United States District Court in Santa Clara County and brings a different perspective as we conclude the story of *A Judicial Odyssey*.

21

# A Brief History of Silicon Valley

*Rick Carroll*

When it all began in the fifties, nobody called the San Francisco Peninsula's electronics corridor "Silicon Valley." The place didn't really have a catchy name. Nor was it yet known as the world center of the technology of the future, the semiconductor industry. It was just a stretch along the Bayshore Freeway from Palo Alto to Santa Clara where engineers in rented warehouses invented devices destined to change everyone's lives.

The transition from rural Santa Clara valley to high tech Silicon Valley was well along by 1957, but farm workers outnumbered computer programmers and John Deere still outsold Mercedes Benz. The orchards soon would make way for tract homes, shopping centers, and freeways but for the moment farmers worked the land, and the roar of the tractor filled the air.

The land barons of the valley were Italian — DiNapoli, Cortese, LoCurto, D'Arrigo, Gianinni — and the perfumed blossoms of their vast orchards made spring the most delightful of seasons in California. Their harvest was unequaled, from dark Bing cherries to fancy Comice pears and world famous Santa Clara prunes. City folks from San Francisco would venture south to take in the annual blossom display and return again in summer to claim a crate or two of tree-ripened fruit from the never-empty cornucopia. The orchards went first, sold in the name of progress, bulldozed and paved over along with the simpler, more traditional life-style. The great canneries disappeared along with seasonal hordes of migrant Mexican workers, and then the roadside fruit stands dried up and an entire industry was gone in a generation, just like that. The land yielded a bumper crop of single-story concrete tilt-up buildings that housed new companies with impossible names like Qantel, Xebec, and Xicor. But nobody complained. It was the best and highest use of the land, planners said.

Housing tracts replace orchards in the Santa Clara valley. (Courtesy San Jose Mercury News.)

The crisp air of the early sixties held a promise of good things to come, new frontiers in easy reach. The stuff of boyhood dreams — a flight to the moon — was possible, and grown men knew it. It was a time of new direction and new hope, a time when people smiled for no apparent reason. Engineers plotting tomorrows with slide rules looked up from their midnight work and grinned. Even the farmers managed smiles as they sold their land and moved on, happy men with fat bank accounts. Life was changing fast, and folks couldn't wait to see what would happen next.

Not all of it was good. A young president was killed in Dallas, a controversial war raged on in Southeast Asia, a generation gap split the nation, drug abuse became widespread and a credibility gap cast doubt on America's leaders. But men walked on the moon, the war ended, and a president who said he wasn't a crook resigned.

Vietnam veterans who returned home to Santa Clara valley found things changed. The sky looked brown and the water sometimes tasted funny, but hell, it was great to be home and great to be alive.

In the valley, where miracles now occurred daily, the high tech flora and fauna of Apples and Coyotes proliferated; things got smaller and cheaper. There were calculators, digital watches, word processors, home computers, video games, and neat things to go with them like floppy disks and joysticks.

The computer age landed square on everyone's doorstep in 1980, and nothing was the same again. Typewriters became antiques and carbon paper was shuffled aside as processors, peripherals, and modems moved into homes and offices. There were new computer languages to learn, like BASIC, COBOL, and FORTRAN. Everyday English was sprinkled with new computer terms like "downtime," "offload," and "interface." Children everywhere huddled before the low glow of computer screens, zapping alien invaders with their joysticks; the young acquired new tastes for real computers and taught their parents a thing or two.

The place got on the map but it was no longer Santa Clara valley. The old name wasn't good enough. It was Silicon Valley now, a made-up name after the vital ingredient in computers, and there were more of those every day. They were like television sets: everyone had to have one. There were predictions that six in ten families would have a home computer by the year 2000; some families already had two or three.

So it was inevitable. The computer got named "Man of the Year" in 1982 by *Time* magazine, the first time in the history of such honors that man lost to a machine. But what a machine! What couldn't it do? The new barons in the valley — Hewlett, Packard, Amdahl, Varian, and Jobs — smiled knowing smiles and delivered the future but Santa Clara valley's sweet bounty was gone and nothing grown or produced there would ever taste so good, again.

## 22

# And There Came a Cry

*Rick Carroll*

Brass letters, bright and shiny, spelled out the mighty presence of the United States government at the superior court in Santa Clara County; it now was "United States District Court."

Two United States marshals guarded the double doors. They wore freshly pressed business suits, carried concealed weapons and looked big and strong. Inside, the judge's bench was ready. The carpet, newly shampooed, still smelled of soap. A large American flag stood to the side of the dais. Spectators filled the first two rows. An attorney stood ready at the defense table. The defendant, a woman, looked nervous. Nobody appeared at the United States attorney's table; the case would start without him. No cameras were allowed, even on this historic day. The year was 1967, the third Monday in January, the beginning of a new era, and there came a cry...

"Oyez! Oyez! All persons having business with the United States District Court for the Northern District of California will now draw near, give your attention and you shall be heard. . . ." A ceremonial cry with roots in Old English law and suitable for bewigged justices of yore, it seemed out of place in this relaxed California courthouse where such formalities were always a stranger.

The clerk, Rosemary Miller, looked uneasy as she called out the ancient refrain that would usher in a new era of jurisprudence in Santa Clara County, indeed, the entire central coast of California; for until this day all federal matters from the academic groves of Stanford University to the distant lettuce fields of Salinas had to be settled in San Francisco at great distance and inconvenience.

The slight discomfort Miller felt evaporated when the beaming, confident judge swept out of his chambers in his new, black robe and flew up the three steps to the bench. At forty-six, Judge Robert F. Peckham, a man with a boyish grin, twinkling eyes and a high, domed forehead, took the bench with such assurance that it seemed he had always been a judge. He had that look about him.

His native judicial demeanor derived, no doubt, from his family which for three generations served the California legal profession. His father, the late Robert F. Peckham, Sr., practiced law in San Francisco and his great-grandfather was a Santa Cruz County judge shortly after the gold rush and later a San Jose lawyer. An uncle, I.M. Peckham, was United States attorney for northern California during the Hoover administration.

No one ever doubted that Peckham would be a lawyer and a judge; it was expected of him by his family and his peers; A Phi Beta Kappa graduate of Stanford University, he studied at both the Stanford and the Yale University law schools and returned to his native San Francisco as an assistant United States attorney. Appointed to the superior court by Governor Edmund G. Brown, Sr. in 1959, Peckham served there seven years before President Johnson nominated him in the fall of 1966 to be the first federal judge in Santa Clara County.

Judge Peckham welcomed everyone and briefly noted the significance of the opening of a federal court in San Jose. Then he directed the clerk to call the calendar, and the very first case commenced.

A routine case of embezzlement of funds from a San Jose credit union by its treasurer, the case is significant only because the United States attorney had balked at commuting to San Jose from San Francisco.

The accused, a forty-two-year-old woman, lived in Los Gatos, some sixty miles south of San Francisco, and, along with her lawyer, Elwood F. DeVilbiss of nearby Campbell, had no desire to drive two hours daily to and from San Francisco for trial. Four days after Judge Peckham began duty on the federal bench in San Jose on November 10, 1966, her lawyer filed a motion to transfer the case from San Francisco and closer to home.

Assistant United States Attorney David Bancroft resisted the move. "In San Jose there is neither courtroom, clerk, nor marshal. No trial date can even be anticipated since no court session has been scheduled. None of the government's witnesses in this case ... has expressed any inability or even inconvenience in attending trial in San Francisco," he protested in the government's response to that motion.

His argument fell on deaf ears.

On December 13, 1966, Federal Judge William T. Sweigert, sitting in San Francisco, ordered the case transferred to San Jose for the convenience of the defendant and witnesses; the upshot of his order was that the reluctant Bancroft would suffer the Bayshore Freeway commute.

By blunder or protest, the prosecutor failed to appear on the first day of trial and apologizing in a phone call to the judge for an inadvertent calendar error, he waived his right to be present on that first, historic day.

The case ended in March with a conviction. That posed a new dilemma: Where should the woman defendant surrender to await transfer to a federal prison? The exchange between the judge and his marshal over the defendant's immediate fate provided the only light moment on her day of sentencing:

THE COURT: Well, there will be a brief period before she goes to Terminal Island?
THE MARSHAL: Yes, sir.
THE COURT: I take it that the county does not have an arrangement with the federal government so that she could stay at Elmwood?

THE MARSHAL: We are checking on that, sir. But she could stay there, forty-eight hours or seventy-two hours.

MR. BANCROFT: That's right.

THE COURT: Yes. Is that agreeable with the sheriff?

THE MARSHAL: Yes sir. She will meet me there and I will —

MR. DeVILBISS: Where is Elmwood?

THE COURT: That is the jail at Milpitas.

MR. DeVILBISS: Oh, sure. I was thinking of another county. All right. Fine.

THE COURT: So that will be the order.[1]

And so it began, one judge in a borrowed courtroom on the fourth floor of San Jose's downtown Superior Court Building, who once or twice a month heard a smattering of routine cases like embezzlement, forgery, and bankruptcy. Not dreary cases but hardly the stuff of headlines. The winds of change that raked the Bay Area in the late sixties sent freshets into the deep and comfortable suburban tracts of the South Bay and stirred up business for the fledgling federal court. The court began to have its first real caseload.

# 23

## A Sampling of Cases

*Rick Carroll*

### The Conscientious Objectors

The war in Vietnam, by 1967, was in full stride and creating a battle at home, one of resistance to the draft, and here they came — young, fresh-faced boys, many still in college, summoned by their neighbors and friends on local selective service boards to stand and fight in the jungles of Southeast Asia.

They chose, instead, to file quietly into federal court and present evidence of conscientious objection, physical ailment, or legal oversight.

They were farmers' sons like a young man from Watsonville, who asked the court to declare unconstitutional the 1967 Selective Service Act on grounds it was "enacted before congressional declaration of war and exceeded the power of government." The first such challenge in the West, it failed in court.

A Berkeley student brought a civil suit to enjoin troop shipments from the Oakland Army Induction Center. The suit was dismissed. There were challenges on every conceivable ground and all of them failed to end the draft or stop the war, but each time the war escalated the resistance intensified.

An Episcopalian cleric in San Jose doused selective service files with napalm on the day before Christmas in 1970 and set them afire. Office workers escaped unhurt but the fire destroyed thousands of the San Jose copies of records for the three local draft boards headquartered in the eleven-story Community Bank Building downtown. Attorney James F. Boccardo, who owned the building, requested the draft boards to vacate the building because of the considerable inconvenience to other tenants caused by the near daily protests.

While the acrid smoke of burning draft cards rose over northern California campuses the hard-pressed United States Attorney's Office in San Francisco was inundated by the

*Protest against the war in Vietnam.
This 1970 photograph shows a march
on First Street by students from San
Jose State University. (Courtesy* San
Jose Mercury News.*)*

paperwork of prosecution. In all, 2,032 young men were criminally indicted for draft resistance in the Northern District of California between 1967 and 1974. In the banner year of 1971, selective service cases numbered 511 out of 868 total criminal cases in northern California, or 59 percent.

When an untold number of resisters fled the country, others took a chance in federal court. Heartfelt cases, they sometimes produced joy when a young man prevailed but more often a profound sadness settled over the court like a summer fog as another young man was convicted. The most celebrated draft resister of the day, a Stanford student named David Harris, then husband of folksinger Joan Baez, was ordered off to prison, but most were placed on probation on the condition that they do two years of work of national importance as directed by the probation officer. Such a disposition was similar to the obligation that the defendant would have incurred if he had been found to be a conscientious objector by his selective service board.

Refusing induction, twenty-three-year-old Robert Michael Preston wrote to his draft board, saying, "I cannot abide by violent means." He stood trial, was convicted but never sentenced. Instead, he took a gun one Sunday in January of 1972 and did what he professed he couldn't do to his fellow man. He killed. Himself.

"It came as a shock to everyone," his saddened attorney, Jerry Berg, told the court on the day Preston would have been sentenced. "The strongest, bravest stand he took in his twenty-three years was refusing to be inducted in an organization that was incompatible with his beliefs.

"The tragedy," Berg said, "is that he had the strength to take this courageous stand but he wasn't equipped with the strength to endure the consequences."

In the very still courtroom, Berg read aloud the young man's last testimony, filled with confusion but strong in opposition to a war that made no sense to him. It was a stand fairly typical of those who refused to fight.

> Thoughout school, our history teaches of the immense freedoms that America affords its citizens and, in most cases, this is true. But I couldn't figure out where the draft fit with these freedoms. "You owe your country a debt," was the answer that I often heard. But with the legality of the Vietnam War in such question by Americans and people of other countries, and the fact that there was no peaceful, constructive way of paying this debt, I began to wonder about the motives of people who support the selective service laws.
>
> I felt that if I were to follow the law of the selective service, I would be forced to help solve mankind's problems in a way contrary to my beliefs and education. I felt that the only way to aid in the ending of the war and to change the law was to break the law.

He broke the law and paid the ultimate price, for reasons known only to him. On the day young Preston was to be sentenced, his body was lowered into a grave at Gate of Heaven Cemetery in Los Altos.

"A victim of our times," the judge intoned on the day of sentence.[1]

The draft soon ended and the war itself was conceded as a lost cause after twelve years of fighting and more than 57,000 American battle casualties.

The last man out of Saigon, a United States Marine, ran for the last helicopter to buzz off the American embassy roof in the early morning hours of April 30, 1975. The Viet Cong took Saigon that afternoon and renamed it Ho Chi Minh City.

Robert Michael Preston would have been twenty-seven.


*The* Stanford Daily *Case*

Stanford University sits like a jewel between San Francisco Bay and the Pacific Ocean in the lee of a coastal range tilted by earthquakes and honed by time into golden rolling foothills dotted with spreading oaks. The 8,000-acre campus, linked to the town of Palo Alto by a lane lined with majestic palms, is strewn with Romanesque and early California mission-style buildings with red tile roofs, flower-filled plazas, and eucalyptus groves.

A more idyllic-looking campus probably does not exist anywhere in the world.

The school community has, in its brief, ninety-two-year history, managed not only to split atoms; transplant hearts; clone cells; find quarks; and invent transistors; but win ten Nobel Prizes, three Pulitzer Prizes, and ten Medals of Science; and produce forty-seven Rhodes scholars. It shares the patent on DNA and is the site of the first work on a cure for the common cold.

Its graduates include Supreme Court justices, presidential advisors, America's first woman astronaut, and sports stars like golfer Tom Watson, tennis ace John McEnroe,

*The April 1971 sit-in at Stanford Hospital. (Courtesy News and Publication Service, Stanford University.)*

and quarterback Jim Plunkett. Its football team, the Cardinal, made history by beating Ohio State and the University of Michigan to win the Rose Bowl. Twice, back-to-back.

The students, many of them the sleek, tan, sports-car driving children of plenty, could scarcely be blamed if they remained immune to the virus of social reform that beset other student bodies in the early seventies.

There had been antiwar speeches, draft card burnings, and militant posturing by various radical groups but nothing at Stanford reached the shrill madness of other student protests. Four students were killed on the Kent State campus during an antiwar demonstration. Armed blacks had taken Cornell University by storm. There had even been tear gas riots over Dow Chemical recruitment at San Jose State, then living down its party school reputation.

Across the Bay in Berkeley, students at the University of California were engaged in the ninth year of a spring offensive when Stanford students rose up with righteous indignation over the firing of a black janitor at the university's medical school and sat down in the hallways to protest.

What started as a sit-in over minority rights escalated to a full-scale student riot and ended as a landmark freedom-of-the-press case in the United States Supreme Court.

The sit-in began peacefully enough but after thirty hours of student occupation, the Palo Alto police decided to clear the hallways. Expecting an easy task, they encountered

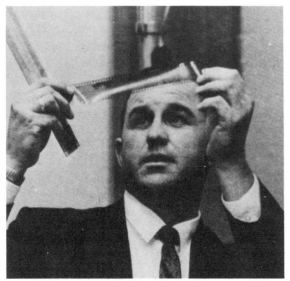

*The Palo Alto police search of the* Stanford Daily *newsroom. In this photograph a police officer scrutinizes film negative for shots of the Stanford Hospital sit-in.* (Courtesy Stanford Daily.)

what Police Chief James Zurcher later called "the most vicious and unprovoked attack on police I have ever witnessed." It was hand-to-hand combat with broken chair legs and billy clubs, a real donnybrook that left fourteen police injured, one seriously; two dozen demonstrators hurt; and the medical center in shambles.

The riot might have slipped into the past and been forgotten except for an even uglier incident that ensued: the infamous police raid on the *Stanford Daily*, the campus newspaper. Three days after the riot, at about 6:00 p.m. on April 12, four Palo Alto police with a search warrant signed by a Palo Alto Municipal Court judge entered the city room of the student newspaper. They came in search of photographs taken during the riot which they hoped to use as evidence to arrest the students who disturbed the peace and assaulted the police. The search party specifically sought unpublished photos, supposedly taken during the riot, of students who attacked the police at the university hospital. They rifled darkrooms, photo files, personal papers, and several cans of trash before leaving at about 6:35 p.m. — empty-handed.

No pictures existed because no student photographer was in a position to take any, university officials informed the Palo Alto police.

Stanford President Richard W. Lyman, first to sound the tocsin, deplored the surprise search as "threatening to the full freedom of the press."[2]

Reportedly the first time in American history that a newsroom had been searched by police, the raid outraged the nation's journalists, polarized editors and police chiefs, and created such a controversy that Sam Bridges, the jobless cause célèbre, was eclipsed in the wake of events and forgotten by nearly everyone but archivists.

"This is something that should not be allowed and it should be fought in court," said student editor Felicity Barringer, now a *Washington Post* reporter. Barringer and six associates, believing the police would conduct "similar searches in similar circumstances," filed suit in United States District Court, seeking a permanent injunction against future police searches of the newsroom.[3]

The suit, seeking declaratory and injunctive relief against Palo Alto police and the

Santa Clara County District Attorney's office, alleged that the student journalists had been deprived of their rights under the First, Fourth, and Fourteenth Amendments to the Constitution because of the search.

Anthony Amsterdam, the law professor and civil libertarian whose cases have involved Ernesto Miranda, Martin Luther King, and Gary Gilmore now took on the defense of the *Stanford Daily*. On July 10, 1972, Amsterdam — his arms full of bulging briefcases and trailed like the Pied Piper by dozens of students, local attorneys, and members of the local press — stepped into the federal court to argue on behalf of the student newspaper, indeed, every news-gathering organization in the land.

"If the court please," he said, "I come heavily burdened, but hopefully we will be able to keep the oral presentation short. I will promise to do that. Whether I will perform or not is another question." His students and the judge alike smiled knowingly as Amsterdam, with his usual spare eloquence, began.

"The harm done by a search isn't what they actually saw. It is the subjection of a newspaper's entire working files, drawers, desks, everything in the office to inspection by authorities with all that implies for the informant who wants to put his trust in the newspaper but is unwilling to have what he confides . . . observed by the authorities.

"The *Daily* is a newspaper. It doesn't matter whether it is the same kind of a newspaper as the *New York Times*.

"The principle of law we contend for is that searches of newspaper offices . . . may not be made unless it is alleged that the newspaper itself is involved in criminal activity.

"We believe that the Fourth Amendment, in short, makes subpoenas the appropriate methods and does not permit searches of persons not themselves suspected of criminal activity for evidence."[4]

The case remained under submission until October 5, when Judge Peckham handed down his landmark decision, accepting the Fourth Amendment arguments.

"A search warrant," he found, "presents an overwhelming threat to the press' ability to gather and disseminate the news, and because less drastic means exist to obtain the same information, third party searches of a newspaper office are impermissible in all but a very few situations."

A subpoena duces tecum, which simply orders the recipient to bring records into court, "obviously is much less intrusive than a search. Newspaper offices are much more disorganized than, say the average law office, and a search for particular photographs or notes will mean rummaging through virtually all the drawers and cabinets in the office."[5]

Peckham awarded the plaintiffs attorney's fees based on 750 hours at $50 an hour, a bargain since Professor Amsterdam had sought no compensation for his seventy-five hours of participation in the case. Peckham enhanced the award by $10,000 because of the high-quality defense work: the total award was $47,500.[6]

The award may have forced Palo Alto city officials to file an appeal to the Ninth Circuit Court of Appeals and, ultimately, the United States Supreme Court. Palo Alto Mayor Scott Carey later claimed that the city appealed "mainly because . . . five city employees were ordered to pay the *Daily's* lawyers $47,500. If the fee had been negotiated down to $5,000 or $10,000, Palo Alto almost certainly would have dropped the case at the United States District Court level."[7] Other legal researchers claimed it was not the award of attorney's fees, but the breadth of the ruling that forced the *Daily* appeal, despite Mayor Carey's statement to the contrary.

The Ninth Circuit Court affirmed Peckham's decision and adopted his opinion. Next the Palo Alto officials pressed their appeal to the nation's highest court. Asking the Supreme Court to review the case, Santa Clara County District Attorney Louis Bergna argued that if the decision stood, "it would strike a massive blow against the public interest in fair and effective law enforcement."[8]

The Supreme Court, reversing Peckham by a five to three vote on May 31, 1978, found nothing in the Constitution to bar third party searches of newsrooms. "At the very least, the burden of justifying a major revision of the Fourth Amendment has not been carried," the Court held.[9]

The federal government and eight states, including California, subsequently passed laws protecting the press from third party searches but, years after the landmark ruling, at least twenty four searches of lawyers and doctors' offices were executed in California counties between 1980 and 1982.

In the end, many agreed that the most remarkable aspect of the case was the ease with which the whole affair might have been avoided. "It need never have happened at all," said Bob Beyers, the Stanford information officer who told the police chief the day of the clash that no unpublished photos existed. "I don't know why, but he never believed me."[10]

### The Legend of Cap'n Crunch

In the shadowy underground of Silicon Valley — and in the secret files of the FBI — John Thomas Draper was known as Cap'n Crunch, the notorious phone phreak and cult hero of the sixties. He borrowed his alias from the popular cereal of the same name, which came with a little toy whistle inside the box. Draper discovered it was much more than a child's prize.

The whistle, he found, could duplicate the telephone company's high-pitched, calliope-like dial tones, enabling him to call anyone, anywhere, anytime, without spending anything. "It's just like fooling a vending machine into giving you a candy bar for a No. 14 washer," he gleefully explained.[11]

When it came to electronics, Draper's ability was considerable and his zeal unlimited. "Anything I do," he once said, "is just for the pure knowledge. I'm a diddler, you know what I mean? I like to know how things work." His interest began in high school but soared in the air force while he served a four-year hitch in England as a radar maintenance man. He learned all he could about the military's phone system which, he said, "never worked right."[12] Bored Airman Draper fished the whistle out of his cereal box one day and made his breakthrough discovery. The world was his for a whistle and a tune, and he called home to California often.

Honorably discharged, he moved to the Silicon Valley in 1968, enrolled in college electronics courses, got a job as an electronics technician, and kept piping his whistle, calling up foreign ports.

It was an imperfect art at best. Sometimes he ended up in Bangkok instead of Baltimore, but it served his needs until the blue box came along. A refined electronic version of his toy whistle, the blue box, duplicated the same signals faster and more efficiently. Draper dismantled it and created a new, improved version, complete with automatic dialing, and set off around the world — by telephone.

The device was a forerunner to the automatic rapid-repeat dialing systems now in widespread use. Its sophistication amazed the FBI agents, trained for the pursuit of white collar criminals but baffled by a high tech world and the crimes that those in the know could commit.

*Cap'n Crunch. This photograph was taken during 1972. (Courtesy San Francisco Chronicle.)*

"He even automated the system by tape recording multi-frequency tones for frequently called numbers, so all he had to do was play the tapes into the telephone," said United States Attorney Paul Fitzpatrick. "We completed calls with this blue box to Australia, Great Britain, and Hawaii," Fitzpatrick said proudly, adding, "with the phone company looking over our shoulder, of course." [13]

On the night of March 27, 1972, Draper telephoned radio station Two M S in Sydney, Australia, to request his favorite song, "Alone Again, Naturally," on the all-night rock 'n' roll show. Unknown to Draper, the FBI was also listening this time, taping all his calls, gathering wiretap evidence to build a federal case against him.

The Cap'n was arrested May 4, 1972, near Los Gatos and charged with fraudulently using the phone company's long distance network, a felony punishable by no less than five years in federal prison.

Defense counsel Frank Ubhaus praised Draper's "fantastic mind: Somebody with John Draper's mind just has to be doing something in electronics." A lenient Judge Peckham, realizing he had a wizard on his hands, let Draper off with a $1,000 fine, five years' probation, and a stern warning. "Your electronic gymnastics may have been thought to be a prank, a frivolity, or a harmless vocational endeavor," said Judge Peckham. "But on the next occasion, if ever there is one, you will receive a prison sentence."

There was a next time. Draper was arrested four years later for cheating the phone company and, true to his word, the judge put the Cap'n behind bars for four months in the Lompoc federal penitentiary. Two years later, the Cap'n was caught in an FBI sting operation in Pennsylvania, clearly in violation of his probation. "You're no stranger to this court," the sorely tested Judge Peckham told Draper on the last occasion. "Is this not simple? You have to pay for your telephone calls."[14]

Draper was off to jail again, a setback for any usual genius but not for Cap'n Crunch. Draper spent the quiet nights in his cell writing computer software programs, including

"Easywriter," a worldwide best-seller which still brings him annual royalties.

He wrote programs for the fledgling Apple Computer firm in Cupertino, gradually weaned himself from telephones to computers and went straight after serving his time.

A wealthy Silicon Valley executive now, Draper is president of Cap'n Software, Inc., specializing in computer programs. He drives the obligatory Mercedes Benz, vacations in such exotic places as the Galápagos Islands, sports a three-piece suit, and owns every high tech gadget ever made — including a Cap'n Crunch whistle, for old times' sake.

### The Bonanno Trial

He sat alone in Tucson, an old man with a bad heart and a head full of memories of a time when America was innocent and he was a young man on the make. By hand, on yellow legal tablets, he wrote in Italian and English about his life and times and men of his tradition, trying to make sense of it all in his autobiography, an absorbing apologia for a life of crime.

It began classically enough: "My name is Joseph Bonanno. I am seventy-eight years old and a grandfather. I've often been described as a gangster, a racketeer, a mobster. I'm supposed to be, or to have been, or to have wanted to be, the 'boss of all bosses,' whatever that means. At one time or another, I have been accused of trying to take over New York, California, Arizona, Wisconsin, Colorado, Alaska, and choice provinces of Mexico and Canada, too. I am not unmindful of my past."[15]

When Bonanno ruled New York, the best that the FBI could do was catch the notorious underworld boss at misdemeanors. But when he retired to Tucson in 1968, agents set out with zeal to put the aging Mafia don behind bars. The campaign lasted fourteen years and involved every trick of the trade: agents infiltrated, bombed, and raided his home; bugged his car; tapped his phone; observed his every move; even plotted his death by crossbow; and always kept close watch on his two sons, Salvatore and Joseph, Jr., in California. The sons would provide authorities the opportunity to nail the "founding father of the modern American Mafia."[16]

Since the early 1970s, the Bonanno brothers, who lived affluent suburban lives in Santa Clara County, had been hauled into San Jose's Federal Court with such regularity it appeared they had no time for malice; their occupation seemed to be perpetual defendants. Their crimes smacked of gangsterism but usually boiled down to little more than bungled alliances with small-time hoods. It was often difficult to tell who the real victims were but the Bonannos always paid the price. They got sent up once for threatening to rough up a child molester.

While the FBI only got the Bonanno brothers on little stuff, they learned enough about them to suspect their father's underworld profits were being funneled into their hands. The two drove the latest cars, wore expensive clothes, and fairly glittered with diamonds and gold but had no visible means of support.[17]

The FBI's suspicions prompted a bizarre undercover operation in concert with Arizona authorities that would last three years and end with Bonanno's first felony conviction.

Agents swapped three-piece suits for greasy overalls to pose as garbagemen and collect Bonanno's curbside trash in Tucson between 1975 and 1978. They seized 6000 handwritten notes in all, from innocent personal reminders to a cryptic but accurate scenario for the murder of San Diego mob leader Frank ("The Bomp") Bompensiero, gunned down February 10, 1977, in a phone booth. The incriminating notes read: "Call Turi p.m. Tell Turi Thursday night with semiautomatic gun (short) 22 that doesn't make much noise." and "Phone booth 9261."[18]

Bompensiero, an FBI informer on Bonanno since 1968, was slain on a Thursday night in San Diego with a silencer-equipped 22-caliber semiautomatic after he was lured to a pay phone. Its number? 273-9261. Turi is Salvatore Bonanno's nickname.[19]

No murder charge was brought against father or son; it would have been nearly impossible to prove. But the secrets of Bonanno's garbage soon yielded new evidence of another crime, this time conspiracy to obstruct justice. In the fall of 1978, a special federal grand jury in San Francisco had begun probing financial records of the defunct Bonanno enterprises: Kachina Fashions of Los Gatos, the United States Mattress and Furniture Company of Campbell, and the Cat House, a pricey seaside Aptos boutique.

The grand jury found no evidence of money laundering but the FBI pieced together hundreds of "trash notes" and discovered instructions from Bonanno to his family members and friends on what to say when they appeared before the grand jury. The piecemeal evidence was sufficient to arrest and charge Bonanno with obstruction of justice along with his nephew, Jack DiFilippi, fifty-four-year-old olive oil importer described as "a loyal soldier" by the Organized Crime Strike Force.

The defense sought immediately to suppress all evidence on grounds by that seizing his garbage, the government violated Bonanno's Fourth Amendment right to privacy.

"The stench of illegality . . . hovers over this entire proceeding," said trial Judge William A. Ingram, who decried the "unlawful and reprehensible" action of Arizona lawmen who "unlawfully tapped phone conversations, falsely swore before state judges . . . and executed false, misleading affidavits." Ingram suppressed Bonanno's 250-page memoir, the nucleus of his autobiography, and privileged tapes of bugged conversations with his lawyers but refused to suppress 40 hours of other taped conversations and 1500 pages of trash notes. "One who puts his secrets in a trash can does so at his peril," the judge ruled.[20] He ordered Bonanno to stand trial in San Jose Federal Court on January 16.

A wise and patient judge, Ingram was known for his tough criminal sentences. In his only other high-visibility case, the retrial of black revolutionary Ruchel Magee, the judge, while a superior court judge, handed down a life sentence in San Quentin with alacrity. Bonanno would get a fair trial and a swift conviction, veteran court reporters agreed.

The on-again, off-again trial took fourteen weeks over five months because Bonanno's frail health and weakening heart forced sudden recesses and long delays even though he took comfort in the judge's chamber and watched his trial on closed circuit television. Sometimes he alerted his attorney, Albert J. Krieger of New York, Miami, and lately, San Jose, by two-way headphone to nuances of the case. He needn't have: Krieger was the best criminal defense attorney money could buy. He specialized in Mafia cases probably because only they could afford his fees, reported to be $10,000 for each day in court.[21]

With a clean-shaven head, booming voice, and a courtroom style at once regal and gritty, Krieger, a master of oratory who often quoted the classics, always drew a crowd whenever he appeared. The day of his final argument every seat in the house was taken.

"May it please this honorable court . . . We've been a long time coming to this point, your honor. I would be less than candid if I were not to say that I do wish this case had ended much, much sooner."

Polite smiles faded as Krieger's strong voice rose to fill the courtroom with argument. "There is no law with which I am familiar," he began, "that says the government can bootstrap substantive accusations into a single, overall conspiracy charge.

"The government has failed in discharging the burden it has voluntarily shouldered in proving the indictment that it crafted . . . they have failed as grossly as if no evidence whatsoever were introduced."

Then, Krieger paused to quote a couplet by poet John Dryden, which, he said, "leaped out to me as what has happened here: 'Thus in a pageant show a plot is made and peace itself is a war in masquerade.'

"The government has been at war with Joseph Bonanno and the government is the aggressor . . . that is why this case has come about. We cannot look at what Mr. Bonanno says or what Mr. Bonanno writes about without full consideration given to the history of the government's atrocious attack upon this man over the years."

He chronicled a history of terror, accused the government of a "venal conspiracy" to put Bonanno, father and son, in jail, and painted the portrait of an old man grown weary, paranoid, and riddled with fear.

"He thought . . . there was a conspiracy in existence to get him through his children or to destroy his children, to destroy his family, to destroy all that he loved, all that he found worthwhile. . . . Bonnano found close family members subpoenaed, found friends of family subpoenaed, and from the notes we can deduce he began to fight with a ghost.

"He could not conceive of this investigation as being anything else other than a carefully orchestrated pageant in which the peaceful appearance of the grand jury would be the war in masquerade and he would be the victim. He knew very well that a mistake by any person appearing before the grand jury . . . could be used by the government as the linchpin to prosecution of the case. So we find, in the beginning notes, his extreme concern about even appearance.

"Bonanno believed that the government was pursuing him for personal gain, that they were willing to spend a fortune of money to obtain his conviction at almost any expense, even if they had to resort to dishonest means."

Krieger scoffed at the notion that Bonanno had such "Svengali and Trilby type control that he could make a person get up on a witness stand in front of a grand jury, look five years straight in the eye, and lie." He dismissed the damaging trash notes as "musings and meditations" of a "harassed man" that "speak in loud and clear terms to an existing paranoia."[22] Finally, he demanded a judgment of acquittal, a verdict of not guilty. It was not to be.

On Tuesday, September 2, 1980, Judge Ingram found Bonanno guilty of conspiracy to obstruct justice. He based his finding on wiretapped phone conversations between the two defendants and 1500 notes from the garbage. The notes, Judge Ingram said, "illustrate the basic agreement and understanding between Bonanno and DiFilippi that prospective witnesses be briefed in advance of their testimony before the grand jury."[23]

"I'm very satisfied with this verdict," said Michael Sterrett, the low-keyed, owlish Strike Force prosecutor. "The evidence inescapably led to that conclusion."[24]

On sentencing day the best seats in the house were reserved for FBI agents from Arizona and California who sat like Cheshire cats as Krieger took his last swing at them and called for "wisdom, mercy, and justice."

"For fifteen years," Krieger said, "this man has been the victim of the most intense suspicion and invasive investigation which produced not one bit of evidence that he was

*Joseph Bonanno leaving the temporary United States Courthouse in San Jose after his sentencing in January 1981. Behind him is his attorney Albert J. Krieger. (Courtesy San* Francisco Chronicle.*)*

involved in any illegality. Time and time again, the government has befouled itself in its effort to convict Joseph Bonanno of a crime it could not name or identify.

"Bonanno believed that his children would fall victim to prosecution upon a mistake, a misunderstanding, a misinterpretation. His fears for his son, Bill, overrode good sense and understanding and a mistake was made."[25]

The silver-haired Bonanno then stood before the judge and in a trembly voice said, "I have nothing to say." He received the maximum possible sentence: five years in prison and a $10,000 fine; and was ordered to surrender his passport and restricted to travel between California and Arizona, pending appeal.

He sank into his brown leather chair at the defense table, a defeated old man with a pinched face. It had taken the government fifteen years to get Bonanno; now only an appeal stood between him and prison.

Eight months later, his conviction was upheld by the Ninth Circuit Court and the United States Supreme Court refused, without comment, to reverse the conviction.

The defense renewed efforts to keep him free on medical grounds. A court-appointed doctor in Tucson found the aging mobster suffered from a leg aneurysm, an enlargement of a weakened artery, and pronounced him too ill to travel to prison.[26]

On November 21, 1983, Judge Ingram sentenced Bonanno to a year and a day in prison. The boss of bosses surrendered to authorities at Terminal Island on December 5 and began serving his first prison term.[27]

### The Harry Margolis Case

Harry Margolis asked permission to commit legal suicide in United States District Court one April morning in 1977; he wanted to discharge his high-powered defense team and represent himself. "I am pretty much convinced that it's indispensable for my defense that I take charge of the defense," said Margolis, fifty-six, a Saratoga tax lawyer who faced felonies enough to put him away until he was an old man.

Slight and balding with a smirking smile, Margolis looked like an overworked accountant instead of a noted tax lawyer and criminal defendant. He stood accused in a twenty-four-count federal indictment of conspiring to defraud the Internal Revenue Service of taxes on 1.4 million dollars by arranging phony tax deductions for singer Barbara McNair, est founder Werner Erhard, Olympic diving star Sammy Lee, and various other wealthy clients. The dark circles under his eyes probably came from anxiety and stress. Trial costs were running $2,000 a day, the government's case looked like ninety court days, and Margolis was getting nervous. He knew he could do a better job than his seven-member defense team which included Leo Branton, Jr., successful co-counsel in defense of Angela Davis. "I've been unable to satisfy myself that anybody of any quality can duplicate my years of experience," Margolis said. "I'm the defendant in this matter and I've got thirty years of life on the line."

The judge asked Margolis to reconsider. "You know as well as I do that the worst lawyer that a man can have is himself," said Judge William A. Ingram. "You simply do not have the necessary objectivity to conduct a trial if you're representing yourself. The course you contemplate . . . in a case such as this is, in my opinion, just plain dangerous. It's a very, very hazardous course to undertake."[28] Fair warning given, the judge granted reluctant permission and Margolis, tax lawyer, counselor to celebrities, and archenemy of the IRS, became a criminal defense lawyer for the first time in his life. He proved he was nobody's fool.

In a classic David and Goliath battle, Margolis single-handedly led a ten-man, two-woman federal court jury through "one of the longest and most complicated tax fraud cases in history." Billed at the outset by the United States Justice Department as "perhaps the biggest breakthrough we've had" in offshore tax havens, the case turned out to be a massive setback, since Margolis won acquittal.[29]

The seven-month trial featured forty-six government witnesses, involved enough evidence to fill a warehouse — 140,000 documents that weighed 1700 pounds — and required three hours for the judge to issue instructions to the jury.

For more than a decade, the Justice Department and the IRS agents had tried to pierce the cloak of secrecy surrounding the many islands of the Caribbean such as the Bahamas, Curacao, and the Netherlands Antilles that served as tax havens for millionaires. The probe, dubbed "Project Haven," was aimed at exposing alleged money laundering and tax evasion which government officials said involved at least $500 million, some of it rumored to be "skim money" from Las Vegas and mob operations.

The Margolis case, the government claimed, would be the first in a long string of

*Harry Margolis, 1977 (Courtesy San Jose Mercury News.)*

prosecutions; it was intended to be the showcase trial and the government expected to prevail — if only prosecutors could explain it simply enough for a jury to understand. United States Attorney James Browning assembled his best: two top assistants well-versed in the tax law, each with a master's degree in the subject from New York University; two veteran IRS agents familiar with the case; and two full-time clerks.

In various court documents, the prosecution explained how the Margolis method of tax planning worked.

> A client borrows $50,000 from company A, an offshore firm that exists only on paper. The client then invests the $50,000 in company B, another paper firm. Then, company B would declare large interest payments to company C, still another paper firm. The client would take a $5,000 deduction for interest charges he supposedly paid to borrow the money from company A. Then he would take another tax write-off of $50,000 because the investment in company B fell through when B took a loss after its huge interest payments to C. While no money actually changed hands ... the client would take a $55,000 deduction on his tax return — and Margolis would be paid a percentage of the savings ... usually a third.[30]

If it seemed complicated, it was; the case was far too complex to grasp for any jury short of one composed of accountants and tax lawyers or Harry Margolis, himself. The jurors, mired by such tax-biz exotica as amortization expense deductions, partnership losses, and interest-expense deductions, fell into the black hole of tax law and returned with a verdict of acquittal. Despite the voluminous evidence, or perhaps because of it, the jurors said they couldn't find "the smoking gun," the damning bit of evidence. Some jurors gave posttrial explanations that amounted to complaints.

"The government took the shotgun approach," said juror Robert Rodine. "They didn't focus on one thing. They tried to show a conspiracy, but we couldn't find it."

"A lot of us wanted to convict Harry," said juror Rosalee Blase, "but the government just couldn't put it together for us. I think this whole case is a bad reflection on our system of justice."

Juror Archie Marshall thought the court was an improper forum, the criminal charges ridiculous. "This case should have gone before Congress. It's up to them to plug the loopholes."[31]

It was a setback of enormous proportions for the government; a turning point in the national mores, perhaps, or maybe the beginning of a new, sophisticated view of the tax system. Something had changed and even the hard-core nail-em prosecutors knew it.

"This trial is a challenge to the entire system of taxation," said Chief Prosecutor Martin A. Schainbaum. "It used to be all right for everyone to pay as little as possible. Now, how much you pay is relative to how much you know and what counselors you have."

In the end, Harry Margolis understood his case best. He had proved his point that anyone, even the "little guy," can operate legally within the loopholed letter of the nation's tax law.

"There's nothing more corrupting to our society than the system of taxation," he said. All he did, he said, was take legal advantage of the system by using the same loopholes used by big business in the same offshore Caribbean tax havens to save money for his clients. "So it's a corrupt system," he said, "but for us it's legal. I would be overjoyed to see them put me out of business, to see a system in which taxes were legitimately levied. All they need is the legislation — let me write the law."

## The IBM-Japan Theft Scandal

From the Asahi, the Yomiuri, and the Sankei Shimbun the Japanese reporters came to California the summer of 1982, to cover their biggest story in America since the war crimes trial of Tokyo Rose. They came from every Japanese news agency to San Jose's United States Federal Building and Courthouse where two Japanese industrial giants and nineteen countrymen stood accused of stealing computer secrets from International Business Machines Corp.

They got caught in a classic FBI sting operation by undercover agents who opened a dummy Silicon Valley computer firm and let the word out that data on top secret goodies were available for the right price. The operation, dubbed PENGEM (PENetration of Gray Electronics Market) attracted the Japanese almost from the first day of business. The swarm of secret agents, mostly high-level Japanese computer technologists from Mitsubishi Electric Company and Hitachi Limited, wanted confidential blueprints for the world's newest, most powerful high-speed computer processing unit, the IBM 3081, before it reached the market.

The Japanese also wanted to view the IBM 3380, capable of storing four times more data than its predecessor, and to obtain the code for the soon-to-be-released MVS/SP Version 2, an enhancement that souped up IBM computers, and various other state-of-the-art devices, all of which could save them "three to five years of development time." Advance inside information about IBM's latest products could increase Hitachi's sales by "at least 100 million dollars a year," experts estimated.[32]

The Japanese offer of $622,000 for the chance to keep pace with IBM computer developments was a pittance; they were prepared to pay "better than one million dollars" just for an IBM 3081 upgrade kit.[33]

Enormous in scope and complicated with detail, the undercover operation played out at 125 meetings, many of them videotaped, over seven months from high-rise Tokyo offices to a Hartford, Connecticut aircraft plant and in swank hotel suites from the Saint Francis on San Francisco's Union Square to the beachfront Colony Surf in Honolulu.

The first meeting occurred in Las Vegas on the fourteenth floor of the Hilton at 3:00 p.m., November 6, 1981. FBI Agent Alan J. Garretson, posing as president of Glenmar Associates of Silicon Valley, met Kenji Hayashi, a senior research engineer for Hitachi, to discuss the purchase of stolen, confidential IBM computer plans. Hayashi said he wanted "early information" on the IBM 3081, manuals for the IBM 3380, and a "viewing" of the machine by a senior engineer from Japan.

Agent Garretson explained the difficulty of breaching IBM's security to steal the documents and warned of the high risks involved in a viewing, but the Japanese knew. "Any kind of trouble . . . it's real trouble for Hitachi," said Jan Naruse, the senior engineer for Hitachi, who paid FBI agents $10,000 in cash to preview and photograph the IBM 3380, then on lease to an East Coast aircraft manufacturing firm.[34]

In a bit of skulduggery right out of the cinema, the Japanese industrial agent and the FBI agent met in a Hartford hotel lobby on the night of November 15, 1981. They traveled to a parking lot near the Pratt & Whitney facility where they met a third man, who gave each of them identification badges. The FBI agent gave the third man an envelope, saying it contained "plenty" of money. The third man drove them to the plant where an armed security guard admitted them. They made their way through the facility until they reached a door, secured by a combination lock, which they were unable to open. The third man phoned another armed guard while the Japanese industrial agent and the FBI agent hid in a darkened office. The guard unlocked the door. The Japanese agent took photographs of the 3380 machine. The $10,000 cash payoff occurred three days later in Silicon Valley where subsequent payoffs were filtered through NCL Data Inc., headed by Tom Yoshida, the sole Japanese-American in the case.

The elaborate charade was one of many in the seven-month undercover operation which ended with the sting in a Silicon Valley parking lot on June 22, 1982, when Hayashi arrived in a van to pick up all the coveted plans in exchange for $525,000. He and four others, including Yoshida, were arrested on charges of conspiracy to transport stolen, confidential computer secrets to Japan.

The scandal strained trade relations between the United States and Japan, sent the Tokyo stock market plunging, and "raised serious concern over the depth of Japan's technology."[35]

"It is a very shocking incident," Prime Minister Zenko Suzuki told the Japanese Parliament. "We must carefully deal with the matter so as not to undermine friendly and cooperative relations between Japan and the United States." But the Japanese media with "wholly disproportionate coverage" exacerbated the scandal by "creating the impression that Japan . . . was unfairly singled out and persecuted by the United States." The case was referred to "day in and day out in the Japanese press . . . with sensational banner headlines . . . as Jap-baiting."[36]

The scandal broke just as America's high tech leaders awoke to realize a technological Pearl Harbor lay ahead as the Japanese pursued their national goal "to become number one in the computer industry by the latter half of the 1990s . . . and establish a

*Journalists swarm for an interview in the IBM case. This photograph was taken in July 1982. (Courtesy San Jose Mercury News.)*

'knowledge industry' in which knowledge itself will be a salable commodity like food and oil."[37]

Like the Space Race of the sixties, the Chip Wars of the eighties would determine world supremacy of much more than engineering. "The computer is at the root of every major future change," said Michael L. Dertouzos, Director of the Computer Laboratory at Massachusetts Institute of Technology. "The Japanese recognize that whoever controls the information revolution has, in effect, some form of increased geopolitical control."[38]

In the history of microelectronic warfare, the IBM-Japan case came to be regarded as an early, important victory and a clear call to action. The CIA assigned at least one agent to Silicon Valley to stem the flow of high technology to foreign countries, estimated at 100 million dollars since 1977. The Justice Department in San Francisco announced creation of a seven member "critical technology task force" to safeguard Silicon Valley's precious secrets. And to maintain world dominance, twelve leading competitors pooled their research to form the nation's first high tech consortium — Microelectronics and Computer Technology Corp. (MCC) — and named Bobby Ray Inman, former deputy director of the CIA, to head the group.[39]

The Japanese press corps engulfed the small makeshift federal courthouse in San Jose as television camera crews shoved boom mikes into the faces of grand jurors and photographed anyone who looked even remotely connected to the scandal.

While they waited outside (cameras are strictly forbidden in United States courts) they took pictures of each other in front of the one-story, mud-brown clapboard building whose sole architectural feature, a covered boardwalk, looked like something out of a Western movie: at best a bunkhouse for cowpokes.

A natural backdrop, the boardwalk appeared nightly on Tokyo television and came to symbolize America's frontier-style justice to the Japanese who believed their country-men had been framed by the FBI sting operation, illegal under Japanese law, except in drug cases.

The courthouse came in for abuse when members of the Japanese press corps tired of complaining about the lack of good sushi bars in San Jose and wondered aloud why the courthouse was such a rustic structure. Their own courtrooms were castles by com-parison and others they had seen in America were elaborate affairs worthy of administering justice. They nodded sagely upon learning that the San Jose courthouse was a temporary one, built a decade before while local folks waited for Washington approval to build a permanent, more striking edifice.

The press corps, foreign and domestic, overwhelmed the courthouse; one day, the Japanese reporters outnumbered the grand jurors summoned to hear evidence and return indictments. Every seat in the courtroom was taken at each session by reporters who then formed long lines outside the clerk's office to collect copies of indictments, pretrial motions, and related documents. Copies in hand, the reporters dashed herdlike across the boardwalk to the lone pay phone, sending a drumbeat echo through the thin walls and shattering the quiet dignity of the court.

Inside, hastily hired defense lawyers from San Francisco sought a change of venue on grounds that the little courthouse was too small, too remote from the big city, too . . . well, just too damned inconvenient. "There are good restaurants in San Jose," Judge Ingram said finally, "and you will discover them." He denied the motion. But he and two other federal judges who would hear the complex cases against Hitachi, Mitsubishi, and the individual defendants lamented privately that the new and spacious federal courthouse was then only blue lines on blueprints and still more than a year from becoming a reality.

When the defense attorneys failed to extricate the case from Silicon Valley and its savvy potential jurors, they tried the next obvious tactic: they charged the FBI with "entrapment and outrageous conduct" and claimed IBM "used law enforcement to harass competitors." The defense claimed the investigation was "a joint venture to prosecute or intimidate (competitors) by a corporate predator, IBM, and their guardian, the FBI."[40]

To prove its claim the defense attorneys for three accused spies sought FBI records of any agreements IBM had with the government; Federal Judge Robert P. Aguilar ordered the FBI to surrender the documents which he termed "indispensable in the interest of justice."[41] The United States Attorney's office in Washington, D.C., balked and ordered no compliance with the judge's order even if it meant a setback to the case.

Aguilar, fifty-one, a liberal, activist judge and the first Mexican-American appointed to the federal bench in California, displayed his usual sympathy for the underdog and dismissed charges against the three defendants.

Federal Judge Spencer Williams confronted similar, but critically distinguishable, defense motions by the defendants the very next day. In a ruling which carefully disarmed any speculation of theoretical inconsistency between Aguilar's dismissing certain defendants for the government's failure to produce certain materials, and which demonstrated his intent to deny the vague and defective discovery requests propounded by the other defendants against the government, Williams established that, despite superficial similarities between the two motions, certain critical legal and factual distinctions required different results. Thus, Williams rejected defendants' motions, and the prosecution proceeded uninterrupted.[42]

From its Armonk, New York headquarters, IBM issued a press release disputing claims the industrial giant directed the FBI to crush its competition. "IBM has nothing to conceal in its relations with the FBI or the Department of Justice," said spokesman Peter Kuhn. "As the victim of the theft," he said, "IBM is disappointed that the charges in this criminal case against three individuals have been dismissed on a technicality."[43]

The Justice Department pressed its case against the others and prepared for a tedious spate of trials. It wasn't necessary. One by one, each defendant pleaded guilty or no contest and received a light sentence of probation or fines of no more than $10,000 each. The payoff funds, of course, were not returned.

The international scandal, probably the biggest case ever to land in the San Jose Federal Court, ended quietly and disappeared from the front pages and nightly television news shows. All that remained was the lingering notion — a new, high tech twist on an old saying — what's good for IBM is good for the country.

# 24

## Epilog

*Rick Carroll*

The evolution from a one-room courthouse to a modern, five-story edifice could hardly be called empire-building; the development lagged far behind the booming South Bay and took eighteen years of effort by many people from lawyers and judges to the United States Congress. A lot has changed since the idea first occurred in 1966: the people, the land, the times, and the court.

In seven years the court had outgrown its borrowed quarters. In 1973 it moved to a modest, temporary facility, appreciated by all but loved by none. "We do not accept it as the long-term solution," said Congressman Don Edwards on June 15, 1973, the day the temporary facility was dedicated.[1]

The facility, with two tiny courtrooms, shaky walls and a noisy air conditioner that forced lawyers and spectators to seat edge to hear key testimony, became known as "the shed." A hand-painted wooden sign declared it to be the "Federal Building and United States Courthouse," reflecting a mix-up in priorities that irked some judges.

The temporary facility would serve for a decade, far longer than anyone ever imagined. All the while the caseload kept growing and more judges were needed to meet the demand.

It took four presidents — Johnson, Nixon, Ford, and Carter — to create the first federal family in the central coast. The judges — Peckham, Williams, Ingram, and Aguilar — all hailed from Santa Clara County but only Peckham of San Francisco and Aguilar of Madera are native Californians.

Like circuit riding judges of gold rush days, they took turns commuting between the courthouse in San Francisco and San Jose which until the spring of 1983 still lacked the authority of a full criminal and civil calendar.

The criminal calendar grew from a local embezzlement to an international scandal over high tech hardware; there was even a dramatic courtroom escape by a bank robber.

While the criminal cases mirrored the times, the civil cases defined them, creating new law, as the yardstick of the Constitution was held up to a wide range of issues from a schoolboy's right to wear long hair to class (he could) to whether computer programs on silicon chips are subject to copyright laws (they are). Other cases were routine or perennial; the case of the overcrowded Santa Clara County jail seemed always before the court.

Soon, other federal agencies began to move into rented offices scattered across the broad valley. The FBI alighted in a shopping center named for a prune; the Secret Service could be found in a downtown bank building; and nobody was ever sure where Internal Revenue agents worked — they preferred it that way. All yearned for the day the federal house would be in order, gathered centrally under one roof.

But San Jose, the first civil settlement in California, founded in 1777, would be the last major city of the West to get a fully operational and permanent United States Courthouse. Even Honolulu had its own, named for the Hawaiian Prince Kuhio.

At last, ground was broken on the south side of San Jose's downtown in January of 1982, and slowly there rose a building of glass, stone, and steel. A magnificent structure wholly appropriate for its time and place — a stark, white, hard-edged monument with a soaring sky grid over a spacious atrium — it set a new, high tech tone for the emerging downtown and Silicon Valley, beyond.

Inside, on a May day full of promise and ceremony, the decades old dream of a United States Courthouse and Federal Building, the name corrected now, and carved in stone, became a reality and there came that old, familiar cry: "Oyez! Oyez! All persons having business . . ."

# Notes

1   *From* Llano de los Robles *to Silicon Valley*

1. O.O. Winther, "The Story of San Jose, 1777-1869: California's First Pueblo," *California Historical Society Quarterly* 14 (March and June 1935): 6. Besides Winther's work, other general histories of San Jose and Santa Clara County include: Frederic Hall, *The History of San Jose and Surroundings with Biographical Sketches of Early Settlers,* (San Francisco: A.L. Bancroft, 1871); J.P. Munro-Fraser, *History of Santa Clara County, California: Including Its Geography, Geology, Topography, Climatopography and Description,* (San Francisco: Alley, Bowen and Co., 1881); Horace S. Foote, *Pen Pictures from the Garden of the World, or Santa Clara County, California,* (Chicago: Lewis Publishing Co., 1888); Eugene T. Sawyer, A *History of Santa Clara County, California,* (Los Angeles: Historic Record Co., 1922); and William F. James and George H. McMurry, *History of San Jose, California, Narrative and Biographical,* (San Jose: A.H. Cawston, 1933). Jan Otto Marius Broek, *The Santa Clara Valley, California: A Study in Landscape Changes,* (Utrecht, Netherlands: N.V.A. Oosthoek's uitg. maatij, 1932), combines history with geography in an informative fashion.

2. Herbert E. Bolton, ed., *Anza's California Expeditions,* (Berkeley: University of California Press, 1930) Vol. 3, 134; Vol. 4, 354.

3. Francis F. Guest, "Municipal Government in Spanish California," *California Historical Society Quarterly* 46 (December, 1967): 325-28; _____, "Mission Colonization and Political Control in Spanish California," *Journal of San Diego History* 24 (Winter 1978): 97-98, 110-12; Elizabeth Eve Messmer, "The Early Years of the Pueblo San Jose," *Historias: The Spanish Heritage of Santa Clara Valley,* Local History Studies, no. 20 (Cupertino: California History Center, De Anza College, 1976), 49.

4. Messmer, "Early Years of the Pueblo San Jose," 54-55; Guest, "Municipal Government in Spanish California," 312-313, 316.

5. Lasuén's comment is cited in Daniel J. Garr, "Planning, Politics and Plunder: The Missions and Indian Pueblos of Hispanic California," *Southern California Quarterly* 54 (Winter 1972): 292. Two anthropological accounts of the Ohlone are: Richard Levy, "Costanoan," Robert F. Heizer, ed., *Handbook of North American Indians* Vol. 8, *California*, (Washington, D.C.: Smithsonian Institution, 1978), 485-97; and Joseph C. Winter, *Tamien: 6000 Years in an American City*, (San Jose: n.p., 1978), chapters 2 and 3.

6. Finbar Kenneally, trans. and ed., *Writings of Fermín Francisco de Lasuén*, Washington, D.C.: Academy of American Franciscan History, 1965) Vol. 2, 284. Debate over treatment of mission Indians has long continued. See Sherburne F. Cook, *The Conflict between the California Indian and White Civilization*, (Berkeley: University of California Press, 1976), parts 1, 2, and 5; Francis F. Guest, "An Examination of the Thesis of S.F. Cook on the Forced Conversion of Indians in the California Missions," *Southern California Quarterly* 61 (Spring 1979): 1-78.

7. Kenneally, *Writings of Lasuén*, Vol. 2, 283-84, 288.

8. Cited in Chester King, "Historic Indian Settlements in the Vicinity of the Holiday Inn Site," Joseph C. Winter, ed., *Archeological Investigations at CA-SCL-128, The Holiday Inn Site*, (San Jose: n.p., 1978), 441.

9. David J. Langum, "Californios and the Image of Indolence," *Western Historical Quarterly* 9 (April 1978): 181-96; David J. Weber, *The Mexican Frontier, 1821-1846; The American Southwest Under Mexico*, (Albuquerque: University of New Mexico Press, 1982), 282.

10. Guest, "Municipal Government in Spanish California," 328-29.

11. Hall, *History of San Jose and Surroundings*, 424-25.

12. *Ibid.*, 50-52; Daniel J. Garr, "A Frontier Agrarian Settlement: San Jose de Guadalupe, 1777-1850," *San Jose Studies* 2 (November 1976): 97.

13. Weber, *The Mexican Frontier, 1821-1846*, examines the relationship between Mexico and its northern provinces.

14. Garr, "Planning, Politics and Plunder." A few mission Indians received grants of land.

15. Robert Archibald, "The Economy of the Alta California Mission, 1803-1821," *Southern California Quarterly* 58 (Summer 1976): 227-40.

16. Richard Henry Dana, Jr., *Two Years before the Mast: A Personal Narrative*, (1840; reprint, New York: New American Library, 1964), 75-81 and *passim* contains classic Yankee comments on Mexican culture. Weber, *The Mexican Frontier, 1821-1846*, 135-39, 203-4, covers the economic impact of Anglo-Americans on Alta California.

17. Winther, "Story of San Jose," 9, 16, 18.

18. Douglas Sloane Watson, ed., *Narrative of Nicholas "Cheyenne" Dawson; Overland to California in '41 and '49, and Texas in '51*, (San Francisco: Grabhorn Press, 1933), 31-35; Charles Wilkes, *Narrative of the United States Exploring Expedition. During the Years 1838, 1839, 1840, 1841, 1842*, (Philadelphia: Lea and Blanchard, 1845) Vol. 5, 216-17; Doyce B. Nunis, Jr., ed., *Josiah Belden, 1841 California Overland Pioneer: His Memoir and Early Letters*, (Georgetown, Calif.: Talisman Press, 1962), 46-48; Edwin Bryant, *What I Saw in California, Being the Journal of a Tour by the Emigrant Route and South Pass of the Rocky Mountains, Across the Continent of North America, the Great Desert Basin, and through California, in the Years 1846, 1847*, (Santa Ana, Calif.: Fine Arts Press, 1936), 296-98.

19. Marguerite E. Wilbur, ed., *Vancouver in California 1792-1794; The Original Account of George Vancouver*, (Los Angeles: Glen Dawson, 1953) Vol. 1, 34-35; Bryant, *What I Saw in California*, 295-96.

20. Robert M. Fogelson, *The Fragmented Metropolis: Los Angeles, 1850-1930*, (Cambridge, Mass.: Harvard University Press, 1967), 25.

21. Hall, *History of San Jose and Surroundings*, 180.

22. James D. Hutton, *Map of the Public Lands of the Pueblo de San Jose 1847. Copied by Geo. Brandon*, (New York, 1852; on file at Bancroft Library, Berkeley).

23. Frederick J. Teggart, ed., *Around the Horn to the Sandwich Islands and California 1845-1850, Being a Personal Record Kept by Chester S. Lyman*, (New Haven, Conn.: Yale University Press, 1924), 242.

24. Julian Dana, *A.P. Giannini, Giant in the West: A Biography*, (New York: Prentice-Hall, 1947), 13.

25. Winther, "Story of San Jose," 16-17, 155.

26. Teggart, *Around the Horn*, 241-57; Carl I. Wheat, ed., "The California Letters of James Carr," *California Historical Society Quarterly* 11 (June 1932): 159-63.

27. William Kelly, *An Excursion to California over the Prairie, Rocky Mountains, and Great Sierra Nevada*, London: Chapman and Hall, 1851), Vol. 2, 293-94, 308-10; Hall, *History of San Jose and Surroundings*, chapters 16, 18, and 19.

28. Winther, "Story of San Jose," 165. Population figures after 1870 are derived from the tabulations of the United States Bureau of the Census.

29. Francis P. Farquhar, ed., *Up and Down California in 1860-1864; The Journal of William H. Brewer*, (New Haven, Conn.: Yale University Press, 1930), 118, 169, 173.

30. Broek, *Santa Clara Valley, California*, chapters 7 and 8; Rodman W. Paul, "The Beginnings of Agriculture: Innovation *vs.* Continuity," George H. Knoles, ed., *Essays and Assays: California History Reappraised*, (San Francisco: California Historical Society, 1973), 27-38.

31. Foote, *Pen Pictures from the Garden of the World*, 179; Broek, *Santa Clara Valley, California*, 109; Janet Humphrey, *From Blossoms to the World; A Study of Fruit Preservation in Santa Clara Valley prior to 1930*, Local History Studies, no. 5, (Cupertino: California History Center, De Anza College, 1970).

32. Thompson and West, *Historical Atlas Map of Santa Clara County, California*, (1876; reprint, San Jose: Smith and McKay, 1973), 30, 55; Mary Dominica McNamee, *Light in the Valley: The Story of California's College of Notre Dame*, (Berkeley: Howell-North Books, 1967), chapers 1-3.

33. Broek, *Santa Clara Valley, California*, 113, 125-26.

34. Benjamin Franklin Gilbert, "Introduction," Everett Hager and Anna Marie Hager, comps., *An Index to Hall's 1871 History of San Jose*, Occasional Paper, no. 2, (San Jose: Sourisseau Academy for California State and Local History and San Jose State University, 1974), 3-4; Hall, *History of San Jose and Surroundings*, 136; Nunis, *Josiah Belden, 1841 California Overland Pioneer*, 19-20.

35. Hall, *History of San Jose and Surroundings*, 359-63, 291-96, 355-59; Farquhar, *Up and Down California in 1860-1864*, 174; Rosemary Lick, *The Generous Miser: The Story of James Lick of California*, (Los Angeles: Ward Ritchie Press, 1967), 35, 38-41, 44, 46-47; James D. Hart, *A Companion to California*, (New York: Oxford University Press, 1978), 236, 327.

36. The fate of different ethnic groups in the San Jose area is reviewed by John M.

Findlay and Donna M. Garaventa, *Archaeological Resources of Downtown San Jose: A Preliminary Planning Summary of Prehistoric and Historic Sites in the Central Business District*, (Hayward, Calif.: n.p., 1983), 23-24, 38, 64-69.

37. Jose Antonio Villarreal, *Pocho*, (1959; reprint, Garden City, N.Y.: Anchor Doubleday, 1970), is an insightful novel about Mexican immigrant culture, set in the Santa Clara valley of the 1930s, and provides a wealth of detail about social conditions. Other useful sources on Mexican-Americans are Margaret Clark, *Health in the Mexican-American Culture: A Community Study*, 2d ed., (Berkeley: University of California Press, 1970); and Armand J. Sanchez and Roland M. Wagner, "Continuity and Change in the Mayfair Barrios of East San Jose," *San Jose Studies* 5 (May 1979): 6-19.

38. *San Jose Herald*, 19 August 1902; James and McMurry, *History of San Jose, California*, 148; Frances L. Fox, *Luis Maria Peralta and His Adobe*, (San Jose: Smith and McKay, 1975), 71; Valeria Ellsworth and Andrew J. Garbely, "Centralization and Efficiency: The Reformers Shape Modern San Jose Government, 1910-1916," David W. Eakins, ed., *Businessmen and Municipal Reform: A Study of Ideals and Practice in San Jose and Santa Cruz, 1896-1916*, Student Papers, no. 1, (San Jose: Sourisseau Academy of California and Local History and San Jose State University, 1976), 12-17, 21; *San Jose Mercury and Herald*, 22 April 1906.

39. Leo Sullivan, *Recollections of Colorful El Dorado Street in Early San Jose*, (San Jose: n.p., 1964), 10; *Commercial History of San Jose*, (San Jose: Metropolitan Publishing Co., 1892), 5, 7.

40. James and McMurry, *History of San Jose, California*, 141-42, 164.

41. Findlay and Garaventa, *Archaeological Resources of Downtown San Jose*, 83-84.

42. On Santa Clara valley in the 1930s, consult Glenna Christine Matthews, "A California Middletown: The Social History of San Jose in the Depression," Ph.D. diss., Stanford University, 1977. The problems facing San Jose after the war were outlined by George Starbird, "The New Metropolis: San Jose between 1942 and 1972," Talk delivered to San Jose Rotary Club, San Jose, 1 March 1972; *San Jose and Santa Clara County: An Economic Survey with Particular Reference to Industrial Development*, (San Francisco: Industrial Survey Associates, 1948), 8-11, 13.

43. Dirk Hanson, *The New Alchemists; Silicon Valley and the Microelectronics Revolution*, (Boston: Little, Brown, 1982), 86-94 and *passim*, uncovers the seeds of Silicon Valley. Ted K. Bradshaw, "Trying Out the Future," *The Wilson Quarterly* 4 (Summer 1980): 66-82, outlines the development of the postindustrial economies of Silicon Valley and other parts of California.

44. Paul F. Griffin and Ronald L. Chatham, "Urban Impact on Agriculture in Santa Clara County, California," *Annals of the Association of American Geographers* 48 (September 1958), 198-99, 201-3.

45. America's Sunbelt has been covered by Carl Abbott, *The New Urban America: Growth and Politics in Sunbelt Cities*, (Chapel Hill, N.C.: University of North Carolina Press, 1981). For varying accounts of San Jose's development, turn to: Starbird, "The New Metropolis"; *Economic Survey and Analysis, Central Business District, San Jose, California*, (San Francisco: Real Estate Research Corporation, 1967); *Goals for San Jose*, (San Jose: San Jose Goals Committee and San Jose City Planning Department, 1969); Stanford Environmental Law Society, *San Jose: Sprawling City; A Report on Land Use Policies and Practices in San Jose, California*, (Palo Alto: Stanford University Press, 1971). How the development of a water supply reflected a "political economy" geared for growth is explained by Richard A. Walker and Matthew J. Williams, "Water from

Power: Water Supply and Regional Growth in the Santa Clara Valley," *Economic Geography* 58 (April 1982): 95-119.

46. Social conditions in Silicon Valley have been discussed by Peter A. Morrison, *San Jose and St. Louis in the 1960s: A Case Study of Changing Urban Populations,* (Santa Monica, Calif.: Rand Corporation, 1973); AnnaLee Saxenian, "Silicon Chips and Spatial Structure: The Industrial Basis of Urbanization in Santa Clara County, California," Working Paper, no. 345, (Berkeley: Institute of Urban & Regional Development, University of California, 1981).

2   *Federal Court's First Arrival in San Jose, April 5, 1852*

1. Ogden Hoffman to Attorney General Caleb Cushing, 15 October 1853, National Archives and Records Service, Records of the Department of Justice, Office of the Attorney General, Record Group 60. The California federal district courts were created by the act of September 28, 1850, entitled "An Act to Provide for Extending the Laws and the Judicial System of the United States to the State of California," 9 Stat. 521.

2. Walter Colton, *Three Years in California,* (New York, 1850), 353-54.

3. Elbridge Gerry Hall to his wife, 31 August and 22 September 1849, Elbridge Gerry Hall papers, Bancroft Library.

4. William Kelly, *An Excursion to California,* (London, 1851), Vol. 2, 312; and A.W. Rawson diary, 24 March and 11 April 1856, Bancroft Library.

5. For the early locations of where the state courts met in Santa Clara, *see* William A. Johnston, *The Court Houses of Santa Clara County, A History,* (1941). This two page typescript was compiled by the San Jose Chamber of Commerce and is available at the San Jose Public Library.

6. It is possible to reconstruct the early cases from Santa Clara County that came before the federal court from a variety of sources, including Common Law and Equity docket books, Vols. 1-2, United States District Court, Northern District of California Archives, San Francisco; Minutes, 3 vols., 19 May 1851-31 August 1861, United States District Court, Northern District of California, Bancroft Library; and Minutes, 1 vol., 1851, Third District Court, Bancroft Library.

7. Oscar T. Shuck, *A History of the Bench and Bar of California,* (Los Angeles: Commercial Printing Co., 1901), 417.

8. *Johnson v. Gordon,* 4 Cal. 368(1854). The act of April 25, 1863, entitled "An Act to Exclude Traitors and Alien Enemies from the Courts of Justice in Civil Cases," only required a loyalty oath from lawyers who sought to practice before the state courts (a similar oath was used in the federal courts). The oath thus inhibited but did not exclude from practicing law those Southern sympathizers who refused to declare loyalty to the federal union.

9. The judicial history of the case can be traced in the California Supreme Court case file of *Gordon v. Johnson,* California State Archives, Appellate Case File No. 218.

10. *See* Clyde Arbuckle and Ralph Rambo, *Santa Clara County Ranchos,* (San Jose: Rosicrucian Press, Ltd., 1968), 31. Gordon's colorful life is told by Albert Shumate, *The California of George Gordon and the 1849 Sea Voyages of his California Association,* (Glendale: Arthur H. Clark Co., 1976).

11. The Judiciary Act of 1789 was entitled "An Act to Establish the Judicial Courts of the United States," 1 Stat. 773. Case file of *Gordon v. Johnson,* Brief for Appellants.

12. Case file of *Gordon v. Johnson,* Points for Appellee.

13. *Johnson v. Gordon*, 4 Cal. 368-69.

14. *Ibid.*, at 373.

15. *Ibid.*, at 373-74.

16. *San Francisco Alta California*, 7 March 1855.

17. Quoted in the *Sacramento Union*, 10 March 1855; *San Francisco Alta California*, 27 February 1855.

18. *San Francisco Herald*, 10 March 1855.

19. California *Senate Journal*, 6th session, (1855), 261.

20. *San Francisco Herald*, 7 March 1855.

21. *San Francisco Alta California*, 7 and 13 March 1855; and *Sacramento Union*, 10 March 1855.

22. *San Francisco Alta California*, 7 March 1855.

23. *Ibid.*

24. *Taylor v. The Steamer "Columbia,"* 5 Cal. 268 (1856).

3   *The History of Monterey's Federal District Court, 1851-1866.*

1. George Cosgrave, *Early California Justice: The History of the United States District Court for the Southern District of California, 1849-1944*, (San Francisco: Grabhorn Press, 1948), 27.

2. Walter Colton, *Three Years in California*, (Palo Alto: Stanford University Press, 1948), 199-200.

3. United States District Court for the Southern District of California, Miscellaneous Case Papers, 1851-1866, Box 1, National Archives and Records Service, Record Group 21, San Bruno, California. For biographical information on Jones, *see* George Cosgrave, "James McHall Jones: The Judge That Never Presided," *California Historical Society Quarterly* 20, (1941): 97-116.

4. Cosgrave, *Early California Justice*, 45.

5. Robert Louis Stevenson, "The Old Pacific Capital," In Robert Reece, *A Brief History of Old Monterey*, (Monterey: Colonial Press, 1969), 59.

6. 64 U.S. 326 (1859).

7. Cosgrave, *Early California Justice*, 50.

8. *Ibid.*

9. Hubert Howe Bancroft, *History of California*, Vol. 21 of *The Works of Hubert Howe Bancroft*, (San Francisco: The History Company, 1886), 238.

4   *Litigation over Mexican Land Grants in Santa Clara, San Benito, Santa Cruz, and Monterey Counties*

1. Rodman W. Paul, *California Gold*, (1947; reprint, Lincoln, Nebr.: University of Nebraska Press, 1965), 55, 349-52.

2. Bruno Fritzsche, "San Francisco 1846-1848: The Coming of the Land Speculator," *California Historical Society Quarterly* 51, (1972): 17-34; Paul W. Gates, "Carpetbaggers Join the Rush for California Land," *California Historical Society Quarterly* 56, (1977): 98-127; Alfred Wheeler, *Land Titles in San Francisco and the Laws Affecting the Same, with a Synopsis of all Grants and Sales of Land within the Limits Claimed by the City*, (San Francisco, 1852), 96-105; W.W. Robinson, *Land in California*, (Berkeley: University of California Press, 1948), chapters 12-14; Paul W. Gates, "Public Land Disposal in

California," *Agricultural History* 49, (1975):158-78; Gerald D. Nash, "The California State Land Office, 1858-1898," *Huntington Library Quarterly* 27, (1964):347-56; and Diane Spencer-Hancock, "State Surveyor General James F. Houghton: The Impact of a Land Speculator on California History," *Pacific Historian* 26, (1982): 42-53.

3. While some of the claims to land were based on grants issued before 1822 and hence "Spanish Grants," the overwhelming number of claims to land in California traced their origin to the Mexican governors, especially during the last decade before the American occupation in 1846. *See* David Hornbeck, "Land Tenure and Rancho Expansion in Alta California, 1784-1846," *Journal of Historical Geography* 4, (1978): 371-90.

Between January 1852 and March 1856, 809 private land claims were presented to the specially created federal land board from which appeals could be taken to the federal courts. Hoffman's Index — prepared by Numa Hubert but so called because it appears in Ogden Hoffman, *Reports of Land Cases Determined in the United States District Court for the Northern District of California*, (San Francisco: Numa Hubert, 1862) — lists 813 claims filed. One of the listed claims was a clerical error, two were preemption claims in San Francisco, and one was the City of Sonora's claim having no reference to a Spanish or Mexican origin, thus they were "land grant claims, but not private land grant claims." (Jacob N. Bowman, *Index of the Spanish-Mexican Private Land Grant Cases of California*, (Bancroft Library: Typescript copy, 1958), preface.)

4. California Senator John Conness in *Congressional Globe,* 38th Cong., 1st sess., 28 March 1864, 1312.

5. David Hornbeck, "Land Tenure and Rancho Expansion in Alta California, 1784-1846," 384.

6. 9 Stat. 992 (1848), article VIII.

7. Act of March 3, 1851, 9 Stat. 630. Paul W. Gates has written on the political maneuvering behind the passage of the bill and its operation; *see* "Adjudication of Spanish-Mexican Land Claims in California," *Huntington Library Quarterly* 21, (1958): 213-36; and "The California Land Act of 1851," *California Historical Society Quarterly* 50, (1971): 395-430. The latter article conveniently lists (in note 28) many of the nineteenth- and twentieth-century critics of the Land Act of 1851.

8. Henry W. Halleck, *Report on the Laws and Regulations Relative to Grants or Sales of Public Lands in California,* House Ex. Doc. No. 17, 31st Cong., 1st sess., 1850, 118, 129-30.

9. William Carey Jones, *Report on the Subject of Land Titles in California Made in Pursuance of Instructions from the Secretary of State and the Secretary of the Interior,* (Washington, D.C., 1850), 26, 27, 38, 39.

10. *See* Paul W. Gates, "The Fremont-Jones Scramble for California Land Claims," *Southern California Quarterly* 56, (1974): 21-22.

11. *See* Paul W. Gates, "Carpetbaggers Join the Rush for California Land," 115, note 80; and Halleck, *Report,* 122.

12. Halleck, *Report,* 124.

13. 9 Stat. 631, section 8.

14. David Hornbeck, "The Patenting of California's Private Land Claims, 1851-1885," *Geographical Review* 59, (1979): 440.

15. *See* Leonard Pitt, *The Decline of the Californios: A Social History of the Spanish-Speaking Californians, 1846-1890,* (Berkeley: University of California Press, 1970),89-91; and *Expenditures on Account of Private Land Claims in California,* House Ex. Doc. No. 84, 36th Cong., 1st sess., 1860.

16. 9 Stat. 631, section 11.

17. Act of June 14, 1860, 12 Stat. 33.

18. On the adjudication of private land claims in the older states, *see* Paul W. Gates, *History of Public Land Law Development*, (Washington, D.C.: n.p., 1968); and Henry L. Coles, Jr., "The Confirmation of Foreign Land Titles in Louisiana," *Louisiana Historical Quarterly* 38, (1955).

19. David Hornbeck, "The Patenting of California's Private Land Claims, 1851-1885," 383-84.

20. David Hornbeck, "Land Tenure and Rancho Expansion in Alta California, 1784-1846"; Halleck, *Report;* Jones, *Report;* and W.W. Morrow, *Spanish and Mexican Private Land Grants,* (San Francisco: n.p., 1923), 15-19.

21. The case files of the claims that came before the Board of Land Commissioners are on permanent loan at Bancroft Library. Access to these historically rich legal documents is greatly expedited by a typescript index of the cases created by Jacob N. Bowman. The original claims were docketed in the federal trial courts by district and number. Thus, the claim of Cruz Cervantes for San Joaquin was filed as 3 Northern District (N.D.).

22. *John Charles Fremont v. United States,* 58 U.S. 542 (1854).

23. *Cruz Cervantes v. United States,* 57 U.S. 619 (1853).

24. Hoffman, *Land Cases,* 10.

25. *Ibid.,* 12.

26. *Ibid.,* 16.

27. *Fremont v. United States,* 58 U.S. 542 at 552.

28. Charles G. Crampton, "The Opening of the Mariposa Mining Region, 1849-1859, with Particular Reference to the Mexican Land Grant of John Charles Fremont," Ph.D. diss., University of California, Berkeley, 1941; and 14 Cal. 279 (1859). After the California Supreme Court had avoided deciding who had title to California's gold for nearly a decade, Chief Justice Stephen J. Field rendered an important opinion which decided that the holder of a patent to a Mexican land grant had title to all precious minerals which might be in the soil. See the companion cases of *Moore v. Smaw* and *Fremont v. Flower* 17 Cal. 199 (1861).

29. Quoted in Charles Warren, *The Supreme Court in United States History* rev. ed., (Boston: n.p., 1937), Vol.2, 350.

30. 58 U.S. 542 at 563.

31. *Ibid.,* at 572.

32. 59 U.S. 539 at 552-53 (1855).

33. *Ibid.,* at 550, 553.

34. For an indication of these preferences among the justices, in particular Taney, Catron, and Daniel, *see* Leon Friedman and Fred L. Israel, eds., *The Justices of the United States Supreme Court,* (New York: Chelsea House, 1969), Vol 1, 635-54, 737-49, and 795-805. *See Fremont v. United States* 58 U.S. 542 (1854); *United States v. Ritchie* 58 U.S. 525 (1854); and *United States v. Reading* 59 U.S. 1 (1855).

35. *United States v. Reading* 59 U.S. 1 at 15.

36. Harte's *Story of a Mine* (1878) is only loosely based on the actual facts of the discovery of mercury deposits on the land and formation of the New Idria Quicksilver Mining Company to exploit the resource. The name New Idria came from the great Austrian quicksilver works at Idria, just as the New Almaden mine in Santa Clara County was named for old Almaden in Spain.

37. Claim for Panoche Grande, 393 S.D. 159, Bancroft Library; *see* Southern District

of California, Miscellaneous Case Papers, 1851-1861, Order to Dismiss Appeals, filed 24 February 1857, Box 1, National Archives and Records Service, Record Group 21; and Robert J. Parker, "William McGarrahan's 'Panoche Grande Claim'," *Pacific Historical Review* 5, (1936): 212-21.

38. *United States v. Andres Castillero,* United States District Court, Northern District of California, Transcript of the Record, (San Francisco, 1859-1861), 4 vols; James Eldredge, "Private Letters on the Fossat-Almaden Land Claims," Bancroft Library; and Kenneth M. Johnson, *The New Almaden Quicksilver Mine, with an Account of the Land Claims Involving the Mine and Its Role in California History,* (Georgetown, Calif.: Talisman Press, 1963).

39. New Almaden claim, 420 N.D. 565, Bancroft Library.

40. The experience of the Berryessa family, in particular, was especially bitter when it came to their landholdings. Although a prominent early California family, they acquired but subsequently lost, large and valuable tracts of land in the present counties of Santa Clara, Napa, Alameda, and Sonoma. The family also had its share of personal tragedy. Sergeant Berryessa was killed by some of Fremont's men near San Rafael during the Bear Flag revolt, allegedly in retribution for the earlier death of two Americans. Even Fremont's biographer, Allan Nevins, has called Berryessa's death "cold-blooded murder" (*Fremont: Pathmarker of the West,* (New York: Longmans, Green and Co., 1955), 276). Still later, a son of Berryessa was lynched as a result of having killed a squatter. Berryessa's heirs had little luck in reaping much reward from the San Vicente rancho, even though Castillero himself believed the New Almaden mine to be on Berryessa land when he made his denouncement.

41. Johnson, *New Almaden Quicksilver Mines,* 32; Paul W. Gates has found that 346 (or 42 percent) of the claims presented to the Board of Land Commissioners were presented by non-Mexicans; *see* "The California Land Act of 1851," 410.

42. *See* Johnson, *New Almaden Quicksilver Mine;* Leonard W. Ascher, "Lincoln's Administration and the New Almaden Scandal," *Pacific Historical Review* 5, (1936); Marc W. Johnston, "Faith with Our Victims; The Litigation of Mexican Land Grants in California after the American Accession — a Case Study of the New Almaden Claims," Senior thesis, Harvard University, 1974; Milton H. Shutes, "Abraham Lincoln and the New Almaden Mine," *California Historical Society Quarterly* 15, (1936):3-20; John W. Wills, "Benjamin's Ethical Strategy in the New Almaden Case," *Quarterly Journal of Speech* 50, (1964):259-65; and Donald C. Brown, "The New Almaden Quicksilver Mine," Master's thesis, San Jose State University, 1958.

43. *San Francisco Alta California,* 12 December 1853.

44. Johnson, *New Almaden Quicksilver Mine,* 59; *also see* Black, *Report,* House Ex. Doc. No. 84.

45. Black, *Report,* 31.

46. *Ibid.,* 32.

47. *Ibid.,* 33; *also see* Alston G. Field, "Attorney General Black and the California Land Claims," *Pacific Historical Review* 4, (1935): 234-45.

48. Black, *Report,* 38; *United States v. Castillero,* 67 U.S. 17 at 102; *Philadelphia Press,* 20 August 1883, cited in Field, "Attorney General Black and the California Land Claims," 242, note 30; and papers of Jeremiah S. Black, Library of Congress, Vol. 37, no. 56671 quoted in Johnson, *New Almaden Quicksilver Mine,* 80.

49. Claim for San Andres, 100 S.D., Bancroft Library.

50. *Ibid.,* 227.

51. *Ibid.*, 114, 116.

52. Los Coches, 289 N.D.; Pasolmi, 410 N.D.; and Ulistac, 323 N.D.; Suisun Rancho in Sonoma County, 392 S.D., Bancroft Library; David Hornbeck, "Land Tenure and Rancho Expansion in Alta California, 1784-1846," 385-88; and 58 U.S. 525 (1854).

53. Claim for Milpitas, 44 S.D. 11.

54. *Ibid.*, 59.

55. *Ibid.*, 4, 11, 33, 57-59.

56. James F. Stuart wrote a series of petitioning letters printed as pamphlets, including: *Titles to Lands in the State of California,* (San Francisco, undated, probably 1888); *Open Letter in Addition to "Titles to Lands in the State of California,"* (San Francisco, 1888); *Relics of the Past,* (San Francisco, undated, probably 1888); *When Are Patents for Lands in California Claimed under Spanish or Mexican Grants Final?,* (San Francisco, 1889); and *Open Letter to the President of the United States, the Secretary of the Interior, the Members of Congress, and the Judges of the Supreme Court of the United States,* (San Francisco, undated, probably 1889).

57. *See* Paul W. Gates, "Pre-Henry George Land Warfare in California," *California Historical Society Quarterly* 46, (1967): 137, note 37; and Paul W. Gates, "California's Embattled Settlers," *California Historical Society Quarterly* 41, (1962):99-130.

5   *The Continuing Connection: Maurice T. Dooling and William F. James*

In addition to the newspaper articles and writings referenced in the text, Mrs. Dettweiler relied on stories told to her by her parents, Mary Devlin Dooling and Maurice T. Dooling, Jr., and family histories compiled by Nevada Kearney, cousin of Maurice T. Dooling, and Jean O'Connell Briare for her biography of her grandfather, Maurice T. Dooling.

1. *San Francisco Examiner,* 28 August 1915.

2. *Ibid.*

3. *San Francisco Chronicle,* 13 February 1918.

4. *Ibid.*, 10 May 1918.

5. *Ibid.*

6. *Ibid.*, 18 May 1922.

7. *Ibid.*, 3 July 1921.

8. *Ibid.*, 26 May 1922.

9. *Ibid.*, 27 May 1922.

10. *Ibid.*, 7 November 1921.

11. Fred L. Thomas, Letter to Calvin Coolidge, 16 July 1927, James appointment file, United States Department of Justice, National Archives, Washington, D.C.

12. George W. Glendinning, Letter to Coolidge, 13 August 1927, National Archives.

13. *Ibid.*

14. *Ibid.*; and T. J. Drais, Letter to Coolidge, 23 September 1927, National Archives.

15. W.S. Clayton, Letter to Coolidge, 27 July 1929; and Glendinning, Letter to Coolidge, 13 August 1927.

16. Information from James's collection of clippings and memorabilia.

17. United States District Court clerk, Northern District of California, Letters to James, 17 and 19 March 1898; and clerk, Letter to J.H. Barbour, 11 February 1906,

United States District Court, Northern District of California Archives.

18. United States District Court clerk, Letters to United States attorney general, 31 July 1900 and 28 January 1901, Archives.

19. United States District Court clerk, Letter to James, 8 February 1906, Archives.

20. United States District Court clerk, Letter to Barbour, 15 February 1906, quoting James letter of 6 February 1906, Archives.

21. *Ibid.*

22. United States District Court clerk, Letter to Postmaster, 8 February 1906, Archives.

23. United States District Court clerk, Letter to Barbour, 15 February 1906, quoting James letter of 6 February 1906, Archives.

24. United States District Court clerk, Letter to James, 15 February 1906, Archives.

25. *Palo Alto Times,* 17 September 1964.

**Part Two**    Politics, Persistence, and Principles in the Struggle for a Federal Court on the Central Coast

In researching the struggle for the court and courthouse, Mr. Franaszek interviewed many of the persons discussed in these chapters. He also relied on a wealth of published and unpublished materials, ranging from memorabilia and newspaper clippings lent to him by Judges Robert P. Aguilar and Spencer M. Williams, to records from the court archives, to personal files kept by Robert Beresford, Judge William A. Ingram, Chief Judge Robert F. Peckham, and Russell Roessler.

6    *A Cornerstone for the Northern District Court*

1. *San Jose Mercury,* 15 June 1973.

2. Advisory Committee — San Jose Federal Court, Agenda, 15 June 1973.

3. *San Jose Mercury,* 16 June 1973.

7    *A Long Road and a Vision*

1. Carl Baar, "When Judges Lobby: Congress and Court Administration," Ph.D. diss., University of Chicago, 1969, 49, 558.

2. *One Day Trips . . . South of San Francisco,* (n.p., 1947), 35.

3. Robert Beresford, Interview with author, April 1983.

4. William Manners, *TR & Will: A Friendship that Split the Republican Party* (New York: Harcourt, Brace & World, 1969), 107.

5. Beresford, Interview, 1983.

6. *Ibid.*

7. Description based on picture in publicity flier, *The Triple-C* (Published by Employees of Continental Can Co., January 1949).

8. Beresford, Interview, 1983.

9. *Ibid.*; and W. Robert Morgan, Letter to George B. Harris, 22 September 1966.

10. Beresford, Interview, 1983.

11. *Western Well Drilling Co. v. United States,* 96 F.Supp. 377 (N.D. Cal. 1951).

12. Beresford, Interview, 1983.

13. Baar, "When Judges Lobby," 51.

14. Beresford, Interview, 1983.

15. George Starbird, "The New Metropolis: San Jose between 1942 and 1972," Talk delivered to San Jose Rotary Club, San Jose, 1 March 1972.

16. *Ibid.*

17. Baar, "When Judges Lobby," 149.

18. Beresford, Interview, 1983.

19. *Ibid.*

20. *Ibid.*

21. Baar, "When Judges Lobby," 162-63.

22. *Ibid.*, 54; and Beresford, Interview, 1983.

**8**   *The Unified Strategy*

1. Russell V. Roessler, Interview with author, May 1983.

2. *California State Bar Journal*, (January-February 1964): 75, 78, 81, 84.

3. "San Jose Discovers How It Feels to Be Rich," *Business Week* (26 September 1964).

4. *Ibid.*

5. John D. Weaver, *Warren: The Man, the Court, the Era*, (Boston: Little, Brown, 1967), 15.

6. Baar, "When Judges Lobby," 322-23; and *Baker v. Carr*, 369 U.S. 186 (1962).

7. Baar, "When Judges Lobby," 267, 302.

8. *Ibid.*, 269.

9. *Ibid.*, 245, 371.

10. *Ibid.*, 353.

11. *Ibid.*, 201.

12. *Ibid.*, 265-66.

13. *Ibid.*, 266-67.

14. Roessler, Interview, 1983.

15. Baar, "When Judges Lobby," 273-75.

16. *Ibid.*, 277.

17. Roessler, Interview, 1983; *see also* Baar, "When Judges Lobby," 327.

18. Baar, "When Judges Lobby," 254.

19. *Ibid.*, 307.

**9**   *Through the Congressional Maze*

1. Roessler, Letter to Don Edwards, 26 January 1965.

2. Weaver, *Warren*, 30, 147.

3. Baar, "When Judges Lobby," 418.

4. Weaver, *Warren*, 347.

5. Resolution of Santa Clara Bar Trustees, 11 June 1962; and Beresford, Interview, 1983.

6. Beresford, Letter to Edwards, 9 January 1963.

7. *Ibid.*

8. Edwards, Letter to Beresford, 19 June 1963.

9. "Federal Court Push Due at Dinner for Rep. Edwards," *San Jose Mercury*, 31 October 1963.

10. Peter Rodino, "That Old Judiciary Just Ain't What She Used to Be," *Washington Star*, 19 March 1981.

11. Baar, "When Judges Lobby," 326, 346-47.

12. *Reports of the Proceedings of the Judicial Conference of the United States, 1964*, (Washington, D.C.), 8; and Baar, "When Judges Lobby," 359-60.

13. Edwards, Letter to Beresford, 2 July 1964.

14. *Ibid.*

15. Baar, "When Judges Lobby," 422-23.

16. House Committee on the Judiciary, *Hearings, Federal Courts and Judges*, 89th Cong., 1st sess., 1965, 20-21.

17. Baar, "When Judges Lobby," 500, 502.

18. House Committee on the Judiciary, *Hearings, Federal Courts and Judges*, 89th Cong., 1st sess., 1965, 177-79.

19. *Ibid.*, 181, 183.

20. Baar, "When Judges Lobby," 508.

21. *Ibid.*, 527-38.

## 10   *Judicious Approval*

1. Baar, "When Judges Lobby," 435; and Roessler, Memorandum to file, 24 March 1965.

2. Roessler, Memorandum to file, 24 March 1965.

3. Baar, "When Judges Lobby," 435.

4. *Ibid.*, 431; and Sherwood Roberts, chairman of Judicial District Subcommittee of the Federal Court Committee, *History of the Establishment of the Southern District of California Federal Court District for the Counties of San Diego and Imperial in the State of California*, (San Diego Bar Association, 4 September 1966).

5. Baar, "When Judges Lobby," 431-32.

6. Roessler, Memorandum to file, 24 March 1965.

7. Beresford, Interview, 1983; and Baar, "When Judges Lobby," 288.

8. Senate Committee on the Judiciary, *New Judicial District in California and New Divison for the Northern District of California*, 85th Cong., 1st sess., 1957, S.Rept. 1158, 11.

9. *Annual Report of the Proceedings of the Judicial Conference of the United States, 1955*, (Washington, D.C.), 6-8; *1956*, 314.

10. *Reports of the Proceedings of the Judicial Conference of the United States*, (Washington, D.C., 1962), 13-15.

11. Baar, "When Judges Lobby," 302.

12. Richard H. Chambers, Letter to John B. Bates, 14 December 1962; and Baar, "When Judges Lobby," 302.

13. Statement of the Ninth Circuit Judicial Council (Circuit Judge Duniway), December 1963.

14. *Ibid.*, Concurrence of Chief Judge Chambers.

15. Baar, "When Judges Lobby," 340.

16. *Ibid.*, 342.

17. *Ibid.*, 337

18. *Ibid.*, 342.

19. *Ibid.*, 357, 359-60.

20. *Ibid.*, 439-40.

21. *Ibid.*, 441-42.

22. *Ibid.*, 444.

## 11  The Reaction in San Francisco

1. Baar, "When Judges Lobby," 454; George B. Harris, Letter to Emanuel Celler, 30 June 1965.

2. Joseph Franaszek, "It Was Decided that the Cat Should Stay and the Judge Should Go — The Impeachment of Judge Harold Louderback," *The Historical Reporter*, Vol. 2, no. 2 (Fall 1982): 6.

3. George B. Harris, "Memories of San Francisco Legal Practice and State and Federal Courts, 1920s-1960s," An oral history conducted in 1980 by Gabrielle Morris, 188, Regional Oral History Office, Bancroft Library, University of California, Berkeley.

4. *Ibid.*, 33.

5. *Ibid.*, 18, 28, 31, 50.

6. *Ibid.*, 9, 187.

7. *Ibid.*, 77, 78, 81, 127, 150-57, 188, 214.

8. *Ibid.*, 139.

9. Harris, Speech given at the Metropolitan Chiefs Conference, 1968, Northern District Archives.

10. *Ibid.*

11. Harris, "Memories," 122-30.

12. Baar, "When Judges Lobby," 284.

13. *Ibid.*, 385-90, 460-63.

14. *Ibid.*, 453-58.

15. Chambers, Letter to Edwards, 3 February 1965; Roessler, Letter to Edwards, 15 March 1964; and Baar, "When Judges Lobby," 453.

16. Roessler, Interview, 1983; Beresford, Interview, 1983; and Robert F. Peckham, Interview with author, May 1983.

17. Baar, "When Judges Lobby," 15, 464-67, 477; 30 June 1965, *Congressional Record*, 89th Cong., 1st sess., 15, 337 et seq.

18. Baar, "When Judges Lobby," 477.

19. *Ibid.*

20. Harris, Letter to Celler, 30 June 1965.

21. *Ibid.*

22. Baar, "When Judges Lobby," 472.

23. Harris, Letter to Celler, 30 June 1965; *also see* House Committee on the Judiciary, *Hearings, Federal Courts and Judges*, 89th Cong., 1st sess., 1965, 297-99.

24. Harris, Letter to Celler, 30 June 1965.

25. *Ibid.*

26. Baar, "When Judges Lobby," 381-82; and Peter Fish, *The Politics of Federal Judicial Administration*, (Princeton: Princeton University Press, 1973), 310-11.

27. Beresford, Letter to Edwards, 17 January 1966.

28. Baar, "When Judges Lobby," 513, 517.

29. *Ibid.*, 510-11.

30. Ramsey Clark, Letter to Celler, 10 August 1965, in *Hearings, Federal Courts and Judges*, 288-89.

31. Harris, Letter to Nicholas deB. Katzenbach, 5 August 1965.

32. Harris, Speech before the Circuit Conference, 1965-66; and Baar, "When Judges Lobby," 486.

33. Baar, "When Judges Lobby," 485-86.

34. *Hearings, Federal Courts and Judges*, 300.

35. Baar, "When Judges Lobby," 490.

36. *Ibid.*, 479.

37. *Reports of the Proceedings of the Judicial Conference of the United States*, (Washington, D.C., 1966), 43-44, 47.

38. Baar, "When Judges Lobby," 512; and Earl Warren, Letter to Lemuel Matthews, 2 June 1965.

39. Baar, "When Judges Lobby," 528-34.

40. 2 March 1966, *Congressional Record*, 89th Cong., 2d sess., 4368, 4374.

41. "United States Court Shift May Spark a Fight," *San Francisco Examiner*, 27 March 1966.

42. Roessler, Memorandum to file, 15 March 1966; Baar, "When Judges Lobby," 530-34; Harris, Letter to Phil Burton, 27 January 1966.

43. Baar, "When Judges Lobby," 530-31

44. Richard Chambers, Letter to Harris, 5 April 1966.

45. Baar, "When Judges Lobby," 534.

**12**    *The Court That Would Not Die*

1. *San Jose Post-Record*, 15 November 1966.

2. Roessler, Letter to Chambers, 21 September 1966.

3. Induction of Judge Robert F. Peckham, Transcript, 10 November 1966.

4. *San Jose Post-Record*, 15 November 1966.

5. Induction, Peckham, Transcript.

6. *San Jose Post-Record*, 15 November 1966.

7. Baar, "When Judges Lobby," 255.

8. *Ibid.*, 542.

9. J.P. Munro-Fraser, *History of Santa Clara County, California*, (San Francisco: Alley, Bowen and Co., 1881), 770-80.

10. *San Francisco Chronicle*, 17 February 1962, 11 March 1953, and 12 July 1956.

11. *Los Angeles Daily Times*, 24 March 1983; *San Francisco Chronicle*, 26 June 1969; *Palo Alto Times*, 10 September 1966.

12. Baar, "When Judges Lobby," 544.

13. *San Francisco Chronicle*, 10 September 1966.

14. Peckham, Interview, 1983.

15. Roessler, Memorandum to file, 14 March 1966; Roessler, Interview, 1983; Chambers, Letters to Roessler, 17 and 30 March 1966; Chambers, Letter to Beresford, 30 March 1966; and Chambers, Telephone conversation with Roessler, 14 September 1966.

16. Harris, Letter to Chambers, 15 September 1966; Northern District of California Rule 2.

17. Chambers, Letters to Harris, 23 August and 16 September 1966.

18. M. Lavine, Letter to Harris, 5 April 1966, enclosing M. Lavine, Letter to Senate Committee on the Judiciary, 1 April 1966.

19. Harris, Letter to Chambers, 15 September 1966.

20. Stanley A. Weigel, Letter to Harris, 7 July 1966.

21. Oliver J. Carter, Letter to Warren Olney III, 6 June 1966.

22. Baar, "When Judges Lobby," 341.

23. Harris, Letter to Chambers, 5 August 1966.

24. Sherrill Halbert, Letter to Beresford, 29 March 1966; and Beresford, Letter to Halbert, 1 April 1966.

25. Roessler, Memorandum to file re: Roessler and Peckham, Television interview, 16 September 1966.

26. Morgan, Letter to Harris, 22 September 1966.

27. William P. Hoffman, Letter to Harris, 22 September 1966.

28. Roessler, Letter to Chambers, 26 September 1966.

29. Roessler, Memorandum to Beresford, 17 September 1966.

30. Roessler, Memorandum to file, 16 September 1966.

31. Roessler, Interview, 1983.

32. Peckham, Letter to George Norton, 28 December 1966; Peckham, Letter to Donald Hubbard, 1 March 1967; and *San Jose Post-Record,* 30 December 1966.

33. Peckham, Letter to Roessler, 23 December 1966; Roessler, Letter to Peckham, 19 December 1966; Peckham, Letter to Harris, 3 March 1967.

34. Peckham, Memorandum to northern district judges, 22 May 1967.

35. Chambers, Letter to Harris, 18 September 1967.

36. William C. Mathes, Letters to Zavatt, 2 and 3 June 1958.

37. Peckham, Memorandum to northern district judges, 12 October 1967.

38. Report of Subcommittee on Federal Court, Santa Clara County Bar Association, 4 December 1968.

39. Peckham, Memorandum to northern district judges, undated.

40. Peckham, Memorandum to Chambers, 30 September 1969.

41. 28 U.S.C. Sec. 137.

42. Peckham, Memorandum to Harris, 19 August 1969.

43. Harris, Memoranda to northern district judges, 3 and 5 September 1969.

44. Peckham, Memorandum to Chambers, 30 September 1969.

45. Alfonso J. Zirpoli, Memorandum to Chambers, 24 October 1969; and Albert C. Wollenberg, Sr., "To Do a Job Well: A Life in Legislative, Judicial, and Community Service," An oral history conducted in 1970-1973 by Amelia R. Fry and James R. Leiby, and in 1980 by Sarah L. Sharp, 242-43, Regional Oral History Office, Bancroft Library, University of California, Berkeley.

46. Roessler, Interview, 1983.

47. Peckham, Memorandum to Chambers, 30 September 1969.

48. Harris, Memorandum to Chambers, 23 October 1969.

49. James P. Welsh, Memorandum to Harris, 7 November 1969.

50. Peckham, Memorandum to Chambers, 30 September 1969.

51. Harris, Memorandum to Chambers, 18 November 1969.

52. Chambers, Memorandum to Harris, 24 October 1969; Chambers, Memorandum to Peckham, 24 October 1969; and Harris, Memorandum to Chambers, 1 December 1969.

53. Chambers, Memorandum to Harris, 19 May 1970; and Harris, Memoranda to Chambers, 22 May and 10 and 11 June 1970.

54. Wollenberg, Sr., "To Do a Job Well," 243.

55. Chambers, Memorandum to Harris, 17 June 1970.

56. *Ibid.*

57. Harris, Memorandum to northern district judges, 18 June 1970.

58. *San Francisco Recorder,* 3 June 1970; and *San Francisco Chronicle,* 2 June 1970.

59. Order of the United States District Court for the Northern District of California, 31 July 1970; and Carter, Memorandum to northern district judges, 30 July 1970.

60. Roessler, Memorandum to file, 27 March 1966; and Peckham, Interview, 1983.

**13** *An Equal Partner*

1. "Statement for Release, 30 March 1983 Re: Full Establishment of Court Operations in San Jose," Robert F. Peckham, United States District Court, Northern District of California.

2. Roessler, Report to the board of directors, Santa Clara County Bar Association, 1969.

3. Peckham, Telephone conversation with Roessler, 11 June 1970; Roessler, Letter to Chambers, 26 October 1970.

4. Peckham, Telephone conversation with Roessler, 11 June 1970.

5. *Ibid.*

6. Lionel M. Allan, Memorandum to Members of the Advisory Committee, 28 September 1970.

7. Noel J. Robinson, Letter to Allan, 28 January 1971; James F. Hewitt, Letter to Roessler, 17 October 1970; *San Jose Mercury,* 11 March 1971.

8. Cortese, Letter to Santa Clara County Bar Association, 21 May 1971; San Jose Advisory Committee Resolution, 12 June 1971.

9. Roessler, Letter to Robert P. Aguilar, 23 December 1971.

10. Roessler, Letter to George Murphy, 6 December 1968; Roessler, Letter to General Services Administration, San Francisco, 8 October 1973; Roessler, Letter to Peckham, 22 October 1973; Edwards, Letter to Roessler, 19 August 1974.

11. Edwards, Letter to Roessler, 30 May 1974.

12. Roessler, Telephone conversation with author, 14 June 1984.

13. *Los Angeles Daily Journal,* 1 November 1982 and 20 April 1983.

14. Aguilar, Conversation with author, 15 June 1984.

15. *Los Angeles Daily Journal,* 1 November 1982; and *San Francisco Examiner,* 20 April 1983.

16. Jess Joseph Aguilar and Robert P. Aguilar, "The Segregation Decisions and the Resulting Problems of Enforcement," *Hastings Law Journal* 9 (1957):42; Robert P. Aguilar and Elva R. Soper, "Uninsured Motorists Coverage," *California State Bar Journal* 36 (1961):205 and "Property Agreements Between Spouses in California," *Santa Clara Lawyer* 2 (1962):52.

17. *Los Angeles Daily Journal,* 1 November 1982; and *San Francisco Examiner,* 20 April 1983.

18. *Los Angeles Daily Journal,* 1 November 1982.

19. *Ibid.;* and *San Francisco Examiner,* 20 April 1983.

20. Aguilar, Conversation with author, 15 June 1984.

21. *San Francisco Chronicle,* 2 December 1965; and *San Francisco Examiner,* 30 January 1966.

22. *San Francisco Chronicle,* 14 March 1966.

23. *Ibid.,* 30 December 1966; and Spencer M. Williams, Conversation with Michael Griffith, 17 July 1984.

24. *San Francisco Chronicle,* 20 January, 21 February, 28 March, 17-19 and 30-31 August, 13 and 28 September, and 4 November 1967.

25. *San Francisco Chronicle,* 8 and 21 February, 24-25 September, 8 October 1969; 9

January, 27 February, 24 April, and 2 June 1970.

    26. William A. Ingram, Interview with author, May 1984.

    27. *Ibid.*; and Beresford, Interview, 1983.

    28. Frederick F. Casucci, Memorandum to Ingram, 4 August 1978; and Tom Hicks, Memorandum to Ingram, 16 August 1978.

    29. *Los Angeles Daily Journal,* 18 January 1983.

    30. Based on accounts of the escape in Casucci, Memorandum to Ingram, 4 August 1978; *San Jose Mercury,* 3 August 1978; Arthur M. Honda, Memorandum to Ingram, 2 August 1978; and Hicks, Memorandum to Ingram, 16 August 1978.

    31. *San Jose Mercury,* 29 February 1960.

    32. William R. Fiedler, Letter to Ronald W. Reagan, 28 March 1969.

    33. From clippings in Judge Ingram's records: *Daily Palo Alto Times,* October 1957; and *San Jose Mercury,* November 1957.

    34. From clippings in Judge Ingram's records: *San Jose Mercury,* April and June 1958, July 1960; and *San Jose News,* 12 May 1962.

    35. *Palo Alto Times,* 17 July and 12 August 1969; *San Jose News,* 29 July 1969; Reagan, Letter to Ingram, 2 April 1971; and *San Jose Post-Record,* 2 April 1971.

    36. *San Jose Mercury,* 5 September 1975.

    37. *San Francisco Examiner & Chronicle,* 28 April 1976.

    38. Ingram, Interview, 1984.

    39. *San Jose Mercury,* 22 October 1975; and *Barristers Bailiwick* 10, no. 11, (December 1976).

    40. Gordon McLean, Letter to Ingram, 4 June 1976.

    41. Ingram, Interview, 1984.

    42. *Ibid.*; and Roessler, Interview, June 1984.

    43. Ingram, Interview, 1984.

    44. *Ibid.*

    45. *Ibid.*; and Lee Benson and Jim Waggener, United States District Court Clerk's office, Interviews with author, June 1984.

    46. Chambers, Letter to Harris, 9 June 1965 and note appended thereto.

## Part Three   An End to the Odyssey — A Home in the Central Coast Counties

### 14  *The United States Courthouse and Federal Building*

The letters, memoranda, and other materials cited in the notes for this chapter have been drawn largely from the Court Archives of the United States District Court, Northern District of California and from the private papers of Judge William A. Ingram, Chief Judge Robert F. Peckham, and Russell V. Roessler.

    1. *San Jose Post-Record,* 27 August 1982; and *San Jose Independent,* 30 August 1982.

    2. Sig Sanchez, Letter to Don Edwards, 11 August 1965.

    3. For replies to Oliver J. Carter's letter, *see* Albert Wahl, Letter to Carter, 4 April 1966; James P. Welsh, Memorandum to Carter, 8 April 1966; Eldon N. Rich, Memorandum to Carter, 11 April 1966. *See also* Carter, Memorandum to fellow judges and Letter to C.E. Keathley, 8 November 1966.

    4. Robert F. Peckham, Letter to Russell V. Roessler, 6 December 1968.

5. Darwin H. Anderson, Letter to Carter, 27 February 1969.

6. Carter, Memorandum to C.C. Eversen, *et al.*, 23 April 1970.

7. Carter, Letter to Anderson, 16 October 1970; and Marci Severson, Memorandum to author, 16 August 1984.

8. Peckham, Letters to Roessler, 11 and 18 June, 4 August 1970; Peckham, Letter to Richard J. Wylie, 4 August 1970; and Roessler, Letter to James R. Browning, 21 September 1970. For the building subcommittee, see Lionel M. Allan, Memorandum to All Members of the Advisory Committee — San Jose Federal Court, 28 September 1970. For the first meeting, see Allan, Letter to Roessler, 27 August 1970 and Agenda for Meeting of Advisory Committee — San Jose Federal Court. *See also San Jose Mercury,* 13 October 1970 and *San Jose News,* 13 October 1970.

9. *See* Anderson, Letter to Carter, 2 November 1970; Carter, Letter to Richard H. Chambers, 10 November 1970; and Carroll A. Hefner, Letter to Carter, 30 November 1970.

10. Peckham, Holograph notes, 17 June 1984.

11. Allan, Memorandum to Austen D. Warburton and Edwin Jones, Jr., 20 October 1970; Sanford Getreu, Letter to Allan, 21 October 1970; Warburton, Letter to Allan, 26 October 1970; Allan, Memorandum to Warburton, Jones, Jr., and Roessler, 18 December 1970; Allan, Memorandum to Warburton and Jones, Jr., 21 January 1971; Getreu, Letter to Allan, 3 February 1971.

12. Allan, Memorandum to Roessler, Warburton, and Jones, Jr., 10 November 1970; Roessler, Holograph notes, 2 December 1970; Allan, Memorandum to Warburton and Jones, Jr., 3 December 1970; Allan, Letter to Paul McCloskey, Jr., 3 December 1970; Allan, Letter to Charles S. Gubser, 3 December 1970; Don Edwards, Letter to Allan, 21 December 1970; Gubser, Letter to Allan, 23 December 1970; and Gubser, Letter to Warburton, 23 February 1971.

13. Dominic L. Cortese, Letter to Santa Clara County Bar Association, 21 May 1971; *San Jose Mercury,* 19 May 1971; Peckham, Letter to Roessler, 6 December 1968; and Peckham, Holograph notes, 17 June 1984.

14. Agenda Advisory Committee — San Jose Federal Court Meeting, San Juan Bautista, 12 June 1971; Advisory Committee — San Jose Federal Court, Resolution; Allan, Letter to Alan Cranston, 16 June 1971; Gubser, Letter to Allan, 21 June 1971; and Peckham, Holograph notes, 17 June 1984.

15. *San Jose News,* 16 June 1973. *See also San Jose Mercury* 12 June 1973; *San Jose Post-Record,* 18 June 1973; and flyer labeled DEDICATION Temporary Federal Building and United States Courthouse.

16. Roessler, Letter to General Services Administration, San Francisco, 8 October 1973; and T.E. Hannon, Letter to Roessler, 17 October 1973.

17. Roessler, Letter to Peckham, 22 October 1973.

18. Gerald Turetsky, Letter to Gubser, 23 October 1973; Gubser, Letters to Roessler, 22 February and 22 March 1974; Edwards, Letter to Roessler, 26 February 1974; *San Jose News,* 6 March 1974.

19. John V. Tunney, Letter to Roessler, 25 March 1974; Roessler, Letter to Stephen Shefler, 15 April 1974; Cranston, Letter to Roessler, 9 May 1974.

20. Allan G. Kaupinen, Letter to Edwards, 15 May 1974; Edwards, Letter to Peckham, 30 May 1974; Edwards, Letters to Roessler, 19 August and 18 October 1974; Roessler, Letter to Gubser, 26 September 1974; Roessler, Letter to Edwards, 26 September 1974.

21. Arthur O. Barton, Letter to Carter, 19 March 1976; Carter, Memorandum to Spencer M. Williams, 2 April 1976; *San Jose Mercury*, 21 January 1975.

22. *San Jose Mercury*, 8 February 1977; Paul Schoellhamer, Telephone conversation with author, 1 June 1984.

23. Schoellhamer, Telephone conversation with author, 1 June 1984; Hearings on Supplemental Appropriations Act, 1978, before United States Senate Subcommittee on Treasury, United States Postal Service, and General Government Appropriations, 27 September 1977; and Supplemental Appropriations Act, 1978, Pub. L. No. 95-240, 92 Stat. 107 (1978)

24. *Reports of the Proceedings of the Judicial Conference of the United States, 1971*, (Washington, D.C.), 63-65; *1972*, 43-45; and *1974*, 138.

25. Peckham, Memorandum to Williams and Ingram, 21 February 1978.

26. *Ibid.*; Hannon, Letter to Browning and Peckham, 10 January 1978.

27. Requests for information on space needed in the new courthouse began in early February. *See* Ingram, Letters to Peckham, 9 and 10 February 1978; Moore, Letter to Peckham, 13 February 1978; Peckham, Williams, and Ingram, Memorandum to G. William Hunter, United States attorney, *et al.*, 27 February 1978. For investigations of the size of other courtrooms, *see* Ingram, Letter to Peckham, 27 February 1978 and Walter T. Moniz, Memorandum to Ingram, 28 March 1978. On the San Jose Advisory Committee, *see* Roessler, Memorandum to All Members of Advisory Committee — San Jose Federal Court, 14 March 1978; and Peckham, Memorandum to Williams and Ingram, 14 March 1978. On the Mineta meeting, *see* Peckham, Memorandum to Williams and Ingram, 21 March 1978.

28. Alden E. Danner, Letter to Peckham, 24 March 1978; and Ingram, Memorandum to Peckham, 31 March 1978.

29. Louis J. Komondy, Letter to William B. Luck, 25 April 1978; Chambers, Memorandum to Browning, 3 May 1978; Peckham, Williams, and Ingram, Letter to Browning, 15 June 1978; Luck, Letter to Peckham, 10 July 1978.

30. Ingram, Letter to Chambers, 4 August 1974. On the escape, *see* Arthur M. Honda, Memorandum to Ingram, 2 August 1978; Frederick F. Casucci, Memorandum to Ingram, 4 August 1978; Frank B. Vasquez, Memorandum to Ingram, 25 August 1978; Tom Hicks, Memorandum to Ingram, 16 August 1978; and *San Jose Mercury*, 3 August 1978.

31. Ingram, Letter to Peckham and Williams, 9 August 1978.

32. For Chambers's suggestions, *see* Ingram, Letter to Peckham and Williams, 9 August 1978; for San Jose ordinances, *see* Ingram, Letter to Chambers, 10 August 1978; and Terry Cox, Memorandum to file, 14 August 1978.

33. Ingram, Letter to Peckham and Williams, 28 August 1978. The head of the Administrative Office sent Judge Browning a letter dated 19 July 1978 requesting the justification.

34. Warren E. Burger, Letter to Browning, 23 August 1978.

35. Peckham, Memorandum to Browning, 13 September 1978; James K. Haynes, Letter to Ingram, 12 September 1978; *see also* Julian Caplan, Letter to Ingram, 7 September 1978; and Carl Hoppe, Letter to Ingram, 11 September 1978.

36. Burger, Letter to Jimmy Carter, 29 September 1978; Ingram, Memorandum to Peckham and Williams, 18 October 1978.

37. Griffin B. Bell, Letter to Jay W. Solomon, 8 January 1979.

38. Burger, Letter to Browning, 9 January 1979.

39. Solomon, Memorandum to all regional administrators, 14 February 1979; Jacqueline Turner, Memorandum to Ingram, 5 March 1979; Komondy, Letter to Peckham, 9 March 1979; Ingram, Letter to Browning, 16 March 1979; Ingram, Letter to Peckham, 20 March 1979; Peckham, Letter to Komondy, 15 August 1979.

40. *See*, for example, *Time Magazine,* (11 September 1978): 22; (25 September 1978): 26; and (2 October 1978): 32.

41. Schoellhamer, Telephone conversation with author, 1 June 1984.

42. The story of the courtroom snafu is documented, although only partially, in Peckham, Memorandum to Ingram, 2 November 1982; Komondy, Letter to Williams, 29 November 1982; Gerry MacClelland, Letter to Komondy, 24 (date unclear) November 1982; Ingram, Letter to William E. Davis, 1 December 1982; and Williams, Letter to Komondy, 19 January 1983.

43. Stanley M. Mix, Letter to Peckham, 11 July 1978; Warren C. Moore and Seymour J. Abrahams, Memorandum to Ingram, 31 July 1978; and Ingram, Letter to Moore and Abrahams, 16 August 1970. For the Bankruptcy Act, *see* Moore, Letters to Ingram, 22 August and 29 November 1978; and Ingram, Letter to Abrahams, 27 November 1978.

44. Moore and Abrahams, Letter to Komondy, 11 December 1979; Komondy, Letter to Abrahams and Moore, 20 December 1979; Abrahams, Letters to Komondy, 14 January and 11 February 1980; Abrahams, Letter to Ingram, 24 January 1980; Komondy, Letter to Abrahams, 30 January 1980; Ingram, Memorandum to Peckham, 18 March 1980; Peckham, Memorandum to Luck, 16 April 1980; Peckham, Letter to Browning, 7 November 1980; Richard Wieking, Letter to Peckham, 22 December 1980.

45. Ingram, Conversation with Joseph Franaszek, May 1984.

## 17 *The United States District Court Clerk's Office*

The letters, memoranda, and other materials cited in the notes for this chapter have been drawn largely from the Court Archives of the United States District Court, Northern District of California and from the private papers of Judge William A. Ingram, Chief Judge Robert F. Peckham, and Russell V. Roessler.

1. *San Jose News,* 13 February 1973.

2. James P. Welsh, Memorandum to Oliver J. Carter, 8 April 1966.

3. Carter, Letter to C.E. Keathley, 8 November 1966; and Carter, Memorandum to fellow judges, 9 November 1966.

4. Carter, Memorandum to United States attorney, *et al.,* 21 December 1967; and Alan Drady, Memoranda to George B. Harris, 2 and 16 February 1968.

5. *San Jose News,* 26 August 1970; Agenda for Meeting of Advisory Committee — San Jose Federal Court; Lionel M. Allan, Memorandum to All Members of the Advisory Committee — San Jose Federal Court, 28 September 1970.

6. Raymond Xavier, Conversation with author, 25 June 1984.

7. Darwin H. Anderson, Letter to Carter, 27 February 1969; C.C. Eversen, Memorandum to Carter, 25 May 1970; Carter, Letter to Anderson, 16 October 1970; Louis J. Komondy, Letter to Spencer M. Williams, 23 March 1978; William L. Whittaker, Memorandum to Williams, 29 March 1978.

8. Jim Waggener, Conversation with author, 26 June 1984.

**20**   *The United States Attorney's and Marshal's Offices*

The letters, memoranda, and other materials cited in the notes for this chapter have been drawn from the Court Archives of the United States District Court, Northern District of California and from the private papers of Judge William A. Ingram, Chief Judge Robert F. Peckham, and Russell V. Roessler.

1. Oliver J. Carter, Letter to C.E. Keathley, 8 November 1966; and Carter, Memorandum to United States attorney, *et al.*, 21 December 1967.

2. Robert F. Peckham, Memorandum to Richard H. Chambers and the Other Members of the Judicial Council of the Ninth Circuit, 30 September 1969.

3. *See* Russell V. Roessler, Letter to George Murphy, 6 December 1968.

4. William W. Stover, Letter to Roessler, 10 January 1969.

5. Peckham, Conversation with Michael Griffith, 5 July 1984.

6. Roessler, Letter to James L. Browning, Jr., 21 September 1970; Agenda for Meeting of Advisory Committee — San Jose Federal Court, 26 September 1970; Roessler, Letter to Browning, Jr., 6 October 1970; Browning, Jr., Letter to Roessler, 6 October 1970.

7. Browning, Jr., Letter to M. Oliver Koelsch, 30 June 1972.

8. Sanford Svetcov, Conversation with Griffith, 1 August 1984.

9. Glen Robinson, James Ledgewood and Anne Miyoshi, Interview with Griffith, 23 July 1984.

10. William A. Ingram, Letter to Stanley M. Mix, 12 December 1978; and Mix, Letter to Ingram, 22 January 1979.

11. Robinson, Ledgewood, and Miyoshi, Interview with Griffith, 23 July 1984.

## Part Four   A Journalist Remembers

**22**   *And There Came a Cry*

1. Criminal Case 41124, Official Court Transcript, 10 March 1967, 8, 9.

**23**   *A Sampling of Cases*

1. *United States v. Robert Michael Preston*, Official Court Transcript, 27 January 1972.

2. *San Francisco Chronicle*, 13 April 1971.

3. *San Francisco Examiner*, 23 May 1971.

4. *Stanford Daily v. Zurcher*, Official Court Transcript, 10 July 1972.

5. *Stanford Daily v. Zurcher*, 353 F. Supp. 124, 136 (N.D. Cal. 1972).

6. *Stanford Daily v. Zurcher*, 64 F.R.D. 687, 688 (N.D. Cal. 1974).

7. *San Jose Mercury*, 24 October 1978, North County edition.

8. *San Francisco Chronicle*, 4 October 1977.

9. *Zurcher v. Stanford Daily*, 436 U.S. 539 (1978). Justice William J. Brennan, Jr. was absent from the bench the day the *Daily* case was argued. Supreme Court students believe that if he had sat with the Court, the division would have been five to four.

10. Bob Beyers, interview with author, 12 July 1983.

11. *San Francisco Chronicle*, 16 August 1972.

12. *Ibid.*

13. *Ibid.*, 30 November 1972.

14. *Ibid.*; and *San Jose Mercury*, 10 March 1979.

15. Joseph Bonanno, Sr., *A Man of Honor*, (New York: Simon & Shuster, 1983).

16. Emerson D. Moran, Jr., "Joe's Secret Notes," *Parade Magazine*, 3 May 1981.

17. *Ibid.*

18. *United States v. Joseph Bonanno, Sr., et al.*, Document 131, 29 July 1980.

19. Author's notes.

20. *San Jose Mercury*, 16 November 1979; and *United States v. Joseph Bonanno, Sr., et al.*, Official Court Transcript, 15 November 1979.

21. Moran, Jr., "Joe's Secret Notes."

22. *United States v. Joseph Bonanno, Sr., et al.*, Official Court Transcript, 24 July 1980, 3066-88, 3104.

23. *San Francisco Chronicle*, 3 September 1980.

24. *Ibid.*

25. *Ibid.*, 13 January 1981.

26. *United Press International*, Tucson, 8 July 1983.

27. *United States v. Joseph Bonanno, Sr., et al.*, Document 287, 28 November 1983.

28. *United States v. Harry Margolis*, Official Court Transcript, 11 April 1977, 2070-81.

29. *San Francisco Examiner & Chronicle*, 25 September 1977.

30. *Ibid.*, 19 December 1976.

31. *San Francisco Examiner*, 7 October 1977.

32. *San Francisco Examiner & Chronicle*, 27 June 1982.

33. *United States v. Hitachi Limited, et al.*, Trial memorandum at 19, (N.D. Cal. 1983).

34. *United States v. Nakazawa, et al.*, Affidavit of FBI Agent Kenneth C. Thompson, 22 June 1982, (N.D. Cal. 1982).

35. *Reuters Wire Service*, Tokyo, 2 July 1982.

36. *United Press International*, Tokyo, 24 June 1982; and *Wall Street Journal*, 2 August 1982.

37. Edward A. Feigenbaum, *The Fifth Generation*, (Reading, Mass.: Addison-Wesley, 1983).

38. "Super Computers — The High Stakes Race to Build a Machine That Thinks," *Newsweek*, (4 July 1983): 58.

39. "CHIP WARS, Chipmakers Pool Their Research to Stay Competitive," *Business Week*, (23 May 1983): 84.

40. *Wall Street Journal*, 13 August 1982.

41. *United States v. Barry Saffaie, et al.*, Official Court Transcript, 28 September 1982.

42. In August 1984 the Ninth Circuit remanded the case for trial, now set for April 1985.

43. *San Jose Mercury*, 29 September 1982.

**24** Epilog

1. *San Jose Mercury*, 16 June 1973.

# INDEX

# Patrons

This book was made possible only through the generosity of the following individuals and organizations. The San Jose Federal Court Advisory Committee is deeply appreciative of their assistance.

Berliner, Cohen & Biagini
Campbell, Warburton, Britton, Fitzsimmons & Smith
Center Foundation
Daniel R. Cowans
Hoge, Fenton, Jones & Appel
Hopkins, Mitchell & Carley
Morgan, Morgan, Towery, Morgan & Spector
Pillsbury, Madison & Sutro